POLITICAL ECONOMY IN NINETEENTH-CENTURY AMERICA

Selected and Introduced by
Morgen Witzel

Volume 2

History of American Thought

Political Economy in Nineteenth-Century America

Selected and Introduced by **Morgen Witzel**

Volume 1
Mathew Carey
Essays on Political Economy, 1822

Volume 2
Francis Wayland
The Elements of Political Economy, 1837

Volume 3
George Tucker
Political Economy for the People, 1859

Volume 4
Amasa Walker
The Science of Wealth: A Manual of Political Economy, 1866

Volume 5
William Graham Sumner
Problems in Political Economy, 1884 and
Essays on Political Economy, 1885

Volume 6
Francis A. Walker
Political Economy, 1892

Printed in England by Antony Rowe Ltd, Chippenham

THE ELEMENTS OF POLITICAL ECONOMY

Francis Wayland

THOEMMES PRESS

Published by Thoemmes Press, 2003

Thoemmes Press
11 Great George Street
Bristol BS1 5RR, England

http://www.thoemmes.com

Political Economy in Nineteenth-Century America
6 Volumes : ISBN 1 84371 048 X

British Library Cataloguing-in-Publication Data
A CIP record of this title is available from the British Library

This book is printed on acid-free paper, sewn, and
cased in a durable buckram.

THE

ELEMENTS

OF

POLITICAL ECONOMY.

BY FRANCIS WAYLAND, D. D.

PRESIDENT OF BROWN UNIVERSITY, AND PROFESSOR OF MORAL PHILOSOPHY.

NEW YORK:
LEAVITT, LORD & COMPANY.
1837.

PREFACE.

THE following work contains, in substance, the Lectures on Political Economy which have been delivered, for some years past, to the Senior Class in Brown University.

When the author's attention was first directed to the Science of Political Economy, he was struck with the simplicity of its principles, the extent of its generalizations, and the readiness with which its facts seemed capable of being brought into natural and methodical arrangement. At the same time, it appeared to him that the works on this subject, in general use, while they presented its doctrines truly, yet did not present them in such order as would be most likely to render them serviceable either to the general student or to the practical merchant. This defect, for the sake of his pupils, he endeavored to supply. What he thus at first prepared for them, he now offers to the public. In how far he has succeeded, it must be left for others to decide.

His object has been to write a book, which any one who chooses may understand. He has, therefore, labored to express the general principles in the plainest manner possible, and to illustrate them by cases with which every person is familiar. In doing this, he is aware that he may at times have become chargeable with repetition. Sometimes, the same case may have been introduced a second time, for the sake of illustrating a different principle. At other times, the same fact may belong equally to two different divisions of the subject. In this latter case, he has preferred introducing it the second time to referring the reader to what has been said before, because he believes that readers rarely take the trouble to make use of a marginal reference.

The principles of Political Economy are so closely analogous to those of Moral Philosophy, that almost every question in the one, may be argued on grounds belonging to the other. He has not, however, thought it proper, in general, to intermingle them, but has argued economical questions on merely economical grounds. For this reason, he has omitted many considerations which are frequently introduced into discussions on this subject. For instance, on the question of protecting duties, it is frequently urged, that, if a contract have been made by the government with the manufacturer, that contract is morally binding. This, it will be perceived, is a question of Ethics, and is simply the question whether men are or are not morally bound to fulfil their contracts. With this question, Political Economy has nothing to do. Its only business is, to decide whether a given contract were or were not *wise*. This is the only question, therefore, treated of in the discussion of this subject in the following work.

It may possibly be urged that the author, having had no experience in mercantile business, should have left this subject to be treated of by practical men. To this he has only to reply, that *principles* belong to all men; that there seemed very little hope that this subject would be undertaken by men engaged in active business; and that he could not perceive why his doing, as well as he was able, a work which seemed to be necessary, should prevent any one else from doing it as much better as he saw fit.

It has been to the author a source of regret, that the course of discussion in the following pages, has unavoidably led him over ground which has frequently been the arena of political controversy. In all such cases, he has endeavored to state what seemed to him to be the truth, without fear, favor, or affection. He is conscious to himself of no bias towards any party whatever, and he thinks that he who will read the whole work, will be convinced that he has been influenced by none. While he cherishes for his fellow citizens who are engaged in political warfare, every feeling of personal respect, he desires it to be believed that he entertains for party itself, whether political, ecclesiastical or social, the opinion which "befits him as an American, a Christian, and a gentleman."*

The first edition of the author's work on Moral Philosophy, owing to causes which he could not control, was unfortunately very incorrect in typographical execution. He hopes that the present work will be liable to no such objection. He has given to the correction of the proof sheets, all the care of which he was capable; and in the performance of this labor, he has also been able to

* Col. Huchinson, when speaking in the British Parliament, respecting the part which he had taken in the King's death.

avail himself of the assistance of some of his literary friends. To the printers, Messrs. Knowles, Vose & Co., of this city, he would also express his thanks for their punctuality and fidelity; and for the interest which they have taken, in presenting the work to the public, in the neatest and most accurate form.

In the hope that these pages will be found subservient to the best interests of science, and that they may be of some practical utility to his fellow citizens, the author respectfully submits them to the judgment of the public.

Brown University,
January 16, 1837.

CONTENTS

AND

PLAN OF THE WORK.

INTRODUCTION.

DEFINITIONS AND DIVISION OF THE SUBJECT.

BOOK FIRST.

OF PRODUCTION.

CHAPTER FIRST.

OF CAPITAL.

CHAPTER SECOND.

OF INDUSTRY.

PART I.

THE OBJECTS AND FORMS OF HUMAN INDUSTRY.

SECTION I.

The different Objects of Human Industry.

SECTION II.

The different Forms of Human Industry.

PART II.

THE MODES BY WHICH THE PRODUCTIVENESS OF HUMAN INDUSTRY MAY BE INCREASED.

SECTION I.

The Use of Natural Agents.

SECTION II.

Of Division of Labor.

SECTION III.

Limitations to the Division of Labor.

SECTION IV.

Effects of the increased productiveness of Human Industry.

CHAPTER THIRD.

OF THE LAWS WHICH GOVERN THE APPLICATION OF LABOR TO CAPITAL.

SECTION I.

SECTION II.

Industry will be applied to Capital, as every man enjoys the advantages of his Labor and Capital.

SECTION III.

SECTION IV.

SECTION IV.

CHAPTER THIRD.

OF A CIRCULATION BY MEANS OF A PAPER CURRENCY.

SECTION I.

Of the Nature of Banks in General.

SECTION II.

Of the Utility of Banks.

SECTION III.

SECTION IV.

BOOK THIRD.

OF DISTRIBUTION.

CHAPTER FIRST.

WAGES, OR THE PRICE OF LABOR.

SECTION I.

The General Principles of Wages.

CHAPTER SECOND.

OF INDIVIDUAL CONSUMPTION.

SECTION I.

Of individual Consumption, for the sake of re-production.

SECTION II.

Of Consumption for the gratification of Desire.

CHAPTER THIRD.

OF PUBLIC CONSUMPTION.

SECTION I.

Of Taxes, or the manner in which the public expenditure is provided for.

SECTION II.

Of the purposes for which the Public Revenue is commonly expended.

ELEMENTS

OF

POLITICAL ECONOMY.

POLITICAL ECONOMY.

INTRODUCTION.

DEFINITIONS, AND DIVISION OF THE SUBJECT.

1. POLITICAL ECONOMY is *the Science of Wealth.* It is sometimes defined the Science of National Wealth. This definition seems not, however, sufficiently comprehensive; inasmuch as, the laws which govern the creation of wealth are essentially the same, whether they are considered in respect to man as an *individual*, or to man as a *society*.

By Science, as the word is here used, we mean a systematic arrangement of the laws which God has established, so far as they have been discovered, of any department of human knowledge. It is obvious, upon the slightest reflection, that the Creator has subjected the accumulation of the blessings of this life to some determinate laws. Every one, for instance, knows that no man can grow rich, without industry and frugality. Political Economy, therefore, is a systematic arrangement of the laws by which, under our present constitution, the relations of man, whether individual or social, to the objects of his desire, are governed.

2. *Wealth.* It has been frequently remarked, that the universe around us is composed of objects suited to gratify

our desire, and thus minister to our happiness. *The capacity to gratify desire*, is, therefore, the first element that enters into our notion of wealth. But as the gratification of our desires, by means of an external object, almost always supposes some change effected in that object; and, as we could have no right to effect that change, unless that object were our own, another element, which enters into the notion of wealth, is *the idea of possession.* Hence, wealth may be defined any object, having the power of gratifying human desire, which is capable of being appropriated. He who possesses many of these objects in abundance, is termed rich. He who possesses few of them, is termed poor. He who possesses a large amount of *money*, is also called rich; because, with money, he can generally procure whatever else of physical convenience he may desire.

3. *Of Value, intrinsic and exchangeable.* The particular quality in any substance, which renders it capable of gratifying human desire, is called its *value.* Thus, that quality of fuel, which constitutes its value, is its power of generating heat, or of gratifying this desire in man. A particular substance may have the power of gratifying either *one* or *several* desires, and thus it may have either one or several values. Thus anthracite coal is at present known to have but one value, namely, that of generating heat. Bituminous coal possesses also another, as it is also used in the manufacture of gas, for the purposes of illumination. Wood has several values, inasmuch as, besides being used for fuel, it may also be used for building, and for the various purposes of the arts. Iron has as many forms of value, as there are uses to which it may be applied, in promoting the convenience of man.

The *degree* of the value of any substance, depends upon the *nature* and *the number* of the desires which it can gratify. If the gratification of that desire to which it is subservient, be necessary to the existence or to the comfort of man, its value will be great. Such is the case with air, water, clothing, food, and fuel. If the gratification which it affords can be easily dispensed with, its value will be small. Such is the case with articles of luxury, or the means of mere amusement. The inferiority of the value of this latter class, is evident from the fact, that, in seasons of scarcity, these are first relinquished. And again, the degree of the value of any substance, depends upon the *number* of desires which it can gratify. India Rubber, or Caoutchouc, a few years since, was used but for one purpose, that of rubbing out pencil marks. It is now used in the manufacture of shoes, and for several other very important purposes. The intensity of its value is, therefore, greatly increased.

We have thus far treated only of *intrinsic* value, or of the power which any particular substance possesses, of gratifying human desire.

If, however, we examine the various articles of value around us, we shall observe a very remarkable difference between them. Some of them may be made the means of procuring for us, *by exchange*, other objects of desire. Such, for instance, are gold, silver, iron, coal, wood, &c. He who possesses a large quantity of either of these, may, ordinarily, procure for himself, by exchange, any thing else that he needs. Others, on the contrary, and those of great intrinsic value, are destitute of this property. What has greater intrinsic value than air, the light of the sun, or water? Yet, we can get nothing in exchange for air or sun-light, and very rarely for water. And again; substances having an exchangeable value, do not possess that value, in proportion to their intrinsic value. Iron has a far greater intrinsic value than gold; yet, an ounce of gold has a far greater exchangeable value than an ounce of iron; that is, an ounce of gold will procure for us far more articles of convenience, in exchange. This latter property, or the power of procuring for us something else in exchange, is called *exchangeable value.*

If, now, we compare those substances which have not, with those which have exchangeable value, we shall find them to differ in the following respects:

1. Those which have no exchangeable value, are every where *abundant* and *inexhaustible.* The supply of the others is limited in *quantity,* or is limited in *place.* Air, and the light of the sun, are inexhaustible every where. Coal is in some places inexhaustible, but it is not so in others. Where it lies, for miles together, immediately upon the surface, and in beds of unknown thickness, it has no exchangeable value. Where it must be carried to any distance, to be brought to the consumer, it then acquires an exchangeable value.

2. The value of the first class of substances has received no *addition from human labor,* but derives whatever qualities it possesses, directly from the gift of God. The value of the other, has always received some addition, and, frequently, it is derived altogether from human labor. Neither air, nor the light of the sun, can receive any additional power of gratifying human desire, from any effort of man. On the contrary, all the most important values of iron, are derived from human skill. A lump of iron ore is as valueless as granite or sandstone. The peculiar properties of the metal, are the result of the processes through which it passes. When, however, a substance which ordinarily possesses only intrinsic value, is placed under such circumstances that human labor must be added to it in order to enable it to gratify desire, it then acquires

exchangeable value. Thus water, which, ordinarily, has no exchangeable value, is frequently sold by the gallon in cities, because it can be procured in purity only from a distance, and hence, before it can gratify the desire of particular individuals, it requires the labor of transportation to be added to it.

We see, then, that every substance on earth may have, and, doubtless, it actually has, intrinsic value. If we then consider all those qualities which are necessary to prepare a substance for the gratification of human desire to be intrinsic values, these may be divided into two kinds; first, those which are imparted to the substance by the immediate act of God; and secondly, those that are imparted to it through the intermediate agency of man. The former, being the gift of God, are gratuitously received, and gratuitously parted with. The latter have cost human labor, and therefore cannot be obtained without an equivalent. Hence it is the latter alone, that enter into computation, in fixing exchangeable value. Thus the exchangeable value of iron and of gold, respectively, does not depend upon the uses to which these metals may be put, but upon the labor which must be employed in preparing them to gratify desire.

Again: Moral Philosophy teaches us, that if a man expend labor in the creation of a value, this labor gives him a right to the exclusive possession of that value; that is, supposing the original elements belonged to no one else. Now, as almost all the qualities which gratify human desire, can exist only by the exertion of this labor, it follows, that all such objects must have already become the exclusive possession of some human being. Hence, he who wishes to possess such objects, must either himself expend the labor necessary for producing them, or else he must procure them by voluntary concession, from some one who has already expended it. But he who has expended labor upon a substance, will never voluntarily surrender it up, either for nothing, or for that which he can obtain without labor. He who makes knives, will neither give them away, nor exchange them for air, or water, or sun-light. Hence, he who wants knives must either make them himself, or else he must offer the knife maker, in exchange for them, some value which he himself has created. Hence, every man who desires the means of happiness, must labor to obtain them. And, as every man has his preference for some particular kind of labor; and as, moreover, every man can succeed better by confining his labor to one thing, than by devoting it to twenty things, every man is desirous of exchanging the value created by himself, for that created by others. So soon as this is the case with any one substance, it then has acquired exchangeable value: that is, just so soon as other men are willing to give me a value which they have created, for that which I have created, then the result of my labor has exchangeable value, and not before.

The *degree* of the exchangeable value of any one substance, depends upon the amount of labor and of skill necessary to create that value. No one would exchange what has cost him two days' labor, for that which has cost another man of the same skill, but one day's labor; because, rather than make such an exchange, he would create this second value for himself. Thus, if a hundred pounds of fish could be procured by a day's labor, and only twenty-five pounds of venison; men would exchange, not pound for pound, but labor for labor: that is, at the rate of four pounds of fish for one pound of venison. The amount of labor expended in the creation of a value, is commonly denominated its *cost*. This is always the standard by which, for long periods, the degree of exchangeable value may be estimated.

When, however, we here speak of labor, we speak of it as simple labor; that is, without taking into consideration the degree of skill which may be combined with it, or the other circumstances which may conspire to create variation in its value. These are to be considered hereafter. We suppose, in the remarks above, that, in all cases, labor of the same kind is to be compared together.

I have said above, that cost forms the standard by which the *degree* of exchangeable value for *long* periods is to be estimated. Temporary circumstances may create a variation from this standard; and may, for a short time, elevate this value above, or depress it below, the cost. These, however, can continue to operate but for a short period; the tendency of exchangeable value is always to gravitate towards cost. The causes of this variation, we will now briefly illustrate:

1. Suppose, that by the use of better tools, or from any other cause, the supply of fish became more abundant, so that a man could, by one day's labor, procure two hundred pounds instead of one hundred pounds. The hunter would not then be willing to exchange as before, since he would now rather catch his fish himself. He would demand eight pounds of fish for one pound of venison: that is, the exchangeable value of fish would fall; or, in other words, it could not procure as much venison in exchange, as it did before. But as, in consequence of this reduction in price, there would be an increased demand for fish; that is, more persons would want it, and they would also want a larger quantity than before, the fisherman would not be obliged to exchange at half the former rate, but would be able to exchange at a rate somewhere above it; say, perhaps, six or seven pounds for a pound of venison. Thus, both parties would be gainers. The fisherman would procure more venison; the hunter more fish, by a day's labor.

Thus, a benefit to one, is a benefit to all. And thus we see, that, other things being equal, the *greater the supply* of any article, the *less* is its exchangeable value; that is, the less amount of other things, can it procure in exchange.

Again: Supposing the labor necessary for taking fish to be doubled; so that, by the labor of a day, no more than fifty pounds could be procured. The fisherman, then, would not sell, as at first, four pounds of fish for one pound of venison; he would rather hunt his venison himself. He would offer but two pounds for a pound of venison. But as, at this rate, the number of his customers would be greatly diminished; and as every person would use less than before, he would find it difficult thus to dispose of the results of his labor, and would be obliged to offer it on more favorable terms, say two and a half, or three pounds, for a pound of venison: thus, with a day's labor, he would procure less venison, and the hunter less fish. That is, the evil would be shared between them; and thus, an injury to one, is an injury to all. Thus we see, that, other things being equal, the *less the supply*, the *greater* the exchangeable value.

Again: Suppose the labor necessary for procuring fish remain the same, but that, from some cause, twice as many persons desired fish as before. Suppose that every person desired five pounds, but that, there was only enough to supply half the population with this quantity. Then there would arise a competition among the buyers, and he who obtained this quantity must obtain it by overbidding his neighbor. Thus, fish would command a larger amount of venison in exchange than before; that is, the exchangeable value of fish would rise, and it would continue at this point, until the demand decreased, or, until a sufficient number of men devoted themselves to fishing, to furnish enough to reduce it to its mean exchangeable value. Thus, the *greater* the *demand*, the *greater* the exchangeable *value.*

And, lastly: Suppose, that, while the labor of taking fish continued as before, the number of purchasers was from any cause diminished, so that, while there was enough caught to supply every person with five pounds, only half the population wanted any. In this case, as a large residue would be left, at the close of every day, on the fisherman's hands, there would be a competition among the sellers; and each one would be desirous of disposing of his stock at a diminished price, rather than lose it altogether. Hence, he would offer to exchange it for a less amount of venison than before; that is, the exchangeable value of fish would fall. It would remain at this point, until, either the demand arose to its natural rate; or a sufficient number of persons turned their attention to some other occupation, to reduce the supply to a level with the demand. That is, the supply being the *same*, the *less* the *demand*, the *less* the exchangeable *value.*

It is the operation of these principles that keeps the supply of any article throughout the world always equal to the demand: and, it is surprising to observe, with what accuracy this effect is produced. In the largest cities, there is always just enough butcher's meat, and vegetables, and clothing, to supply the wants of the inhabitants, and no more. The moment the price of an article falls below cost, it ceases to be produced, until the price rises. As soon as it rises above ordinary profit, capital and labor are directed to it, and it is produced in sufficient quantity to meet the unusual demand. Thus, also, we see why the high price of any article is commonly followed by a low price of the same article, and the contrary. When the price of any article is low, men leave off this kind of production in too great numbers, and hence follows a comparative scarcity of the product which they furnish. When the price is high, men rush, in too great numbers, into this sort of production, and hence arises a temporary glut, and a depreciation of its exchangeable value.

Again: It will be seen that this variation in the exchangeable value of any article, is dependent greatly on its *perishableness.* An article which is not liable to be destroyed by keeping, will neither fall so rapidly, nor so low, by either a diminution of demand, or an increase of supply, as one which is, in its nature, rapidly perishable. Thus, iron will keep for years, without decay; and hence, its exchangeable value cannot greatly vary, from increase of supply or decrease of demand: that is, it is an article not liable to great or sudden fluctuation. On the contrary, fish, fruits, and articles of this nature, very often, in the course of a few days, vary one or two hundred per cent.

Another source of variation in the exchangeable value of products, is the *time* necessary for their production. When any amount of a commodity may be produced on demand, its rise of price will not keep pace with the diminished supply; because, every one will know that, by waiting, he can be provided with it at a reasonable price. Thus, a small rise of price in a manufactured article, when the material is abundant, will cause the quantity produced to be greatly increased; hence, the rise is never excessive. But when a long time is necessary for the production of an article, and it is an article of prime necessity, the rise of price is frequently great.

And again: It will be seen, that, so far as the seller and the buyer are concerned, these variations balance each other. When products rise on the merchant's hands, he charges an additional price: when they fall, he is obliged, frequently, to sell at a reduced profit, or even to sell below cost. The gain, in one case, makes up for the loss in the other. Hence, as no one sympathizes with the merchant, when he sells at a loss, no one should complain, when he sells, for a short time, at more than an ordinary gain.

If, now, we sum up what has been said, we shall come to the following general conclusions:

1. *Cost;* that is, labor bestowed; is the foundation of exchangeable value, and from this, it can never, for long periods, materially vary: that is, an article can always be had for what it costs to produce it; including in this, the ordinary profit to the producer. Notwithstanding this, there will, however, arise various fluctuations, depending upon the following circumstances:

Other things, then, being equal—

2. The greater the supply, the less the exchangeable value.

3. The less the supply, the greater the exchangeable value.

4. The greater the demand, the greater the exchangeable value.

5. The less the demand, the less the exchangeable value.

6. And, in general, cost being fixed, exchangeable value is inversely as the supply, and directly as the demand.

7. Or, still more generally, at any particular time, exchangeable value will be as the cost, *plus* the effect produced by the variation in supply and demand.

Hence, wealth consists of all objects which have an exchangeable value.

Exchangeable value is slightly distinguishable from price. The first, is the power which any object possesses of procuring for us any object whatever. The second, *price*, is the power that it has to procure for us one particular object; that is, *money*.

Of Production. From what has been said, it is easy to explain the nature of Production. It is the act by which we confer a particular value upon any object whatever, or by which we give to any object its adaptedness to gratify desire. We can neither create nor annihilate any thing. All that we can do, is, to modify what already exists. When we so modify any thing, that it is capable of gratifying a desire which before it was not capable of gratifying, our so doing is called *production*.

The modifications which objects need, in order to render them capable of gratifying desire, are various. Sometimes the *elements of the substance*, sometimes *its form*, and sometimes *its place*, require to be changed. Whenever human industry accomplishes any of these results, it is called *production;* the person who exerts this agency is called a *producer*, and the substance itself, on which this agency is exerted, is called *a product*.

In some cases, we find the substance, as, for instance, ore in the mine, or stone in the quarry, in its natural state; in others, we receive it from those who have imparted to it one value, and we add to it another. The material which, in either case, we obtain for the purpose of combining it with our own industry, and forming it into a product, is called *capital;* and, after the labor has been exerted, and the value created, it is called *a product*.

Thus, the same article may be *product* to one, and *capital* to another. Leather is the *product* of the *currier*, and the *capital* of the *shoemaker*.

The term *capital* is not merely applied to the *material* on which industry is to be exerted, but also to all the *instruments* by which human industry is assisted ; as well as to *whatever is necessary to the support* of that industry.

Of Exchange. I have said, above, that the mode of every man's industry is decided by his individual tastes and circumstances. It is commonly, however, confined to the creation of one kind of product, inasmuch as it is thus vastly more available. His desires, on the other hand, are as innumerable as the objects created to gratify them. He creates but one value, and he wants a thousand. Hence, he can be gratified by means of no less than nine hundred and ninety-nine exchanges. He thus parts with various portions of the value which he has created, for the sake of obtaining the values which others have created. Hence the necessity of universal and ceaseless *exchange*. Hence the reason why so large a portion of mankind devote themselves to the business of effecting exchanges. Those who do so, are called *merchants*. Those who are employed in the transportation of wares or merchandise by sea or by land, are all engaged in effecting the same object.

Distribution. In even the very first stages of society, it is found that the productive result of human power is greatly increased by union of effort and division of labor. Ten men, laboring together, will accomplish much more than ten men laboring separately. Specially is this the case where the various parts of a process are divided, and each one performs that part for which he is best adapted.

And, as capital accumulates, it is commonly the case, that one who owns the capital, unites in production with another or others, who perform the labor. When the product is realized, and the gains are to be divided, some equitable law is to be adopted, in the distribution. Different laborers are entitled to different wages: and there are just proportions to be observed between the wages of labor and the wages of capital. The principles of this adjustment are treated of by Political Economists, under the head of *Distribution.*

Consumption Suppose, now, the value to be created, and brought within the reach of him who desires it; he uses it, and, in the very act of use, its value is destroyed. We exchange labor, or money, or wheat for fuel: we use the fuel in our fire places, and its value is destroyed. We purchase bread; we eat it, and its value ceases forever. A baker purchases flour, and makes it into bread; the flour ceases to be flour: its value, in this respect, is gone forever. This act, by which we annihilate any particular value, is called consumption. It is exactly the opposite to production.

Sometimes the utility is destroyed, with no other result than merely the gratification of desire. Such is the case with fire-works, shows, and amusements of almost every sort. At other times, the value or utility is destroyed; but it reappears, in another and much more valuable form. Thus, a side of sole leather is cut up into soles, for shoes: its value, as a side of sole leather, is destroyed forever; but its value reappears, in another form, and with an increased exchangeable value. The food which we eat, disappears; but its value reappears, in reanimated health and vigor, by which we are prepared for subsequent labor. The former is termed *unproductive*, the latter, *productive consumption*.

The whole subject of Political Economy, may be therefore divided into four parts.

The First Part treats of PRODUCTION, or the laws which govern the application of labor to capital in the creation of value.

The Second, or EXCHANGE, treats of the principles which govern men, when they wish, by means of their own labor, to avail themselves of the labor of others.

The Third, or DISTRIBUTION, treats of the laws by which those who have united in the creation of a product, receive, respectively, their portion of the result.

The Third, or CONSUMPTION, treats of the laws which should govern us in the destruction of value.

Each of these subjects will be treated of, in the above order, in the following work.

BOOK FIRST.

PRODUCTION.

It is obvious that when man was first created, there existed nothing but this earth, with its various substances, their qualities and relations; and man, with his various physical, intellectual, and moral powers. The difference between the *present state* of man and of the universe around him, and the *original state*, consists in this; that the qualities and relations of things have now been discovered, and rendered available to the service of man; and the intellect of man has been cultivated, and his skill improved, so that he is able, more successfully, to avail himself of these qualities and relations. And it is also obvious, that this change in the external world has been produced by the physical and intellectual faculties of man; that is, by human industry. The whole wealth of the world has been created by the union of human industry with the materials which God had originally spread around us. Hence, all that is necessary to the creation of wealth, is capital and industry. But, it is also obvious, that the application of industry to the materials around us; that is, capital, has not been at all times either equally strenuous, or equally successful. There must, therefore, exist some rules, by which this application of industry to capital is governed, and some conditions under which it is more successfully exerted, than under others.

The subject of Production is, therefore, naturally divided into three parts. 1st. *Capital.* 2d. *Industry.* 3d. *The principles by which the application of industry to capital is governed*

CHAPTER FIRST.

OF CAPITAL.

FIRST. *The nature of Capital.* The word *capital* is used in two senses.

When used in relation to product, it means any substance on which industry *is to be exerted.* After that industry *has been exerted*, it then becomes product. Thus, leather is the *capital* of the shoemaker, and shoes are his *product.*

When used in relation to industry, however, it has a much wider signification. It then signifies the material on which industry is *about to* confer value, that on which it *has conferred* value, and the *instruments* which are used for the conferring of value, as well as the *means of sustenance*, by which the being is supported whilst he is engaged in performing the operation. The capital of an individual, if it be examined, will be found to be composed of all these. Thus, also, the capital of a nation is composed of raw material, of articles ready to be consumed, of buildings, ships, manufactories, and also of the various substances, by which human life is prolonged and rendered desirable.

SECOND. *The forms of Capital.* Hence it must be seen, that the forms of capital must be as various as the various employments of man.

1. The *Farmer* possesses seed, manure, breeding animals, &c.

The *Manufacturer* possesses cotton, wool, flax, iron, leather, wood, and, in general, all the material on which, according to his particular calling, he desires to exert his industry.

The *Merchant* possesses sugar, tea, coffee, iron, &c., or the various substances to which, by transportation, he has added, or to which he intends to add, value.

2. But, in order to effect this intended creation of value, it is found that intermediate agents must, in all these cases, be employed. A farmer could not reap with his fingers, nor a miner dig with his hands, nor a manufacturer labor without tools. All these *instruments*, the use of which is necessary to the creation of value, are, therefore, also termed capital.

Thus, the ploughs, harrows, spades, carts, and working animals of the *farmer*, are a part of *his* capital. To the same class also, perhaps, belongs his land.

The axes, planes, hammers, of the *mechanic*, and the buildings and machinery of the manufacturer, are their capital.

Under this division of capital, may also be included the

ship of the merchant, the wagon of the teamster, and the railroad and locomotive of the railroad proprietor.

3. But, besides all this, all these several persons must be fed and clothed, whilst they are exerting the industry by which value is given to these various products. Hence, under the head of Capital, must be comprehended all the various kinds of food, clothing, and houses, which are necessary, in order to give *sustenance* to a human being. These are generally the same, in all kinds of industry.

4. But, besides all this, every individual, in each of these departments of human industry, will retain some portion of the product which he has created, but which he is ready to part with for something else. The farmer has grain, which he has raised; the manufacturer, cloth, which he has fabricated; the merchant, commodities, which he has imported, or bought for sale. These form another item of capital.

THIRD. *Of the changes which Capital undergoes.* From what has been already said, it is evident, that capital derives its value from labor, and that the effect of labor exerted, is to produce some change in it. Hence, capital, in every industrious country, must be always undergoing changes; and hence, also, it frequently re-appears, in forms very different from those in which it at first existed. The form, however, is of no consequence, if a superior value be the result. Political Economy, unmindful of the form, looks only at an augmentation, either of the *amount*, or of the *degree* of value.

1. The *material* undergoes changes.

The seed and manures of the *farmer* are changed into vegetables, and these again into the grain of the harvest.

The cotton and wool of the *manufacturer* are changed into the fabrics which he produces. The wood and nails of the *carpenter* are changed into houses.

The commodities of the *merchant* undergo changes. He exports cotton, rice, wheat, or manufactures; and imports calicoes, silks, wine, hardware, &c.

2. The *instruments*, or *machinery*, employed by these several classes of persons, undergo changes. These several instruments, in the course of production, are gradually destroyed, or consumed. The plough and cart, and animals of the farmer, the tools of the mechanic, the machinery of the manufacturer, and the ships and vehicles of the merchant, are worn out and rendered worthless. But if they have been profitably used, they have re-appeared, in the increased value, which they have conferred upon the various objects upon which they have been employed.

The various kinds of food, clothing, and shelter, necessary for the existence and comfort of the human being, are also changed. They are consumed, from time to time, and their value re-appears, in that new vigor imparted to his body and mind, which forms a fresh capital, to be employed again in the work of production.

3. And lastly: The *mature product* of every laborer is constantly changing. As soon as he has created a product, he is anxious to dispose of it to some one else, that he may invest its increased value in some other material which he may again, with increased advantage, unite with industry. As soon as the farmer has raised grain or fat cattle, he wishes to dispose of them, that he may invest their value again in seed, or manure, or agricultural improvements. As soon as the manufacturer has finished

his fabric, he exchanges it for the means of subsistence, materials, or machinery; and so of the merchant, and of every other laborer.

We see, then, that capital is undergoing perpetual changes, and that the course of these changes is constantly from a state of less, to a state of greater value; that is, from a state more remotely adapted to the gratification of human desire, to a state less remotely adapted to it; and that so soon as it has become precisely adapted to this gratification, its change ceases, and it is consumed in some mode or other. And if it be profitably consumed, it again re-appears, in some form adapted to create a further increase of the means of enjoyment. And hence we see, that, that country is the most prosperous which is the most rapidly accumulating, by the results of its labor, the greatest amount of the ultimate products, in proportion to its number of inhabitants. The greater the share of these products which falls to the lot of each individual, the greater are the means of physical happiness in his possession.

FOURTH. *The increase of Capital.* In all these changes, which we have considered, it is always to be remarked, that there is, in the very act of change, a destruction of value. He who changes iron into steel, consumes the iron, destroys that particular value, and creates another in its place. He who sows wheat, destroys the value of that wheat, for food; and he who spins cotton, destroys the value of cotton wool *as* cotton wool. That is, neither of these substances can ever be used again for the purposes to which they were before adapted. If, however, the industry of the laborer have been skilfully directed, the product will have acquired an exchangeable value sufficient to replace the original material in additional quantity, and also to repay him for his labor, and pay the

the interest of his capital. The amount of difference between the exchangeable value of his original material, together with his labor and the exchangeable value of his product, is his profit. The annual amount of these profits, is his annual gross revenue. The annual amount of these profits in a nation, is the gross national revenue.

It is obvious, that it matters not in what form capital re-appears, if it only re-appear in a form bearing a greater exchangeable value. The smith exchanges gold or silver for coal; he burns up this coal, and nothing is left but ashes. But it has produced an invisible substance, called caloric, by means of which he has been able to give such an increased value to iron, as will not only replace his gold and silver, but also the iron itself, and will also pay him for his labor. The farmer exchanges his gold or silver for manure, but this manure will so increase his harvest, that he will be able to replace his gold and silver, and also be abundantly repaid for his labor. The principle is the same, in all cases of change of capital. It matters not into what we change our capital, nor how valuable the substance is that is exchanged, if we only receive, in return, a greater amount of exchangeable value, or that which will procure for us a greater amount of objects of desire.

We see, hence, in what manner nations and individuals grow rich. It is by uniting the industry of this year to the capital of last year, and, by this process, creating an augmentation of capital. This augmentation will be either greater or less, in proportion as our industry has been successful in giving additional value to that value which previously existed. If we destroy a value, and produce only another simply equal to it, we lose our *labor*. If we destroy a value, and reproduce nothing, we lose both *labor and capital*. It is only as the value created is superior to the value of labor and capital employed, that we are enriched. Hence we see, that wealth is acquired by small, but oft repeated accumulations. The gross amount of these accumulations will be decided by our skill and industry. But, as from these our various expenditures must be subtracted, our nett revenue will depend, not only on our skill and industry, but also on our frugality. Though a man earn much, yet, if he spend all, he will grow no richer. Hence, *industry* and *frugality* are the great sources of wealth. Nor is this the less true of nations. Hence it is, that wars, unnecessarily expensive governments, or high taxes for whatever purpose, may keep the most enterprising and industrious nation always poor.

Of Productive and Unproductive Capital. Productive capital is that, which, being in any manner united with industry, is in the process of augmentation. Unproductive capital is that, which, not being united with industry, remains, at the end of the year, just the same as it was at the beginning. Money at interest, capital undergoing the various transformations effected by industry, tilled land, and manufactories in operation, are productive capital. Money lying in coffers, materials unsaleable, manufactories unoccupied, and land lying waste, are unproductive capital.

When capital is unproductive, it may be considered as losing for us, annually, its ordinary rate of interest; because it must have been purchased with that which would have yielded that interest. Hence, although we still own the principal, if it remain long unproductive, its annual losses may amount to as much as though we had lost it all at the beginning. Hence it is, that every sound economist is anxious to have the whole of his capital productively invested. He who acts otherwise, is ignorant of the principles of production, indolent, or slovenly. The farmer who allows a heap of manure to lie in his farm yard for a year, instead of spreading it on his land; the merchant who allows his ships to lie idle, or his goods to be scattered, unsold, over several warehouses; or the manufacturer who owns twice as much machinery as he is able to employ, are annually losing all the accumulation which this capital, properly invested, would produce. And still more, as we have seen that all gains are by small and successive accumulations, it is manifest that habitual negligence of this sort must greatly diminish, if it do not entirely consume, all the nett revenue of an establishment. The effort of every man should be, to unite every fraction of his capital with industry, and to keep it so united, continually. Any gain, even the smallest, if it be sure, is better than no gain at all.

From what has been said, it is evident that the process of accumulation, in all branches of production, is the same. It will also appear, that where capital is free, that is, where there are no restrictions upon the use of it, there can be no great permanent difference in the rate of accumulation, between the different modes in which it is employed. If the profits of one kind of business are above the average rate, other capital will flow into that channel. If the profit in any branch of production be below the ordinary rate, capital will be withdrawn from it. If commerce be unusually lucrative, men will leave other pursuits, and devote themselves to commerce, until, by competition, they reduce the profits to the ordinary rate. If commerce be depressed, men will leave it, until, by the reduction of the supply of commercial facilities, the rate of profit is increased. Rates of profit cannot be rendered permanently unequal in any other manner, than by oppressive legislation. The differences in profit, in the various departments of industry, are, therefore, more apparent than real.

When profit is sure, it is of course less than when it is uncertain. But, how much soever individual cases may differ, it will be found that the average is, for long periods, very nearly equal.

Of Fixed and Circulating Capital. The capital from which the owner derives profit only by exchanging its form or place, is circulating capital. Thus, the wares of the merchant, the products of the manufacturer, the harvests of the farmer, are circulating capital. On the other hand, the instruments which each of these producers uses, in performing his various operations, are fixed capital. Such are the ships and warehouses of the one, the machines and buildings of the other, and the tools and land of the third.

The amount of fixed capital employed in some branches of industry, is much greater than in others. Some mechanical trades require no more fixed capital than a cheap set of tools. Others, as large manufacturing establishments, require a large fixed investment. In proportion to the amount which must be thus employed, must be the amount of accumulated property necessary to be possessed by him who wishes to employ himself in that particular department of industry. Sometimes, by far the greater part of the investment is fixed capital, and is also very great in amount. In this case, it is frequently apportioned among individuals, who each subscribe and pay a part of the cost. Such is the case with railroads, canals, and works of public improvement, generally.

It will be seen, from what is here said, that circulating capital is, in general, that which is already prepared for the gratification of human desire, or that which is in a course of preparation for this state. Fixed capital, in general, consists of the instruments, or fixtures, which, in some form or other, assist us in accomplishing this result. Tools, machinery, houses, ships, roads, canals, and improvements on farms, &c., are fixed capital. Circulating capital is generally rapidly consumed. It is commonly an annual product, and subject to an annual consumption. Fixed capital is not an annual product, and may last for a year, a life time, or indefinitely. It is, however, still liable to gradual decay, which decay must be replaced, or else the possessor would find himself growing poorer, inasmuch as these tools and machinery are the means by which his labor is rendered productive.

But besides this, there is an obvious tendency, in the nature of things, to convert circulating, into fixed capital. As circulating capital is annually consumed, it must be annually replaced, or mankind, after the first year, would all perish. It is replaced by the annual productions of the earth, either vegetable, animal, or mineral. But, if the industry of man has been successfully exerted, the amount of annual production will be sufficient, not only to supply the ordinary wants of the producers, and to repair the waste and wear of fixed capital, but also to leave a surplus unappropriated. Now, as this kind of capital is annual, and as it is also perishable, if it be not *used* in some way, this surplus must be a total loss. If it be appropriated to the multiplication of annual capital, it will only increase that surplus, which is already too great. Hence, it can be usefully employed only in the creation of fixed capital. To accomplish this result, it is offered in the form of wages, to mechanics, artisans, and those persons who employ themselves in the manufacture of those articles, in which fixed capital consists. Hence, the wages of this class of persons will rise, and a portion of them will be drawn from the production of circulating capital. This might at first be supposed to diminish the amount of circulating capital. Such would be the result, were it not for the fact, that the very object of fixed capital, is, to enable us to create circulating capital, with a less amount of labor. A society, in which a part of the members are devoted to the making of useful machines, will create a greater amount of annual products, than one in which all are devoted exclusively to the creation of annual products. Thus, in a short time, the annual surplus is greater than before, and a greater number of persons is employed in creating fixed capital, and that kind of fixed capital, which involves, in its creation, a greater amount of expense. It is thus that a society, age after age, grows rich, and each successive race of men leaves the world more richly provided with the means and facilities of production, than it found it.

This may all be illustrated, by a few very familiar instances. A savage, who obtains peltry by his bow and arrows, having provided enough for the food and clothing of his family, will, if he be industrious, possess a surplus which must now be useless to him. He would naturally exchange his surplus for a rifle; a kind of fixed capital, by means of which, his circulating capital would be greatly increased. This increase of capital would enable him, besides procuring better clothes and more annual conveniences, to add to his fixed capital by purchasing a horse, or a plough, or by erecting a house. These, in their turn, would augment his circulating capital; and thus, with every year, his fixed and circulating capital would steadily increase. Hence, very soon, there would arise a demand for the services of men who employed themselves in creating fixed, instead of circulating capital. That is, mechanical arts would be practised; and the artisans would be, as we find that in such a state of society they always are, exorbitantly paid for their labor.

Again: Suppose a farmer enters upon new and untilled land. His first care is to produce the necessities of life, for himself and his family. When this is accomplished, he appropriates a part of his labor to creating fixed, instead of annual capital: that is, he erects fences, purchases carts and animals with his produce, builds barns and outhouses, and thus renders his farm a much more productive instrument than before. With his increasing surplus, he purchases more land, if he needs it, and brings it all into such a state of cultivation as he thinks desirable. By all these means, his annual surplus is rendered greater, and he is enabled to extend the amount of his fixed capital, by building a better house, purchasing better ploughs, harrows, carts, and various machines by which his future labor will be rendered more productive. But we see that this could not be done by the farmers of a neighborhood, unless some portion of them abandoned farming, and devoted themselves to the creation of fixed capital. There would, therefore, arise a great demand for mechanical labor. And as there would hence arise the necessity for a great number of exchanges, some portion of the society must devote themselves to effecting them; that is, must become merchants. In this manner, circulating capital first gives rise to fixed capital, and fixed capital increases again the amount of circulating capital; and thus they go on, year after year, mutually augmenting each other.

Thus, also, the merchant, whose business it is to augment the exchangeable value of a given amount of circulating capital by transportation and exchange, produces, by his operations, an annual surplus. This he adds to his former capital, for a while, but soon purchases fixed capital, as ships, to facilitate his operations. When he has enough of these, and as large an amount of circulating capital as he wishes to employ, he then begins to invest his surplus in some permanent works of public improvement, as bridges, roads, canals, or in something which, besides facilitating the productiveness of the society, will also yield him a revenue, or else he employs it in manufactures, according to the condition of the country, and its natural demands and facilities.

From what has been remarked above, we may easily see the natural course which a nation takes, in its progressive accumulation of wealth. Its first productions are, circulating, or annual capital; the products of the field, of the forest, or of the ocean. Next follows improvement in permanent conveniences, and the construction of instruments for agricultural production; then the exchange of its own products for other circulating capital, or for the annual necessaries of life; and then the exchange for fixed capital of the most necessary kind. Thus, the Dutch, on their first settlement in this country, used to import their bricks from Holland. Commerce being thus commenced with an older country, they soon engage in it themselves, and invest a large portion of their annual surplus in ships. Before manufactures had commenced in this country, previously to the Revolution, the commerce of the colonies had become already extensive. All these prepare the way for the investment of capital in manufactures, which, in their proper and natural time, *must be* established; and when that time arrives, they *will be* established, without the aid of legislative enactment, and by the very laws by which accumulation is governed.

From what has been remarked, we also see that the advantages which we enjoy over savage nations result, principally, from the possession of a greater amount of fixed capital; or, in other words, the permanent results of pre-exerted industry. That advantage consists in this, that this capital, besides affording to its owners the ordinary rate of profit, enables men to produce at a much cheaper rate; that is, at a less expense of labor. Thus, a cotton factory, besides affording a fair profit to the owner, enables him to do, by one hour's labor, what would otherwise require the labor of days or of weeks. By all this difference, therefore, we have the advantage over savages, or over those who went before us. Hence, a nation, which does not possess the results of pre-exerted industry, must be poor, unless its natural advantages enable it to avail itself of those of other countries.

Hence, we also see the reason why the traffic between savage and civilized nations is so greatly in favor of the latter. The latter are enabled to offer in barter what is of inestimable value to the savage, but which the civilized man can produce with a very small portion of labor. An axe would cost a savage the labor of weeks or of months, while a smith in New England would make it in a few hours. Hence, it is not wonderful that the one should be willing to give for it vastly more than it cost the other. And, on the other hand, the commodities of the savage are of very little value to *him*, but of high value to the mechanic or artisan. Hence, the gain to him also is great. An Indian who exchanges peltry, which is worth in New York fifty or one hundred dollars, for a rifle, powder and bullets, has improved his condition, by means of the purchase, really more than the gunsmith, who has made so exorbitant a profit.

Of Money. It will be observed that, thus far, I have not mentioned money as an item of capital. Although this is not the place in which to treat of the functions of money, yet it may be proper here to add a single remark concerning it.

Money forms but a very small part of the capital of any

country. Every one may easily judge of this, from his own observation. How very small a portion of any one's possessions is in money. And if this be true of every individual separately, it must be so of all the individuals collectively.

The sole use of money, is to facilitate exchanges. It is an instrument for the saving of labor, and for the performing of labor with greater accuracy. Of this, any one may convince himself in a moment, if he will imagine two cases, in the one of which he was obliged to make several exchanges without money, and the other in which he could make them with it.

Money gains nothing by exchange, but rather loses in value, like every other machinery which is worn out while it accomplishes its object. Hence, it belongs to the class of fixed capital. It is subject to slow wear, which must be replaced out of the circulating capital of the country.

And, hence, as any country may have a greater amount of any particular kind of fixed capital than it needs, as, for instance, of any particular kind of machinery; and as, when this is the case, it sends it abroad, or in other words, makes it an article of export, or changes it into circulating capital, so is it with money. If a country has more money than is sufficient to accomplish its exchanges, it sends it abroad, and receives back something that it needs more. Such is, permanently, the case in mining countries; and such is, temporarily, the condition of almost every commercial nation.

CHAPTER SECOND.

OF INDUSTRY.

Having, in the previous chapter, explained the nature and changes of *Capital;* we now proceed to treat of *Industry*. In doing this, we shall consider: 1st. The different *objects* of Human Industry. 2d. The *forms* of Human Industry; and, 3d. The *modes* by which the productive power of Human Industry may be increased.

PART I.

THE OBJECTS AND FORMS OF HUMAN INDUSTRY.

SECTION I.

THE DIFFERENT OBJECTS OF HUMAN INDUSTRY.

It has been seen, in the previous chapter, that the increase of capital; that is, the means of physical happiness to man, can be effected only by producing change, of some kind, in capital. But it is evident that this change cannot be produced without labor, since no valuable change is spontaneous. Hence, the great object of human industry is, to produce some valuable change in capital.

Now, the changes which may be produced in the substances of nature, may all be reduced to three; change in the *elementary form*, change in the *aggregate form*, and *change in place*. To effect one or the other of these, all valuable human labor is directed.

1. Man may change the *elementary form* of matter. The farmer, by means of seed, manure, and cultivation, aided by the agencies of the sun and the earth, of rain, and the atmosphere, transforms the elementary forms of carbon, gases, and water, into wheat. The chemist changes the elementary forms of acids and alkalies into salts. The dyer changes the elementary forms of iron and tannin into coloring matter; and the case is the same with the various other forms of human occupation.

2. Man may change the *aggregate form* of matter. The cabinet-maker changes the form of a board into that of a desk or a table; the smith, a piece of iron into a horse shoe or a nail; the mason changes a pile of bricks and mortar into a wall; the cotton spinner, a bale of cotton into thread; the weaver, this thread into cloth. And, in general, the labor of *mechanics* and *manufacturers* is employed in effecting changes in the *aggregate* forms of matter.

3. Man may change *the place* of matter. Thus, the shipmaster transports a cargo of cotton from New York to Liverpool, and brings back a cargo of cotton goods, of crockery or of hardware. The teamster receives a wagon load of merchandise in one town, and transports it to another. The owner of a canal boat receives manufactured goods in Albany, transports them to Buffalo, and brings back to Albany, in return, a freight of agricultural produce. The agent of a railroad receives a hundred boxes of merchandise in Manchester, and transports them to Liverpool. And thus, also, a large number of the inhabitants of every populous town derive their subsistence, and frequently grow rich, simply by transporting wares and merchandise from one part of the town to another.

These divisions, in general, correspond with the agricultural, mechanical and commercial departments of human industry. I have adopted a different terminology, simply for the reason that it seems to me to form a more generic and better limited division, and one more conformable to the facts in the case.

1. Concerning these divisions, it is proper to remark, that, though these are the various objects of human industry, yet it frequently happens that, he who labors in one, is also obliged to labor in one or both of the others. Thus, the farmer who raises a crop, is obliged to *transport* the seed to the field, and frequently to transport his harvest to market. The cabinet maker who *manufactures* a table, may *transport* his materials from the lumber yard. The engineer, on the railroad, is obliged to change the *elementary* form of wood, in order to produce the caloric, necessary to move his locomotive. We designate the class of laborers to which a man belongs, by the ultimate object which he has in view, in exercising his profession.

2. Each one of these forms of industry is equally important in conferring intrinsic value upon substances; that is, in giving them capacity to gratify human desire. Thus we see that the ore in the mine has no power to gratify desire, until it is made into iron or steel. The steel is valueless for the purpose of cutting, until it is transformed into a knife, an axe, or some cutting instrument; and, if I want to make a pen in New York, a knife is utterly valueless to me for this purpose, while it remains in Sheffield or Liverpool. Unless these several values are all conferred upon it, it would be of no service to me. Hence, in purchasing a knife, I pay for them all, and do it willingly.

3. Hence we see how incorrect is the notion sometimes advanced, that all wealth is the production of one or of two, and not of all these forms of human industry. All these

changes must be effected in almost every article which we consume, and if either of them were to be suspended, our desires would not be gratified, and the other two must also be discontinued. He who transports flour, performs an act of as essential importance to the sustentation of the human race, as he who raises wheat. He who brings a knife from Liverpool to me, performs a labor as important to me, as he who manufactures the knife; for, if it were three thousand miles off, it might, for all the purposes for which I want it, as well not be in existence. And yet more, if the one should cease, the others must soon cease with it. Of what value would wheat or wool be to the farmer, if they could not be transported from his farm? And again: what gain could be derived from either, if there were no means of grinding the one, or of manufacturing the other? Hence we see that all the forms of industry mutually support, and are supported by, each other; and hence, also, we see that any jealousy between different classes of producers, or any desire on the one part, to obtain special advantages over the other, are unwise, and, in the end, self-destructive. The fact is, that if left to themselves, they all flourish, and they all suffer together. Nor can either one be depressed, for any considerable period, without injuriously affecting both the others.

These various forms of human industry enter, in different degrees, into the value of different articles of use. For instance, butchers' meat and green vegetables derive almost their whole value from the first kind of labor, as they require very little modification, and will bear but short transportation. On the contrary, salted provisions may derive a large portion of their value from change of place. Clothing, cutlery, and what are commonly denominated manufactures, derive the greater portion of their value from change in the *aggregate form.* The original material constitutes, in general, but a small part of their price, and, not being of great bulk, their transportation is not very expensive. The steel that would make a pair of razors, and the cost of transporting them from Sheffield or Paris to New York, would form but a very small portion of their price. On the contrary, bulky articles, such as coal and iron, derive a very large portion of their cost from transportation. Coal, that has scarcely any exchangeable value in the coal mines of Pennsylvania, is sold for eight or ten dollars a ton in Providence. And all the labor employed upon it, is that necessary for breaking it in pieces, and removing it from its bed to the house of the consumer.

As, however, the human race is scattered over the face of the globe, and as their wants in all latitudes are so nearly the same, while no country affords facilities for supplying more than a very small number of these wants, it is evident that the labor employed in change of place must, in civilized countries, be the most universal, and must enter essentially into the greatest number of commodities. Of this every one will be convinced, who will take any article of dress, of furniture, or of food, and consider the amount of transportation that has entered into its production; and, specially, if he take into account the transportation which has entered into the formation of the instruments by which it has been produced. The same truth is also illustrated by the fact, that whole nations, with very small natural advantages, as Holland and Venice, have, in a short period, become immensely rich, merely by conferring change of place on the merchandise and productions used by other nations. Water communication, in the early stages of society, greatly diminishes the cost of transportation, and, of course, increases the facilities of exchange. It is on this account that the first settlements of nations are always either on the shores of the ocean, or along the banks of navigable rivers.

It may also be worthy of remark, that, thus far, in the progress of society, the ingenuity of man has been more successful in devising means for increasing the productiveness of labor in the second and third, than in the first kind of human industry. Improved agricultural utensils, a better knowledge of the nature of soils, and of the different kinds of grain and edible vegetables, and of manures have added considerably to the quantity of product that can be raised by a given amount of labor. But this increase bears no sort of proportion to that effected by the use of machinery in the case of the cotton manufacturer, the use of locomotive and many other forces. It is, doubtless, wisely ordered that it should be so. Agricultural labor is the most healthy employment, and is attended by the fewest moral temptations. It has, therefore, seemed to be the will of the Creator that a large portion of the human race should always be thus employed, and that whatever effects may result from social improvement, the proportion of men required for tilling the earth should never be essentially diminished. It is also to be remarked that division of labor, which so greatly increases the productiveness of human industry in the other modes of production, can be applied but in a small degree to agriculture. No man can devote himself exclusively to ploughing, sowing, or reaping; because, only a small part of the year can be employed in either of these occupations. The farmer must, therefore, practise them all, at different times; and, of course, every farmer must be able to perform not one, but all the several operations required in his trade. This forms another reason why the increase of productiveness of human industry, in this department of labor, has not kept pace with that which has been witnessed in manufactures and commerce.

SECTION II.

THE DIFFERENT FORMS OF HUMAN INDUSTRY.

INDUSTRY, is any form of human exertion employed for the creation of value. This, of course, includes exertion, both of *body* and of *mind.*

The object of industry, as we have seen, is to produce change of some sort; since change is necessary, either to the creation or to the increase of intrinsic value, and is always necessary to the existence of exchangeable value.

We have also seen that all the changes which human industry can effect in matter, may be reduced to three, namely: Change in *elementary form;* change in *aggregate form;* and change in *place.*

But when man puts forth exertion to effect change, it is not any change at random, but some specific change which he has directly in view. Were it otherwise, his labor would be worse than useless, and, like the effort of a maniac or an idiot, would, in nine times out of ten, destroy, instead of creating value.

It is also evident that the changes which can be effected in matter, are not produced at random, but, *in obedience to certain laws.* If we wish to make a fire, it is not any kind of effort that will do it, but effort exerted in obedience to the laws of combustion. If we wish to raise wheat, it is not every kind of labor that will do it, but labor exerted in obedience to the laws of vegetation. And so in general, if we wish to effect either of the three kinds of change mentioned above, we must act in obedience to those laws of the Creator, to which this kind of change has been subjected.

Again: Supposing the laws of nature, in respect to a particular change to be known, it is also necessary to know the *manner* in which they may most successfully be applied to the accomplishment of a particular result. The laws of combustion and of gravitation may be known, and yet a very important effort of human ingenuity may be required, before we ascertain the best method of so applying them, as to be able to construct a good fire-place. The expansive power of steam was known long before a steam engine was invented; and still longer before any application of it was devised by which it might be used for propelling vessels on the water. And still further, a man may understand the general laws of physiology, and yet be unable to apply them to the cure of diseases. A man may understand the general principles of jurisprudence, and yet not know how to avail himself of them, in such a manner as to procure either defence from injury, or redress of grievance.

But suppose this also to be known: it still remains for us to put those means into operation, by which, in obedience to the laws of nature, a given result may be accomplished. He who understands the laws of combustion and gravitation, and the mode of their application, may now set himself to work, according to these laws, and build a chimney. He who understands the laws of hydrostatics and the mode of their application, may now set himself to work, to build a boat. It is, however, true that there would still be required a certain degree of skill and dexterity, before he could perform either of these operations well; although he now could perform them, in some way or other. This skill can be acquired only by practice; and the power of acquiring it, is, in general, very universally bestowed upon men.

From what has been said, it is evident that the industry of which man is suceptible, is capable of assuming three different forms, namely: Industry of *discovery or investigation;* Industry of *application or invention*; and Industry of *operation.*

1. *Industry of Discovery or Investigation.* Under this class of laborers, is to be comprehended those who discover the laws of nature, and those who make them known to mankind, after they have been discovered. Newton labored in this department, when he discovered the laws of gravitation, optics, and of the motions of the heavenly bodies; Franklin, when he discovered the laws of electricity; and Sir Humphrey Davy, when he discovered the alkaline bases, and the laws of their combination. The labor of each of these men is also of the same kind, when they made known these laws to the public. The labor of those who are called *philosophers*, belongs to this class.

2. *Industry of Invention or Application.* It is very rarely that a simple law can be of any use, without some adjustment by which we may avail ourselves of its advantages. Hence, a very important department of human industry is that which teaches us how to make the application of the principle, so as to accomplish a particular purpose. Newton performed this labor, when he invented the telescope; Hadley, when, by means of the quadrant, he applied the laws of light to the measurement of angles; Franklin, when he invented the conductor, or lightning rod; and Sir Humphrey Davy, when he invented the safety lamp; and Fulton, when he invented that modification of the steam engine, by which vessels may be propelled through the water.

Under this class, I think, may also be comprehended professional labor, generally. The business of the clergyman is to teach us in what manner we may avail ourselves of the *moral laws* of the Creator. The lawyer teaches us how to avail ourselves of the laws of that *civil society*, of which we are the members. The physician teaches us how to obey the *physiological laws* under which we are created, so that we may be relieved from sickness, or preserved in health.

3. To the third class of human industry belong all those who *put forth the physical effort* necessary, in order to create the values desired. They are the laborers who produce those changes, either in elementary form, in aggregate form or in place, of which we have already spoken, and they compose by far the most numerous class of society.

It may here be remarked, that two of these forms of labor are frequently performed by the same person. For instance, he who discovers a law, sometimes also teaches us how to apply it. Thus, as we have already shown, Sir Isaac Newton, Franklin, and Sir Humphrey Davy, were all of them both discoverers and inventors; that is, they performed both the first and the second kinds of industry. Thus, the second and third are also frequently united; that is, the individual who labors at a particular operation, also invents some machine by which a particular process in that operation is improved. Thus, Sir Richard Arkwright, a mechanic, invented the spinning machinery now in common use; and, in general, many of our most important inventions have been made by operative laborers. And there can be no doubt that, if a knowledge of the laws of nature were more generally diffused throughout this class of society, the progress of invention would be inconceivably more rapid. I know of nothing which would promise more for the general improvement of the useful arts, than a wider diffusion of the knowledge of principles among those whose business it is to employ those principles in their daily practice.

Although I have arranged the several forms of human industry in the above order, I by no means assert that this is the order in which they actually appear among men. The reverse is, on the contrary, far more commonly the fact. Men commence by creating, at first, the simplest forms of value, and those absolutely necessary to their actual existence. Still, in order to create these values, with certainty and with regularity, they must very soon have discovered, by experiment, some *rules* by which the process must be conducted. Men would very soon discover that stones would not burn, and that a fire could not be built in a pool of water. As they advanced, by successive experiments, they invented tools, by which, without knowing why, they found themselves able to accomplish their purposes with less labor and with greater success. Thus, a man would construct a raft to transport himself and his property over a river, before he knew any thing of the laws of hydrostatics; and he would employ a wedge, before he understood the doctrine of forces. The last labor required, is to ascertain the laws by which these changes are governed. As soon as this is done, a great improvement is at once effected in all the former inventions; and new inventions arise, which otherwise would never have been suggested. Thus, a knowledge of the laws of combustion has greatly improved the construction of instruments for warming our houses. A knowledge of the laws of hydrostatics, has greatly improved the construction of ships. And a knowledge of the laws of steam, has given birth to all the machinery connected with the steam engine. And, it seems not too much to hope for, that the knowledge of the laws of nature will be yet so universally diffused, that invention shall almost cease to be the work of accident, but, that, when an instrument is wanted, men will proceed to discover the law and invent the application, just as Sir Humphrey Davy proceeded, when he was requested to invent the safety lamp.

OF THE DIFFERENT PRODUCTS OF THE VARIOUS FORMS OF INDUSTRY.

1. The product of *operative* industry, is a change of form or of place in *matter*, by which its intrinsic and exchangeable value is increased. As the exertion of this labor confers this value, it gives to the laborer a right either to the whole, or to an equitable part of the matter on which it is exerted. This right is easily ascertained and enforced; for the laborer may enforce it, by seizing either on the matter itself, or on such part of it as may be sufficient to satisfy his demand.

2. The change which is thus produced, could not be effected by a less amount of labor, than that which the laborer has exerted. If a man make a table with suitable skill, such a table could not be made by any one else with a less degree of skill and a smaller amount of labor; and hence, the cost of tables must, in the same place and at the same time, be very much the same. Besides this, there is no power in tables to multiply themselves. Hence, the laborers in this or any other department, have a sort of monopoly of this kind of production, inasmuch as no one can produce it cheaper, and none but themselves can produce it as cheap.

But all this is reversed, in the case of the first two kinds of labor. For,

1. The product which the discoverer or inventor creates, is *immaterial.* It is *knowledge*, or a change effected on *mind*, the immaterial part of man. By creating this change, a man does not acquire a right to the whole, or to any part of the *substance*, in which the value resides. The substance cannot be appropriated, nor can it be divided; and, were this possible, the laborer could make no use of it. Nor is the change one which is cognizable by the senses of others, but only by the consciousness of the person in whom it is wrought. Hence, this marks a broad distinction between these and the other forms of labor.

2. Although the discovery of the laws by which the changes in matter are governed, may require the exercise of the most unusual talent, and may demand both protracted and most expensive labor; yet these laws may be *promulgated*, after they are discovered, by men of the most ordinary talent. Hence, there is no ratio between the labor or skill necessary to create it, and that necessary to promulgate it after it has been discovered. Hence, he who first creates knowledge, has no means of monopolizing it; nor can the exchangeable value be sustained, by the consideration that no one could create it, afterwards, with less labor.

3. The product which he creates has an indefinite power of self production. If a man discover a law and reveal it to his neighbor, that is, create this change in his mind, his neighbor may create the same product in an hour, in the minds of a thousand persons, and each one of these in the minds of a thousand more. And specially, by means of the press, this power is multiplied indefinitely. Hence, as the supply of the product can at any moment be illimitably increased, it very soon ceases to have any exchangeable value.

From these reasons it will be seen, that the ordinary rules of supply and demand, and cost and labor, do not enter into view, when we speak of intellectual products. They can therefore be adjusted by no fixed rule. Nevertheless as immaterial products are of the greatest importance to the prosperity of a country, the Political Economist may point out the circumstances most favorable to their production, and the rule by which their labor should be remunerated. The above considerations are suggested, in order to explain, why Political Economy, so commonly, treats almost exclusively of *material* products.

It may, however be remarked, that civil society observing that immaterial products are necessary to the well being of a community, and that those who create them, are liable to remain altogether unpaid; has frequently devised means by which some remuneration may be reaped from the exercise of this kind of industry. Such are the laws of copy, and of patent right. By the first of these, an author is allowed, for a limited time, the exclusive control over the publication of his work ; and by the other, the inventor is entitled to the exclusive control over the use of his invention. In this manner, both of these classes of laborers are enabled to derive some portion of benefit from their productions. Were it otherwise, all their reward would consist in whatever of consideration they might obtain in the community, and in the gratification of benevolence from the consciousness of having improved the condition of their fellows. But, inasmuch as every other man who is usefully employed, obtains these rewards also, and receives pecuniary advantage in addition, there is no reason why the intellectual laborer should receive only the first, and be excluded altogether from the second.

From what has been said, another difference between

these two forms of product may be seen. The product of operative labor, being united with matter, and being limited in quantity and fixed in cost, may be exported to another country, and will command a correspondent amount of exchangeable value in the products of that country. Hence, a nation may grow rich, either by agriculture, manufactures, or commerce. But this is not the case with immaterial products. We cannot send abroad a given amount of knowledge, and bring back a correspondent amount of material products. The smallest amount of knowledge, is capable of such indefinite multiplication, that the demand may be instantly supplied. Hence, a society composed solely of philosophers, or inventors, or professional men, would never grow rich, but must, if they did nothing else, of necessity starve. Laborers of this class add greatly to the value of other labor, though their product, if no other were created, would be valueless in exchange. They may be compared to the steam in an engine, which, when it is combined with proper machinery, produces the most surprising results, but which, when left to itself, is dissipated into air. While the separate parts of the machinery, though they might be of some use as raw material, yet, if the steam were withdrawn, would, without it, become a mere mass of cumbersome and valueless lumber.

Thus, we see that all the classes of laborers are mutually necessary to each other. Without a knowledge of the laws of nature, we should all be savages. Without the skill and labor of the mechanic, there would neither exist the opportunity of acquiring knowledge, nor would our knowledge, if acquired, be of any practical value. Nothing can, therefore, be more unreasonable than the prejudices which sometimes exist between these different classes of laborers, and nothing can be more beautiful, than their

7

harmonious co-operation in every effort to increase production, and thus add to the conveniences and happiness of man.

PART. II.

THE MODES BY WHICH THE PRODUCTIVENESS OF HUMAN INDUSTRY MAY BE INCREASED.

It is obvious, that if the capital and number of laborers be at any one period the same, the annual amount of product created will be as the amount of industry exerted. Were the laborers all sickly, so that they could work only for four hours a day, there would be but half as large a product created, as if they all labored for eight hours a day. If, by a palsy, they were all deprived of the use of one of their arms, a correspondent decrease of production must ensue. On the contrary, if, while the cost of their support remained the same, their ordinary power of labor could be doubled, there would be twice the usual amount of value created. And hence, in general, we see that, other things being equal, just in proportion as more labor is bestowed, the desires of every one are more fully gratified, that is, he grows rich; and, on the contrary, as labor is diminished, the laborer suffers, or grows poor. This result every one witnesses every day. Sick, aged, and idle people suffer, because they either do not, or cannot, bestow the labor upon capital necessary to create a sufficient amount of product for their subsistence.

But the physical power of man is extremely limited. There is an average amount of fatigue which a human being can undergo, which can rarely, and but for very short periods, be exceeded. If he be worked too hard, he sickens and dies; and probably dies from being overworked more readily and more commonly than any other animal. When, therefore, the whole physical power of man is employed upon the capital which he possesses, this may be considered the *natural* limit of human productiveness.

1. But, it is evident, that if by any means we could increase this power ten fold, there would be a tenfold increase of production. If we could, by any means, enable a man with one day's labor, to execute as much change in capital as he could before execute with ten days' labor, there would be just ten times as many changes effected; that is, ten times as much value created, and ten times as much product to be either enjoyed by himself, or to be exchanged for equivalent means of happiness. And, if the power of effecting changes is increased in other men in the same ratio, the product of the whole society will be increased in the same proportion. This is *one* of the effects produced by the use of natural agents; and hence it is, that, just in proportion as they are used, the condition of man is annually and rapidly improved.

2. But this is not all. There are many values which are necessary to the happiness and even to the existence of man, which he could not create by his unassisted powers. Thus, he needs shelter, cooked food, and clothing. But he could not, with his teeth and nails, cut down a tree, and fashion it into a cabin. He cannot, by his hands, either cook his food, or manufacture a fabric suitable for clothing. All these can, however, be done by other agents which he can command and control. Thus, iron can be made to cut down and fashion a tree, fire to cook

his food, and a spinning wheel and loom can be made to furnish him with clothing. Thus we discover the *second* use of natural agents. They enable him to *create values* necessary to his existence, *which, without their aid, could never be produced.* Thus, an additional power for the creation of product is given to human industry.

3. But this is not all. It is found that a man, by devoting himself to one particular pursuit, is able to create a vastly greater amount of product in a given time, than if he devoted himself to several pursuits. Hence, if there are ten products to be created, and there are ten men to create them, they will in a day, create a vastly greater amount, if each one labors entirely upon one, than if each one labors upon them all. The product of the whole ten, therefore, by such a division of labor, will be greatly augmented. This is the *third* method by which the productiveness of human industry may be increased.

We see, then, the modes in which the productive power of man may be exerted. 1. Man may, unassisted, labor up to the extent of his physical ability. 2. He may multiply his power, by availing himself of the *agents of nature*, either to *facilitate* the creation of products, or to *create* products which he could not create himself; or, 3d. He may *economize* his labor, by such arrangements, as will enable him, in a given time, and with a given amount of fatigue, to accomplish a greater amount of result.

It is in this manner, that is, by adopting these means, that the human race advances from the savage to the civilized state. With nothing but his hands and feet, man could not subsist, except in the most temperate climates. His food would be wild fruits, and the animals which he could run down in the chase. This is the lowest point of human wretchedness. It is a most laborious and incessant struggle to obtain the bare means of prolonging existence. He invents a bow and arrow; this is a natural agent, or a tool by which he avails himself of the elasticity of wood. By this simple tool, his condition is materially improved. Still, he is destitute of most of the comforts, and frequently, at times, of the necessaries of life. Hence, in cold climates, great numbers of savages every winter perish from cold and famine. He next becomes a shepherd. Here he avails himself of the use of natural agents. The sheep furnishes him with wool, and the herds with milk. He now begins to taste the blessings of a regular and sufficient supply of food and clothing. He next becomes an agriculturist. Here, in addition to the agents formerly employed, he makes use of the earth, manures, and implements, and begins rapidly to accumulate capital. His wants increase, and a division of labor is necessary to supply them. He here advances with rapid progress, and at every step, employs either new agents, or else old agents more successfully; and divides his labor more skilfully, until he at length arrives at all the blessings of mature civilization.

If it be asked, how far may this increased productiveness of human industry be carried, we answer, it is impossible to tell, unless we can ascertain how great are the blessings which God has in reserve for man. Who can estimate the benefits conferred on man by the magnet, or by steam, or by the printing press? And what reason have we to suppose that the gifts of God are exhausted, or that there are not other and more excellent natural agents to be discovered, or other modes of using those which we are already acquainted with, that shall produce yet more surprising results than any which we have yet witnessed? Before the discovery of these agents, the most vivid imagination could never have conceived of the benefits which they have already conferred upon society. There is no reason to suppose that we are now more capable of fathoming the goodness of God, than our ancestors were, three or four hundred years ago.

And hence we see the inconceivable importance to a nation, of science, and of the labors of those who are devoted to the discovery of the laws of nature, and to the invention of new modes of applying these laws, to the service of man. What would be the condition of the world at the present moment, if the knowledge of navigation and magnetism, and of the laws of chemistry were abolished. Undiscovered knowledge is just as rich in the means of human happiness, as discovered knowledge. And hence, that nation which is cherishing within itself, the means for availing itself of the benefit of all the laws of the Creator, will, most rapidly provide itself with the comforts and conveniences and luxuries of life, in the greatest abundance, and at the least possible cost. Who can tell the benefit which will result to this country, when Geology has revealed to us the riches which at present remain hidden from our view, beneath the surface of the soil.

SECTION I.

OF THE USE OF NATURAL AGENTS.

We shall now proceed to consider the several means by which the productive power of industry may be increased. This section will treat of the *use of natural agents.*

A natural agent, is any quality or relation of things which can be used for the purpose of assisting us in production.

Thus, the light and heat of the sun are natural agents, without the aid of which, we could not create vegetable products.

Caloric, or artificial heat, is a natural agent, without which we could neither cook our food, prolong our lives in cold climates, give any valuable quality to metals, nor create steam for the purposes of machinery. Magnetism is a natural agent, by which we are enabled, in any part of the earth, to know in what direction we are moving.

The various powers and instincts of animals are natural agents, by which we accomplish purposes which could not be accomplished without them. Thus, the farmer avails himself of the muscular power and docility of the ox and the horse; the huntsman, of the fleetness and scent of the hound, &c.

Wind, the gravitating power of water, and steam, are natural agents, by means of which, we create the momentum necessary to the several operations in the arts.

A tool, or *a machine*, is any combination of matter, by means of which, we are enabled to avail ourselves of the qualities or relations of a natural agent. Thus, a lens or burning glass, is a tool, by means of which we concentrate, for useful purposes, the rays of the sun.

A stove, or *a fire place*, is an instrument, or tool, by which we avail ourselves of the calorific properties of fuel.

A mariner's compass is a tool, by which we avail ourselves of the peculiar quality of the magnetic needle.

A water wheel is a tool, by means of which we avail ourselves of the gravitating power of water.

A steam engine is a tool, by means of which we avail ourselves of the expansive power of steam.

The only difference between a tool and a machine is, that the one is more complicated than the other. A common hammer is a tool, by means of which we avail ourselves of the gravity and density of iron, and of the power of the lever. A trip-hammer, by which large masses of iron are fashioned and wrought, is called a machine, but the principles employed are, in both cases, the same, only that the trip-hammer is moved by a natural agent, water or steam, while the common hammer is moved by the hand.

Now, it will be easily perceived, from what has already been said, that the qualities and relations of natural agents are the *gift* of God, and being his gift, they *cost us nothing*. Thus, in order to avail ourselves of the momentum produced by a water-fall, we have only to construct the water-wheel and its necessary appendages, and place them in a proper position. We then have the use of the falling water, without further expense. As, therefore, our only outlay is the cost of the instrument by which the natural agent is rendered available, this is the only expenditure which demands the attention of the political economist.

If we reflect upon the various natural agents employed by man, we shall see that some of them can be used without any tools whatever. Such is the case in agricultural labor, with air, and the light of the sun. Others require only such simple instruments, that the effect of them upon price is not appreciable. Thus, a mariner's compass, which would last for twenty years, and assist in the transportation of half as many millions' value of merchandise, would cost but a few dollars. Others are used by few persons, and for particular and unusual purposes, as the lens, or the microscope. It is only those agents which require, in order to their employment, machinery, of which the cost is appreciable, and which are of so general necessity, that their use enters into consideration in estimating the expenses of living, that require to be specially noticed in Political Economy.

The means most universally required for creating change, is momentum, or, as it is commonly called, power. Without this, in agriculture, no change in elementary form, and, in mechanics, no change in aggregate form, and, in transportation, no change in place, can be effected. The instruments necessary to avail ourselves of the natural agents which create momentum, or which enable us to use it in particular methods, are very numerous and very costly, and form a large portion of the fixed capital of man. The natural agents which man uses for this purpose are, therefore, those which particularly claim our attention; and, to these, the remainder of this section will be devoted.

The natural agents connected with the use of momentum, may be divided into two classes:

1. Those which *create* momentum.

2. Those which enable us *to use it.*

1. *Of those which create momentum.*

This class of agents may be subdivided into two kinds: 1st. *Animate;* and, 2d. *Inanimate.*

1. *Animate.* These are, beasts of draft and burden, generally. The most common of these are, the ox, the horse, and the mule; others in use in particular districts, are the camel, the elephant, and the dog.

The subjection of animal power to the will of man marks an era in the progress of civilization; and teaches us that the first important step has been taken in the improvement of the condition of man, and in the productiveness of human industry. The ox and the horse have much greater physical power than man. They may also be sustained at a much less expense. Their food is the spontaneous production of the earth, which, for a large part of the year, they gather for themselves, and which requires no labor in preparation. They need no clothing in any latitude, and, in the warmer parts of the temperate zone, need no shelter. But, in consequence of his superiority in intellectual endowment, man can direct and govern the physical power of several of these animals, and, by attaching them to agricultural machines, can command that power at his will. If, then, by the use of animals, one man can wield a physical force equal to that of ten men, he will be able to produce, by the labor of a day, ten times as much as he could, before the introduction of animate agents. He will, therefore, by the same amount of labor, produce ten times as large an amount of objects of desire; that is, of means of human happiness. He will have a larger surplus to employ in *fixed capital* for the next year, and this surplus will be annually increasing, and increasing at the rate of compound interest. He will have a larger portion *to exchange;* hence, he will be able, also, to enjoy a larger amount of his neighbor's products. He will be able to exchange with a greater *number of producers;* hence, he will have a larger number of his desires gratified. And when once this first step has been taken, capital, unless destroyed by man's perverse moral dispositions, must increase so rapidly, that the mechanical arts soon commence, and permanent improvements and intellectual cultivation will follow in rapid succession.

In the earlier stages of society, animate power must be used for the production of momentum, in all the three departments of human industry. In the labors of agriculture, it is still employed, and must probably be thus employed forever. Nothing has yet superseded it, and there is reason to doubt whether any thing ever will supersede it. In this respect, therefore, so far as the means for the creation of momentum are concerned, the early and the later periods of society remain on a level. The improvements that have been made by the introduction of other creative forces, have generally been connected with the other modes of operative industry.

2. *Of Inanimate Natural Agents.* The inanimate agents most commonly in use, are: *The explosive force of Gunpowder; Wind; The gravitating power of Water;* and *The expansive power of Steam.*

1. *Gunpowder* is used in the blasting of rocks, in hunting, and in war. Its value, in the blasting of rocks, is very considerable. By drilling a small hole, which may be done by one man in a day, and by the use of a few ounces of gunpowder, a force may be exerted in an instant, producing an effect which, twenty men, for several days, could not otherwise have exerted. Hence, it is of very great use in all works of internal improvement, where rocks must be removed, in order to admit the passage of railroads and canals. In fact, it is doubtful whether many of the most important of these works could ever have been executed, but for this agent. Others, if the execution of them were possible, must have been accomplished at so great an expense, that the investment of capital in them

would not have been profitable, and, of course, it would not have been made.

Gunpowder is also used extensively in war. If war be beneficial, or even necessary, gunpowder is an agent of the utmost importance ; for, by no other means yet discovered, is it possible to destroy so many men, with so little physical suffering, and with so little personal labor. It has also a moral advantage over other methods of slaughter, inasmuch as the destruction of human life in this manner, excites less sensibly the ferocity of the human heart. On this account, wars, since its introduction, have been conducted on more humane principles than formerly. It has also been a valuable auxiliary to the progress of civilization, since it has conferred on civilized, an undisputed mastery over uncivilized nations. There has not been, for centuries, any danger to Christendom from barbarian invasion. Besides, the more energetic are the means of destruction in war, the less is the loss of life in battle. Hence, of a given number of combatants in an engagement, a much smaller proportion is now slain than formerly. This might almost give rise to the seemingly paradoxical hope, that some means of destruction might yet be invented, so overwhelming in its effects, as to put the smallest number of men on a level with the greatest, and hence to put an end to wars altogether.

2. Another agent used for the creation of momentum, is *Wind.* Wind, as a stationary agent, is an important mechanical power, in countries destitute of water power, or of the fuel necessary for the production of steam, or of the capital which must be invested in the machinery required in the use of more expensive agents. Its principal advantage, is its cheapness. It costs nothing to create it, and the machinery by which it is applied, is simple, and easily constructed.

The disadvantages of wind, are its uncertainty, both in quantity and in time, and the difficulty with which it is regulated. In consequence of the *irregularity* of its *force*, it is impossible to employ it in labor requiring delicacy of operation; and, in consequence of its *uncertainty* in *time*, it could not be employed where the labor of many persons was dependent on its assistance.

As a locomotive power, on water, wind is almost universally used in navigation. Though the direction in which it acts, is variable; yet, nautical skill enables us to use it when blowing from almost any point whatever. Its variation in the quantity of force, is here also a matter of less consequence, since this circumstance can affect the operation to be performed, only in respect to time. And variation, even in this respect, has, in a great degree, yielded to science and enterprise. It is astonishing to observe with what precision and certainty, voyages are now made between New York and Liverpool. Hence it is, that this agent is made use of in all foreign navigation. Steam has taken its place in the navigation of rivers, and along the coast; and attempts are now in progress to employ it upon the ocean, but with what success, it remains yet to be seen. It is probable that, for packet ships, it may be used with advantage; but for vessels of burthen, it is doubtful whether any thing will ever take the place of wind. The splendid discoveries of Dr. Nott, by which anthracite coal has been successfully introduced, as a fuel for the generation of steam, will probably greatly facilitate the use of this agent in foreign navigation.

3. Another agent used for the creation of momentum, is the *gravitating power of Water*. This is used only as a stationary agent. Its advantages are, that it is cheap, tolerably constant, and frequently, is capable of exerting great mechanical force. Its disadvantages are, that it is

stationary; that is, that it can be used only in situations where it has been created by nature. Hence, it is frequently at a considerable distance from the seaports whence the manufacturer derives his supplies, and whence he exports his products. In such cases, the cost of transportation must be deducted from the profits of the establishment, and of course are, to this amount, a diminution of its value.

Water cannot always be commanded in *sufficient quantity.* Very few mill seats are secure from the liability to suffer from the want of water. This is a great inconvenience, inasmuch as, in seasons of drought, a large number of the laborers must be unemployed, and a large portion of the expenses of the establishment must be incurred, without yielding any remuneration to the proprietor.

Another disadvantage of water power is, that it is liable to danger from inundation. Though this may be guarded against, in many cases; yet, it frequently can be done only at an expense which reduces greatly the cheapness of the agent. Notwithstanding these disadvantages, water power will probably be always used, where great mechanical force is required; where the machinery to be employed is simple; and where the operation does not require the greatest possible nicety of execution.

4. The power, however, most commonly in use at present, is *Steam.* Its advantages are, that it can be used to create any required degree of mechanical force; that it is perfectly under human control; that it may be created in any place where fuel can be obtained; that it can be used at will, either as a stationary, or a locomotive power; and that it can be made to act with perfect regularity. Its only disadvantage, is its expensiveness. The ma-

chinery by which it is generated is costly, and requires frequent repairs; and the fuel, by which it is maintained, is a very serious item of consumption. The price of engines, however, will be gradually reduced, as the demand for them increases. And it is probable, that, by improvement in their construction, the consumption of fuel will be greatly diminished; while increased facilities for transportation will materially reduce its price. The introduction of steam power has greatly reduced the price of fuel in Great Britain.

The question whether steam or water power should be used in any particular case, is, I suppose, to be decided by their relative expensiveness. This will be decided, principally by the place in which the power may be required. Where water power can be procured in abundance, and sufficiently near to a market or to tide water, it will generally be the cheaper. But where it is variable in quantity, or is at a considerable distance from the place of delivery, the cost of transportation will frequently overbalance its other advantages, and render steam power the more economical. Machinery propelled by steam, can be erected and carried on upon a wharf, or in the midst of a city; and hence it avoids all the cost of unnecessary transportation. Machinery propelled by water power, can be erected only at the place where the water power exists, and, of course, is subject to all the expense of transportation between that place and the market.*

* Whilst these sheets are passing through the press, I observe it stated in the public prints, that at Lowell, Massachusetts, the expense of steam, is to that of water power, as one hundred to one hundred and twenty-five, or, as four to five. I have not, at the instant, the means of ascertaining the truth of this statement. If it be true, it is of vast importance, and teaches us that manufactures may be established, in any part of our country, where fuel can be procured at a reasonable cost. The fuel employed at Lowell, is, I presume, brought from Pennsylvania.

The ADVANTAGES of *inanimate over animate natural agents, are several.*

1. Inanimate agents can, within a small compass, and with comparatively little weight, produce a vastly greater amount of momentum, than animate agents. Thus, a steam engine of one hundred and fifty, or two hundred horse power, occupies but a small space, and forms but a small part of the cargo of a vessel. But, so great a number of horses could scarcely be carried in any vessel designed to transport either freight or passengers; and besides, no mechanical arrangement has yet been devised, by which such a number of animals could profitably be employed upon one operation.

2. They are *continuous;* that is, they are never liable to fatigue, and never need rest. Animals must spend the greater part of their time, in feeding or in repose. Specially is this the case, if they are worked rapidly. During this time, the labor which they perform must either be suspended, or else other animals must take their place. A horse cannot labor severely, more than eight hours in twenty-four. Hence, if the uninterrupted labor of horses were required for twenty-four hours, three relays must be provided. Thus, if a boat were required to perform a voyage in twenty-four hours, she must employ three relays of horses; that is, a steam boat worked by a power equal to that of one hundred and fifty horses, would require four hundred and fifty horses, in order to create the necessary momentum.

3. Hence, there is a great gain in *Economy.* The first cost of inanimate, is generally less than that of animate agents; they are liable to no diseases; they require no food; and create expense, only while they are performing their work. Were the labor now performed by steam, to

be performed by horses, the price of the ordinary necessaries of life would be quadrupled, and many articles of ordinary use would be placed out of the reach of any but the most opulent. Nor is this all. The substitution of inanimate, for animate power, has a great tendency to reduce the cost or to increase the supply of all agricultural products. Suppose, that, by the use of steam, one thousand horses can be dispensed with. A horse requires for sustenance, throughout the year, as much agricultural produce as would support eight men. If, then, these one thousand horses can be dispensed with, there may be produced, on the land which was formerly employed for the production of hay, as much grain as will support eight thousand men. This must, at first, reduce the price of grain; but as, in the end, the price of grain would rise to the general average, the result would be, that the district would support eight thousand more men than before.

4. There is, also, commonly a gain in *personal safety*. Inanimate agents act under laws which may be known and obeyed, and of which the results may be commonly foreseen and guarded against. Animals are endowed with passions and will, which we can frequently neither control nor influence. Besides, the greater expensiveness of the individual machines employed in theuse of inanimate agents, renders it for the interest of the proprietor, to employ men of experience and responsibility to manage them. This very sensibly diminishes the risk. When we reflect upon the vast amount of travelling, by steamboats and railroads, it must be evident that, notwithstanding the accidents to which they are liable, a vastly greater amount of human life would be sacrificed, if the same number of persons were transported by horses. It is also to be remembered, that the use of steam is yet in its infancy, and that greater experience and skill will

materially reduce the number of accidents to which this mode of conveyance is at present liable.

5. Inanimate agents can be used *without the infliction of pain*. Inanimate agents are insensible. Where the labor to be accomplished is either severe, or where it requires great speed, animals must be rapidly consumed. This exposes them to great suffering. A horse, in a stage coach, can rarely travel, *rapidly*, more than ten miles a day; and most horses will endure even this labor but for a short time. From this suffering, inanimate power is exempt. It never endures pain, from being over driven.

6. Animate power decreases with velocity. Hence, we must soon arrive at a point, beyond which it can no further be used to create momentum. If we represent the tractive force of a horse, when moving at two miles an hour, at 100, his force, at the rate of three miles, will be 81; at the rate of four miles, 54; at the rate of five miles, 49; at the rate of six miles, 36; while, at the top of his speed, he can carry nothing more than his own weight. An engine, on the contrary, works as powerfully at one degree of velocity as at another. In all cases, therefore, in which both great power and great velocity are required, inanimate power must, of necessity, be employed.

From these causes, we see that inanimate is rapidly taking the place of animate power, both where stationary, and where locomotive force is required. By the additional speed which it is capable of producing, it gives rise to great economy of *time*. This, to all persons engaged in active employments, is a consideration of vast moment. Being a continuous agent, it is also enabled to act with the greatest certainty. Hence, men may adjust their transactions, in different places, with entire precision. This is also another source of economy, both of time and capital. And besides, notwithstanding the expensiveness of the arrangements for the use of locomotive forces, yet the amount of additional travelling to which they give rise is so great, that the expensiveness of transportation between different places is, in general, materially diminished.

II. *Of the natural agents by which momentum is* APPLIED.

It is obvious that a great addition is made to human power, where the agents for *creating* momentum have been discovered. But this is not all. There may be formed several combinations of matter, by which mere human force may be greatly assisted, and which, by being united with the agents for creating momentum, may greatly increase, and vary, and give adaptation to, its utility. These are called the mechanical powers, which are treated of at large, in works on Mechanics and Natural Philosophy. In their simple form, they are, the lever, the wheel and axle, the inclined plane, the screw, the pulley, and the wedge. They are variously combined, for producing the different results of mechanics, but may be all reduced to these simple elements.

By means of these, the muscular power of man is enabled greatly to increase its effect; that is, a man, by his own strength, can now accomplish labor which he could not have accomplished without them. Though these instruments give no new strength, yet they greatly increase the effectiveness of that which already exists; and hence, their invention marks an important era in the progress of civilization. It is also to be remarked, that their origin, in point of time, is far in advance of the discovery of the creative agents. Archimedes had made great progress in the discovery and application of these *modifying* powers, when the use of *creative* agents was almost unknown.

The triumph of human skill is, however, achieved, when these two forms of natural agency are combined in a single machine. By the *one*, we *generate* power, to what extent soever we choose; and, by the *other*, we *modify* it in any form, give to it any application, and direct it to any purpose that our convenience may require. It is in this manner, that man renders all the various powers of nature tributary to himself. He can thus create, and use as he pleases, as great a power as he desires. He devolves the labor upon nature, and he has only to fabricate the instruments, and give them their direction. He is successful, just in proportion as he does this; since nature always works with undeviating accuracy, with unerring skill, with indefatigable perseverance; and she always works for nothing.

It may be useful to specify some of the results accomplished by the various instruments, which man employs for modifying that momentum which is exerted by the first class of natural agents.

1. We are thus enabled to *change the direction* of the power. Thus, in the cylinder of the steam engine, the momentum is created in perpendicular or horizontal strokes. This being, by means of an arm and a crank, changed into a circular motion, moves the paddle-wheels of a steamboat. Thus, also, in the machinery for moving a trip-hammer, a circular is changed into a perpendicular motion, by the striking of the cogs of a wheel, upon the short arm of a lever, while the hammer is attached to the other arm.

2. We exchange *power for velocity*. This is done in all spinning machinery. By water or by steam, we cause a large wheel to revolve ten, twenty, or thirty times in a minute, and with a power equal to that which could be

produced by fifty or one hundred horses. In spinning, however, we need small power, but great velocity. Hence, by the combination of various large and small wheels, we produce a velocity, in a thousand spindles, equal to many thousand revolutions in a minute. The whole of this fifty or one hundred horse power, is thus spread over a large manufactory, and adapted, by various contrivances, to every degree of velocity, and every form of motion that may be required.

3. We are thus enabled to *exert forces too great for animate power.* By water power, or by steam, we can generate as great a force as we please; and we have only to combine with it the proper adjustments, in order to exert any momentum which we desire. The power required to roll and hammer iron, or copper, to propel steamboats, to forge anchors, and that used in several other of the arts, is greater than could be exerted by any force with which we are acquainted, unless it were exerted by means of some combination of the mechanical forces.

4. We are thus also enabled to execute operations too delicate for human touch. Very delicate operations, soon weary the nervous system by the excessive attention which they of necessity require. Thus, to spin the finest thread on a spinning wheel, there must be great accuracy, both in the velocity of the wheel, and in the muscular power exerted in drawing out the thread. This requires an effort of attention, which the human system cannot long maintain, and, of course, the thread will frequently be uneven. But, by means of machinery, both of these operations may be adjusted with mathematical accuracy; and, as machines have no nerves, they will be pefectly faithful to that adjustment. Thus we invariably see that the most delicate fabrics are those that are wrought by natural agents. Hence machinery is of necessity used in the

manufacture of such articles as require for their formation identity of result, such as screws, types, &c.

5. By means of machinery, we are enabled to *accumulate power.* We thus exchange a continuous and small force, for a sudden and violent one. Such is the case with the pile-driver, and the common beetle or mallet, when used in combination with the wedge.

6. By the same means, we are enabled to *exchange a short and irregular effort for a continuous and regular movement*, or to spread the action of a short, over a long period of time. This is done in clocks, watches, and other similar machinery. Here we spread the action of a minute, over a day, or a week, and with almost mathematical accuracy.

In consequence of the above mentioned application of machinery, various other advantages are realised in production. For instance; there is frequently a great saving of material, as in the change from making boards with the adze, to that of making them with the saw; and again the labor of natural agents is so much cheaper, that many articles which would otherwise have been worthless, are now deserving of attention, as they may now be profitably endowed with some form of value.

I close these remarks, upon the use of natural agents, with an extract, very graphically describing the power of the steam engine, which has commonly been ascribed to Francis Jeffrey, Esquire, of Edinburgh:

"It (the steam engine) has become a thing, stupendous alike for its force and its flexibility; for the prodigious power which it can exert; and the ease, precision and ductility with which it can be varied, distributed and applied. The trunk of an elephant, that can pick up a pin or rend an oak, is as nothing to it. It can engrave a seal, and crush masses of obdurate metal before it; draw out, without breaking, a thread as fine as a gossamer; and lift up a ship of war, like a bauble in the air. It can embroider muslin, and forge anchors; cut steel into ribands, and impel loaded vessels against the fury of the winds and waves.

"It would be difficult to estimate the value of the benefits which these inventions have conferred upon the country. There is no branch of industry that has not been indebted to them, and in all the most material, they have not only widened most magnificently the field of its exertions, but multiplied, a thousand fold, the amount of its productions. It is our improved steam engine, that has fought the battles of Europe, and exalted and sustained, through the late tremendous contest, the political greatness of our land. It is the same great power, which enables us to pay our national debt, and to maintain the arduous struggle in which we are still engaged, with the skill and capital of countries less oppressed with taxation.

"But these are poor and narrow views of its importance. It has increased, indefinitely, the mass of human comforts and enjoyments, and rendered cheap and accessible, all over the world, the materials of wealth and prosperity. It has armed the feeble hand of man, in short, with a power to which no limits can be assigned; completed the dominion of mind over the most refractory qualities of matter; and laid a sure foundation for all those future miracles of mechanical power, which are to aid and reward the labors of after generations."

SECTION II.

OF DIVISION OF LABOR.

We have shown that the productiveness of human industry may be greatly increased by the discovery of the qualities and relations of things, and by the invention of instruments, by which those qualities may be applied and modified. In this manner, the power of man receives an almost incalculable augmentation. But this is not all. It is found that the result of human effort may be still farther very greatly increased. Thus: supposing the agents of nature, and also their mode of application to be known, and that a given number of men are about to perform an operation, they may make such arrangements among themselves, as will, in a given time, and with a given expenditure of labor, enable them to accomplish a vastly greater result than could be accomplished without such arrangements. The mode in which this is effected, is by *division of labor.*

Division of labor, is always, to some degree, employed where different individuals are engaged in the different branches of human industry. Thus labor is divided, when different persons employ themselves in the several departments of discovery, application, and operation. Labor is still further divided, when those employed in these great departments, are separated into distinct classes, each class devoting itself to the accomplishment of one particular object. Thus, one man investigates the laws of mechanics; another, those of astronomy; and a third, those of vegetation. One man is devoted to the profession of law; and another, to that of medicine; while each separate trade, is employed in the execution of a particular operation. By all these divisions, it is manifest that the result of the whole is greatly increased. It is only the savage, that combines in his own person, in all their departments, the character of philosopher, inventor, and operator. He approximates to the civilized state, only in so far as he begins to confine himself to some particular calling. And it is always in the most advanced periods of civilization, that division of labor is carried to its ultimate limits.

But, besides this, the different parts of a single operation may be analyzed; and to each part the whole labor of a single individual may be confined. Thus, the labor of making a pin may be divided into wire drawing, wire straightening, pointing, heading, tinning, &c. In political economy, labor is said to be divided, just in so far as these several processes are assigned to separate operators. It is found, by experience, that such an arrangement increases the productiveness of human labor to an extent, which, to a person who had not examined the facts, would appear wholly incredible. The principles on which this increased productiveness of labor depends, are the following:

1. Division of labor shortens the period required for learning an operation. The more complicated the operation, the longer is the time necessary for acquiring the skill requisite to the performing of it successfully. But this time spent in learning, is useless to the operator and to society, only in so far as it is necessary to the creation of the product. The longer the time necessary for learning an operation, the higher must be the wages of the operator, for the remainder of his life; and also, of course, the greater must be the price of his products. If this can

be lessened, the price of course will fall. Now, that this is lessened by division of labor, is evident from an obvious example. Suppose a given process, say the making of nails, consists of seven operations; and that each of these operations required one year's practice, before it could be successfully performed. Now, if seven men were to learn this occupation, and each one were obliged to learn every operation, the time required would be $7 \times 7 = 49$ years; whereas, if each of them were required to learn but one, the time would be but $7 \times 1 = 7$, or, the difference would be, $49 - 7 = 42$ years of human labor, or six-sevenths of the whole time, which would thus be saved. There would be six years more of productive labor, in the life of each of these men; and, as they had spent less time in acquiring their art, they could afford to exercise it for lower wages.

But, besides this, there is, intimately connected with this cause, another, of considerable importance. Every one, in learning an art, must, by unskilfulness, destroy a considerable portion of capital. And this amount of capital will be in proportion to the number of operations which he is obliged to learn. Thus, suppose a man learns seven operations, and, in learning each, destroys ten dollars' worth of capital, the amount which he will destroy, in acquiring his whole trade, will be $7 \times 10 = 70$. If he have to learn but one, it will be but ten dollars; and thus, the difference will be $70 - 10 = 60$ dollars, upon every such individual. A difference, so great as these two combined, when spread over the whole face of society, will have no inconsiderable effect upon the annual nett revenue of a community.

2. When one man performs all the operations required in a complicated process, much time is lost in passing from one operation to another. By division of labor, this loss is avoided.

The effect of habit is known to every one. It renders any operation easy, which is frequently repeated. The mind and the muscles become adapted to a particular form of labor; but, if that form of labor be suspended, and our attention be directed to another, it requires a considerable time before we can acquire a different habit, and, in the mean time, the good effects of the preceding habit, are, to a considerable degree, lost. Hence, he who is frequently passing from one occupation to another, is in the condition of him who is, during his whole life, *forming habits;* and never in the condition of him, who has the advantage of habits *already formed.* Besides, this long habit produces in the muscles a capacity for continued exertion. He who is in the *habit* of performing an operation, can perform it, without sensible fatigue, for hours together. Every one who has ever sawed wood, or used a spade in a garden, is sensible of this fact. Now, all this advantage is lost, by turning frequently from one operation to another.

3. Where complicated tools are to be used, and there is no division of labor, much time is also lost in adjusting them to the different kinds of work. By division of labor, this disadvantage is obviated. Suppose that nails, of different sizes, are to be made, and it is necessary that the machinery, in order to adapt it to the different kinds of work, should be frequently adjusted; the time so occupied produces nothing, and is lost. If, on the contrary, one machine is permanently used for the manufacture of nails of one particular size, all this loss is avoided. This is also more obvious, when the adjustment involves expense; as, for instance, when a furnace is used. If a furnace be heated, and then suffered to cool while the operator is performing some other labor, the fuel consumed, after he leaves it, and that which is used to bring it again to the requisite temperature, are a total loss, in addition to

that of the time and labor required in lighting the fire, and in waiting for the rise of temperature. By dividing the labor, so that one person shall be always employed at the furnace, whilst others are employed at other parts of the process, much capital and labor will be saved.

4. By constantly pursuing the same occupation, a degree of skill and dexterity is acquired, which greatly increases the productiveness of human labor. This advantage is lost, by employing the same individual upon several operations. Adam Smith informs us, that a blacksmith, who occasionally makes nails, but whose whole business is not that of a nail-maker, can make but from eight hundred to one thousand nails a day; whilst a lad, who has never exercised any other trade, can make upwards of twenty-three hundred a day. All who have been accustomed to visit manufactories, must have been surprised to observe the dexterity which is acquired, even by children, in performing the operations in which they are exclusively engaged. It is probable that the performers of jugglery or sleight-of-hand, derive their skill, almost entirely, from this cause. They seldom perform more than a few operations, but by practising these, and these alone, for a great length of time, they at last attain to a proficiency, which, to a spectator, is incomprehensible.

5. Division of labor suggests the contrivance of tools for the performance of the operation in which it is employed.

The more completely any process is analyzed, the simpler must become the individual operations of which it is composed. And the simpler any operation is, the easier is it to contrive a tool, or an adjustment, by which it may be performed. Adam Smith informs us, that, in the first steam engines, boys were constantly employed to open a communication between the boiler and cylinder, according as the piston ascended or descended. One of these boys observed, that, by tying a string from the handle of the valve which opened this communication to another part of the machine, the valve would open and shut without his assistance, and leave him at liberty to play with his fellows. One of the most important improvements of this machine was thus, by division of labor, brought within the capacity of a playful boy. It would have been very difficult to invent machinery for the making of nails, when all the processes were considered as a complicated whole. But after the several operations are divided, and are assigned to individuals separately, it becomes comparatively easy to construct an adjustment, by which any one of them, singly, could be performed.

This is the first step in invention. But this is not all. After these several single instruments have been invented, the next step is to combine them together. This is the most finished effort of mechanical genius. This is the principal difference between a tool and a machine. A tool performs one single operation; a machine combines several tools together, and accomplishes either the whole, or a considerable part, of a complicated process.

6. Every one, at all acquainted with manufacturing employments, must have observed, that some of the operations, in a given process, require greater muscular power, or greater skill, or greater dexterity than others. Some, for instance, can be performed only by the most experienced workmen, while others can be perfectly well performed by children. Now, by division of labor, a manufacturer is enabled to employ, upon each operation, precisely the labor adapted to it, and is obliged to pay for each portion of the labor no more than it is actually worth. This must greatly diminish the cost of production. Thus,

the manufacture of pins is divided into ten different operations, and each operation employs one laborer. But some of these laborers are men; others are women and children; and their wages vary from six shillings to four and a half pence sterling a day. If the labor were not divided, one person must understand the whole process, and, therefore, must be employed at the highest price of labor; and hence, he must be paid at the rate of six shillings a day, for that part of the work which is worth only four and a half pence a day. Every one must see that this would greatly increase the price of pins, and also occasion a great deficiency in labor. It is by this means, also, that ocpation is provided for the weak and the aged, for females and for children, who would, otherwise, be unable to earn any thing. Thus, all the labor of the community is rendered productive, and an immense amount is annually added to the revenue of a country. Nor is the gain to be estimated at simply what is thus earned. The whole community is thus acquiring those habits of industry and self-dependence, which are essential to its happiness and well-being, no less than to its rapid accumulation of capital.

Nor are the benefits of the division of labor confined to mechanical processes. Their results have been equally interesting, in those cases where this principle has been applied to intellectual labor. The effect of such a division is seen in the following account, which I introduce here, not only because it very happily illustrates this whole subject, but also because it may suggest to scientific men, some other cases in which it may be again applied with similar benefit.

During the period of the French revolution, the government was desirous of producing a series of mathematical tables, in order to facilitate the extension of the decimal system, which had been recently adopted. They directed their mathematicians to construct such tables on the most extensive scale. The superintendence of the work was confided to M. Prony. It happened that shortly after he had undertaken it, he opened, in a bookstore, Adam Smith's "Wealth of Nations," and, by accident, turned to the chapter on division of labor. The thought immediately suggested itself, that this might be adopted in the work in which he was engaged. He immediately followed out the suggestion, and arranged his plan accordingly. He divided the persons who were to execute the labor, into three sections:

The first section was composed of five or six of the most eminent mathematicians of France. Their duty was to ascertain the analytical expressions which were most readily adapted to simple numerical calculation, and which could be performed by many individuals employed at the same time. The formulæ on the use of which it had decided, were to be delivered to the second section.

The second section consisted of seven or eight persons, of considerable aquaintance with mathematics, whose duty it was, to convert into numbers the formulæ put into their hands by the first section; and then to deliver out these formulæ to the members of the third section, and to receive from them the finished calculations. These they could verify without repeating the work.

The third section consisted of sixty or eighty persons. They received the numbers from the second section, and using nothing more than addition and subtraction, returned to that section, the finished tables. Nine-tenths of this class had no knowledge of arithmetic beyond its first two rules; and it is remarkable that these were usually found more correct in their calculations, than those that possessed a more extensive knowledge of the subject. The extent of the labor, which was thus executed in a remarkably short space of time, may be estimated, when it is stated that the tables thus formed are computed to occupy seventeen large folio volumes. And yet, we see that the greatest part of the labor was actually accomplished by persons who might be employed at very small expense, and who could do the work assigned to them, as perfectly as those whose labor was the most expensive.*

We thus see the manner in which the productiveness of human labor may be increased. 1st. By discovering the various agents of nature which God has created for our benefit; 2d. By applying these agents to the service of man; 3d. By so arranging and adjusting human industry, that the labor necessary to be employed, may operate with the greatest possible advantage. In one or other of these methods, must every improvement in the physical condition of mankind operate. And, civilization advances just in proportion as all of them combined are brought to bear upon the work of production; that is, of creation of objects of desire, in other words, of means for human happiness.

SECTION III.

THE LIMITATIONS TO THE DIVISION OF LABOR.

We now proceed to another branch of the subject, *The limitation to the division of labor.* These are of two kinds 1st, *from the nature of the process*, and 2d, *from other causes.*

* Babbage, on Economy of Machinery.

I. From the nature of the process. Every process can be analyzed into its ultimate elements; that is, into the various simple processes of which it is composed. Thus, the straightening of a wire is one operation, the cutting it into equal lengths is another, the sharpening of the points is another, the heading of a pin is another, &c. But when we have reduced it to its simple operations, we can now proceed no farther. Hence, here is our necessary limit; for it is no *division of labor* to employ two men to perform precisely the same operation. Hence, an establishment which carries division to this limit, will be able from what has been said, to undersell another which does not carry it to the same degree of perfection. And hence, in establishing a manufactory, it is important so to adjust the number and kind of workmen, that, when the different operations of a process have been assigned to different persons, *these persons may be in such proportions as exactly and fully to employ each other.* The more perfectly this is accomplished, the greater will be the economy. And, this having been once ascertained, it is also evident, that the establishment cannot be successfully enlarged, unless it employ multiples of this number of workmen.

II. *Division of labor may be limited* by other causes. These are: 1st. *Capital.* 2d. *Demand.*

1. *By Capital.* Division of labor in manufactures, cannot be carried on, unless the proprietor have sufficient capital to employ, at the same time, all the persons necessary to such a division, and to keep them so employed, until the proceeds of their work enable him to furnish them again with fresh material. This is, of course, a considerable outlay, and supposes a considerable accumulation of the proceeds of pre-exerted industry. Hence, in a poor, or in a new country, there is but little division of labor. No one has more than enough capital to employ

himself, and perhaps one or two laborers ; and hence, each individual performs all the operations of each process, and frequently those of several processes. The same individual is the farrier, blacksmith, cutler, and perhaps wheelwright, for a whole settlement. To illustrate this by a single instance : If a nailer be able to purchase no larger amount of iron and coal than he can use in the manufacture of nails in a day, he must perform all the parts of the process himself ; and, of course, must labor very disadvantageously. As soon, however, as he is able to double his capital, he may employ another person to work with him, and they may then introduce a division of labor. When he has tripled his capital, he may employ another workman, and carry his division still farther. He may thus go on, until he have reduced the process to its simplest elements. When he has gone thus far, the accumulation of his annual capital, will enable him to invest something in fixed capital. He will thus be able to purchase some of the simpler machines, by which some of the parts of his process may be executed. To these he will add others, as he advances in wealth, until his accumulated means enable him to combine them into one machine, for completing the whole process. Thus, he becomes a manufacturer, and derives the larger part of his revenue, from the use of his fixed capital. It is not pretended that all these changes always, or frequently, take place within the life-time of a single individual. The progress of society is not generally so rapid. Yet they sometimes occur, in the manner which I have stated. I give the illustration, to show the tendency of things, and the power of accumulated capital. But, whether the results are comprised in the life-time of one, two, or three individuals, the principle is the same.

2. Division of labor is controlled by *the demand* for the article produced. Suppose that, in a given district, there

is a demand for one hundred pounds of nails per day, and that these can be made by two men. If three men could, by division of labor, make two hundred pounds per day, there would be but small gain, either to the workmen or to the public; because these men would, of course, lie idle half of their time, and, for this time, they must be paid, as well as for the time in which they were employed. Or, if they did not lie absolutely idle, that portion of their time which was employed on other labor, would be of comparatively small value; and they, by attending to other business, would lose the skill which complete division of labor confers; and which is one of its principal benefits. The case is still stronger, if we take into view the fact, that division of labor supposes a large investment of fixed capital, and that those who are educated to any manufacturing business, can rarely employ themselves upon any thing else. If the laborers at any of our manufactories were employed only half the time, their wages must be doubled; for their families must eat one day, as well as another, and the interest of the whole investment must be charged upon half the quantity of product. These causes, together with the loss of skill in workmen, would more than double the price of products, and would, of necessity, carry back the division of labor, to its less perfect state.

But this demand must depend upon several circumstances. The most important of these are the following:

1. The *number of the consumers.* When the number of inhabitants is small, as in a newly settled country, or in an isolated situation, the demand must, of course, correspond to their number. One hundred men will require but one-tenth as many hats, or shoes, as one thousand men. It is on this account that wealth accumulates most rapidly on navigable waters, because the market of the producers is not limited to themselves, but may be easily extended to other places.

2. By *the wealth of the inhabitants.* Demand does not signify *simple desire* for an article, but *desire* for it, combined with the *ability* and *willingness* to give for it what will remunerate the producer. Hence, the greater the ability, in a given population, to remunerate the producer, the greater will be the demand. The demand for hats, in a population of one thousand men, would be limited to those persons in that population who *were able to buy a hat.* The larger the proportion of such individuals, the better it would be for the hatter, and for every other producer. Hence we see, that every individual is interested in the prosperity of every other individual in the community.

3. *By the cost of the article.* The greater the cost of a product, the smaller will be the number of persons who are able to purchase it. Hence, the less will be the demand; and hence, also, the less opportunity will there be for division of labor. And, besides, the greater the cost of the article, the greater amount of capital is required, in order to produce it by division of labor. Hence, this cause operates in two ways to prevent the employment of this means of effecting the reduction of price. Thus, if a community consist of one thousand men, and of these, one hundred be worth one thousand dollars per year; four hundred be worth five hundred dollars; and the remainder be worth but two hundred and fifty dollars per year; and an article be produced within the reach of only the first of these classes, it can have but one hundred purchasers; if it come within the reach of the second class, it will have five hundred; and if it come within the reach of the third class, it will have one thousand purchasers. Hence it is, that division of labor is but sparingly used in the manufacture of rich jewelry, and in articles of expensive luxury; while it is so universally used in the production of all articles of common use. Hence we see,

that the benefits of the use of natural agents and of division of labor, are vastly greater, and more important to the middling and lower classes, than to the rich. These means of increased production, reduce the cost of the necessaries and of the essential conveniences of life to the lowest rate, and, of course, bring them, as far as possible, within the reach of all.

4. *By facilities of transportation.* This is evident, from what has been said. The cost of an article depends not only on the cost of its *original* production, but also upon the cost necessary to *bring it* to the consumer. Coal may be very cheap at a coal mine, but if it must be borne on the shoulders of men to the consumer, it would, at a few miles from the mine, become so dear, that no one would be able to use it. The demand would be so small, that there would be no profit either in investing capital in machinery, or in employing division of labor to raise it from the mine. But if horses be used to transport it to the consumer, the demand will increase. Again, if, for horses, canals and railroads be substituted, it will become cheap, and the demand will increase still more; and, with every such improvement, the circle of consumption expands, of which the mine is the centre. The same principle applies to manufactures, specially those of iron or heavy ware, and it applies, just in proportion as transportation forms a large or a small part of the cost to the consumer. And thus, in general, we see the principle on which facilities for internal communication improve the condition of both the other branches of industry. For this reason, the price of land and of grain, rises in a district through which a canal or a railroad passes; and for the same reason, manufactories may, at one time, be successfully established in situations where they at another time would have been useless, if not ruinous to the proprietor. And, still more generally, we see how all the branches of

labor mutually assist each other. A railroad or a canal can never profitably be constructed in a country where there is nothing to be transported. But where agriculture, manufactures and commerce are productive, and hence require a large amount of transportation, there, these facilities are immediately in demand. Were Liverpool and Manchester to decline, of what use would be the railroad between them? And, on the other hand, the railroad between them, by reducing the cost of all articles bought and sold, diminishes the cost of living in both places, enables the producer to come into market with greater advantages, increases the profit in all kinds of industry, facilitates the accumulation of capital, and thus adds greatly to the annual revenue of both cities.

I have thus far considered the division of labor, as it exists among the inhabitants of the same place, and in the same situation. The same principle, however, applies to people of *different districts*. Here, it is not merely a matter of choice, but, in a great measure, of necessity; that is, it is required by the very conditions of our being.

It is manifest that the different portions of the same country possess different facilities for producing the objects of human desire. No district possesses advantages for producing every thing. And yet more, almost every district possesses peculiar facilities for producing something. Now, natural advantages are clearly nothing more than means of increased productiveness of labor, in the creation of any particular product. If one soil will produce forty bushels of wheat to the acre, with the same labor that another will produce twenty, the labor of the first is twice as productive as that of the second; that is, the owner of the one has a machine, by which he can, with the same labor, produce twice as much as his neighbor. But, perhaps the soil which will produce only twenty bushels of wheat, will produce forty bushels of corn per acre, while the other soil will produce only twenty. This second soil is, therefore, an instrument which gives a double productiveness to labor, in the raising of corn. Now, it is manifest, that if each one devotes himself to the production of that for which nature has given him peculiar facilities, his amount of production will be greater, he will himself be richer, and the whole community will be supplied at a diminished cost. Suppose each occupied twenty acres, and each produced the crop for which he had the greater advantages; the result would be, $20 \times 40 = 800$ of wheat, and the same of corn; $= 800$ bushels of wheat, and 800 of corn. Suppose, again, they divided their crops, and each appropriated ten acres to wheat, and ten to corn; the result would be, $10 \times 40 = 400$ wheat and $10 \times 20 = 200$ of corn, and $10 \times 40 = 400$ of corn, and $10 \times 20 = 200$ of wheat; that is, 600 of wheat, and 600 of corn; that is, there would be 600, instead of 800 bushels of each raised, and the loss to both, and to the community, would be 200 bushels of each a year. By so much would they both be poorer than by devoting themselves wholly to that product for which each had the greatest natural advantages.

Or, to take another case. Suppose one district rich in soil, and adapted to the production of wheat, but level and far inland, and therefore, unadapted, by position, and want of the proper natural agents, to the production of manufactures; and another district, on the sea board, hilly and sterile, adapted to manufactures, but unadapted to the culture of wheat. On the first, with one day's labor, a man may raise two bushels of wheat; but could produce but four yards of cloth. On the other, by the same labor, a man can produce twelve yards of cloth, but can raise but one bushel of wheat. Now, it is manifest, that by each district's devoting its labor to that kind of production, for which it has the greatest natural facilities, the production of the whole country will be increased. It is also evident, that a man in the wheat district will provide himself with cloth at a cheaper rate, by raising wheat, and procuring cloth by exchange, than by manufacturing it himself; and on the other hand, that the manufacturer will provide himself with wheat, at a much cheaper rate, by making cloth, than by raising wheat himself. Thus, by this form of division of labor, the productive power of both is increased; their desires are gratified at the expense of less labor; and thus, both are rendered richer and happier.

All this seems obvious, if only the several districts of the same country be compared. And it is obvious, because every one perceives that God has bestowed upon different districts of the same country, different advantages, which it is for the interest of that country that each district should improve to the utmost. But every one may see, that the same principles apply to different nations inhabiting the different quarters of the globe. The separation of the earth into warring nations, is nothing but the arbitrary work of man; it alters neither the qualities nor the relations which God has given to things, nor the laws under which he has constituted man. If a man own a farm, of which one part is suited only to tillage, and another part only to grazing, and he divide it, and sell the pasture land to his neighbor; this does not alter the nature of the soil. Will it not be just as profitable to appropriate each part to the purpose for which God designed it, after the purchase, as before.?

Every man needs, for the gratification of his innocent desires, nay, for his conveniences and even necessaries, the productions of every part of the globe. To be convinced of this, we have only to enumerate the articles which furnish our houses, the food that covers our tables, and the raiment which clothes our bodies. How greatly would all our means of happiness be diminished, were we deprived of the iron, the furs, and the hemp of the North; the coffee, teas, sugar, rice, fruits, and spices of the South; or the wool, the wheat, and the manufactures, of temperate climates. Every one must be convinced that the happiness of every man is increased, in proportion as he is furnished with the greatest number of these objects of desire; and furnished with them, in their greatest perfection, and at the cheapest rate.

But, it is evidently the will of our Creator, that but few of these objects, every one of which is necessary to the happiness of every individual, should be produced except in particular districts. Others, if they can be produced in several places, can be produced much cheaper, and in greater perfection, in some places than in others. Every part of the globe possesses peculiar advantages for the production of something; but no part possesses advantages for the production of every thing. Hence we see, on the principle illustrated above, that the annual production of the globe will be greatest; that is, there will be the largest amount annually to the share of every individual; that is, every individual will be richer and happier, when each portion of the globe devotes itself to the creation of those products for which it has the greatest natural facilities. If a man in New York can raise, by one day's labor, one hundred pounds of flour, but could not raise more than one ounce of coffee; and a man in Cuba can raise twenty-five pounds of coffee, but cannot raise more than one pound of flour, and they exchange, as we have before seen they must exchange, labor for labor; the one will produce, by a day's labor, twenty-five pounds of coffee, instead of an ounce; and the other, one hundred pounds of flour, instead of a pound. Is not this better than for the New York farmer to raise his coffee in a hot-house, at the expense of a day's labor for an ounce; and the West Indian to raise his wheat on the mountains, at the expense of a day's labor for a pound? Such are the advantages of that division of labor suggested by geographical position.

And the final cause of all this is evident. God intended that men should live together in friendship and harmony. By thus multiplying indefinitely their wants, and creating only in particular localities, the objects by which those wants are supplied, he intended to make them all necessary to each other; and thus to render it no less the interest, than the duty of every one, to live in amity with all the rest.

Nor is the application of this principle confined to geographical localities. The simple fact that a nation possesses facilities, be they either natural or acquired, for creating any product at a cheaper rate than any other nation, is a reason why that nation should devote itself to the creation of that product; and why another nation should, for the same reason, improve its own peculiar advantages. Thus, there are certain states of society, and certain amounts of accumulation of capital, most favorable to the creation of certain products. A nation in this state, and with this accumulation, can furnish these products cheaper than her neighbors; and this is a reason they should purchase them of her. Could not one of our old States supply one of the new States with manufactures, cheaper than the new State could produce them itself? And is not this a reason why the new State should procure them by exchange, rather than by direct production? Is it not cheaper for an Indian to buy a rifle of an European, than to attempt to make one for himself?

This is, however, by no means to assert that such arrangements and relations are to be permanent. As a country accumulates fixed capital, it creates its own facilities for creating every kind of manufactured product. One nation will naturally begin to do this at the same point of accumulation at which another began to do it. And the way in which to arrive at this point the soonest, is to become rich as fast as possible; that is, to buy as cheap as we can, or, in other words, to procure, annually, as many objects of desire as possible, for a given amount of labor. A tribe of Indians would much sooner be able to make rifles for itself, by purchasing, at first, rifles of an European, than by determining that it would never use rifles, until it could manufacture them for itself. As the use of a rifle would render industry more productive, and thus render the tribe richer, it would bring them one step nearer to that degree of accumulation, at which they might begin to make rifles for themselves. But the resolution not to purchase of others, would have no such tendency, inasmuch as it would do nothing whatever towards accumulating production; but would, on the contrary, shut them out from the very means offered them for most rapidly benefitting their condition.

To sum up what has been said. It will be seen that production will be increased; that is, men will be richer, and therefore may be happier, as the following conditions are complied with:

1. As the laws of nature, designed by our Creator for our benefit, are understood;

2. As the means are devised for availing ourselves, in the most successful manner, of the utility of these laws;

3. As the human labor necessary to be expended, is so arranged as, with a given expenditure, to produce the greatest and most perfect result; and

4. As the inhabitants of the earth in different localities, devote themselves most exclusively to the production of those objects of desire, for the production of which they have received, either directly or indirectly, from their Creator, the greatest facilities.

Or, still more generally, production will be abundant; that is, man will enjoy the means of physical happiness, in proportion to his individual industry, both of mind and body; and to the degree of harmony and good feeling which exists between the individuals of the same society; and also between the different societies themselves.

SECTION IV.

EFFECTS OF THE INCREASED PRODUCTIVENESS OF HUMAN INDUSTRY.

This subject has been already so frequently alluded to, and all the points on which it depends so distinctly stated, that it will not be necessary to examine it so fully, as might otherwise be required.

The result of *industry* applied to *capital* is *product*, *value*, or *the means of gratifying human desire.* The result of *increased* productiveness of human industry, is, with the same labor, *increased* product, value, or means of gratifying human desire. That is, in general, increased productiveness is equivalent to increased means of human happiness. This simple statement would seem sufficient to explain the whole subject. In order, however, to obviate any objections that may arise, we will proceed to show its practical operation, by several illustrations.

Take the case of a single individual. Suppose a man, by the same amount of labor that he spent last year, to be able this year to create twice as much value. Suppose that a farmer has twice as large a harvest; that is, that his instrument is twice as good this year as it was last year. The result is, he will be able to satisfy the desire which that product gratifies, twice as abundantly as he did last year. He will have more to exchange with other producers, and hence he will be able to gratify other desires more abundantly. He will be able to make exchanges which were before out of his power; hence, he will be able to add to his mode of living, new means of happiness. And, on the other hand, as he is able to make exchanges with others with whom it was before impossible, others in return, are able to avail themselves of his product, or means of happiness, who were before unable to do so. Hence, he is not only happier himself; but the very means by which he becomes so, renders him the instrument of greater happiness to others. Hence, it is a benefit to a whole neighborhood, for a single member of it to become rich. In other words, increased productiveness in one branch of labor, increases productiveness in every branch of labor.

Let us call this first individual A, and suppose that before the productiveness of his labor had been increased, he exchanged with another individual B, on equal terms. If the labor of A and B were 10 per day, they would exchange with each other at the rate of 10 for 10. But, suppose now, that by some new invention, A's labor produced 20 per day. He would offer to exchange on the same terms as before, but he would offer 20, and expect from B 20 in return. But, in consequence of the inferior productiveness of B's labor, he would not be able to purchase so much; he could afford to buy only 10, as before. A, therefore, in order to induce him to exchange, that is, to buy, would abate his price; that is, would offer to exchange on better terms, and would offer him at the rate of 20 for 15, or in some such proportion. What B would not purchase at the rate of 10 for 10, he might be willing to purchase at the rate of 15 for 20. Thus, we see, they would, in this case, share the benefit between them. But let the labor of B now be increased in productiveness, so that it shall be equal to that of A; that is, be also at the rate of 20 per day. They will now exchange at the same rate as before; that is, at the rate of 20 for 20, with this difference, that for one day's labor, they will both have twice as many objects of desire as before, or as many objects of desire, with half a day's labor; that is, both will be twice as rich as before. Thus, the increased productiveness of B, is now a benefit to A, inasmuch as he now receives 20 for 20, when before, he only received 15 for 20. Now it needs but a little reflection to perceive, that the case of A and B, is the case of the whole community.

But the case is made still stronger, when the effect of competition is taken into the account. Let the productiveness of labor in any department be ever so great, where labor and capital are free, competition will always reduce profit in one department, to the same average per cent. that it affords in other departments. Hence, let the productiveness of labor and capital, in any one mode of employment, be ever so great; interest and wages in that employment, will be no higher than they are, other things being equal, in other employments. That is, while the capitalist and the laborer receive the same interest and wages as the rest of the community; in other words, while the community pay no more for this capital and labor than they pay for any other, they receive a greater amount of value in exchange, and, as much more, as the productiveness of that labor and capital has been increased. Thus, capital and labor in the cotton manufacture is not better paid, upon an average, than in other modes of investment and industry. If it were, capital and labor would flow into it, until the equilibrium was restored. But, while this is the fact, we obtain a yard of cotton cloth for one fourth the price, or at one fourth of the labor, at which we formerly obtained it; that is, we receive four times as much as formerly, in return for what we pay for the cost and labor of making cotton cloth. And thus, over the whole world, every instance of increased productiveness, whether it be from the use of natural agents, or from the division of labor, whether in our own country, or in another country, if we choose to avail ourselves of it, enables every man, by paying the producer the same as before, to procure a larger amount of value; that is, of objects for the gratification of desire; that is, enables every man to become both richer and happier.

The above remarks will, I hope, be sufficient to illustrate the general principle. As, however, there are several consequences resulting from increased productiveness of human labor, especially from the use and improvement of natural agents, which seem at first view to be at variance with what we have here advanced, it may be necessary to pursue the results somewhat more minutely, and to consider the objection commonly made, that the use of labor-saving machinery is prejudicial to the interests of the laboring classes.

It may, however, be here premised, that the objection made against natural agents, is not to their *use*, but to their *improvement*. Men object to the use of a spinning *jenny*, but not against the use of a spinning *wheel.* They dislike a rake *by horse power*, but do not dislike a *rake.* But every one must see, that this sort of objection, if it be founded in truth, is by no means sufficiently extensive. A spinning *wheel*, or a *hand* loom, or a *hand* rake, is a labor-saving machine; and it involves the use of natural agents, just as truly as as spinning *jenny*, a *power* loom, or a *horse* rake. If the use of natural agents be injurious, we should abandon it altogether, and spin, and weave, and rake, with our fingers. But if this would be unwise, and it be conceded that we must use natural agents, in some form or other, why not use the best that we can procure; that is, the best that God has given us? If, as all must allow, the use, up to a certain point, has been an incalculable benefit, what reason have we to suppose, that *additional* improvement in the use of them will not be still *additional* benefit.

But, passing this, I proceed to consider the effects of increased productiveness of labor, both upon *Producers* and *Consumers*.

I. *The effect of natural agents upon* PRODUCERS.

These are either *immediate*, or *ultimate*.

1. *Immediate.* It is said that every *improvement* in machinery enables the work to be done by fewer laborers, and hence many persons are thrown out of employment; and that every change in the *manner* of labor, deprives many persons of the use of that skill, which is their whole means of subsistence.

So far as change in the *manner* of labor is concerned, but little need be said, as this is but a temporary inconvenience. If a new kind of work is to be done, some person must learn to do it, and must be paid for learning.

If a man do not choose to learn it, although he would be paid for learning it, and be supported by his labor, after he has learned it, it is his own fault. He may quarrel with his own obstinacy, but he has nothing else to blame. Nor, is the simple change of employment a peculiar hardship. Few men pass through life, without, at some time or other, materially modifying their mode of employment, from choice, instead of from necessity.

The main difficulty, therefore, which is supposed to result from the use of improved methods of production, is, that they employ a *less* number of laborers; and, hence, that many laborers are thrown out of employment.

In reply to this it might be asked, what is the testimony of facts, in this case. Improvements in machinery have been going on, ever since the creation. Has the demand for labor diminished? Improvements have been made in particular districts. Have the laborers been, by these means, driven away; or, on the contrary, are not these the very districts, to which they inevitably resort for employment?

But, aside from this, let us examine the assertion, that some laborers are thrown out of employment. Let us, however, first endeavor to ascertain how great the evil is.

1. It is not *universal.* The improved mode of labor always requires some labor, and, of course, a *portion* of those formerly employed must still find employment. To these, there results no other disadvantage, than that of a change in the mode of employment; but with the meliorating circumstances of higher wages and less fatiguing labor.

2. It is, by necessity, *gradual.* Improvements in ma-

chinery, are made by slow degrees. Although the total change may show a greatly increased productiveness of labor, yet no one single change is often, of itself, great enough to produce a great change in the demand for laborers. Again: Let the change be ever so great, it cannot be introduced at once, over a whole nation. Hence, its effects will be, at first, to reduce the wages of those engaged in the former methods of manufacturing. The consequence will be, that no new laborers will learn the trade. This will tend to keep up the wages of those who remain in it. And, lastly: If a new instrument is to be employed, there must be an additional number of men employed to manufacture it. This will, of course, require an additional number of laborers, who must be withdrawn from other employments. This will tend to raise the price of labor, and, of course, either to furnish employment for those who wish to leave the former occupation, or else to keep up their wages while they remain in it.

3. The infelicity here spoken of, is no other than that which belongs to the tenure of all property whatsoever. Skill and labor, as well as capital, are always liable, in the revolutions of society, to depreciate in value, or even to become worthless. "Riches *make to themselves* wings, and flee away." The wisdom of man, since the creation, has never yet discovered any link strong enough to connect a human being, indissolubly, with any sublunary possession. The laborer, therefore, in this case, holds his property precisely as any other man holds it, and is subject to no peculiar hardship.

Let us however proceed to consider the *ultimate effects* of increased productiveness upon *producers*.

1. The producer shares with the rest of the community in the benefit derived from increased productiveness;

that is, if he earn the same wages as before, he is richer; and, if he earn less, he is less poor than he would have been, if no such change had taken place. That is to say, money, or, in other words, a given amount of labor, is capable of procuring for him a greater amount of objects of desire, than before.

2. From this increased productiveness, there must be, throughout the whole community, an increased demand for labor. Suppose a community of one hundred men to acquire, by their labor and capital, every year, just enough to support themselves, after defraying the expenses of their several establishments. So long as this state of things continued, there would be no increased demand for laborers; for there would be no additional capital with which to maintain them. The young must therefore emigrate, or else there will be a competition among laborers for work, and thus wages will fall. But, suppose, that by some new mode of increased productiveness, the capital be increased, in a single year, twenty-five per cent., there will then be a demand for the industry of a greater number, say twenty-five additional laborers; since this additional capital can produce nothing, unless it be united with labor. If there be not twenty-five additional laborers to be immediately procured, wages must rise, because there will be a competition between capitalists for labor; and children and persons, who with the former prices could earn nothing, will now be employed. And, if the demand for labor, arising from this increase of capital, could not be thus supplied, those engaged in less profitable employment in other districts, and other countries, would come in to supply the deficiency. Such is always seen to be the fact. Population follows capital. It goes where capital goes, and it concentrates where capital accumulates, and it leaves when capital leaves. And hence, in a whole country, where the number of inhabitants is limited, the

increase of capital must raise the rate of wages. And hence, by just so much as increased productiveness of labor increases the amount of capital, must it also tend to raise the price of labor throughout a whole country. That is to say, the obvious tendency of the use of natural agents is, to increase the wages of laborers in general.

3. But, thirdly; the tendency of the use of machinery is to increase the wages of laborers, in that very department of industry, in which they are employed. The reason for this is obvious. Reduction of price produces an additional demand, more than sufficient to compensate for the diminished amount of labor necessary for the creation of the particular product. That this must always be the case, can, I think, be conclusively shown.

Suppose that with the present machinery, one hundred men are able to manufacture cotton cloth at fifty cents per yard, and that the amount which they produce is precisely sufficient to supply the wants of the district for which they labor. At this price, no consumers, but those worth one thousand dollars per year, can afford to purchase cotton cloth, and, of course, the demand is limited exclusively to them. Suppose now, that improved machinery enables fifty men to manufacture as large an amount of cotton cloth as one hundred men could manufacture before, and the consequence is, that cotton cloth is sold at twenty-five cents per yard. It is evident, that if the demand be precisely doubled, there will be wanted just as many laborers as before; so that their condition will be in no manner altered, except by change of labor, with its correspondent advantages, and the gradual rise of wages, spoken of above. And, it is also evident, that every degree of increase of demand, *beyond what is sufficient to produce this equilibrium, must be for the benefit of those engaged in this sort of labor.*

But it is evident, for several reasons, that the reduction of price one half, must more than double the demand for cotton cloth. Thus, when the price was fifty cents per yard, only those consumers worth one thousand dollars per year, could purchase cotton cloth; and the sale was, of course, limited to them. But now that it is at twenty-five cents, the class worth only five hundred dollars per year is just as able to purchase it, as those worth one thousand were formerly. Now, if this class were only of the same number as that worth one thousand, the demand would be doubled, and, of course, the laborer would suffer no injury. But the fact is, that the class worth five hundred dollars, is three or four times as large as that worth one thousand. Hence, by all this difference, the laborer is the gainer, and a larger number of laborers is required. But this is not all. There are various classes between those worth one thousand dollars, and those worth five hundred dollars, as, those of nine hundred and fifty, eight hundred, seven hundred, and six hundred, each one of them larger than the class of first purchasers, who now can purchase the article. All these unite to increase the demand for this kind of labor. And again: The class worth one thousand dollars will now use much more cotton cloth than formerly; and cotton cloth will now be used for purposes to which it could never before have been appropriated, and it will supersede the use of many articles, with which it could never before have come into competition. All this is to be added to the benefits conferred, by the introduction of machinery, or by increasing the productiveness of labor, upon the laborers in this particular department. Every one must see that this benefit, thus resulting from increase of demand, which is the thing now in dispute, is absolutely incalculable.

It may be said, that this is an exaggerated case. I answer: The case is not given for the sake of accuracy in *numbers*, but for the sake of illustrating a manifest tendency. And, that, in this respect it is accurate, the whole history of manufactures bears ample testimony. Compare those states of society in which machinery is not used, with those in which it is used, and inquire in which of them the wages of the laborer are higher, and in which his habitation displays the greater number of comforts, and in which his shelf is covered with the greater number of books. Examine the statistics of a particular branch of manufacture, and inquire in what period there has been, in proportion to the whole population, the greatest number of laborers required in that particular manufacture. Has this demand for this particular kind of labor been greater in the period when natural agents and machinery have been used, or in that in which they have not been used? The answer to these questions is given in the history of the progress of the cotton manufacture, the manufacture of books, of nails, of pins, and every other article of common use; and these alone are of any consequence in such an estimate. This shows that the above illustration is *true*, so far as it teaches the *tendency*, which is all that is necessary in the present case.

But this is not all. Suppose the demand for cotton cloth be doubled, there must be twice the amount of cotton produced; twice as many vessels built, to transport it; twice as many men to navigate them; besides the number of men required to construct machinery to fabricate it. Suppose the number of books be doubled; there must be twice as much paper made, twice as many rags purchased, twice as many types made, and twice as much transportation required for the supply of the market. All this must add to the demand for labor, and must tend, by just so much, to increase the wages of the operative. And hence, if these considerations be compared, it will be seen,

1. That the introduction of machinery reduces the price of articles of consumption; that is, renders *the wages*, whatever they may be, of the operative, *of more value.*

2. That, by the more rapid multiplication of capital, it produces a greater demand for labor *in general* that is, it makes the wages of *all labor greater;* and

3. That its tendency is to create an increased demand for labor; that is, to produce a rise of wages in that *department of industry*, into which natural agents are specially introduced; and it does this according to the degree in which they are introduced. That is, in general, the introduction of machinery renders the wages of the laborer *more valuable;* it raises the wages of labor *in general*, and raises the wages of labor *specially*, in that department into which natural agents are introduced. What any man can reasonably ask for, more than this, I do not distinctly perceive.

II. The effects of increased productiveness upon *consumers* may be easily explained, on the principles already illustrated. I need not, therefore, enlarge upon this subject, as it has already been so frequently alluded to.

1. By increased productiveness, every consumer is richer; that is, he is able, by the same amount of labor, to procure a greater amount of the objects of desire. This is evidently the same thing to him, as though his income were increased. If I am able, this year, with two hundred dollars, to purchase as much as I could purchase last year for four hundred dollars, and I can earn two hundred dollars as easily as before, it is precisely the same thing, as if, at the former prices, my wages had risen from two hundred to four hundred dollars.

2. Production is more perfect. This has already been illustrated, as one of the effects of the use of machinery; that is, the consumer not only obtains more of the same article for the same sum of money, but he also obtains a better article. Every one must have observed, that calicoes, crockery, and many other articles of ordinary consumption, are not only much cheaper, but also much more beautiful, than they were a few years since.

3. A vast number of articles is thus added to the means of happiness of the human race, of which, otherwise, they must, from necessity, have been deprived. All that we possess, above the comforts of the naked savage, is the result of the use of natural agents, and of division of labor; that is, of the increased productiveness of human labor.

4. Nor is this all. While all the labor of man is necessary to support mere physical existence, there can be no opportunity for intellectual cultivation. As soon, however, as he arrives at that condition of productiveness of labor, in which he is able to provide for his physical wants, with less than all his time and effort, opportunity is afforded for intellectual development. At this point, then, commences the dawn of intellectual improvement. As increased productiveness affords more and more leisure, improvement advances. As soon again as, by improved intellectual power, man begins to discover and apply the laws of nature, a vast accession is made to the power of human productiveness. Henceforth, these two forces conspire to assist each other. Increased productiveness, affords increased time for investigation, discovery and invention; and discovery and invention increase the power of productiveness. The more actively these act and re-act upon each other, the more rapid is the progress of society, and

the more rapidly accelerated is the movement of civilization.

If this be so, we see how puerile is the prejudice which frequently exists against the use of labor-saving machinery, since the introduction of such machinery, more than any thing else, tends permanently to improve the condition of the laborer. We see, also, how groundless is the opinion, that education and science are without *practical* benefit, and that philosophers and students are merely a useless burthen upon the community; since it is *knowledge* which has given to us all the advantages which we possess over savages, and it is the *application* of that knowledge, which furnishes employment for nine-tenths of the whole community. We see, also, how short-sighted is that national selfishness, which desires to limit and restrict the intercourse between nations; since it is for the interest of each nation to improve to the utmost its own advantages, and to procure, by exchange with other nations, those productions for the creation of which it possesses, by nature, inferior facilities.

CHAPTER THIRD.

OF THE LAWS WHICH GOVERN THE APPLICATION OF LABOR TO CAPITAL.

We have, thus far, considered capital and labor, separately, and have endeavored to analyze the nature and functions of each. It is manifest, however, that we have not yet exhausted the subject. In many countries, a vast amount of capital and of labor has never yet been employed. In other countries, capital and labor have been united at different periods, with different degrees of activity. Hence, while some nations have rapidly accumulated wealth, the wealth of others has remained, for years, stationary; and in others, it has diminished. The most fertile soils of Europe and Asia, once the garden of the world, now under the despotism of Turkey, scarcely maintain their sparsely settled inhabitants. It remains for us, therefore, to proceed with our investigation, in order, if possible, to ascertain the laws which influence the application of labor to capital.

SECTION I.

THE CONDITIONS OF OUR BEING, ON WHICH, THE LAWS ON THIS SUBJECT ARE FOUNDED.

In order to arrive at the truth with the greater certainty, it will be proper to consider the circumstances under which man is placed, with reference to the universe around him, so far as this subject is considered.

1. God has created man with physical and intellectual faculties, adapted to labor. He has given us a mind, adapted to investigate the laws of the universe, and a body adapted to perform all those operations, by which, in obedience to those laws, the objects of desire may be produced.

2. Labor has been made necessary to our happiness. No valuable object of desire can be procured without it. Intellectual power cannot be attained without intellectual discipline; nor knowledge of the laws of nature, without study. Neither physical comforts, nor even physical necessaries, can be obtained, unless labor be first expended to procure them. The universal law of our existence, is, "In the sweat of thy face shalt thou eat thy bread, until thou return to the ground."

3. Labor is necessary to the healthful condition of our powers, both physical and intellectual. Without intellectual labor, the mind becomes enfeebled; and, were this labor wholly intermitted, it would sink into idiocy or madness. Without physical labor, the body, feeble and enervated, becomes a prey to pain and disease.

4. That labor, *per se*, is pleasant, it is not necessary to assert. It is sufficient to our purpose, that it is less painful than idleness and the results of idleness. The laborer complains of his toil, but, deprive him of his opportunity for toil, and he becomes miserable. When men are, in our penitentiaries, condemned to solitary confinement, and labor or idleness are left purely to their own choice, they have never been known to continue longer than a few days, without beseeching, importunately, for work. The veterans who are supported at the Greenwich Hospital, England, at the public expense, wholly without labor, are said to be, in general, very unhappy. The uncontrollable desire of children, for some sort of employment, illustrates the same truth. Those persons who consider labor as degrading, obey the same law of our nature, in another form. The gymnastic exercises of the Greeks and Romans, and the hunting, riding, shooting and travelling of the moderns, are nothing more than expensive modes of exercise or labor. The poor man exercises himself, the rich man employs a horse to exercise him. The one does, expensively and unproductively, what the other does, without expense and productively. Both equally, yield obedience to the law of our creation; and, in what manner soever it is obeyed, both reap advantages, from the mere fact of obeying it.

5. On the contrary, the Creator has affixed several penalties, which those, who disobey this law of their being, can never expect to escape. He who refuses to labor with his mind, suffers the penalty of ignorance. The amount of this penalty may be estimated, by considering the blessings, both physical and intellectual, of which ignorance deprives us; and by contrasting the comforts of savage, with those of civilized nations, where the physical effort, made by both, is the same. He who refuses to labor with his hands, suffers, besides the pains

of disease, all the evils of poverty, cold, hunger and nakedness. The results which our Creator has attached to idleness, are all to be considered as punishments, which he inflicts for the neglect of this established law of our being.

6. And, on the other hand, God has assigned to industry, rich and abundant rewards. "The hand of the diligent maketh rich." "Seest thou a man diligent in his business, he shall stand before kings; he shall not stand before mean men." The pleasure, the independence, and the power arising from knowledge, are the rewards of intellectual industry. "*A wise man* is *strong*, yea, *a man of understanding increaseth strength.*" And, it is only by physical labor, that the riches of the earth are appropriated, and the laws of nature made available to the happiness of man. At the first, there existed nothing in our world but the earth, with its spontaneous productions, and capabilities, and helpless and defenceless man. All that now exists of capital, of convenience, of comfort, and of intelligence, is the work of industry, and is the reward which God has bestowed upon us, for obedience to the law of our being.

7. If such be the facts; if God have given to all men faculties for labor; if he have made labor necessary to our happiness; if he have attached the severest penalties to idleness, and have proffered the richest rewards to industry; it would seem reasonable to conclude, that all that was required of us, was, so to construct the arrangements of society, as to give free scope to the laws of Divine Providence. If he have excited us to labor by sufficient rewards, and deterred us from indolence by sufficient penalties, it would seem that our business must be, to give to these rewards and penalties their free and their intended operation. These, at any rate, should be the

means first tried, in order to facilitate production; nor should any others be resorted to, until these have been tried and found ineffectual.

The effects of this constitution, under which we are placed, will, I think, be fully exerted, in proportion as the following conditions are observed:

1. As every man is permitted to enjoy, in the most unlimited manner, the advantages of labor.

2. As every man suffers the consequences of idleness.

And, these being equal,

3. Labor will be applied to capital, according to the ratio which subsists between the whole amount of capital, and the whole number of laborers; that is, the greater the ratio of capital to the number of laborers, the more active will be their industry, and *vice versa*. And,

4. Labor will be applied to capital, in proportion to the knowledge which men possess of the advantages which they shall obtain by labor; that is, the greater the intelligence, the greater the industry. To these several topics, the remaining sections of this chapter will be devoted.

SECTION II.

INDUSTRY WILL BE APPLIED TO CAPITAL, AS EVERY MAN ENJOYS THE ADVANTAGES OF HIS LABOR AND HIS CAPITAL.

Although God has designed men to labor, yet he has not designed them to labor without reward. Hence, when men devise some form of labor, even for exercise, they always connect with it some result, as the game of the huntsman, the watering place of the traveller or tourist, or the reward of victory of the gymnic. Thus, also, as it is unnatural to labor without receiving benefit from labor, men will not labor continuously nor productively, unless they receive such benefit. And, hence, the greater this benefit, the more active and spontaneous will be their exertion.

In order that every man may enjoy, in the greatest degree, the advantages of his labor, it is necessary, provided always he do not violate the rights of his neighbor, 1st. *That, he be allowed to gain all that he can;* and, 2d. *That having gained all that he can, he be allowed to use it as he will.*

1. *It is necessary that every man be allowed to gain all that he can;* that is, that the arrangements of society be so constructed, that every man be able to render his labor, in the highest degree, available to himself. This will require,

1. That property be divided. When property is held in common, every individual of the society to which it

belongs, has an equal, but an undivided and indetermined, right to his portion of the revenue. Hence, every one is at liberty to take what he will, and as much as he will, and to labor as much or as little as he pleases. There is, therefore, under such an arrangement, no *connexion* between *labor* and the *rewards* of labor. There is rather a premium for indolence than for industry. In such a case, there will be no regular labor, if, indeed, there be any labor at all; and, what is still worse, even the scanty and spontaneous productions of the earth will frequently be gathered before they are ripe, since every one fears, that if he do not seize them now, he will never enjoy them at all. The forest of an Indian tribe, is held in common, and a few hundred families almost starve, upon a territory which, were it divided and tilled, would support a million of civilized men. The little that it produces to him, is the result of division of property. His bow and arrows, his wigwam and his clothing are acknowledged to be, in the fullest sense, *his own*. Were these to be held, like his land, in common, the whole race would very soon perish, from want of the necessaries of life.

On the contrary, as soon as land with all other property is divided, a motive exists for regular and voluntary labor, inasmuch as the individual knows that he, and not his indolent neighbor, will reap the fruit of his toil. Henceforth, he begins to create a regular supply of annual product. With increased skill, this annual product increases, and he begins to convert it into fixed capital, a form of wealth which could scarcely exist, without division of property. Every accession to his fixed capital, renders his labor more productive, and, hence, it creates a stronger stimulus to increased exertion. With increased exertion, his annual capital is increased, and a greater surplus remains to be changed into fixed capital. Thus, increased production, stimulates industry, and increased industry results in more abundant production. And thus we see, that division of property, or the appropriation to each, of his particular portion of that which God has given to all, lays at the foundation of all accumulation of wealth, and of all progress in civilization.

Hence, we see the reason why property held in common, is so generally prejudicial to the best interests of a society. A common, where every one, at will, may pasture his cattle; and a forest, from which every inhabitant may procure his fuel; are severally encouragements to indolence, and serve to keep a community poor. Thus, also, funds left at large for the support of the poor, on which every one is supposed to have an equal right to draw, have generally been found to foster indolence. Poor laws, in so far as they are to be considered a fund for this purpose, have the same sort of injurious tendency.

2. But the division of property would be of no avail, unless the right of property were enforced; that is, unless every one be protected in the undisturbed possession of whatever he has rightfully acquired. As no one will labor, unless he knows that he shall reap the fruit of his toil, so no one will take the pains to reap the fruit of his toil, unless he also know that he will be able to hold it, and appropriate it to the purposes of his own gratification. And, hence, we see that human labor is exerted in different countries, very much in proportion as the right of property is both understood and enforced.

Moral Philosophy teaches us that the right of property may be violated by the individual or by society. It is violated by the individual, by cheating, stealing, robbery, and violation of contracts. And we universally see, that just as these crimes prevail, production languishes, industry diminishes, and the richest soil fails to support its few and impoverished inhabitants. Such was the case in Europe, during the feudal oppression. There was no encouragement to labor, because no one knew whether he, or a baronial tyrant, would reap the fruit of his industry.

Hence, we see the economical importance of all means which shall prevent the *individual violation* of the right of property. These means are two.

1. The first is, the inculcation of those moral and religious principles, which teach men to respect the rights of others as their own, that is, to obey the law of reciprocity; and which present the strongest conceivable reasons for so doing. This is the most certain method of preventing the violation of the right of property, inasmuch as it aims to eradicate those dispositions of mind, from which all violation proceeds. It is also the cheapest, as it aims at *prevention*, which is always more economical than *cure.* It is also necessary; inasmuch as good laws will never be enacted, or, if enacted, will never be obeyed, only in so far as there exists a moral character in the community sufficiently pure to sustain them. In proportion as these are efficacious, all other means are needless. Hence, we see the reason why moral and religious nations grow wealthy so much more rapidly than vicious and irreligious nations. The feeling of perfect tranquillity and security, which a high social morality diffuses over a whole community, is one of the most beneficial, as well as one of the strongest stimulants to universal industry. This is one of the temporal rewards which God bestows upon social virtue. And, inasmuch as no one can enjoy this reward, simply by being virtuous himself, but only as his fellow citizens also are virtuous, we see the indication in our constitution, that it is the duty, as well as the interest of every man, to labor to render other men more virtuous.

2. But inasmuch as all men are not influenced in their conduct by moral and religious principles; it is necessary that aggression be somehow prevented, and violations of property, in so far as possible, redressed. Hence, the importance of wholesome and equitable laws, of an independent and firm judiciary, and an executive, which shall carry the decisions of law faithfully into effect. Hence we see, that the expense necessary for the most perfect administration of justice, is among the most productive of all the expenditures of society. Good law, and the faithful administration of it, are always the cheapest law, and the cheapest administration of it. Hence we see, that the interests of man require that law should be invariably executed, and that its sovereignty should, under all circumstances, be inviolably maintained.

But the right of property may be violated by *society*. It sometimes happens, that society or government, which is its agent, though it may prevent the infliction of wrong by individuals upon individuals, is itself by no means averse to inflicting wrong or violating the right of individuals. This is done, where governments seize upon the property of individuals by mere arbitrary act, a form of tyranny, with which all the nations of Europe were, of old, too well acquainted. It is also done, by unjust legislation; that is, when legislators, how well soever chosen, enact unjust laws, by which the property of a part, or of the whole, is unjustly taken away, or unjustly subjected to oppressive taxation.

Of all the destructive agencies which can be brought to bear upon production, by far the most fatal, is public oppression. It drinks up the spirit of a people, by inflicting wrong through means of an agency which was created for the sole purpose of preventing wrong; and which was intended to be the ultimate and faithful refuge of the friendless. When the antidote to evil, becomes the source of evil, what hope for man is left? When society itself sets the example of peculation, what shall prevent the individuals of the society from imitating that example? Hence, public injustice is always the prolific parent of private violence. The result is, that capital emigrates, production ceases, and a nation either sinks down in hopeless despondence; or else the people, harassed beyond endurance, and believing that their condition cannot be made worse by any change, rush into all the horrors of civil war; the social elements are dissolved; the sword enters every house; the holiest ties which bind men together are severed; and no prophet can predict, at the beginning, what will be the end.

Hence we see the importance to the industry of a country, of a constitution which guarantees, to the individual, immunity not only from private, but also from public oppression. Wherever this immunity is wanting, the progress of a nation in wealth, will be slow. It is owing rather to the freedom of her institutions and the equity of her laws, than to her physical advantages, that Great Britain has so far outstripped all other European nations in the accumulation of wealth, and in every thing that confers social power. It is almost superfluous, however, to add, that a free constitution is of no value, unless the moral and intellectual character of a people be sufficiently elevated to avail itself of the advantages which it offers. It is merely an *instrument* of good, which will accomplish nothing, unless there exist the moral disposition to use it aright.

To sum up what has been said: Labor will be applied to capital, in proportion as every man is allowed to gain all that he can; that is, as property is most perfectly divided; and as this division is most strictly enforced; that is, as the right of property is guarded by the most equitable laws; and as there exist the strongest guarantees that these laws will be inviolate, whether they relate to individuals or to society.

II. The second part of the condition mentioned in the beginning of this section is, that the individual be allowed to use his own as he will. To this, is of course to be added the condition, that he use it in such manner, as not to interfere with the rights of his neighbor.

A man's possessions are his talents, faculties, skill, and the wealth and reputation which these have enabled him to acquire; in other words, his industry and his capital. In order that industry be applied to capital with the greatest energy, it is necessary that every man be at liberty to use them both as he will; that is, that both of them be free.

The reason of this is obvious. The aptitudes of men for different employments are very dissimilar. The choice of every man naturally leads him to that employment for which he is best adapted. By allowing every man, therefore, to employ his industry as he chooses, every man will be employed about that for which he is best adapted; and hence, the production of all will be greatly increased, because we thus avail ourselves of the *peculiar* productiveness of every individual. Nor is this all. By allowing every man to labor as he chooses, we very greatly increase the happiness of every individual. And every one knows that a man will labor with better success when his labor is pleasant, than when it is irksome.

The case is the same with respect to capital. Every man is more interested in his own success, than any other man can be interested in it. Hence, every man is likely to ascertain more accurately in what manner he can best employ his capital, than any other man can ascertain it for him. If every man, therefore, be allowed to invest his capital as he will, the whole capital of a country will be more profitably invested, than under any other circumstances whatever. And, since, when he is left thus at liberty, there will be the greatest gain to the capitalist, there will also be the greatest stimulus to his industry; for the stimulus to labor is always in proportion to the rewards of labor. And, on the contrary, in just so far as, by any means, this productiveness is diminished, the stimulus to labor is also diminished with it.

It may be said that men, if left to themselves, will be liable to invest their capital unwisely. Granted. Man is not omniscient, and therefore this liability cannot be avoided. The question, therefore, is, how shall it be rendered as small as possible. Will a man, who reaps the benefit of success and suffers the evils of failure, be less likely to judge correctly, than he whose faculties are quickened by no such responsibility? Nor is this all. Not only are legislators, who generally assume the labor of directing the manner in which labor or capital shall be employed, in no manner peculiarly qualified for this task; they are, in many respects, peculiarly disqualified for it. The individual is liable to no *peculiar* biases, in making up his mind in respect to the profitableness of an investment. If he err, it is because the *indications* deceive him. The legislator, besides being liable to err by mistaking the indications, is liable to be misled by party zeal, by political intrigue, and by sectional prejudice. What individual would succeed in his business, if he allowed himself to be influenced in the manner of conducting it, by such considerations? And must not like causes always produce like results?

Besides, every man feels, instinctively, that he has a right to use his capital and his industry as he pleases, provided he interfere not with the rights of another; and that, to restrict him in this use, is injustice. We have before said, that nothing paralyzes industry like oppression, and it is as true in this case, as in any other. If this sort of interference be violent or frequently repeated, capital and labor, whose motto like that of Dr. Franklin is, "Where liberty dwells, there is my country," will emigrate to some more congenial social atmosphere. And if the interference be not so intolerable as to produce these results, yet, in just so far as it has any effect, it is all of this kind, and, by its whole operation, must diminish the incitements to industry.

And, on the contrary, just as every individual is free to employ his industry and capital as he chooses, and thus both to receive a larger compensation for his labor, and also to labor more happily, will be the inducements to industry and to the investment of capital.

If this be so, we see the impolicy of several forms of legislative interference, in relation to this subject.

1. We see what must be the effect of monopolies. A monopoly is an exclusive right granted to a man, or to a company of men, to employ their labor or capital in some particular manner. Such was the exclusive right granted to the East India Company, to import into the ports of Great Britain, or her territories, the productions of all countries east of the Cape of Good Hope. Such were the privileges granted formerly by Spain, to particular individuals or companies, of importing foreign commodities into the ports of her colonies in South America. The result of this exclusion was to prevent all other persons, except those thus favored, from the right of investing

their capital in this manner; and hence, to reduce the value of that capital, by precisely the amount of this effect. The tendency of this system may be easily seen; for, were all the modes of employing capital thus restricted, the additional capital that might be accumulated, would be utterly worthless. Nor is this all. Those who hold this exclusive privilege, being liable to no competition, may charge for their commodities whatever they choose. Here is, therefore, a two-fold injustice; first, the means of the consumer are diminished; and secondly, the price which he must pay, is enhanced at the mere will of his oppressor.

These remarks, of course, do not apply to patent and copy right, which are a species of monopoly. They however differ from that which we have described, in this, that they leave the consumer at option to use the invention or not, as he chooses. If a man invent a valuable machine, he is under no obligation to make it known to others, but has a right to use it, if he choose, for his own exclusive benefit. By the law of patent right, he and the community enter into a mutually advantageous agreement. He agrees to surrender all exclusive claim to it, on condition of having the exclusive right to vend it for a certain time. If, at the price he asks for it, it is an advantage to the rest of society, they will purchase it, and are, by this advantage, the gainers. If, at this price, it is no advantage, they do not use it, and they are in no respect the losers. In both cases, after the period of patent right has expired, they have the use of the improvement for nothing.

2. Hence we see the impolicy of obliging an individual, or a class of individuals, to engage in any labor, or to make any investment, contrary to their wishes. Thus, we are told that during the French revolution, some indi-

viduals were punished, capitally, for raising cattle, instead of wheat. Men may call this *legislation*, but the true name for it is *robbery*. To oblige a man to raise a crop worth fifteen dollars per acre, when he would otherwise have raised one worth twenty dollars per acre, is just the same thing as to let him do as he pleases, and then rob him of five dollars an acre afterwards. The wrong is the more intense, in the former case, inasmuch as it is done under the semblance of justice, and by men who claim, as the robber does not, that they have the *right* to do it. Such legislation as this will, in any country, soon produce a famine.

3. Another form of injury under this class, is seen in the restrictions upon industry, formerly, if not now, existing in many of the countries of Europe. By these regulations, artisans were prohibited the exercise of more than one trade; they were not allowed to exercise that trade, unless they had served a prescribed apprenticeship; nor, unless they joined a particular trade-society, and bound themselves to comply with certain restrictions, as, for instance, to sell at particular prices, and never to employ beyond a certain number of apprentices. The result of all this oppression is most iniquitous. It reduces the value of skill and industry, the sole estate of the laborer; and places him in the power of those, whose interest it is to reduce the supply as much as possible, in order to secure to themselves the most exorbitant profit. In such cases, a large amount of available industry must be kept out of employment; and, of course, production is, to this whole amount, diminished.

4. The same effect is partially produced by any mode of legislation, by which, in consequence of favor shown to one party, which of course another party must pay for, men are obliged to exchange an employment which they

prefer, and for which they have peculiar facilities, for another which they do not prefer, and for which they have not the same facilities. The manner in which this would lessen the stimulus to industry, has already been illustrated. Thus, should our government believe that commerce was more valuable to this country than manufactures, and therefore not only leave every one at liberty to engage in commerce, but, also lay a tax upon all American manufactures, in order to increase the amount of foreign transportation, and also remove all duties from imports, this would drive manufacturers out of business, and oblige them to become merchants and agriculturists. I think that every one must see that this would diminish the stimulus to industry throughout the whole country. Men would not voluntarily engage in manufactures in preference to commerce, unless they found manufactures to be the more profitable; and to oblige them to exchange the one for the other, is, therefore, to oblige them to leave a more productive for a less productive mode of employment. By all this difference is the country the loser, and the incitement to industry is diminished.

5. Hence, we also see the impolicy of laws regulating consumption. Such are sumptuary laws; or those which limit the degree of expensiveness in our dress, clothing or equipage. These were formerly common in Europe. Such, also, are laws which forbid or restrict the expenditure of money for the purposes of benevolence, religion, or any thing of this sort. Every one must see that one of the incitements to industry, is the pleasure which men expect to derive from expenditure. Now, if this expenditure be innocent, it matters not what sort of expenditure it is. Society has nothing to do with it; and it can in no manner interfere with it, without doing injustice, and taking away one of the strongest inducements to industry.

SECTION III.

LABOR WILL BE APPLIED TO CAPITAL, IN PROPORTION AS EVERY MAN SUFFERS THE INCONVENIENCES OF IDLENESS.

If God have made labor necessary to our well-being, in our present state; if he have set before us sufficient rewards to stimulate us to labor; and, if he have attached to idleness correspondent punishments, it is manifest that the intention of this constitution will not be accomplished, unless both of these classes of motives are allowed to operate upon man. We shall, therefore, co-operate with Him, in just so far as we allow his designs to take effect in the manner he intended. "We taught you," saith the apostle Paul, "that if a man will not work, neither shall he eat."

Now this result will be accomplished,

1. By the division of property. When property is perfectly divided, and every thing is owned by some one, and every one knows what is his own, nothing is left in common. Of course, no man can then obtain any thing more than he has, unless he obtain it by labor. And as every man has faculties capable of labor, and as these are exclusively his own; and as every one who possesses capital desires to employ labor with which to combine it, every man who possesses his natural faculties, has the means by which he may obtain something for his subsistence. The division of property is thus favorable to the laborer; inasmuch as, in consequence of it, every one needs his labor, and also has something to give him in exchange for it.

3. But, suppose property to be universally divided. A man may possess himself, either dishonestly or by begging, of the property for which he has not labored. The dishonest acquisition of property, as by cheating, stealing, or robbery, will be prevented by the strict and impartial administration of just and equitable laws. Hence, we see that the benefit of such laws is two fold. They encourage industry, first, by securing to the industrious the righteous reward of their labor; and secondly, by inflicting upon the indolent the just punishment of their idleness; or rather, by leaving them to the consequences which God has attached to their conduct. Being thus thrown upon their own resources, they must obey the law of their nature, and labor, or else suffer the penalty and starve.

If any man complain that this is a hardship, he must mean that this hardship has reference to our relations either to man, or to God. So far as our relations to man are concerned, there can certainly be no hardship, for every thing that we see is the result of labor, and is either the result of the labor of him that holds it, or of him who voluntarily parted with it for an equivalent in labor. Now, as every thing we see is the result of labor, the question is, who shall enjoy this result of labor, he who has labored, or he who has not. If it be a hardship for a man not to enjoy that for which he *has not labored;* it would certainly be a much greater hardship for a man not to enjoy that, for which he *has labored.* So that, the hardship would be greater if the system were arranged to suit the complainant, than it is now, under the system of which he complains.

If the hardship turn upon our relations to God; that is, if a man complain because God made him to labor; it is a difficulty which the complainant must settle with his

Maker. We have nothing to do with it. But since God has ordained it, we cannot help it, and an indolent man has no just cause of grief with his fellow men, if they see fit to act according to it.

II. But secondly: Men may be relieved from the necessity of labor, by charity. It will be understood that I here speak of men as poor from indolence, and not by visitation of God. I do not here refer to the sick, the infirm, the aged, the helpless, the widow, the fatherless, and the orphan. When God has seen fit to take away the power to labor, he then calls upon us to bestow liberally, and he always teaches us, that this mode of expenditure of our property, is more pleasing to him than any other. With this mode of charity I have now nothing to do. I speak only of provisions for the support of the poor, simply because he is poor; and of provision to supply his wants, without requiring the previous exertion of his labor. Of this kind are poor laws, as they are established in England, and in some parts of our own country; and permanent endowments left to particular corporations for the maintenance of the simply indigent. Now, such provisions we suppose to be injurious, for several reasons.

1. They are at variance with the fundamental law of government, that he who is able to labor, shall enjoy only that for which he has labored. If such be the law of God for us all, it is best for all, that all should be subjected to it. If labor be a curse, it is unjust that one part, and that, the industrious part, should suffer it all. If, as is the fact, it be a blessing, there is no reason why all should not equally enjoy its advantages.

2. They remove from men the fear of want, one of the most natural and universal stimulants to labor. Hence, in just so far as this stimulus is removed, there will be in a

given community less labor done; that is, less production created.

3. By teaching a man to depend upon others, rather than upon himself, they destroy the healthful feeling of independence. When this has once been impaired, and the confidence of man in the connexion between labor and reward is destroyed, he becomes a pauper for life. It is in evidence, before the committee of the British House of Commons, that, after a family has once applied for assistance from the parish, it rarely ceases to apply regularly, and, most frequently, in progress of time, for a larger and larger measure of assistance.

4. Hence, such a system must tend greatly to increase the number of paupers. It is a discouragement to industry, and a bounty upon indolence. With what spirit will a poor man labor, and retrench to the utmost his expenses, when he knows that he shall be taxed to support his next door neighbor, who is as able to work as himself; but who is relieved from the necessity of a portion of labor, merely by applying to the overseer of the poor for aid.

5. They are, in principle, destructive to the right of property, because they must proceed upon the concession, that the rich are under obligation to support the poor. If this be so; if he who labors be under obligation to support him that labors not; then the division of property and the right of property are at an end: for, he who labors has no better right to the result of his labor, than any one else.

6. Hence, they tend to insubordination. For, if the rich are under obligation to support the poor, why not to support them better; nay, why not to support them as well as themselves. Hence, the more provision there is of this kind, the greater will be the liability to collision between the two classes.

If this be so, we see, that in order to accomplish the designs of our Creator in this respect, and thus present the strongest inducement to industry,

1. Property should be universally appropriated, so that nothing is left in common.

2. The right of property should be perfectly protected, both against individual and social spoliation.

3. There should be no common funds for the support of those who are not willing to labor.

4. That if a man be reduced, by indolence or prodigality, to such extreme penury that he is in danger of perishing, he be relieved, through the medium of labor; that is, that he be furnished with work, and be remunerated with the proceeds.

5. That those who are enabled only in part to earn their subsistence, be provided for, to the amount of that deficiency, only.

And hence, that all our provisions for the relief of the poor, be so devised as not to interfere with this law of our nature. By so directing our benevolent energies, the poor are better provided for; they are happier themselves; and a great and constantly increasing burden is removed from the community. It has been found that alms-houses, conducted on this plan, will support themselves; and sometimes, even yield a small surplus revenue. This revenue, however, should always be given to the paupers, and should never be received by the public. The principle should be carried out, that the laborer is to enjoy the results of his industry.

For the same reason, penitentiaries and State prisons, should always be places of assiduous and productive labor. Idleness is a most prolific parent of crime. If the vicious could be accustomed to labor, one half of their reformation would be effected. Besides, by this means, a great diminution would be effected in the expense to the community. There can be no reason why a hundred able-bodied men, and such are generally the tenants of our prisons, should not both support themselves, and pay for the superintendence necessary to their labor. In a well-regulated prison, they will always do this. There must always be something faulty in the arrangements of such an institution, where this is not the result.

And thus, where a society is so organized, that every man is left to suffer the results of idleness; that is, where labor is made necessary to the acquisition of every thing desirable, and where the results of that labor are most perfectly secured to the laborer, there will exist the greatest stimulus to labor, and, of course, production will be most rapidly augmented.

SECTION IV.

THE GREATER THE RATIO OF CAPITAL TO LABOR, THE GREATER WILL BE THE STIMULUS TO LABOR.

The principle to be considered in this section may be thus illustrated. Capital is useless; that is, will yield no revenue, unless it be united with labor. A farm will yield nothing, unless it be tilled, and the grain be harvested; cotton wool, and a manufactory, will produce nothing, unless there be workmen to labor in it. Hence, every man who holds capital, is desirous of uniting it with industry, that he may share, with the laborers, the profits of the resulting product. On the contrary, he who has industry, is desirous of uniting it with capital, because, unless he can so unite it, it will yield nothing in return. A man can earn nothing by spending his whole time in beating the air. Hence, when the number of laborers is great; that is, where labor is abundant, and the amount of capital small, there will be a competition of laborers for work, and the price of labor will fall; that is, the laborer will receive a less compensation for his work. On the contrary, when the number of laborers is small, and the amount of capital great, there will be a competition among capitalists for labor; that is, the price of labor will rise; that is, the laborer will receive a greater compensation for his work. Thus, we see, the greater the amount of capital, in proportion to the number of laborers, the greater will be the rate of wages, and, of course, the stronger the stimulus to industry.

It deserves, however, to be remarked, that this principle is liable to some important modifications. Thus, it is practically true, only in so far as men continue to be operated upon by the hope of reward. When this ceases to operate, and wages are so low as to render the utmost amount of labor necessary to avoid starvation, they will work more assiduously, the lower the wages; that is, the nearer they are to actual starvation. But, to this, there is also a limit. For men cannot long endure so great toil, under the depressing influences of despair, Many very soon die, and thus, a diminished population again raises the price of labor. Another common result of such a condition of laborers, is domestic insurrection. Men who have long stood on the borders of starvation, become desperate.

They know, that by no change could their condition be made worse; hence, *cupidi rerum novarum*, they unite under any agitator who promises them bread; the whole fabric of society is prostrated; and civil war and anarchy succeed.

Another modification of this principle, is the following: I have said above, that the stimulus to labor is in proportion to the wages of labor. This will be true, only of those cases where the facilities of gratifying desire are equal. Although wages be high, yet if only few objects of desire can be procured in exchange for them, there will be wanting one important element in stimulating the human being to labor. Hence, the stimulus to labor will be the most effective, when the wages are highest, and when, by means of wages, the greatest number of desires can be gratified.

Thus, in a newly settled country of great fertility, wages are high, because a vast amount of land is open for cultivation, and a proprietor can afford to give a high price for labor. Still, industry is not active in proportion to the rate of wages, because, the desires which can be gratified in a new country are few, and a man can procure all that is procurable with a less amount of labor than he is able to exert. Hence, the reason why men labor so intensely in prosperous seasons, in large cities. The remuneration at such times is high, and the desires which wealth can gratify are innumerable. A merchant in New York, during the season of business, when profits are high, will cheerfully impose upon himself labor, which he knows will, in all probability, ruin his constitution; labor, which, he would not, on any account, impose upon a slave.

Hence, we see that the accumulation of capital is more for the advantage of the laborer than of the capitalist.

The greater the ratio of capital to labor, the greater will be the share of the product that falls to the laborer. The greater the ratio of labor to capital, the greater will be the share of the product that falls to the capitalist. Hence, the laboring classes are really more interested in increasing the capital of a country, than the wealthy classes. Hence, we see, that when one class of the community repines at the prosperity of another class, they repine against their own mercies, and the means of increasing their own rate of compensation.

It is, however, evident, that the accumulation of capital, in any nation, does not depend simply upon its annual production, but upon the proportion that its annual production bears to its annual expenditure. A country that annually expends all its production, let it produce ever so much, will never increase its capital. A country that produces ever so little, if it annually expend somewhat less than its revenue, will be accumulating something; and must, in progress of time, become richer than its more highly favored neighbor. This explains the fact, that the countries blessed with the richest soils, and the greatest natural advantages, have not generally become the richest nations. The result has, within moderate limits, been almost the reverse.

Hence, we see, that every mode of unnecessary expenditure, whether individual or national, by diminishing the annual accumulation of capital, tends directly to lower the rate of wages, and thus injure the condition of the laboring classes. The millions which are wasted and destroyed by intemperance, if saved, would add to the capital of a country, and thus increase the demand for labor. All unnecessary expenditure for the maintenance of civil government, has, of course, the same tendency. Hence arises, also, one of the most afflicting consequences of war. Had the almost incalculable sums which Great Britain has expended in wars, for the last hundred years, been added to her operative capital, and, but for these wars, it would have been so added, all her inhabitants would have found, at all times, abundant employment, and, at a rate of wages, which would, by this time, have banished almost the recollection of poverty from her shores.

SECTION V.

INDUSTRY WILL BE APPLIED TO CAPITAL, IN PROPORTION TO THE INTELLECTUAL IMPROVEMENT OF A PEOPLE.

Intellectual cultivation tends to increase the industry of a people, in two ways. 1st. *By exciting a people to exertion;* and, 2d. *By directing that exertion.*

1. *Intellectual cultivation excites a people to exertion.* Ignorant men are indolent, because they know not the results that may be accomplished, nor the benefits that may be secured by industry. This is one of the most common causes of the great indolence of savage nations. An Indian, who knows of no condition better than his own, of no covering better than a skin, of no habitation better than his wigwam, and of no weapon better than his bow and arrow, has no motive to industry, beyond what may be adequate to procure these simple necessaries. Let him know that, by additional effort, he can provide himself with a blanket, and by a still additional

effort, that he can exchange his bow and arrow for a rifle, and his wigwam for a comfortable house, and you present motives to additional labor. His industry will thus expand with the occasion. The case is the same with a nation, at a more advanced period of its history. Hence, the impulse which is always given to industry, by any important improvement in the intellectual character of a people. It was a knowledge of the conveniences and luxuries of the East, which the crusaders brought back to western Europe, that was the precursor and the cause of that dawning of improvement which succeeded the night of the dark ages.

2. *Intellectual cultivation directs to a profitable end, the industry* which it has previously excited.

Agriculture will be successfully prosecuted, only in proportion as men are acquainted with the best modes and seasons of culture, the laws of vegetable and animal physiology, and the probable existence of that demand which it will be most profitable to supply.

Manufacturing labor will be successful, in proportion as the manufacturer is able, by his knowledge, to avail himself of the improvements of other countries, to understand the laws of nature, and invent means of applying them to his own advantage, and as he is able, by his intelligence, to modify his occupation in any manner that may be for his interest.

The Merchant will succeed, in proportion as he is able to select the most profitable places and times for exchange, to foresee the probable changes of the market, and to avail himself of the fluctuations of capital which are always taking place, in various parts of the civilized world.

And, in general, it is evident that, with a given amount

of labor and of capital, production will be exactly in proportion to the knowledge which the operator has of the laws which govern that department of production in which he labors, and to the degree in which his labor conforms to his knowledge. If, then, labor will be in proportion to the benefits which it confers; and if, by knowledge, these benefits are increased, we see how manifestly labor must be stimulated by intellectual cultivation. Thus we see how it is, that an intelligent people is always industrious, and an ignorant people always indolent. Hence, one of the surest means of banishing indolence, is to banish ignorance from a country.

But, it is evident, that improvement in knowledge, in order to be in any signal degree beneficial, must be universal. A single individual can derive but little advantage from his knowledge and industry, if he be surrounded by a community both ignorant and indolent. Just so far as they improve their condition, and become useful to themselves, they become useful to him; and both parties thus become useful to each other. This is specially the case, where a government is, in its character, popular; that is, where laws emanate from the more numerous classes. In such a case, not only is an intelligent man not benefitted, but he is positively injured, by the ignorance and indolence of his neighbors. Hence, the reason why every man has a personal interest in the intellectual improvement of every one of his fellow citizens; and why the education of the whole population should be the care of the government; that is, of the whole country.

The efforts of a government may be usefully directed, in this respect, to two objects. 1st. The *increase;* and, 2d. The *dissemination* of knowledge.

First. The increase of knowledge. This may be promoted in several ways.

1. By the establishment of colleges, universities, and other seminaries of learning. These, I suppose, should be furnished by the public, with libraries, apparatus, and all the means for instruction, investigation and discovery. They should be so governed, and the remuneration so adjusted, that teachers should be placed under the strongest stimulus to labor for the promotion of science, and to communicate, most successfully, knowledge to their pupils. Colleges and universities should, at all times, be places of strenuous effort, and vigorous mental discipline, on the part of both instructors and pupils. As soon as they become the places of literary leisure, and intellectual indolence, they are not only useless, but hurtful; inasmuch as they retard, rather than advance, the progress of science.

For this reason, I doubt whether endowments, for the support of professorships, are useful; at least, so far as they tend to render a teacher's support, independent of his own exertions. For the same reason, a teacher should not be remunerated by a fixed salary, but by the sale of tickets of admission to his lectures, or by a salary, varying with his ability and success. Large foundations for the support of students in colleges, if under the control of the college itself, so far as they render the number of students in no way dependent upon the ability and faithfulness of the instructor, will have a tendency to remove from him one of the most valuable stimulants to industry.

2. By rewarding those who have been successful in the advancement of science.

1. This may be done, first, *Directly*, as by bestowing premiums, rewards, grants of money, &c., to those who have made discoveries of pre-eminent utility. This is frequently done by the British government; and I see no reason why it is not done wisely. In this country,

however, it is, I believe, never practised. The only rewards which we ever confer, are for military or naval service. The propriety of those, I by no means, in this place, dispute ; yet, I think it would be difficult to show, that warriors are the only benefactors of mankind, or, that Whitney or Fulton did not deserve as well of their country, for the invention of the cotton gin and the application of steam to navigation, as they would have done, had they captured a fleet on the ocean, or routed a tribe of Indians in the forest.

2. *Indirectly*, by granting to those who labor in science or invention, the right to derive advantage from their discoveries or inventions. This is done by laws of copy and patent right. The justice of this provision we have elsewhere shown. We here see the manner, in which, by stimulating intellectual labor, by hope of reward, it tends to increase knowledge, and hence, facilitate production. We hence see the reason, why such laws should be rigidly enforced, and why a violation of them is prejudicial to the best interests of society.

Secondly. A government may improve the intellectual character of a people, by the *dissemination* of knowledge. This will be done, so far as provision is made for the universal instruction of a people in the elements of a common education. The interest of every man demands that all his fellow citizens should be able to read and write, to keep accounts, to understand geography ; and thus possess the means of self-improvement, to whatever degree they may be disposed to carry it.

The effect of such a diffusion of knowledge, has already been illustrated at sufficient length. It will be necessary here only to allude to the means, by which this result may be best attained.

1. As a stimulus to intellectual improvement, probably, the right of suffrage should be restricted to those who are able to read and write.

2. Provision should be made, in every neighborhood, for the education of all children under a certain age.

3. The expenses of this provision may be borne, *partly*, by a general fund. This fund should, however, never defray more than a portion of the expense; for no man values, highly, what he gets for nothing. If a fund be raised for this purpose, great care must be taken that it be not abused.

4. Without a fund, the same result will probably be better accomplished by obliging every district containing a given number of inhabitants, to provide itself with a school, on penalty of a fine to be paid to the school districts in its neighborhood, for the purposes of instruction.

5 To complete this arrangement, it would, probably, be necessary that seminaries should be provided for the purpose of educating teachers for the primary schools. This would ensure a supply of instructors, of assured qualifications, without which, such a system could not go into successful operation.

And now, to sum up what has been said: It will be seen that the inducements to labor, and, hence, of course, the wealth and means of happiness, in any given country, must depend, principally, upon two conditions: 1st. The degree of its intelligence; and, 2d. The purity of its moral character.

1. On its intelligence will depend its knowledge of its own advantages, of the laws of nature, and of the means

by which it may avail itself of those laws, for the promotion of its own happiness. A nation without knowledge, like a blind man in the garden of Eden, might be surrounded with every thing lovely to the eye or delightful to the taste, without ever being able to ascertain, either where a single object of desire was to be found, or how the possession of it might be secured.

2. On the moral character of a nation depends the justice of its laws, its respect for individual right, security of property, individual and social virtue, together with the industry and frugality which are their invariable attendants.

Of these two, the latter is the more important to national prosperity. For, where virtue, frugality, and respect for right exist, riches will, by natural consequence, accumulate; and intellectual cultivation will, of necessity, succeed. But, intellectual cultivation may easily exist, without the existence of virtue or love of right. In this case, its only effect is, to stimulate desire, and this, unrestrained by the love of right, must eventually overturn the social fabric which it at first erected. Hence, we see that the surest means of promoting the welfare of a country is, to cultivate its intellectual, but especially its moral character. Until this have been done, no permanent foundation for a nation's prosperity has yet been laid. And, if any one will take the pains to examine, he will find, that, other things being equal, the wealth, and happiness, and power of every nation, are in exact proportion to its intellectual and moral character.

And, here, it may not be amiss to add, that all true benevolence may be defended, no less upon principles of political economy, than of philanthropy. The circulation of the scriptures, the inculcation of moral and religious truth upon the mind of man, by means of Sabbath schools, and the preaching of the gospel, are of the very greatest importance to the productive energies of a country. The argument is very short, but it seems very conclusive. No nation can rapidly accumulate or long enjoy the means of happiness, except as it is pervaded by individual and social love of right; but individual and social love of right will never prevail, without the practical influence of the motives and sanctions of religion; and these motives and sanctions will never influence men, unless they are, by human effort, brought to bear upon the conscience.

The same principles will defend, upon economical grounds, the efforts of benevolence on behalf of foreign nations. Intelligence, virtue, and equitable laws, will have the same effect upon other men, that they have upon us. They will render men industrious, frugal, and consequently rich, and raise them from a savage to a civilized state. Just in proportion as a nation is thus transformed, are its products increased; the riches of the whole world are augmented; the portion of wealth which falls to the share of each man is rendered greater; and the ratio of capital to labor is higher. Just as a nation becomes intelligent and rich, its wants are multiplied, and the means for supplying them are provided. Hence, it becomes a better customer to other nations; it gives an additional impulse to their industry; and it repays them for their products, with whatever God has bestowed upon it, which will add to the happiness of others. Can any one doubt that Great Britain and France reap incomparably greater advantages from each other, in their present condition of advanced civilization, than either of them would, if the other were in the condition in which it was found by Julius Cæsar? What demand would Great Britain make upon the productions of France, if she were, at this moment, inhabited by half naked savages? Or again: How much greater benefits does North America confer upon the world, than it would if it were peopled by its aboriginal inhabitants? How great a stimulus would be given to the industry of the world, at this time; and how greatly would the comforts and luxuries of men be increased, if Africa were peopled by civilized and christianized men? Now, if these things be so; and that they are so, I see not that any one can dispute; it seems to me, that civilized nations could in no way so successfully promote their own interests, as by the universal dissemination of the principles of religion, and the means of education and religion.

SECTION VI.

ON THE EFFECTS OF DIRECT LEGISLATION, AS A MEANS OF INCREASING PRODUCTION.

I have thus far said nothing upon the effect of legislative enactments, by means of bounties and protecting duties, as a means of increasing production. The reason is, that I have not yet been able to discover in what manner they produce this effect. Nevertheless, since many persons suppose them to be of great importance, it might seem that a discussion of this subject was incomplete, if they were passed over in silence. I shall devote this section to a consideration of their effects.

Of discriminating, or, as they are frequently called, protecting duties.

1. Duties of this sort are to be considered apart from duties levied for the support of government, because they are either not necessary for this *purpose*, or else they are levied for a different *object*. Thus, if five per cent. on an import be necessary to the support of government, and ten per cent. be levied, in order to favor, or, as it is said, to protect one branch of industry, the additional five per cent. is levied for a distinct object, aside from that of the support of government. It is only this latter part of the duty which we propose to consider; that is, so much of the duty as is levied for the purpose of favoring one particular product.

2. Now, if such a duty have any effect upon the productiveness of a nation, it must be in one of these ways. It must either first increase the *capital* of a country; or, secondly, increase its *number of laborers;* or, third, create a greater *stimulus to labor.* I think it evident, from what has already been shown, that every condition which affects production, must exert its influence in one of these three methods.

3. I think it evident, that legislation of this sort cannot increase the *capital* of a country. The capital of a country, at any moment, is its present amount of annual and fixed capital. Now, a law cannot create capital; since, if it could, there would be no necessity for any other labor than that of legislation; and, in order to grow rich, a nation would have nothing to do but meet in public assembly, and spend its whole time in making and hearing speeches, and enacting laws. I believe, however, that this mode of growing rich, has never been found remarkably successful.

If it be said that, in this manner we shall attract foreign capital to our own country, I answer: this depends not upon legislation, but upon the rate of interest, and the security of property. If these conditions be more favorable here than in another country, capital will flow hither. If they be more favorable in another country than here, it will flow thither. The system of Great Britain has been exclusive, but capital does not go from this country to be invested there.

4. Legislation of this kind cannot increase the actual *number of laborers.* The number of laborers is as the number of inhabitants. Legislation has never been supposed to have any power to create men. It is true, population is found always to increase with the increase of the means of living; that is, with the increase of the productiveness of labor. Population will increase or diminish, just in proportion as a laborer is able to procure more or less for the product of a day's labor; that is, as every thing is cheap or dear. Whether the tendency of duties is to render productions cheap, remains to be considered. It must, however, be evident to all, that laws do *not create human beings;* of course, they add nothing to the number of laborers, that is, of human beings in a country.

It may be said, we may thus induce laborers to come from other countries. To this it may be answered; this will depend upon the wages of labor. If laborers be better paid here than elsewhere, they will come here, and not otherwise. But it may be said, that we shall thus induce more of them to come. But then, just as we increase the proportion of labor to capital, we diminish the wages of labor. In what manner we encourage *domestic* industry, by inviting foreigners to come and underbid our own citizens, I believe has not yet been explained. Besides, what is called protection changes only the *mode* of labor; that is, it takes men from one mode of labor, to employ them upon another. Suppose, then, that it attracts foreign laborers to one branch of industry; it deters those in another branch of industry from imigrating. If, for instance, manufactures are protected, this will tend to encourage manufacturers to imigrate; but it will, in a correspondent proportion, discourage agriculturists.

5. If, then, discriminating duties produce any effect upon production, it must be by *stimulating* industry; that is, while the amount of capital and the number of laborers remain the same, by stimulating men to labor more, and thus to create a greater amount of production than they would under other circumstances. This, I believe, is supposed to be the way in which the system produces its effect. This is the point of view in which we shall now proceed to consider it.

The manner in which this is done, is the following: Suppose a country to be under a free system, and that every one is devoting himself to agriculture, commerce, or manufactures, as he finds either the most for his interest; under these circumstances, there will be a certain aveerage of productiveness, both of labor and of capital. Woollen cloth can be procured by exchange, for five dollars a yard; but it cannot, in the present state of the country, be manufactured under ten dollars a yard; that is, capital and labor are, in every thing else, so productive, that they could not be abstracted from other employments at the same rate of profit, unless the manufacturer could receive ten dollars a yard for his cloth. Now, suppose that, in order to enable him to do this, a duty of five dollars a yard is levied on imported cloth, by which the price of all cloth is raised to ten dollars a yard, that thus it may be in the power of a manufacturer, to employ his capital and labor in this manner. There is no doubt that thus the cloth manufacture might be established.

Now I think it evident, upon inspection, that the productiveness of labor, is not by this operation, increased. The reason why cloth was not manufactured before, was, that the productiveness of labor and capital, in this mode of investment, was lower than the average productiveness of labor and capital in other modes of investment. All that has been effected is, to raise the productiveness *here*, to the general average *elsewhere.* There has been nothing done to render it any greater, either in this or in any other employment; for, I presume that no one will contend, that one kind of industry should be really more highly paid than another; nor that, if it were desired, it could be effected, without the aid of a direct monopoly.

But the manufacturer now gets ten dollars for that, which before would bring only five. Let us inquire whence this additional five dollars comes.

It is evident that government possesses nothing. All that it possesses, is precisely so much taken from the annual revenue of individuals. In this case, therefore, it really bestows nothing, but only causes a transfer of annual revenues, from one party to another. The case is, therefore, the same as it would be if, while there had been no duty laid, every man had been allowed to buy cloth for five dollars a yard, but had been obliged, for every yard that he bought, to pay five dollars to the manufacturer. It would be the same thing to both parties as at present. The consumer would then, as now, pay ten dollars a yard for cloth, and the manufacturer might sell it for five, if he received five more as an additional gratuity. The five dollars that is *added* to the revenue of the one, is precisely five dollars *taken from* the revenue of the other.

Now, if this be the fact, inasmuch as what is added to the productiveness of the industry of the one class, is taken from the productiveness of the industry of the other class, it would seem that what the one gained, the other lost; and hence, that there could be no increased stimulus to industry *on the whole*, since, by as much as the *one* is stimulated, the *other* is depressed. But this is not all. What you have given to the one class, has only raised his mode of labor to the point of productiveness, at which that of all the other classes was before ; while the means by which this has been effected, has, to the whole amount of its effect, reduced the productiveness of all the other classes lower than it was before. By just as much as *this productiveness has been diminished*, by so much has the stimulus to industry been, upon the whole, decreased.

But yet more. As the *price* of the article is increased, the *demand* for the article is diminished. This has been before illustrated. There will, therefore, be less of the article made, because less of it is wanted. By all this *diminution* is the demand for labor diminished ; the price of labor must, therefore, fall, and the stimulus to labor *be, by so much*, decreased.

This effect will take place, in what manner soever the discriminating duty may operate. Suppose, that from scarcity of wool, the price of imported cloth had, without any duty, been doubled? The result would have been, that the demand would so have fallen off, that multitudes would have been thrown out of employment, and whole establishments would have been ruined. Suppose that, by a duty, we exclude the foreign cloth, and make it ourselves. There is still a less quantity *made*, than before. But the imported cloth was not to be had for nothing. Some of our own population were obliged to raise the products, which we sent in exchange for it. As we do not take their *cloth*, they cannot take our *produce.* Of course, all those who labored in the products which *were exchanged for cloth*, are out of employment. There was a demand for a sufficient amount of their labor to purchase one thousand bales of cloth; suppose, now, there is a demand for labor sufficient to make only five hundred bales of cloth. By all the difference, therefore, between the labor necessary to *procure* one thousand bales by exchange, and that necessary to *manufacture* five hundred bales, is the demand for industry diminished, and, of course, the stimulus to industry weakened.

Again: The system of discriminating duties proceeds upon the principle, that the more of our own labor we employ upon a product, the greater is the encouragement to our own industry. This is the reason why we are advised to do our own labor, and manufacture our own goods, instead of allowing other nations to manufacture them for us. Now we have no disposition, at present, to deny this assertion, and are willing by it to test the system in question. In the one case, we *import* cloth for *five* dollars a yard, and, in the other, we *make* it for *ten* dollars a yard. When we make it for ten dollars, we employ only the labor necessary for making it. When we import it, we employ, *first*, the labor necessary in making the articles which we send abroad, with which we purchase it; and *secondly*, the labor necessary to transport those articles to a foreign port; and, *thirdly*, the labor necessary to transport the cloth here, together with the labor necessary for the construction of shipping, for the two voyages. Now it is manifest, if these things be taken into consideration, that our labor makes up a much larger portion of the price of the *imported cloth*, than *of that which is made at home.* By all this difference, therefore, the imported cloth creates a larger demand for domestic industry. This would be the case, even where the quantity annually consumed was the same. By how much more is this the case, when it is considered that, by the augmentation of price which this system occasions, the quantity absolutely consumed must be greatly diminished.

We see, then, what is the tendency of a system of this kind. So far as the manufacturer is concerned, it cannot increase his profit beyond the average profits of every other employment; for, if competition be allowed, capital and labor will flow into it, whatever may be its advantages, until its profits fall to the general level. In the mean time, the demand for other labor is diminished, by the reduced consumption created by a rise of price, and by using an article into which less of our own labor enters as a constituent of price; and also, as this rise of price increases the expenses of living, it makes even these reduced wages of less value than they were before. Hence the tendency is, to reduce the profit of capital and labor in the whole community lower than they were before such duty was imposed. To this reduced average, manufacturers must conform; and hence, by this very operation, they themselves must suffer. Hence we see the reason why, when once a duty is imposed for the protection of a particular branch of manufactures, it is not long before a larger protective duty is demanded; and also why a protective duty, which at first is followed by great manufacturing enterprise and success, is so commonly afterwards followed by so universal a depression of manufacturing industry.

Nor is this all. The rise of prices must, of necessity, follow a protecting duty; for this is its very object. Its object is, to raise the price of some particular product, so that it may be created where it could not be created before. If it produce no rise of prices it is useless.

Now, a rise of prices raises the cost of production, and, by its whole effect, must raise the price of every product which we create. By this whole effect, therefore, is our foreign market injured. If we can raise cotton at ten cents a pound, and bring it into market as cheap as other nations, we have as good an opportunity as they, for selling it. If we can raise it at nine cents, we can undersell them, and supply the whole market; or, if we sell it at the same price as before, we gain one cent more on the pound. If, by increase of the expenses of living, we cannot raise it for less than eleven cents a pound, they will undersell *us*, and we shall be obliged to give up the raising of cotton, either partially or altogether; and the industry engaged in raising and transporting the cotton, and what we receive in exchange for it, must be either partially or wholly thrown out of employment. Every one must see, that the manufactures of England could be afforded much lower; that is, would be able much better to compete with those of other nations, if, by abolishing her duties on corn, her manufacturers could be supplied with the necessaries of life at half the present cost. At the same profit to the laborer and capitalist, her products could be afforded at a price less than at present, by all the diminution of the expenses of living. By this difference, she would both undersell other nations and increase the demand for her manufactures, thus reaping, at once, a double advantage.

But once more: It is seen that, by such a system, the course of industry and of capital in a nation, must be greatly changed. Thus when an article is imported, one class of producers must labor to create the article which we exchange for it; another class must build ships to transport it; and another class must carry on the transportation. By a discriminating duty, all these classes must, either in whole or in part, be thrown out of employment, and this capital be either reduced in value, or rendered wholly useless. Now this is a serious injury, both to the capitalist and the laborer. The property of the one and the skill of the other are rendered useless, and by so much is it a total loss to the country. It may be said, let them seek other employments. True; they *must do this*, or starve; but this renders it not the less true, that there has been *so much loss*. If a man's house be burned down, it is easy to say to him, move into another house; but this does not alter the fact, that his house has been burned down, and that he has suffered loss to precisely this amount.

But, suppose he turn to the other employment. It has been shown that the average of profit, in this employment, cannot be higher than the average of profit was, in the employment which he left. He is then no better off than he was before, and, in the mean time, he has lost the skill and capital which he spent years to acquire. By all this amount of depreciation, therefore, is he, and of course, the whole country, poorer by the exchange.

Of Bounties. The principle of bounties is the same as that of discriminating duties. The manner in which they are bestowed, is the following: If a manufacturer cannot produce cloth for less than ten dollars a yard, and the imported cloth can be procured at five dollars, a bounty of five dollars a yard is given him, for every yard he manufactures, or for every yard he exports. The cloth, then, is sold, either at home or abroad, at five dollars, and he also receives five dollars as a gratuity.

The principal reasons urged above, apply to bounties. They are, however, less objectionable, for several reasons:

1. The price of the article is not visibly raised, and the consumption, therefore, on this account, is not so much diminished.

2. The encouragement given, in this manner, is cheaper; that is, we pay only for what is made, while, by discriminating duties, we pay the same, whether any thing is made or not. We pay a very heavy duty on cutlery in this country, while not a hundredth part of the cutlery used, is made here. It would be one hundred times cheaper, to pay a bounty equal to the present duty on cutlery, and it would be, for aught I can see, just as good for the cutler. The whole effect of this mode of encourgement is, to pay one man as much more as the bounty amounts to, for producing an article, than we should pay another man; that is, one man will do it for five dollars, and we engage another to do it for five dollars, and give him five dollars besides, for the sake of economy.

I have, thus far, considered this subject solely in respect to its connexion with economy; that is, as it is favorable or unfavorable to production. It is, however, obvious, that an entirely distinct argument might be constructed on another, that is, a moral ground. It might be asked, by what right does society thus interfere with the property of the individual? when did the individual surrender this right? and how wise would it be for him to surrender it? It is in vain here to urge, that society has the right to destroy individual property, in cases of extreme necessity; because, in order to render this plea available, it must be shown that this is a case of extreme necessity. And besides, if society destroy individual property in case of extreme necessity, it is always bound to make good the loss to the individual. I think that, if the protected interests were obliged to make good the loss which the system inflicts upon all other interests, the demand for protection would be less unjust than at present; and protection would be considerably less injurious.

But, as these are questions of *right*, and belong rather

to Moral Philosophy than to Political Economy, we shall not, in this place, discuss them any further.

But, in opposition to what has been offered, several objections have been urged. It may be proper to notice here, some of those which are most commonly advanced.

I. The above argument is made to turn upon production alone, and proceeds upon the supposition, that the prosperity of a nation depends upon the abundance of the productiveness of its industry, more than upon any thing else. In order to meet this view of the case, it has been said, that *production* is a matter of no consequence to a nation's prosperity, and that, in order to make a nation rich, happy and powerful, all that is necessary is, to encourage and stimulate *consumption.*

1. To this it may be answered, that this assertion leaves the above argument untouched, so far as production is concerned; that is, it does not deny that the effects of discriminating duties upon *production,* are such as we have shown.

2. But secondly: If a man assert that the wealth of a nation is the result of its consumption, and not of its production, he must also assert that the hand of the *prodigal,* and not that of the *diligent,* maketh rich; that industry and frugality are the sources not of *wealth,* but of *poverty;* that fire and sword, devastation and murder, are national blessings; that *we* ought to pay other nations, instead of their paying *us,* for spoliations of property; that incendiaries should be rewarded, instead of being hanged; and that the way to render a city rich, happy and prosperous, is to reduce it to ashes. If a man really *believe* this; I do not say if he *assert* it; his case is beyond the reach of ratiocination; and he must be recommended to the kind attentions of a discreet and judicious medical adviser.

II. It has also been urged, that the only method of rendering products cheap, is to encourage competition; that competition is the great source of increased productiveness of labor, and that to excite competition among our own manufacturers, by means of higher duties, is the only sure method by which to cause any article of necessity to be produced at the lowest possible rate.

To this objection we reply, that the principle assumed *is erroneous;* and that the reasoning from it is *self-destructive.*

1. The principle assumed *is erroneous.* Although free competition is necessary, to reduce prices to their *natural rate;* yet beyond this, competition, within long periods, can have no effect whatever. The price of every article is determined by the cost of its production; that is, by the labor and capital necessary to produce it. Its price can be reduced in no other manner than by reducing this *cost.* If the materials can be furnished cheaper, and it can be produced by less labor, its price will fall; but it can fall from no other cause. If it be a monopolized article, the producer may, over and above a fair remuneration for his expenses, demand an excessive profit. If there be a free competition, his profits will be reduced to the general average of other capital and labor. A competition which obliged a producer to sell for less than cost, would, of course, ruin him, and would be a loss to the community. Such is the case in times of manufacturing depression, when the producer is obliged to sell at a loss. These are surely not times of prosperity. The result of such competition is, to drive a portion of the producers out of employment; a less amount of the product is created, competition is diminished, prices rise to their natural level, and the whole effect of competition is at an end. If, then, when there is no monopoly, competition, be it

ever so great, can reduce the price of no article permanently below the cost and charges of its production; and that by this cost, its price will always be determined, be the competition whatever it may; it is evident, that the only way in which the price of any thing can be *really reduced*, must be by diminishing the price of the material and labor employed in creating it; that is, by rendering every thing as cheap as possible. And it is also evident, that by raising the price of articles of consumption; that is, of the articles of living, we shall raise the price of whatever is produced, let the competition be ever so great.

But, *secondly*, the argument drawn from the assertion is self-destructive. If it be the fact that competition is the great and proper cause of reduction of price, then, the wider the competition, the greater will be the reduction of price. If this be so, we should not only open our ports to every other nation, but should abolish import duties altogether, even for the sake of raising a revenue, and sustain the expenses of civil government, altogether by direct taxation. It would, however, be a new mode of encouraging competition, if the citizens of New York should forbid every one, not a native of that city, to exercise the trade of a carpenter or joiner, within the limits of their jurisdiction. In what manner such an act would reduce the prices of house-building, I confess myself unable to discover.

I think, therefore, that the system of discriminating duties cannot be defended on the ground that they, by competition, tend to reduce prices.

III. Again: It is asked, is it not better to labor for ourselves, than to have others labor for us?

I answer, undoubtedly, We *must* labor for ourselves, unless we mean to live either by begging or by stealing. And this is really the only alternative which the Creator has left us. On this point, therefore, there is no dispute. It is agreed, on both hands, that it is better to labor for ourselves, than to have others to labor for us.

Whatever either a man or a nation possesses, except by robbery or begging, must be the production of its own labor. The question then, is, whether it is better for us to receive a greater, or to receive a less result from our labor. Every man must labor for a coat. But is it better for him to procure it by labor, for five dollars a yard, or for ten dollars? Is it better that he should, by exchange, earn it by five days' labor, or make it for himself, by fifteen days' labor? He procures it as much by labor in the one case, as in the other. I do not see that there can be any question, in which way his labor can be most profitably expended. If a manufacturer wish for oranges, he can procure them in no other way than by labor. The question is, whether he shall procure them by labor in manufactures, or by labor in raising them. In the first case, a day's labor will produce, by exchange, a hundred; in the second case, it will cost several days' labor to produce one. The question is, which is the preferable way, in which, by labor, a manufacturer shall produce oranges?

IV. But it is said, although we may be obliged, at first, to procure manufactures at a higher price, yet, having once introduced them, they will, in the end, become cheaper than before; and thus, our ultimate benefit will more than repay our temporary loss.

In order to consider this objection, it will be necessary to refer to what we have already remarked on the nature of annual and fixed capital.

It is evident, that, in the first stage of any society, there exists nothing but the earth with its capabilities, and man to labor upon it. The labor of man produces an annual capital. If he have been industrious and frugal, there will have arisen an annual surplus, which must, of necessity, be transformed into fixed capital; and it is so transformed, for the purpose of increasing the annual capital. Thus, every addition to the fixed capital for this year, lays the foundation for the investment of a larger amount of fixed capital for the next year; and thus nations grow rich, and the demand for fixed capital is annually increasing.

It is evident that the investment in fixed capital will be, *first*, in those instruments themselves, necessary for the direct increase of annual production, as ploughs, fences, houses, barns, &c.; and, *secondly*, in the machinery necessary to the creation of these, and of the productions for annual consumption; that is, it will be in manufacturing establishments. But, inasmuch as the capital of a country is at first small, a nation will, of necessity, at first invest its annual surplus in those manufactures which require the least capital, and of which the price is most enhanced by transportation. As capital increased, it would be able to make larger investments of fixed capital. Manufactures, which it would have been impossible for it to conduct profitably in its tenth year, it may conduct profitably in its fiftieth year; and what it could not conduct profitably in its fiftieth year, it may very profitably conduct in its one hundredth year. And the reason of this variation is two fold. In the one case, it did not, and in the other case it did, possess the capital necessary for the investment in this particular branch of manufactures; and, in the second place, though it possessed the requisite capital, that capital could not be taken from the employments in which it was at present engaged, and invested in any thing else, without a loss, that is, a diminution of profit. As soon, however, as the most necessary investments have been made, their annual product will enable the nation to commence something else. By the multiplication of capital, interest is diminished, and a nation is gradually enabled to produce for herself every thing for which she has the natural facilities. And hence, the time when any manufacture can be profitably established, in a country which possesses natural advantages for it, is decided by the amount of the capital of that country; the amount of annual investment which it is able to make in fixed capital; and on the rate of interest of capital at the period in question.

Now, suppose that the system of discriminating duties left the prices and means of accumulation unaffected. In this case, the period of profitably producing the article in question would arrive, at the *same time* as if no such system had been adopted. Previously, therefore, to *this time*, the article must have been purchased by the whole community, at an additional and unnecessary expense; since, when this time arrived, in the natural course of things, the manufacture in question will commence, just as though nothing had been done, and just as every other manufacture had previously commenced. In this case, then, I see not that there would be any gain. All that has been paid, therefore, is so much unnecessary expense, withour rendering this kind of investment profitable to the whole community, any sooner than it would have been, had no such expense been incurred.

That, however, a discriminating duty does not increase productiveness, but that, on the contrary, it diminishes it, has, I think, been already shown. Now, by just so much as it diminishes productiveness, and of course diminishes annual capital, by so much it *postpones* the period, at which the manufacture in question can be profitably established. Hence, the state of the case is this: In the present condition of capital and labor, the manufacture of a particular product is unprofitable. In order to produce it *now*, instead of producing at a *later* period, we diminish the productiveness of all other labor. And the only effect of this imposition which we have laid upon ourselves, is, instead of hastening the period of its profitable establishment, to postpone it to a still more distant period.

But, this is not all. We see that this is all done, and all this expenditure is increased, without any certain knowledge of the result. It cannot be certainly known when the period will arrive, at which the manufacture, in favor of which we have laid the discriminating duty may be profitably commenced, or whether, indeed, it can ever be commenced at all. If it can never be commenced, we have thus imposed a duty by which we are all made so much the poorer, without the prospect of any benefit. And if it may profitably be established at some future time, but we know not when that time will arrive, we are paying out our money at random; that is, we know not whether we shall gain or lose by the exchange. Supposing a benefit in fact to result, it is worth a given sum, and no more; but we have no means of knowing whether the sum which we pay, is only equal to the benefit, or whether it is ten times greater. Now, that it is very possible for a nation thus to pay for an advantage, supposing an advantage to be gained, vastly more than it is worth, is manifest.

To illustrate the amount which has been frequently expended to gain this supposed advantage, I subjoin the following instances from the Edinburgh Review, for October, 1829:

"The French duties on iron, from 1814 to 1822, have directed much capital to the iron trade. In 1818, 1,140,000 quintals of unwrought iron were produced, in France; in 1825, 1,976,000; in 1829, 2,269,000. Thus far, the system has succeeded.

On the contrary, as foreign iron is imported at a duty averaging twenty francs, the price of the whole 2,269,000, above what it could have been imported for, is 40,538,800 francs, the *direct cost* for protection. This is about £20 sterling a-piece to every person engaged in the iron trade. The effect of these measures is, to add fifty francs to the price of a plough, and to render cotton machinery one-third dearer than it would be, if imported. The price of charcoal has been doubled or trebled, and, from twenty-five to fifty per cent. has been added to the price of iron and wood. So great is the injury to other branches of production.

And yet, the iron trade is *depressed.* This is owing to the fact that too great a portion of capital has been directed to the iron trade; and also, to the increased price of charcoal. It must also necessarily follow, from what has been said above. This pressure which has been brought upon other branches of production must reduce the average ratio of profit; and to this average the iron trade must sink, as well as every thing else. Here there is an injury done to every other branch of business, and yet the iron business is not at the average rate of profit; that is, it it depressed. There is a great annual loss; but where do we see the prospect of a subsequent benefit.

The Sugar Trade. To encourage her colonies, France lays a duty of fifty francs per quintal, on all foreign sugars. This has increased the quantity made at home and at her islands. So far, it has succeeded; but,

2. The difference between the duty on foreign and the

duty on her own sugars, amounts to 32,945,000 francs. This is the bounty paid to the sugar growers of Martinique, and at home.

3. The quantity of sugar consumed is probably less, by one-third, than it would otherwise be. England, with half the number of inhabitants, consumes two and a half times as much sugar as France.

4. But it is said, that by this means, beet-root sugar will yet supply France at the ordinary price. It must, however, take twenty years, under the present system, in order to do this. The present protection costs £1,400,000 per annum. Suppose this to continue for twenty years, it will amount to £28,000,000 sterling, the interest of which, at five per cent., will buy, at two and a half pence per pound, 126,000,000 pounds of sugar per annum; or nearly the whole annual amount of sugar now consumed in France.

The Cotton Manufacture. By pushing forward those products, for which she has no capabilities, she has diminished those to which she is adapted. Countries which formerly bought of her, now that she refuses to receive their products, refuse to receive hers. Hence, the exports of wine, her natural product, have fallen off. Before the Revolution, her export of wine, averaged 100,000 tons per annum. Since 1820, it has varied from 39,000 to 63,000 tons. The result upon her silk trade has been the same. She has obliged other nations to raise silk for themselves."*

Such are some of the certain evils of such a system. These, surely, ought not to be voluntarily imposed upon

* I have marked the above passage as a quotation, although I have abridged the extract, without giving the exact words.

ourselves, without equal certainty of future benefit, and a benefit so much superior to that which we should otherwise have reaped, as to compensate us for all the evils and expenses which we impose upon ourselves. And if it do no more than this, we are the losers, by all the cost of the agency for doing that which would as well have been done without us. But, if the system itself do nothing towards hastening the time of profitable investment in manufactures, then it is an immediate and a very great and wide-spreading evil at present, and it tends to nothing but evil for the future.

For these reasons, I do not believe that the *direct* efforts of government are to be numbered among the means for encouraging the application of labor to capital. Their good effect, if it exist, must, therefore, be sought, not in their effect upon production, but upon something else.

But, it may be asked, can a government do nothing to promote the industry of a people, and to increase the amount of their production? I answer; they can do much.

1. They can enact wise, wholesome, and equitable laws, and thus protect the individual in the exercise of his right of person and property.

2. They can do much to accomplish the universal diffusion of the means of knowledge, by the promotion of education among all classes of people.

3. They can do much for the promotion and extension of science, by fostering seminaries of learning.

4. They can originate that knowledge, which must otherwise be obtained at great individual expense. As,

1. By experimental farms, of which the results should be accurately registered, and published to the whole community.

2. By experimental manufactures, which might show, from time to time, what branches of manufacture could profitably be introduced into a country, and how they might be most successfully conducted.

In this manner, much might be done, and at small expense. When these means have been tried, and have failed, it will be time enough to make other and more expensive experiments.

4. They can do much, by confining themselves to their own appropriate duties, and leaving every thing else alone. The interference of society with the concerns of the individual, even when arising from the most innocent motives, will always tend to crush the spirit of enterprise, and cripple the productive energies of a country. What shall we say, then, when the capital and the labor of a nation are made the sport of party politics; and when the power over them, which a government possesses, is abused, for the base purpose of ministering to schemes of political intrigue?

So far as I am able to discover, such are the most important conditions on which the productiveness of any society depend. They are briefly these: *Industry* and *Frugality*, *Virtue* and *Intelligence.* Possessed of these, no nation, with the ordinary blessing of God, can long be poor. Destitute of either of them, whatever be its natural advantages, no nation can ever long be rich. Patriotism, no less than religion, would, therefore, teach us to cultivate these habits in ourselves and in others; and he is the purest patriot, who cultivates them most assiduously.

BOOK SECOND.

BOOK SECOND.

EXCHANGE.

Exchange, is a transaction, in which two individuals mutually and voluntarily transfer to each other the right of property, to a given amount, either in capital or labor.

This transfer must be both mutual and voluntary by both parties, or else it is robbery by the one party. If property, without the right of possession, be given in exchange, it is fraud. If I give a horse in exchange, which does not belong to me, I confer no right of property; for I have none to confer; since the real owner may reclaim him, at any moment. The exchange may be either of capital by both parties, as if A and B exchange wheat for corn; or of capital for labor, as when A gives B a bushel of wheat for a day's labor; or of labor for labor, as when A agrees to work for B to-day, on condition that B shall work for him to-morrow. Exchange is of three kinds, viz.:

I. Barter in general or exchange in kind.

II. Exchange by means of a metallic currency.

III. Exchange by means of a paper currency.

CHAPTER FIRST.

OF BARTER OR EXCHANGE IN KIND.

SECTION I.

OF THE PRINCIPLES IN THE PRESENT CONSTITUTION, WHICH GIVE RISE TO EXCHANGE.

1. It has been already shown, that human labor, of some kind, is necessary to production; that is, to the creation of whatever has the power of gratifying human desire. Hence, without labor, no desire would be gratified; that is, the race would speedily perish. As we have said before, the law of our being, imposed upon every individual, enacts that, by the sweat of our face we shall eat our bread.

2. But we are taught, by Moral Philosophy, that by labor exerted upon any substance, in such manner as to give it value, we establish over that value, either in whole or in part, the right of property. If the original capital were our own, we possess that original capital, together with all the additional value, which the change that we have effected has created. If, by labor upon the capital of another, we have raised its value, we establish a right to a portion of it, to be estimated by the respective values of the labor and capital employed. Nay, this capital is

nothing but the result of pre-exerted labor. So that the capitalist contributes his *past*, and the laborer his *present* labor, and they share the product between them.

3. Hence we see, from the very conditions of our being, that the very act of creating a value appropriates it to a possessor. This holds true of every thing not the spontaneous gift of God. Hence, every thing created by man, belongs to some man; that is, he possesses over it the right of property. And this right of property is *exclusive;* that is, he has the right to use it as he will, to the exclusion of every man and of all men. And, provided he do not interfere with the rights of others, no man can interfere with his use of whatever product he has created, without a violation of moral law.

4. Different men are constituted by the Creator with different aptitudes for different pursuits, and with different dispositions towards those pursuits. One man is adapted to investigate, and another to apply to practice, the laws of nature, and another to perform the operation by which those laws are made to create value. And these aptitudes are still further subdivided. One man is better adapted to investigate physical, another intellectual, and another moral laws. Thus, also, in the various pursuits of operative industry, one man prefers agriculture, another manufactures, and another navigation. And it is found, as might be expected, that the *disposition* towards a particular operation, severally corresponds with a man's *aptitude* for it; that is, that, in general, a man is most strongly disposed to devote himself to that particular occupation, for which God has given him the greatest aptitude. Indeed, the disposition, in most cases, will do very much to create the aptitude. A man always labors more successfully in an occupation which he likes, than in one which he dislikes.

5. Hence, a great public, as well as private advantage, arises from every one's devoting himself to that occupation which he prefers, and for which he is specially fitted. Inasmuch as he *likes it best*, he is thus happier than he would be in the pursuit of any other. Every one thus being able to do that which he likes best, every one will derive from this source, all the happiness which it is able to confer. And, inasmuch as he is *better fitted for it*, he will, with the same labor, create a greater amount of value than he will by labor in any other employment. He will also create the value much more perfectly. The annual amount of value created in a community, will thus be greatly increased, with the same amount of labor, and, with a much greater amount of happiness. If every man labored at that employment in which he could create an amount of value equal to *twenty*, there would be, by the whole society, just twice as much created, as if, by changing occupations, each one labored at that for which he could create a value equal only to *ten*. If all the different classes of laborers were, for a year, to be obliged to exchange work with each other, every one can perceive that, for that year, production would almost absolutely cease.

Were this all, though every man created his own particular value with the greatest possible success, yet each man would, manifestly, possess but *one* value. The wheat grower would have nothing but granaries full of *wheat*; the carpenter, nothing but ranges of houses; the stonecutter, nothing but piles of stone; and the shoemaker, nothing but thousands of shoes. But while there exists in every man, both the *aptitude* and the disposition for the creation of a *particular* value, there exists equally in every man, a *desire* to enjoy *every* value that can be created. A man may like to create a value of which he desires to use but very little himself; nay, for which, in itself, he perhaps has even less desire than most other men. The man who is the fondest of fishing, may be, by no means, a great lover of fish. He who is the fondest of hunting, may be, by no means, the fondest of game. No man supposes, because a man is fond of fox-hunting, that he is fond of fox-eating. Thus, we see, that the desire for the creation of value, is *one thing*, and the desire for using the value created, *is another*. The one is limited to a single object, and the other is as widely extended as the objects to which it can be directed. And it is evident, that the one form of desire is as much intended to be gratified as the other. He who created the desire, and also created the object which would gratify it, intended the one for the other, restricting man only to the modes and degree of gratification which He has appointed. Civilization and social happiness advance, just in proportion as the greatest number of the desires of man are gratified, in conformity with the laws of the Creator.

7. We see, then, that man is created with the aptitude and the desire for the *creation* of *one* product, but with the *desire for the enjoyment* of a *thousand* products, and, that the gratification of one of these forms of desire is as much the intention of his Creator, as the gratification of the other. He is intended to produce *one* thing, and to hold this thing produced by the right of property, while at the same time, every man is intended to require, for the gratification of his desires, a thousand things. Now, it is the existence of these contrary indications in his nature, that creates the necessity for exchange. The right to use his product as he pleases, is also the right to transfer it to whomsoever, that is, to exchange it with whomsoever, he pleases, and for whatever he pleases. By doing this, all the indications of his nature are fulfilled. The right of property is preserved inviolate. Every one may employ his own capital and industry as

he pleases, that is, as will best promote his own happiness, and also as will add the most abundantly to the wealth of the whole community; and, at the same time, by means of the products of his single branch of industry, he may procure every object of desire that every other man has created. And, inasmuch, as by division of labor, on the principle of which we have spoken, a larger amount will be created, and in greater perfection, he will procure every object at less labor, and in more perfect condition, than would be possible in any other manner.

We see, therefore, that the necessity of exchange, as truly enters into the conditions of our being, as that of production. Without exchange, there could be no division of labor, and, of course, only the smallest possible amount of production. Without exchange, there would rarely be any stimulus to labor; for labor could add but little to our means of gratification, beyond the most absolute necessaries of life. There would be no stimulus to form societies, since, as man depended solely upon himself, he might as well be solitary as social. Hence, all progress in civilization would be hopeless, and each generation would tread in the footsteps of that which had preceded it.

8. I have, thus far, spoken merely of exchange between the individuals of the same society. I think it evident, however, that the same principles apply with equal force to the exchanges between different societies.

The aptitudes of different nations for the creating of different products, has, in many cases, been fixed by unchangeable, geographical, and physiological law. Cotton, coffee, spices, dye-stuffs, sugar, rice, and many of the most valuable fruits and medicines, can be cultivated only in southern latitudes. Wool, wheat, and bread stuffs generally, flax, and the most valuable animals, are found only in temperate climates. Iron is found in northern latitudes; and furs, hemp, and feathers are brought from climates still further north. Besides, one country is better adapted to commerce, another to agriculture, and another to manufactures.

Besides, as we have already shown, a society, at one period of its history, is better adapted to one sort of production than to another. When capital is scarce, and land is cheap and fertile, a nation is better adapted to agriculture; when capital becomes abundant and land dear, it becomes gradually better adapted to manufactures: that is to say, nations, as well as individuals, both by original endowment and accidental circumstances, have their special adaptations to the creation of particular products. I suppose it unnecessary to state, that nations, that is, people, if left to themselves, are, like individuals, disposed to avail themselves of the peculiar advantages bestowed upon them by their Creator. Self-interest teaches them this lesson with sufficient clearness, and they willingly practice it, if left to their own natural instincts.

It is also evident that, by each nation's devoting itself to that branch of production for which it has the greatest facilities, either original or acquired, its own happiness will be better promoted, and a greater amount of production created, than in any other manner. And while all nations thus appropriate their industry, a much greater amount of annual value will be created for the whole human race, than by any change that could possibly be made. If Cuba should relinquish the raising of coffee and sugar, and devote herself to the raising of wheat; and New York, relinquishing the culture of wheat, should betake herself to the raising of coffee and sugar, would not both communities be poorer, and would not the price of coffee, sugar and wheat be increased over the whole world; that is, would not all the world, and these countries especially, be poorer than they are now?

But, whilst it is thus evident that every nation is intended by the Creator to improve its own advantages, that is, to create that product for the creation of which it has the greatest facilities; it is also the fact, that every nation, and every individual of that nation, desires the productions of every other nation; and is happy in proportion as it enjoys them. What nation could be happy without the cotton of the South, the hemp and iron of the North, or the wool, wheat, and manufactures of temperate climates? Nay, let any individual look at the clothes which he wears, the furniture of his room, or the food and utensils of his table, and he will be immediately convinced, that every latitude of both hemispheres, and almost every country on the globe, are tributary to his happiness. His own country has peculiar adaptations, but they are adaptations for but few products, while every citizen of that country requires for his convenience, nay, almost for his existence, the productions of every other country. These desires can be gratified only by national exchanges. Hence we see, that *national* exchanges enter as much into the constitution of things under which we are created, as *individual* exchanges.

And the final cause of this constitution is, in both cases, equally evident.

Individuals are made thus dependent upon each other, in order to render harmony, peace, and mutual assistance, their interest, as well as their duty. Where men are mutually dependent upon each other, the prosperity of one, is the prosperity of all; and the adversity of one, is the adversity of all. No one can enjoy many of the blessings which God has intended for him, only in so far as others enjoy them also; and no one can be deprived of them, unless others are deprived of them to a considerable degree also. Thus, we see that the individual progress of man, is, by the constitution of things, indissolubly connected with, if not absolutely dependent on, his social progress.

And, for the same reason, nations are dependent upon each other. From this universal dependence, we learn that God intends nations, as well as individuals, to live in peace, and to conduct themselves towards each other upon the principles of benevolence. Where all are mutually dependent, as in the former case, no one can prosper without increasing the prosperity of all, nor suffer without bringing suffering upon all. Hence, it is as truly our interest to seek the happiness, peace and prosperity of other nations, as it is to seek the happiness, peace and prosperity of our own nation.

9. From the above constitution it is evident, that universal exchange is as necessary to the welfare, and even to the existence of the human race, as universal production. We have already seen, that in all the departments of human industry, a great saving, both of time and expense, is effected by *division of labor.* This is as true of labor in exchange, as in any other case. Since, then, exchanges must be made, it will be better for *the whole,* if a *part* of a society devote themselves exclusively to the business of making them.

Thus; suppose that, in a given society, the labor is divided, so that each individual devotes himself to the creation of a given product. One man raises wheat, another rye, another wool; one labors upon iron, another upon wood, another upon leather, &c. Now, these persons can procure the productions of each other, only by exchange. But if every one, every time he needs any thing, is obliged to leave his labor to find a purchaser for his product, he will lose much time himself, and will consume a large portion of the time of all his neighbors. It would frequently take as much time to exchange a pair of shoes, as it would take to make them. This additional *time* must enter into the *price* of the shoes; and hence, these, and every other article of consumption, would rise in price accordingly.

In such a case as this, it would clearly be a great benefit to the whole society, if some one should devote himself exclusively to the business of making exchanges. Every producer might then deposit with him, whatever he had to exchange, instead of going in search of a purchaser. When this was done, every one, by going to him, might ascertain immediately, what was to be exchanged, throughout the whole community, and at what price; and also, what was required in exchange. He would thus be able, at once, to procure, by his own product, whatever was procurable for it; and to know what he must produce, in order that he may procure what he may need. Thus, the labor of a whole day, or of several days, might be accomplished in a few minutes, in a much more perfect manner, than by any other method. Hence, as all the time unnecessarily consumed in the other method would be saved, there would be much more time to be appropriated to production. As, in a given time, and with given labor, there would be greater production, every thing would be cheaper, that is, every one would be richer; and, at the same time, a reasonable profit would remain for him who devoted his time to the labor of exchange.

Hence, we see that *exchangers* are as necessary to the *cheapness* of production, as producers themselves. Hence we also see, how absurd is the outcry sometimes raised against them, because it is said they *produce nothing*. Did not a large class of the community devote themselves to this employment, it is impossible to conceive what would be the price of the most common and necessary utensil. Were the farmer obliged to carry his wheat or his cattle to Sheffield, to exchange for needles for his wife, or for a sickle for himself, who could estimate what these utensils would cost? If the laborer were obliged to go to Birmingham for a spade, which he must use in New-York, what would be the price of a spade, and how would he ever be able to gain a subsistence? The laborer may sometimes complain that the merchant is rich, and that he is poor; that the merchant stands at his desk, while he labors in the street; that the merchant rides in his carriage, while he travels on foot. But it may be to him some consolation to remember, that were not the merchant rich, the laborer would be still poorer, for every article would be dearer, and besides, there would be no one to pay for the labor with which alone he is able to purchase it. Were not the merchant to be at his desk, the poor man would have no labor to do in the street; and were not the merchant able to ride in his carriage, the laborer would be obliged to go barefoot. And accordingly, we see that whenever mercantile business, that is, the business of exchanges, is the most successful, then are the means of living cheaper in proportion; and then are the operative classes richer; and the avenues to riches are the most widely open to all.

The persons who conduct the exchanges of a community are called *merchants*. They are of two classes, viz.: *Retail Merchants*, and *Wholesale Merchants*.

The *retail merchant* carries on exchanges, between the inhabitants of the same country. He purchases of the manufacturer or the importer, in quantities too large for the means of the individual consumer, and sells again, in any quantities that the consumer may desire. This produces a great saving of time, and, of course, of expense, to the whole community. Were the manufacturer obliged to leave his labor, to sell a yard of calico, the price of calico would be trebled. Were the importer obliged to open his hogsheads, to sell a pound of sugar, he must charge accordingly. And besides, as each importer and manufacturer is supposed to confine himself to one particular product, the purchaser would be obliged, frequently, to go great distances, and transact, with a great number of persons, business, which he may now be able to accomplish with a single individual. Every one must thus perceive, that a consumer saves much time by purchasing his sugar, tea, coffee, pepper, salt, &c., at one shop, instead of going to the wholesale importers of these articles individually; specially, if, as is frequently the case, they lived some hundreds of miles asunder. So, therefore, it is much more economical to buy needles, tape, cotton, calico and silk, at one shop, than to go to the several individuals, in different places, who have imported or made these articles in large quantities. In consequence of this advantage to the community, the retail dealer is able to charge a profit on all the articles which he sells, and at the same time, to furnish them at a much lower price than that at which the purchaser could procure them, in any other manner. The purchaser not only procures them cheaper, but he procures them of a better quality. It is the business of the retail dealer to understand the quality of every article in which he traffics, and it is for his interest to purchase it as cheaply, and of as good quality, as it can be purchased in the market; since it is on the goodness and cheapness of his articles, that his custom depends. Hence, the consumer is thus enabled to employ for his benefit, a skill vastly greater than his own; and at a much less cost, than that, at which he could accomplish the business himself. Hence we see, that retail dealers are as necessary to the prosperity of a country, and to the cheapness of productions, as any other class of persons. And it will be found very universally, that it is much more economical to employ their services, than for a man to undertake to do their business for himself.

The *wholesale merchant*, conducts the exchanges between the individuals of different nations. He exports, in bulk, the commodities of his own country, and imports, in return, the commodities of another country. His own interest induces him to export whatever is at the lowest price in his own country; that is, of what may be there in the greatest abundance; and bring back in return, whatever will command the highest price at home; that is, of which there is the greatest need. And his own interest will, of course, teach him to procure what he brings home, at the place where it can be had at the cheapest rate; so that he may be able to furnish it at the highest profit to himself, and at the lowest price to others. Hence his interest, and that of the community, are the same. It is for the interest of the community that those commodities of which we have a superfluity, should be exported; and the fact of this superfluity is known by the reduction of their price, in comparison with the price of other commodities at home, or of the same commodity in other countries. It is for the interest of the merchant to export the same commodity, because, the lower the price at which he purchases it at home, on the better terms he can exchange it abroad. It is for the interest of the community, that those objects of desire which are most wanted should be brought back in return; and the rise in their exchangeable value is the proof that they are so wanted. It is for the merchant's interest, also, to bring back these very commodities; for, from these alone, can he expect gain, and that gain will be the greater, in proportion as he procures them on the most favorable terms; that is, as he procures them where they are the cheapest and most abundant. Hence, his gain will be in proportion as he can transfer the productions of the earth from those regions where they are least wanted, to those regions where they are most wanted. And this is precisely what the interests of society require should be done.

To the merchant, it is, of course, a matter of no consequence, what he exports and what he imports. Unless a commodity were more wanted at home than that for which he would exchange it, he could have no motive to make the transfer. And that it is so wanted, is evident from the fact, that the community is willing to give a higher price for it than for that which is exported. If he desired it, he could not make any profit, except by consulting the wants of the community; and that profit will be the greater, in proportion as he is able to consult those wants with the greatest possible nicety. His gains are the gains of the community, and his losses are the losses of the community. Hence, there is no reason why he should, in any manner, be restricted in the nature or the quantity of the articles which he exports or imports. The constitution of things, and his own self-interest, provide all the regulating forces which the nature of the case requires.

SECTION II.

THE GENERAL DOCTRINES OF EXCHANGE.

I. *Of the rate of Exchange, or the exchangeable value of Products.*

If two men have created their respective products, and are prepared to exchange them, it is manifest that they will not commonly exchange them, quantity for quantity; because, a given amount of labor will procure a much larger amount of some products than of others. The same labor which will procure an ounce of gold, will procure a hundred pounds of iron. Hence, the gold miner will offer to exchange labor for labor; that is, an ounce of gold for a hundred weight of iron. And if the miner of iron will not exchange on these terms, the miner of gold will procure his iron for himself. Since, if he can thus procure it for himself, by a less amount of labor, than by exchange, he will do so. Hence it is, that the general rate at which every thing is exchanged, is, the amount of labor which it costs to produce it.

But we have previously seen, that labor appears in two forms, that of annual capital, and of fixed capital. Both of these enter into consideration, when we speak of labor as determining the exchangeable value of products.

For instance: Suppose I purchase wheat, and grind it by hand; I sell it again, at an additional price, proportioned to the labor which I have bestowed upon it. Suppose I thus earn money enough to erect a wind-mill; I shall then be entitled to the same amount of wages per day for my labor, and also to an additional sum sufficient to pay the interest of what was expended in my wind-mill, and also to pay for its wear and tear, in performing the operation. The price of grinding was, at first, only that of immediate labor; it is now the price of immediate labor, together with interest on the amount of pre-exerted labor. It is, however, to be observed, that notwithstanding I am receiving emolument from two sources, and am growing rich faster than before, it is on terms vastly more favorable to the community, inasmuch as I can, for the same remuneration, give ten times as much in return as I could before.

The case is the same, if two separate individuals are employed in the operation, the one owning the capital or stock, and the other performing the labor. In this case, the cost consists of the wages of labor and the interest on, and the wear and tear of the capital. Here, however, as before, the community is the gainer; because, for the wages of labor and interest of capital, it receives a much larger product than it received before, for the wages of labor alone. Thus, if a machine cost one thousand dollars, and there were paid for the use of it, one hundred dollars a year, this, added to the wages of labor, at a dollar a day, would be four hundred dollars, allowing three hundred working days a year. This would be but one hundred dollars more than would be paid for the labor of the man alone. But a man, with such an instrument, would, probably, in a year, accomplish ten times as much work as he could accomplish without it. All the gain of the change is, therefore, for the benefit of the public. We see, therefore, that labor and the interest of capital, must, necessarily and justly, enter into the price of every product which is offered in exchange. The producer can never, for a long period, charge more than a fair remuneration for his labor and capital; because, then, it would be cheaper for the other party to produce it for himself. He cannot, for *a long period*, charge less; because, in this case, he will be ruined, and must leave the employment; and thus the number of producers will be diminished, and the value of the product will rise to the average rate of profit.

Nevertheless, *for short periods*, the exchangeable value of any product may be raised above the reasonable rate of profit. If the demand exceed the supply, there will be a competition among the buyers; the more wealthy will overbid the less wealthy, and the price will rise. This rise of price will induce others to devote themselves to supplying the demand, and thus the price will fall. If the supply be greater than the demand, there will arise a competition among the sellers, and the price will fall, and will remain depressed, until either the demand increase, or else until so many leave the employment, as shall reduce the supply to the average demand.

It is evident that it makes no difference, as to the result, whether the ratio between supply and demand be disturbed by a change in supply or in demand. If the demand continue the same, a diminished supply produces the same effect as would be produced by an increased demand, while the supply remained the same. And, on the other hand, demand being the same, an increased supply produces the same result as, when, supply being the same, the demand is decreased; that is, in the one case, the exchangeable value of the product will rise; in the other case, it will fall.

It deserves, however, to be remarked, that this effect produced by the disturbance of the ratio between supply and demand will be greater or less, according to several circumstances. These are:

1. The durability of the commodity. If it be one which, unless it be consumed immediately, will become worthless, the fall of price, from increased supply, is great. Such is the case with oranges, lemons, figs, fresh fish, &c. If, on the contrary, it be a commodity which will endure for years, without loss of intrinsic value, the effect will be less. Thus, an increased supply of iron, produces in the market a comparatively small variation in the price.

2. Variation of price, from this cause, depends, also, upon the ease or difficulty with which the supply may be increased. Thus, manufactured articles can *generally* be produced in a short time, and, if necessary, in a much more than usual quantity. Agricultural products, on the contrary, require a year, in order to be brought to perfection. Hence, if a crop fail this year, we know that there must be a diminished supply in the whole country, for the remainder of the year; and hence, as there must be a scarcity, every one is prepared to give as much as he is able. But, if cotton cloth be high, unless the rise of price be owing to a diminished production of the material, this high price will cause more cloth to be made, and hence, before long, the price will fall. We therefore purchase only what we absolutely need, and wait for the favorable change.

3. It will be affected by the nature of the demand for the article. If it be an article of universal necessity, it will rise more rapidly by scarcity, and sink less rapidly by increased supply; while, if it be an article of mere luxury, it will rise less rapidly by scarcity, and sink more rapidly by increased supply. When every one must have a commodity, the demand is constant, and every one is alarmed at the prospect of suffering; hence, he purchases it at any price. And, on the other hand, if the supply be abundant, the holder knows that the ordinary con-

sumption will soon reduce the quantity in market, and rather than sell at a reduced profit, he will wait for the change of price. On the contrary, if an article of luxury be scarce, men begin to abandon it, and thus the demand is quickly reduced. If it be abundant, the number of purchasers does not increase with the supply, because men have not yet learned to use it; hence, its fall in price is rapid, being not sustained by a correspondent increase of demand.

These, I think, are the principal circumstances which enter into the exchangeable value of products. They are variously combined and modified, so that they may sometimes counteract, and sometimes exaggerate each other. But, I think, that, by applying them to the actual occurrences of life, we may generally be able to explain the fluctuations of price, which are daily taking place in the market.

II. *When an article of produce is offered for exchange, the producer has conferred upon it his last value, and it is now ready for the consumer.*

By the consumer, here, I do not mean him only who gratifies his desire by the ultimate destruction of the product, but also him who receives it for the purpose of giving to it some other modification. The exchanger confers upon it no new value. It is the same when it passes out of his hands to the consumer, as when it came into his hands from the producer: that is, in general, exchange confers no value at all upon products; since they receive no modification by passing from the hands of one person to those of another.

1. Hence it will be seen, that the more rapidly exchanges are made, the better. The more rapidly they

are made, the less is the loss of interest, and the smaller the advance which the exchanger must charge for his labor. If a merchant purchase to-day a thousand dollars' worth of iron, which he sells to-morrow, he charges for his labor and skill, and adds only the interest of one day upon his capital. If he must keep the iron a whole year before he sell it, he must also charge the interest of a whole year, or else he will be the loser by his operation.

Nor is this all. If he sell his iron to-morrow, he may invest the same sum in iron, and sell it again fifty times in the course of the year; and thus receive a profit fifty times a year upon the use of his skill and labor, while, in the other case, he receives this profit but once. Hence, when exchanges are rapid, he can afford to exchange at a less rate for his labor and skill, than when they are slow. And hence, brisk exchanges are for the benefit of both buyer and seller; and a benefit to the one, is a benefit to all. It is for this reason, among others, that we can frequently purchase at a cheaper rate in a large city, than in a country town.

2. And hence we see a reason, why the profit upon one operation in some kinds of exchange, is greater than that in others. The profits of the wholesale merchant are, for instance, greater than those of the retail merchant. He who sends his capital to the East Indies, and receives in return, a load of teas, must charge interest and risk, for the whole time consumed, from the day that he parts with his property, until the day that he receives it again. This may be nearly two years. The retail merchant, who purchases one of those chests of tea, may sell it all in a week, and thus invest it fifty times in the course of a year. Now, if the profit on exchange, were as great in the one case as in the other, the gains of the retail merchant would be exorbitant. These are reduced, by competition, to the

average level; and hence, his gains on any single operation are much less than those of the wholesale merchant. The same principle applies to production. The greater the time consumed in an operation, the larger the profit on each article which justly belongs to the producer.

But, though the act of exchange add nothing, either to the intrinsic or the exchangeable value of the commodity, it adds greatly to the convenience both of the buyer and the seller; inasmuch as it enables both to gratify a desire, which, otherwise, would have been unsatisfied. If I want a pen-knife more than I want a dollar, and a hardware merchant wants a dollar more than he wants a pen-knife, we make the exchange with each other. The dollar is the same as before; it will buy no more in his hands, than it will in mine. The pen-knife is the same as before; it has neither gained nor lost; and I might, if I chose, exchange it with the next man I met, for a dollar. But, both the merchant and myself are benefitted by the exchange. I can use the knife for purposes for which I could not use the dollar; and thus render my labor per day much more valuable. The merchant has received a full remuneration for his labor, capital and skill, and is, by so much, richer than he was before. That both of us have been benefitted by the exchange, is evident from the fact, that neither of us would make the exchange back again. If a hungry man have a piece of silver, and a baker have a loaf of bread, they will readily exchange with each other. The silver is the same, and the loaf is the same, as before; but still, both parties are richer and happier; and neither would the hungry man take back the same piece of silver for his loaf; nor would the baker take back the loaf for the silver.

The case is the same with nations. If a nation exchange iron, of which it has more than it can consume, for wheat, of which it does not raise enough for consumption, with a nation which has more wheat than it can consume, but produces no iron; the wheat and the iron are the same as before; but each nation is richer and happier; each has one more desire gratified than before, and is able, the next year, to increase more largely its stock of production. That both are happier than before, is evident; because neither would reverse the exchange, if it were in its power. And thus, in general, whenever two nations mutually wish to exchange their productions with each other, and are mutually gratified when the exchange is made, it is evident that both are made happier, and that the exchange has been advantageous to both parties.

Hence we see, how fallacious is the notion formerly entertained, that, by exchange, only one party is benefitted; and consequently, that what one party gains, the other party loses. Were this the case, no country could grow rich by exchange, unless by impoverishing every other country; and the gain of one nation, would be nothing else than a transfer of the wealth of other countries to itself. On the contrary, precisely the reverse is the case. The most favorable commerce to any one country, is that, by which the riches of both countries are the most rapidly increased. A merchant, whose gains were all derived from the impoverishment of his customers, would very soon have none but paupers for neighbors. A nation, whose traffic caused the impoverishment of another nation, would very soon be obliged to discontinue commerce. The only traffic of this sort, is the African slave trade, and the result has been the almost entire depopulation of the slave coast. And thus, we see, in political economy, as in morals, every benefit is mutual; and we cannot, in the one case, any more than in the other, really do good to ourselves, without doing good others; nor do good to others, without also doing good to ourselves.

In what I have said of exchange, it is to be observed that I have spoken of exchange simply, and not as combined with the labor of transportation. The labor of transportation gives an additional value to an article; that is, it confers upon it change of place. This has been already spoken of. It is true, a merchant frequently performs this labor, or causes it to be performed. In this case, he is entitled to a double profit; first, for the labor of transportation, and secondly, for the labor and skill of exchange. He who labors in either of these employments, is entitled to the profit of that in which he labors; and, he who labors in both, is entitled to the profit of both. In speaking of the profit of *exchange*, it is always to be observed, that the profit of the merchant is derived *partly* from his labor and skill, and partly from his *capital*. He who exports to France one hundred thousand dollars' worth of cotton, must first buy the cotton; that is, he must have one hundred thousand dollars to invest in this exchange. He exchanges the cotton for silks or for calicoes, and replaces his first investment. He is entitled to interest and risk on that capital, for all the time that it is out of his hands, besides the remuneration for his labor and skill.

III. *Of the conditions on which the frequency or infrequency of exchanges depends.*

It is manifest that the more numerous are the exchanges, the better must it be for a community. As no one exchanges, except to gratify his desires, and to improve his condition, the more numerous the exchanges, the more desires will be gratified, and the more universally will the condition of a people be improved. It is also evident, that facility of exchange is one of the greatest stimulants to production. If a man cannot transform his products into what he desires, he will labor for nothing but the mere necessaries of life. But in just so far as he is able, by exchanging the products of his labor, to procure objects of desire, his motives to industry will be quickened. And the same is true of nations. Every one, whether poet, or philosopher, or traveller, in setting forth the prosperity of a country, has described its harbors thronged with ships, its roads covered with merchandise, and its sails whitening every ocean. But all these are only so many forms of expressing the general fact, that a nation's exchanges, both internal and external, are abundant and prosperous; that is, that its producers are able, by their own labor, easily to avail themselves of every other production which they may desire.

We have said that exchange is a voluntary and mutual transfer of the right of property.

If this be the case, there must exist, in each party,

1. A mutual desire for the property of the other, greater than the desire for his own.

2. Mutual ability; that is, each party must be able to offer to the other, such a consideration as will induce him to make the exchange.

Where both of these exist, exchanges will, of course, take place. If A have a dollar which he wishes to part with for B's knife, and B has a knife which he wishes to part with for A's dollar; as soon as each knows the wish of the other, they will mutually gratify each other, and the exchange will take place.

3. As, however, the right of property alone is frequently transferred, while the property itself is not delivered at the time of the exchange, there is always, in every such act of exchange, a liability to fraud. Besides, a commodity may not prove to be as good as it was represented, or the owner's title may not be satisfactory. In all such cases, there is an opportunity for the practice of dishonesty; and the risk of suffering from such dishonesty, would, of course, diminish the frequency of exchanges. Hence, frequency of exchanges will depend upon security of the right of property, and the existence of the means for enforcing that right.

If we now reflect upon these facts, I think we must perceive, that the *desires* of a people for exchange, will depend, principally, upon their *intelligence.* Their *ability* will depend upon the *productiveness* of their *labor and capital;* and the *security of property* will depend upon their *individual and social morality.* That is, exchanges will be frequent, in proportion to the *intelligence*, *wealth*, and *moral character* of a people.

1. Exchanges will be frequent or unfrequent, in proportion to the *intelligence or ignorance* of a people. It is only by the diffusion of knowledge that men ascertain how their desires may be gratified. It is by knowledge that the desires of man are brought into relation with the objects intended by his Creator for their gratification. Every one knows how the dormant desire for exchange is awakened in the bosom of a child, the moment he enters a toy shop. I suppose that strangers rarely pass through the streets of a large city, without being strongly, if not successfully, tempted to lighten their pockets, before the termination of their journey. Every reader knows, how strongly his desire for books is enkindled, by passing a few minutes in a book store. And thus we see, how

instantaneously a desire for exchange arises in the breasts of savages, as soon as they are brought into contact with civilized man. A multitude of objects for the gratification of desire, of which they were before ignorant, is set before them; and they are frequently stimulated to exchange, to their own disadvantage. The early voyagers give us striking illustrations of this fact. They represent themselves as overwhelmed with these rude people offering every thing which they supposed their visiters would desire, for nails, beads, pieces of looking-glass, iron hoops, and almost every thing on which they could lay their hands.

When, however, I speak of intellectual cultivation in this connection, it is to be understood that I by no means refer exclusively to the knowledge and mental discipline which is acquired by the reading of books. Books, though essential to the intellectual progress of a country, are only one means of introducing and circulating knowledge. Knowledge is gained by observation, and by conversation; and it is, if I may say so, absorbed from the intellectual atmosphere which we breathe; it is derived from the general spirit of the community in which we live. Thus, a man rarely goes from home into another country, or into another section of the same country, without obtaining a knowledge of various conveniences of which he was before ignorant. Familiar intercourse between men of different pursuits, conduces to the same result. Newspapers, filled with advertisements, circulated over every district of a country, have, in this respect, a powerful effect. All these causes combine to show every individual what he can produce which other men want, and how he may, by exchange, procure from them what he wants himself.

We see all this illustrated, in every district separated

by nature from the surrounding country, as a valley inclosed by mountains difficult of access, or an island which has but rare communication with the main land. The progress of such a population in the arts, and in possessing themselves of the conveniences of life, is always much less rapid than than that of their more highly favored neighbors. They know but little of what is going on around them, and their desires are but feebly stimulated to improve their condition. The state of such a population is always suddenly and rapidly improved, by any means of easy communication with their neighbors. They are stimulated at once to develope their own resources, and thus to share in the benefits enjoyed by those around them. Thus the Pastor Oberlin, a truly great and good man, when he wished to improve the condition of the Ban de la Roche, commenced by inducing his people to repair their roads. Hence we see, how important, in this respect, to a nation, are all means of internal communication, and the facilities for the universal circulation of the commonest forms of knowledge.

2. Exchanges will be numerous, in proportion to the *productiveness* of a country.

We have already seen, that simple desire, in both parties, is not sufficient to effect exchanges. Each party must both possess, and be willing to part with, so large a portion of the product desired by the other party, that the other is willing to make the desired exchange. Every man desires a horse and carriage, and every man who either raises horses or manufactures carriages, is willing to part with them for an equivalent. But until every man have something to offer for a horse and carriage, which will be sufficient to induce the other parties to make the exchange, every one cannot be so accommodated. If A have wheat which he is willing to exchange for rye, but if B either have no rye which he is able to offer in exchange, or have it not in sufficient quantity to remunerate the labor of A, no exchange can take place. But if both have been prospered, and each have enough of his own product for his own use, and is also able to offer, on fair terms, a portion in exchange, they may then exchange with advantage, and, of course, they will do so.

Or, again: If A and B have only so much surplus product as will enable them to make this one exchange with each other, much as they may desire the product of C and D, these last desires must be ungratified; since no further exchange can take place. Or, on the contrary, if A and B have abundance, but C and D have been unfortunate, and have nothing which they can part with, the same result will take place. But let A, B, C and D be all blessed with abundance, and all have surplus products which they are willing to exchange with each other, and in such proportions as will reward each other's industry; and they will all exchange accordingly. And hence we see, that exchanges must always be most numerous, in the most prosperous condition of a country; or, as every one knows, mercantile business is most prosperous, that is, exchanges are most abundant, when manufacturing, agricultural, and all other kinds of industry are most productive.

And we see, moreover, that this principle is of universal application. A good harvest in one country, is a benefit to every other country; because the favored country desires a larger amount of the productions of her neighbors, and has a larger fund wherewith to pay for them. Hence, the exchanges between such a country and every other country, are increased. On the contrary, a famine, or a war, or any other calamity happening to one country, is a calamity to every other country, because the unfortunate country wants less of the productions of its neighbors; since it has less wherewith to pay for them. Its exchanges, therefore, are of necessity diminished. Hence, that merchant is short-sighted, as well as morally thoughtless, who expects to grow rich by short crops, civil dissensions, calamity, or war, in the country with which he traffics. A wiser and farther-sighted reflection, would teach him that it is very difficult to grow rich by trading with beggars, and that the benefit of one is always the benefit of all. To illustrate all this by a single case, let us ask what would be the amount of exchanges effected by the inhabitants of Great Britain, France, and the United States, either among themselves or with each other, if the productiveness of these several countries, were no greater than it was in the time of Julius Cæsar.

3. Exchanges will be numerous in proportion to the *moral character* of a people.

1. Individual morality is highly favorable to exchange, inasmuch as it lessens the liability to fraud, and, of course, the risk to which exchanges are exposed. No one will, if he can avoid it, trade with a knave. In proportion to the prevalence of knavery, will be the disinclination to exchange.

2. On the general moral character of a people depend the equity of their laws, and, of course, the full enjoyment of the right of property. As has before been remarked, exchanges are not always completed at the instant. One party frequently parts with his property to-day, on condition of receiving the property of his neighbor a month hence. Here is a liability to fraud. Unless the one party have, by means of just and equitable law, the power of enforcing contracts, exchanges will be greatly restricted.

3. On the morality and intelligence of a people, will greatly depend the freedom of its civil constitution; that is, the accuracy with which it limits the power of the society, that is, of the government, over the person and property of the individual. When these are improperly understood, or insufficiently guarded, the property of the citizen is liable to suffer from the avarice or oppression of rulers. To this evil, property, undergoing exchange, is specially liable. Exchange exposes to the view of the public, the possessions of the parties, and, of course, enables a tyrant to seize upon them with the greater certainty. For this reason, exchanges are frequently, under bad governments, made in secret; and, for this reason, under such a government, they are always as few as possible, and at great expense to the consumer.

Hence we see, in general, that the frequency of exchanges will be in proportion to the wealth, and to the intellectual and moral character of a people. And since, as the progress of a nation, in these respects, will promote her mercantile prosperity, we may easily see what will depress it. The frequency of exchanges will diminish, as a nation decreases in intelligence and virtue. Of the truth of this remark, all history is filled with illustrations. After what has already been said, it will not be necessary to enlarge upon this topic. These effects, moreover, are principally to be observed, by comparing the condition of a country at long periods; and tracing the effects of measures and events in those directions which are not always obvious to every observer.

While, however, the government and laws of a country remain the same, there frequently occurs a temporary diminution of exchanges, which is denominated *a stagnation* of business. This deserves to be noticed. As the business of a merchant is to execute exchanges; that is, to perform the labor of exchanging, for those who wish to exchange their products, a stagnation of mercantile business must occur, when there is less of this operation to be performed; that is, he is ready to perform the exchange, but a less number of persons desire it to be performed.

The reason why the merchant feels this more seriously than any other man, is obvious. All his capital is invested in this kind of operation. He buys of one party, that is, invests his capital in one kind of product, and sells to another, that is, receives his product in exchange, and he supports himself by the profit of these two operations. The moment exchanges cease, his means of support are dried up; for he is supported only by making them. He can buy, but he cannot sell. Hence there arises, as it is called, a stagnation of business; that is, a cessation or diminution of exchanges. The principal causes of this, are the following:

1. It may arise from a *diminished desire* for a particular product. Thus the decrease of the Catholic religion, during the wars of the French revolution, diminished the desire for fish, which the Catholics eat in Lent, and on fast days. This produced a stagnation of business in the fish trade.

It may arise from change of *fashion*. Thus, when shoe-strings were substituted for shoe-buckles, the demand for shoe-buckles ceased; the manufacturers of shoe-buckles were thrown out of employment; and there was a stagnation of business in this kind of trade.

It may arise from the fact, that one particular product has been supplanted by another. Thus the increasing cheapness of cotton cloth, has materially diminished the demand for linen.

Whenever, from any cause, the desires of men change, then the traffic in the article neglected, must be diminished; since it is very difficult to sell to a man a commodity which he knows he does not want. To this disadvantage, all articles which derive their value from fashion and caprice are exposed; and, on this account, they are always sold at a higher profit, in order to compensate for the additional risk.

2. Stagnation in business may arise from a *failure in production*. This must, of necessity, produce it; since, as we have already seen, two men cannot exchange, unless they both have something to part with; and the amount and number of every man's exchanges will be in proportion to the amount which he is able to part with, and the amount which others are able to offer him in exchange. Thus, if the crop of sugar should be reduced one half, there would be a stagnation in the sugar business; that is, there would be but half the quantity of sugar to be exchanged, and half the quantity of other things to be exchanged for it; in other words, half the number or amount of exchanges would be made. And, in general, the failure of any crop, or the diminution of any kind of production, must cause a stagnation of business in the traffic in that article itself, and also of whatever is usually exchanged for it. Thus, also, if production languish from civil war, or from insecurity of property, exchanges of all kinds diminish, towns are depopulated, harbors are deserted, and the accumulated treasure of past generations insensibly melts away.

A partial glut, or stagnation of business, may also arise from poverty in one of the parties making the exchange. If a nation is able to produce but one hundred thousand dollars' worth of exports, it can purchase but one hundred thousand dollars' worth of imports. This, then, will generally be the annual amount that will be brought to its market. But if, from any cause, a larger amount, say one hundred and fifty thousand dollars' worth, is brought thither, there will arise a glut, or temporary stagnation of business. There will be fifty thousand dollars' worth more than can be exchanged. The reason is not, that they do not want the additional fifty thousand dollars' worth of the productions of other countries, but that they have nothing with which to purchase it. Hence, after one hundred thousand dollars' worth have been purchased, there will be sellers, but no buyers. It will be seen, however, that such a case can generally exist only in new, small, or in very unproductive countries, or for short periods; or else in respect to articles of which the consumption of the whole community is but small.

3. A stagnation of business may be the effects of *legislation*. Suppose the importation of coffee into this country be a million pounds per annum. This must be paid for, in some way, by the productions of our own industry; and the demand for those productions to this extent, is for the sole purpose of paying for this coffee. There must, of course, be a great variety of exchanges required to collect these products, to bring them to the sea ports, to exchange them for coffee, and again to circulate this coffee throughout the country. Now, let a duty be laid upon coffee, which shall double its price, and thus diminish its consumption one half. The demand for one half of the products by which it was paid for, ceases, the demand for coffee, to this extent, also ceases; and the labor of transportation on both articles is reduced one half. Here must be a stagnation of business, in both of these articles; and half the shipping thus employed, will, for a time, be useless. Hence, there must, of course, arise a stagnation of business; that is, a permanent diminution of exchanges, in all the departments of industry affected by this arrangement.

IV. *Of the effects of legislative enactments on Exchange.*

I think it too obvious to need remark, that duties on imports can have no favorable effect on *exchange*. Their only effect must be, to raise the price of the products, and, of course, to diminish the ability in both parties to exchange. Every one knows that the exchanges between two places are diminished, by any natural obstacle to communication. If a road were so bad that it cost five dollars per hundred weight to transport merchandise between two places, every one knows that exchanges between these places would be fewer than they would be if the road were improved, so that transportation could be effected for twenty-five cents per hundred weight. Now, it makes no difference whether this additional four dollars and seventy-five cents be the result of the badness of the road, or of a transit duty between the two places. The diminution of exchange which it causes, will be precisely the same. In a severe winter, our northern harbors are closed, for weeks or months, by the ice. This is a natural tariff, and imposes a large protecting duty, inasmuch as exchanges must be effected, if they be effected at all, at a vastly greater price than in summer. I suppose it is not generally believed that this has no effect on the number of exchanges; and I have never heard it mentioned, as specially favorable to domestic industry.

I therefore think it evident, that governments can do nothing to facilitate exchanges by means of *discriminating duties*. They have, however, attempted to accomplish this result, by means of *bounties* on particular exports.

The manner in which this is accomplished, is this. Suppose we were not able, profitably, to produce and offer to other nations in exchange, some particlar article, say, for instance, iron. To encourage this export, a bounty is granted on every ton of iron exported, equal to the difference between our cost of producing it, and that at which other nations produce it. Our producer can then sell it in a foreign port, as cheap as the producer from another nation. But where does this bounty come from? Why, it is from a duty laid on some other import, or else from a tax laid on some other product. The iron worker is no better off than any other man, and all the other exchangers or producers, or both, are just so much worse off; and the value of capital and labor is, by the whole operation, diminished, as we have shown in the article on the effect of legislative enactments upon production. Did any merchant ever grow rich by selling under cost, for the sake of competition with his neighbor? It would be very difficult to show how a nation can grow rich in the same way. But, as the principles on which this discussion depends, have been already treated of in the article above alluded to, I need not here repeat them.

If, then, governments can do nothing in this manner to promote the business of exchanges, in what manner may exchange be affected by legislation?

We have said that exchanges are the natural result of mutual desire and mutual ability. In what manner may these be influenced by legislative enactments?

1. *Of Desire.* If by desire, be meant the original impulses implanted in the bosom of man, it is evident that these can be neither increased nor diminished. These are a fixed quantity, with which we cannot interfere. These desires, however, generally remain dormant, until they are awakened into exercise by the presence, or by the knowledge, of their appropriate objects. It is by a knowledge of the existence of these objects, therefore,

and of the modes by which they may be obtained, that the desire for exchange is excited. Hence it is plain, that the desire for exchange may be increased:

1. By the general diffusion of knowledge, especially of that sort of knowledge by which man is taught how he may benefit his condition. This will be accomplished, generally, by an universal diffusion of the means of common education.

2. By removing all impediments to the diffusion of knowledge. In this respect, duties on imported books, which is really a tax on knowledge, are, in a free government, absurdly injudicious.

3. By increasing the physical means for the dissemination of knowledge and intelligence. This will be done by allowing every facility for internal improvement; by an efficient and cheap post-office system, pervading every portion of the country, and bringing to every man's door the information circulating throughout the civilized world.

I do not know that a government can do more than this to excite in a people the *desire* to exchange.

2. *Of Ability.* The ability to exchange depends, as we have shown, upon productiveness. Hence, every means by which the productiveness of industry is increased, will also benefit exchange. These have already been alluded to, in the former book, and need not here to be repeated.

There is, however, one branch of productive industry which is more immediately connected with exchange, than any other, and which deserves, on that account, in this place, a more minute consideration. I refer to internal improvements. On this, I shall offer a few remarks.

An internal improvement, is any means by which the operation of change in place may be performed at a less expense than formerly. It is, in fact, a labor-saving machine, peculiar to this branch of industry. Of those at present in use, the most common are roads, railways, and canals.

What is peculiar to these machines, is, *First,* they are very costly, and hence, in general, require more capital than can be commanded by a single individual; and, therefore, must be owned by a number of persons associated together. *Secondly:* they must pass through the lands of various individuals who have no special interest in them, and are thus liable to interfere with the right of property. This interference can be allowed only by the whole community; and, hence, there arises a necessity for legislative enactment, granting permission to this effect.

Now, inasmuch as such machines, if properly constructed and skilfully managed, are greatly for the benefit of the whole society, it is manifestly the duty of society to grant all suitable facilities for constructing them. Inasmuch, however, as they, like any other privileges, are liable to be abused, and may, in the end, injure the interests which they were intended to benefit, it becomes a legislature, on all such occasions, to reserve, at the outset, the right of visitation; and the power to modify or amend, on equitable terms, the privileges granted, in such manner as the exigencies of the public may require.

Whether a government should itself undertake the work of internal improvement, is, however, not so clear. On this subject, it may be suggested:

1. If it *will not* be profitable; that is, if capital thus invested will not be as productive as that invested in other employments, it ought not to be undertaken by the public, because the capital thus invested must be taken from other employments; that is, it must be taken by force from a more productive, to be invested in a less productive employment. If it be said, though it be not itself productive, it may enrich the district in which it is constructed; the answer to this is, then let that district pay for it, unless it can be shown to be either wise or just, to impoverish one district, for the purpose of enriching another.

2. If it *will be* productive, private associations, in an intelligent community, will, with proper encouragement, be ready to undertake it. And of the question of profitableness, private individuals will judge much more accurately than a government, because the facts are equally known to both; the degree of intelligence is likely to be as great in the one case, as in the other; and the one party can be influenced by no motive but self-interest, which is here also the interest of the public; while the other party may be influenced by party politics, sectional jealousy, love of power, and a thousand disturbing causes.

3. A work of this sort will be executed at much less expense by private individuals, than by a government. The costliness of all public works, is every where proverbial. The greater the number of intermediate agencies by which any work is performed, the more imperfectly is the work done, and the greater is the unnecessary expenditure. Now, government is itself an agent. It must perform the work by means of another set of agents. Under these, may be half a dozen others, in the form of contractors and sub-contractors. All these unnecessary agencies must be paid out of the public purse, and their

accounts adjusted by those who have no special motive to encourage economy. All this is reversed, when those who conduct the work pay for it themselves, and whose profits, in the end, must depend upon the goodness of the work and the cheapness of its execution.

4. A work of this kind will be more faithfully superintended by private, than by public owners. The private owner knows that he must conduct his operation economically, and maintain the favor of the public, or else he will gain nothing by his investment. A government is under no such salutary check.

5. But a still stronger objection to the confiding of such works to the public, is, the amount of patronage which it must, of necessity, place in the hands of a government. The power to make roads and canals whenever it pleased, and to employ upon them whomsoever it pleased, once placed in the hands of a party, would perpetuate it in office forever, in spite of any violation of right which it might perpetrate, or any corruption of which it might be guilty. This, of itself, seems to me a sufficient reason for declining to confide this power in the hands of any government.

There is, however, another class of improvements, of very great importance, which belongs, of necessity and of right, to a government; it is that class of improvemenis which reduce the expense, and lessen the risk of external commerce. Among these, the most important are the removal of obstructions from harbors; the location of buoys and the erection of lighthouses; the execution of accurate surveys; and the publication of accurate charts of its whole coast. The more perfect these become, the less is the risk of shipwreck, in leaving and approaching a coast; of course, the less is the cost of insurance, and the less the price of every thing imported and exported. Hence, a nation offering these advantages, becomes a better market for all other nations, and they will the more readily resort to her for exchanges. Improvements of this sort are one of the most economical forms of national investment; they frequently save, in a single year, the whole cost of their erection. The loss of property and life, by shipwreck, on almost every coast, is enormously great. The greater part of this loss might probably be saved, by judicious expenditure upon improvements on the coast, and proper regulations for the government of pilots.

I have said, above, that exchanges will be effected by the security or insecurity of the right of property. Hence, legislators can do much to promote the prosperity of a country, by the enactment of wholesome laws, by which contracts shall be enforced, wrongs redressed, and injuries prevented. And they should be specially careful that they are not guilty, in their social character, of what they forbid to others in their individual character. They should be scrupulous in the observance of individual right, and should remember, that a single individual is as important as a nation, when the question of justice is concerned.

And the same principles apply to the treatment of foreigners. No foreigner can traffic with another country, without placing his property in the power of the citizens of that country. If his rights be respected, and he be assured of the benefit of equal laws, he will invest his property abroad as freely as at home; and will, with confidence, and on the most moderate terms, effect exchanges to as great an extent as he is able. Hence, under these circumstances, exchanges will be effected to the greatest advantage of both countries, and they will naturally flow from other countries to such an one as this. And the reverse will be the case, if the rights of foreigners are disregarded. Other nations will desire their custom, if we do not. Commerce will leave our shores, and we shall be left in the well-known condition of the dog in the manger. The fable, I believe, informs us that he was starved to death.

CHAPTER SECOND.

OF EXCHANGE BY MEANS OF A METALLIC CURRENCY.

SECTION I.

OF THE USE OF A CIRCULATING MEDIUM.

In the preceding chapter, I have endeavored to illustrate the general principles of exchange, and the conditions by which it is regulated. Exchange, however, like every other benefit which we enjoy in this life, can only be accomplished by labor. But in this, as in every other case, it holds true, that a great advantage is gained by increasing the productiveness of labor; that is, by enabling the same individuals by the same labor, to accomplish a greater amount of exchange. And it holds true in this, as in other cases, that the result of labor is more perfect, just in proportion as the productiveness of labor is increased.

But, in order to accomplish this, an intermediate instrument or tool must be used. A man who cannot split a log by the direct use of his hands, will find no difficulty in splitting it with a beetle and wedges. So, also, he who would find it impossible to effect a dozen exchanges in a day, if he insisted on exchanging the products themselves, will find no difficulty in doing it in a few minutes, by means of the instrument which has been invented for this purpose, and he will not only thus do it in a shorter time, but also on better terms, and with much greater exactitude.

This instrument, of so much importance in exchange, is *money;* to a consideration of the nature and uses of which, we shall devote this and the succeeding chapters. The present chapter will be confined to the consideration of a *metallic* currency. We commence with the *use* of a circulating medium.

In treating of this subject, we shall *first* consider the difficulties which must necessarily embarrass exchange in *kind;* and, *secondly,* the manner in which these difficulties are removed by means of a circulating medium.

I. *The difficulties which attend upon exchange in kind.*

By exchange in kind, I mean exchange of commodity for commodity, as when a farmer exchanges wheat for sugar, or pork for iron, &c.

1. Suppose a producer to have prepared his product for consumption. If he be obliged to exchange in kind, it may be a long time before he finds another person who wants the article which he has created. If he be obliged to wait long, his product, if it be perishable, is either destroyed or deteriorated. He must go in search of a purchaser; and, if he at length find one, he may have consumed, in the search, as much time as the article originally cost. This must be added to the cost of the article, or else he will be a loser. But, by this additional cost, the product is no better; it is only dearer. This must, of course, decrease the demand; and hence, by all this additional cost, both parties are poorer.

2. But it is to be remembered, that the producer not only wants to part with his product, but also to part with it for some definite object of desire. He who has raised wheat, does not wish simply to part with his wheat, but also to receive in exchange for it, tea, or coffee, or iron, or salt, or clothing. He must, therefore, in order to effect the exchange which he desires, not only find some one who wishes for wheat, but, also, some one who is able to give him, in return, the precise product he desires. If he desire clothing in return, it will not be sufficient to find some one who offers him bread, or shoes, or butcher's meat. This, also, increases the difficulty of exchange, and, of course, the labor and the cost necessary to effect it.

3. But this is not all. Men who wish to exchange, do not always wish to exchange in equal amounts. A grazier who brings a fatted ox to market, may find persons enough who want a few pounds of beef, but very few who want a whole ox. The grazier cannot divide his ox, and give a part of it for a few pounds of coffee or tea; nor, probably, does he require one fourth of the value of the ox, in any article which can be purchased in the town where it may be sold. He wishes to obtain, by the sale of the ox, additional provender for the support of his remaining herd. This he cannot, perhaps, procure, except in the country; or, if he could procure it, the merchant who owns the provender, would not want a whole ox for butcher's meat. Thus, exchanges would be arrested; or must be made very rarely, and at great cost, and under every possible disadvantage.

4. Such are the difficulties which attend upon the exchange of *material* products. But it will be manifest, at once, that material products give rise to but a small part of the exchanges which are, by necessity, made among men. One great article to be exchanged, is *labor*. This,

every man produces, and must produce, by the law of his nature; and this, every man is able to offer in exchange for the objects of desire. Now, were exchange only in kind, a man who had nothing but labor or skill to offer, would not be able to labor for those who *wanted* him, and who would give him the *greatest wages* for labor; but he must labor for those who were willing to give, in ever so small quantity, the articles which he *needed for* his support. The laborer in a furnace, would be obliged to take his pay in iron. But, as he could not exchange his iron with the baker, the butcher, or the clothier, he must go and work for them, for any compensation by which he might obtain for himself the necessaries of life. The workman of the baker must take his pay in bread. But he would want only a small portion of bread for himself, and he must spend his time in exchanging it for whatever else he needed. If he could not thus procure tea, coffee, clothing, and other necessaries, he must leave his occupation, and work for those who wished to exchange them for his labor. The physician must take his fee in iron, or bread, or butcher's meat; and, if any of his patients produced what he did not want, he must either attend them gratuitously, or they must die without assistance. Besides this, there are many products incapable of division. If a hundred men engaged in building a ship, or a house, how would they take their pay in kind, without taking the ship in pieces, and thus rendering their work wholly useless?

5. Hence we see, that were exchange only in kind, there would be no division of labor, except in its most imperfect form. No man could perfect himself in any one art; because, by the exercise of that alone, he could not possibly procure the means of sustenance. I have already shown, how impossible it would be for him to do this by the practice of any one of the ordinary mechanical trades. How much much more, when these trades are minutely

divided. I have elsewhere stated the advantages of this subdivision. But how could this be effected, if exchange were made only in kind? Suppose a man employs his time in the single process of heading pins, or in forming the rivets for the handles of penknives; how could he subsist by exchange in kind? Who would give him what he needed for subsistence, for his pin-heads, or for his knife-handle rivets? Hence, we see that division of labor, so essential to the productiveness of human industry, to the progress of society, and to the use of natural agents, could exist only in its most elementary forms, were exchanges limited to exchange in kind.

And, if it be said that this inconvenience could be avoided by establishments for barter, it will at once appear, that these could remedy it only in part. They could assist in the exchange of nothing but *material* products, and of those which were not rapidly perishable. They could present no relief for exchanges of labor. Hence, they would do almost nothing to facilitate division of labor, and could carry forward the progress of society in no respect beyond its most rude beginnings.

From such causes as these, arises the necessity of a circulating medium; and it will be easily seen, in what manner, by means of a circulating medium, they are remedied.

1. Suppose that the producer can always exchange his product, not for the article which he immediately wants, but for some other article which is universally wanted, and wanted at all times, and in all quantities. As soon as the producer has, by exchange, possessed himself of this commodity, he may then, on account of its universal desirableness, easily procure, by another exchange, whatever he may need. In this manner, by means of two

exchanges made at the same instant, the labor of days or of weeks may be accomplished. Thus, if salt were this commodity, and every one wanted salt in all quantities, at all times, and at a fixed value; by exchanging every thing for salt, and then exchanging salt for whatever we might desire, the labor of exchanges would be vastly diminished.

2. This convenience, however, will be much increased, if the article of universal desire be small in bulk; because, in this case, much of the labor of transportation will be avoided. Were the lace-maker obliged to exchange his lace for salt, he would be obliged to furnish himself with a cart, in which to receive his payment. And thus, in general, instead of a purse, in which to carry our money, we should require, for this purpose, the use of a wagon and horses.

3. If this circulating medium be also minutely divisible, it will possess still greater conveniences. The producer may then part with all, or with a part of his product; and he can procure, with the circulating medium, as small a portion of that which he wishes in exchange, as he may choose. The farmer, instead of exchanging one part of his wheat for tea, another part for coffee, and another part for clothing; or else, exchanging it all for tea, and then endeavoring to find customers for his tea, may exchange it all for the circulating medium, procure as much of each as he pleases, or, if he choose, make no farther exchange whatever.

4. The case is still stronger, when *labor* is one of the articles to be exchanged. The laborer will now no longer be obliged to labor at any price, for him who is able to give him in exchange what he immediately wants; but he may

labor for any one who will give him, in return, this object of general desire. Hence, he is now at liberty to labor for him who will give him the best wages; that is, where his industry and skill will be employed most advantageously to himself. With this he can procure whatever he wants, in such portions as he may desire.

5. The practicability of the division of labor now becomes immediately apparent. If the laborer be paid in the article of universal desire, it makes no difference whether the person who produces what he wants, needs or does not need, his particular product. He wants the object of universal desire, and this is enough; for, by this, the laborer can effect exchanges with him or with any one else. If he can procure this circulating medium by means of pin-heads, or knife-handle rivets, this is all that he wants. He is now as independent as though he produced that which every one wants; since, by means of what he produces, he can procure that which every one wants. Thus, we see, that every man is, in this manner, able to devote himself to that in which his skill will be most productive to himself. And all men thus making the first exchange in this object of universal desire, all are equally independent; and all are able, in the most successful manner, to avail themselves of the fruits of their own industry.

Now, whatever it is that performs the office of thus facilitating exchanges, is called a *circulating medium.* So great has been the necessity of some such instrument, that even the rudest nations have always been found adopting some such contrivance with advantage.

Thus, the natives of the African coast were formerly in the habit of using, as money, small white sea-shells, denominated cowries.

In pastoral nations, cattle were frequently used as a circulating medium. Thus we are told, by Homer, that the armor of Diomede cost nine oxen. Sheep, probably, were also used for the same purpose. The ordinary mode, among such nations, of estimating the wealth of an individual, was by the number of his flocks and herds. Hence, probably, arose the custom, among the Greeks and Romans, of stamping their earliest coin with the figure of an ox or a sheep. Hence, also, the Latin word *pecunia,* is supposed to be derived from *pecus,* a sheep.

From reasons which will easily suggest themselves, all other substances soon gave place to the metals, as a circulating medium. Different metals were, however, used at first by different nations. The first instance on record of the use of metals, as a medium of exchange, is found in Genesis 23:16. "And Abraham hearkened unto Ephron. And Abraham *weighed* to Ephron the silver which he had named, in the audience of the sons of Heth, four hundred shekels of silver, current money with the merchant." We see that at this time the money was weighed; that is, was not paid by tale. I presume that the metals were used as a circulating medium for a long period before they were fashioned into coin. At a much later period, the baser metals were used as money by the Greeks and Romans. Thus the Lacedemonians, under Lycurgus, established iron as the circulating medium. The Romans used copper or brass in the early ages of their history. Hence, *æs* signifies, in Latin, both brass and money. These, however, in all places, have long since given place to gold and silver, which are hence denominated the precious metals. These are now used for the purposes of money, throughout the known world, except among the rudest and most barbarous tribes. Copper is used only in the payment of sums less in value than the lowest denomination of silver coin. In some countries, both gold and silver are made a legal tender in payment of debts; in other countries, only one of these metals is used. In this country, both are established by law. In Great Britain, gold is the only legal tender for all sums greater than twenty shillings, and silver, for all sums of less amount. Copper is used only in payment of sums less than six-pence.

SECTION II.

OF THE QUALITIES NECESSARY TO THAT WHICH CONSTITUTES THE CIRCULATING MEDIUM.

In order to render any substance available as a circulating medium, the essential quality required is, that it be *universally desired as such.* Its object is to facilitate exchanges, but it can accomplish this object, only by means of the willingness of the whole community to exchange for it every thing which they are willing to part with. If one individual of a community prefer one substance, and another individual another, exchanges will be embarrassed, by unnecessary multiplication, and by the useless consumption of time. And if, on the other hand, any substance be thus universally desired, on account of the great facilities which it offers, and the great saving of labor which it effects, it will be immediately used for this purpose. And it will be so used, without any agency of government; and even although a government did not exist; just as a man will use any other instrument for increasing the productiveness of his labor as soon as he can procure it; simply for the reason that it is for his advantage.

If the exchanges of a country were wholly internal, it would be sufficient that such a circulating medium were universally acceptable among themselves. But, inasmuch as every nation has important and extensive exchanges with other nations, it is an additional advantage to have the same substance used as a circulating medium by all. We have already seen, that that exchange is the most profitable for a country, in which it exports what is relatively most abundant at home, and imports that which is relatively most wanted at home; and imports it from that country in which, what it exports is most wanted, and what it imports is most abundant. Now, it is evident, that the circulating medium may be accumulated in any country, so that it shall be relatively lower in price than other commodities. Thus, the precious metals may be so abundant in this country, that a merchant can procure more iron in Russia by sending a given amount of silver, than by sending the flour which would here be equal in value to the silver. It is, therefore, for his advantage to send the silver, and it is equally for the advantage of his country. And, for the same reason, if in this country, there be a relative scarcity, it will be for the advantage of other nations, as well as for our advantage, that they should send silver in exchange for our products. In this manner, exchanges are made, of that which is least wanted by both parties, for that which is most wanted by both. This enables both parties to supply themselves at the lowest rates.

Besides, it is a great advantage, for the value of the circulating medium, in proportion to other values, to be as little as possible liable to fluctuation. The reason of this is plain. When once any substance is adopted as a circulating medium, all contracts are henceforth adjusted with reference to that substance. A man agrees to pay his neighbor a certain amount of value, not in cotton, or coffee, or sugar, but in the circulating medium. Now, if this circulating medium be liable to great fluctuation, the contract, though the same in words, will express a very different reality at different times. If I agree to pay six dollars a barrel for flour, three months hence, and if dollars be worth twice as much, that is, represent twice as much value, in three months as they do now; though I pay what I promised in name, I pay twice the amount of value. If they have fallen to half the value, the seller will receive only half the value which he expected. This would be a great disadvantage, and would materially diminish the utility of any substance when used for a circulating medium. But, if the same substance be used in all the civilized world, this fluctuation, if not absolutely prevented, will be so restricted, as to produce the least possible amount of evil. When exchanges between countries are frequent and numerous, and the prices of all commodities are universally known by the merchants of both, as specie may be sent abroad with very little cost of transportation, a very slight advance in its relative value will cause it to flow in from other countries, and a very slight surplus will cause it to flow to other countries, until the common equilibrium be restored. In this manner, we see how the universal employment of the same substance, by all nations holding intercourse with each other, will be an advantage to all; inasmuch as it will prevent any great fluctuation in its relative value in any particular country.

While, however, it is the fact, that any thing which is thus universally acceptable will be used as money, there are various circumstances on which this acceptableness depends. Some of these are the following:

1. Its cost, or, in other words, the amount of labor necessary to its production, must be as invariable as possible.

Hence, it could not be a vegetable product, because the variations in the productiveness of labor thus employed are very great. An abundant harvest produces a rapid fall, and a dearth produces a rapid rise, in the price of wheat, which bears a large proportion to its average value. On this account, a metal is preferable; because, here the amount produced, is directly and immediately dependent on the labor employed in producing it, and is less liable to be influenced by disturbing forces.

2. It should be an article of high price; that is, within a small bulk, it should concentrate a large amount of value, or represent a large amount of labor. This is, of course, a great advantage, by saving the labor of transportation. Every one sees that the commerce of the world, at its present state, must instantly cease, if we were obliged to exchange our gold and silver for the iron money of Lycurgus.

Yet, to this remark there is a limit. As a substance may not be of a price sufficiently high, so it may also be of a price too high for the purposes of money. Precious stones are minerals, and they cost all the price at which they are sold; but they are too dear to be used for this purpose; that is, though they might answer for the exchange of great values, yet, for all common exchanges, they would be utterly unsuitable, because they would be of so small bulk, as to be very easily lost.

3. The substance must be capable of division, without loss of value. As it is desirable that provision be made for facilitating all sorts of exchanges, the substance used as money, should be capable of division into such portions as may suit the convenience of every one, without itself suffering, by this division, any diminution of value. On this account, also, the precious stones would be unsuitable

for this purpose, because their value is not proportional to their size. A large diamond is worth several times its weight of small diamonds. If it be divided, its value is very greatly diminished; and having been once divided, its value can never be restored. On the contrary, a lump of gold may be divided into one hundred pieces, and the value of all the pieces together, is equal to the original value of the whole. They may, if occasion require, be again united into one lump, and the value of the whole is the same as before.

4. The substance should be of such a nature, that it can be easily verified; that is, it should be susceptible of such preparation, that every one can readily assure himself of its purity and weight; that is, of its value. Unless this can be done, at every exchange, every one must examine and try every piece by itself. This would consume much time, would require the possession of great skill in every individual, and would, by its frequent repetition, soon wear away the substance itself. Hence, it is of advantage that the metals used for money, should be peculiar in their weight and color, and that their appearance should attract attention, so that their peculiarities may be easily learned and distinguished. The brilliant lustre of silver and gold, therefore, adds very much to their fitness for coin. Their weight, also, presents a ready means for the detection of adulteration. Platina, which is used in Russia for the purpose of money, has the advantage of both of them in weight; but it has no lustre, and, in appearance, it very much resembles the baser metals. This will be an objection to its universal acceptableness.

5. It should be, as little as possible, liable to fluctuations in value, either from decay, or from other causes. Were it easily destructible, great losses would constantly occur; as the loss must fall upon the individual in whose

hands it happened at the time to be. And besides, were it from any cause liable to great fluctuation in value, it could never be used as a circulating medium. No one would contract to pay for a house, in a stated quantity of wheat, or in a stated quantity of fish, in twelve or eighteen months from a given time ; for he could not know how many causes might diminish the quantity of wheat, or vary the price of fish ; and, of course, he might be obliged to give twice as much as he expected. Could the circulating medium always bear the same relative price to other commodities, it would probably be advantageous. But as this is impossible, it is manifest, that that commodity which is liable to the least fluctuation, is, by this circumstance, the best adapted to this purpose.

6. As we sometimes desire to make small, and sometimes large exchanges ; and, as the substance best adapted to the one, is not always best adapted to the other, there is an advantage in employing two metals for this purpose. For this reason, both silver and gold are commonly employed in most civilized countries. For exchanges of less value than the smallest silver coin, copper is also generally used. And, if silver should ever become so abundant and cheap as to be too bulky to be used for effecting small exchanges, it would take the place of copper, and its place would be supplied by gold. Should gold become as abundant as silver, it would take the place of silver, and some dearer metal, as platina, would be used in its stead.

Inasmuch as gold and silver possess all the essential qualities which are required in a circulating medium ; and, as the condition of man so manifestly points to the necessity of some such instrument, it is not remarkable that they have so long and so universally been adopted for this purpose. But it is always to be remembered, that we use them as a circulating medium, because *we want a circulating medium*, and because *they accomplish the purpose.* We do not use them as a circulating medium, because *we see a stamp upon them*, nor because government *has made them a legal tender;* but because we know that *they represent a given amount of value*, and we therefore know, that we can exchange them for the same amount of value, whenever we please. If a bushel of wheat sell for a dollar, we know that it costs as much labor to produce a dollar at the mine and bring it to us, as to produce a bushel of wheat and bring it to us. Hence, we know that until some new and vastly more productive mines are discovered, this dollar cannot be produced for less labor, nor represent a less amount of value. And, as every body wants a dollar, and no one can furnish it at a less cost, we know that it will bring, in exchange, the same as we have given for it.

We remarked, when speaking of exchangeable value, that the demand for any product, and, of course, its exchangeable value, was affected by the number of desires it would gratify. The greater the number of desires which it will gratify, the greater the number of persons who will want it; hence, they will overbid each other; and, unless there be some improved, that is, cheaper method, of producing it, its exchangeable value will rise. This principle applies to whatever is used as money. The precious metals are used for ornament, for domestic utensils, and for coin. If the use of them for one of these purposes should be discontinued, the demand would be less; and, as they are not liable to decay, their relative price would fall.

Hence it is, that the amount of plate and utensils formed of the precious metals, in a country, is no criterion of its wealth, but, frequently, an indication of the reverse.

Should commerce be unproductive, and exchanges diminish, and our intercourse with other nations be cut off, and we be reduced to the condition of Europe in the dark ages, there would be but little need of the precious metals as an instrument of exchange, and their price would fall. Hence, they would be melted down, by the rich, into plate. And, on the other hand, when they have been used for plate, and the demand for them, and their consequent price have, from any cause, subsequently increased, the temptation to use them, productively, is too great to allow them to be employed in this manner; and the plate is melted into coin, and its place supplied with porcelain, or plated ware, or glass, or any other material of equal beauty, but of inferior costliness.

SECTION III.

OF THE FUNCTIONS OF MONEY.

Let us now suppose metals to have been selected by the whole community as the circulating medium, and that they have been so divided and verified as to be fitted to accomplish this purpose. We shall proceed to consider some of the functions which these metals would discharge.

Money is the instrument for facilitating exchanges. This, when considered as money, is its only office. By accomplishing this purpose in the least time, and at the least expense of labor, and transportation, and wear, it reduces the cost of every product, and thus adds immensely to the productiveness of human industry.

The principles on which it accomplishes this result, have been already alluded to. They are briefly as follows:

1. The cost, or price of the money employed in every exchange, is equal to the cost or price of the article which is exchanged for it. If a barrel of flour in Lima be exchanged for ten ounces of silver, the cost of producing the flour, and of transporting it to Lima, is equal to the cost of producing the silver and transporting it to the same place. If a barrel of flour in New York, be exchanged for seven ounces of silver, the cost and transportation of the one at the place of exchange, is equal to that of the other. If the flour merchant wishes for a thousand ounces of silver, he can procure it more cheaply by producing flour, than he can by going to the mines of Mexico, and working it out from the ore. And, if the miner wishes for flour, he can procure it more cheaply by working in the mine, than by attempting to raise wheat and manufacture flour on the mountains of Potosi.

That this is so, is evident from the fact, that if the cost of the precious metals change, their exchangeable value varies, like that of any other product. Thus, if new and richer mines are opened, so that the cost of producing the precious metals is reduced, or, in other words, so that mining labor is more productive, the price of the precious metals falls. In such a case, we receive more silver for a day's work, for a bushel of wheat, for a pound of wool, or for any other product. Money is thus rendered cheaper, on the same principle that when a wheat harvest is abundant, we receive a larger amount of wheat for a day's work, or for a pound of wool, than at other times. This is exemplified, in the great change of prices which occurred throughout the world, after the discovery of the mines of South America. And, on the other hand, when the price of producing the precious metals is increased, their exchangeable value rises. This has been the case, for some time past, in consequence of the civil wars of South America. Hence, there has been, for some time past, a gradual rise in the price of the precious metals; that is, the price of other things has fallen; that is, in general, if the cost of the production of the precious metals diminishes, while that of the production of wheat remains the same, we shall receive more silver in exchange for a bushel of wheat. If the cost of producing an ounce of silver is increased, while that of producing a bushel of wheat remains the same, we shall receive less silver in exchange for a bushel of wheat; that is, in exchanging products for the precious metals, as for any thing else, we exchange on the principle of labor for labor.

Besides, the price of the precious metals, like that of any other commodity, is influenced, in short periods, by the fluctuations of supply and demand. There is, in any country, the course of whose industry is not distorted by legislation, a supply of money, equal to the ordinary wants of the community, for the purposes of exchange. The price of both articles, is, in such a case, based upon the cost of the production of specie, compared with the cost of the production of the several articles for which it is exchanged. But, suppose that while this amount of specie remains the same, there should happen a year of universal productiveness in all the departments of agricultural, manufacturing, and commercial industry. In this case, the number of exchanges, and the amounts exchanged, would be proportionally increased. The instrument with which exchanges were to be made, would be relatively scarce; the demand for it would rise; and there would be competition among the bidders for it. Hence, its exchangeable value would rise; that is, we should give more wool, and wheat, and cotton, for an ounce of silver; that is, every thing would be cheap; or, in other words, for an ounce of silver, we should procure a larger amount of other products; as we always do, in a season of universal productiveness. And, on the contrary, if, while the ordinary amount of specie remained in the country, there occurred a very unproductive season, the number of exchanges would proportionally diminish, and there would be less demand for the instrument of exchange. There would arise a competition among the sellers, and the relative price of money would fall; that is, we should give more money for every other article of necessity; that is, every thing would be dear, as every one knows it is, in a season of scarcity.

We see, then, that the exchangeable value of money, is not derived from its shape or color, from the stamp of the mint, or from the enactments of the government; but that, like every thing else, it is based upon the cost of its production, varying, slightly, and for short periods, like every thing else, with the accidental fluctuations of supply and demand. And hence, the reason why a man exchanges a bushel of wheat for two ounces of silver, and a yard of broadcloth for six ounces, is, that it costs as much labor and capital to produce the one at the place of exchange, as the other, and that no one can produce the given amount of silver, by mining, or in any other way, without expending the same amount of labor and capital, that the flour merchant or the manufacturer has expended in the creation of his products.

As, then, every man, when he exchanges his products for the precious metals, knows that he receives a commodity of as much cost; that is, which represents the same amount of labor and capital, as that for which he exchanges it; and, as he knows that every one wants this commodity; that is, he can procure with it any thing which any one else has to exchange; and, as no one who wants it, can procure it on any better terms from any one else than from himself, every one is willing to exchange for money, and would rather exchange for it than for any thing else. As this feeling is universal, every one acts upon the same principle; and hence, all exchanges are either made in money, or else are regulated by it.

Hence, we see again, the great importance of adopting, as a circulating medium, a commodity which is not liable to fluctuation. If I exchange a bale of cotton for a hundred ounces of silver to-day, when both the articles represent the same amount of labor, I do it upon the supposition, that no one can furnish the silver, next week, on better terms than myself. But if, in a few days, the relative cost of silver should fall one half, every one would be able to furnish it at a less cost, and I should be underbidden; that is, I should be obliged to sell my silver at half price; that is, for half the amount of labor which I gave for it.

II. But the question will naturally arise, if the value of the silver be equal to that of all the amounts exchanged for it, must not the value of the precious metals in the community, be equal to the value of all the other commodities?

We answer, this would be the case, if all exchanges were actually made in money, and actually made at the same instant. But the contrary is the fact.

No man exchanges *all* his products at once, but exchanges them in *successive portions*. If two men possess one thousand dollars' worth of commodities; for instance, if A have wool and B have wheat, and they exchange the whole at once, and use money as the instrument, they must both possess also one thousand dollars with which to make the exchange; that is, A must give B one thousand dollars for his wool, and *vice versa*. But, if they exchange in portions of the value of ten dollars, at one hundred successive times, ten dollars in the possession of each, and the same identical ten dollars, would accomplish the whole object. Now, as it is evident, that on any particular day, only a very small part of the whole amount of values in the possession of the community, is exchanged, it is evident that only so much of the instrument of exchange is necessary, as will accomplish the exchanges which the convenience of the community requires. No one supposes, because there is a million tons of merchandise in a city, that there must have been vehicles capable of carrying a million tons at once in order to bring it there. A locomotive, carrying fifty tons at once, if it went and returned frequently, would speedily accomplish the whole work.

2. But this is not all. A large amount of exchanges is constantly made in *kind*. A buys wool of B, and B buys cloth of A. They both estimate the value of their product in money, because, as this is the usual medium of exchange, and that by which they are obliged to estimate cost, this method of estimation is most convenient. Each charges the other with all that he purchases, at its value in silver. At the close of the year, they adjust their accounts with each other. If A and B have both received of each other the same amount of value estimated in silver, the one account balances the other; and thus, no money at all is required. If one have received more than the other, he pays merely the difference, either in silver, or else in his own product, at the option of his creditor. In this manner, a large proportion of the exchanges actually made,

is conducted. In this manner, *book-keeping* tends greatly to diminish the amount of the circulating medium necessary for the exchanges of a community.

3. We see that this is still more emphatically the case, in respect to all the exchanges which take place between different districts, and different nations. Inasmuch as no society can gain possession of the objects of desire, except by its own labor, it must pay for what it receives in the product of the labor of others, with what it sends away, in the product of its own labor; that is to say, the exports of any country must be substantially equal to its imports. If, then, the transactions between two nations should be precisely equal, there would be no need of the transmission of any money at all between them. If A send ten thousand dollars' worth of cotton to Liverpool, and import ten thousand dollars' worth of calicoes from Manchester; he authorises the manufacturer in Manchester to receive in payment, the ten thousand dollars which are due to him from the merchant in Liverpool; and, thus, the whole matter is adjusted. If we receive from England, values to a larger amount than she wishes to receive in our own productions, we send some of our productions to a third country, and thus procure for England, what she wishes from the third country, in sufficient quantity to pay the residue. If we can get her products, in this manner, cheaper than we can make them ourselves, it is for our interest to do so. If they thus cost more than we could produce them for, ourselves, we shall relinquish the trade, and begin to manufacture them. In either case, there is no necessity for the use of money. And hence, the only reason why money is sent from one country to another, in the transactions of commerce, is the same reason as that for which tea, or coffee, or cotton, or flour, is sent; that is, because it is so much cheaper in the country from which it is sent, than in that to which it is exported,

that a larger value can be procured for it, than for the same value of any other commodity. In this case, it is for the advantage of both countries that it should be so exchanged.

The amount of the circulating medium, in any one country, and, of course, in all countries, must, therefore, be very small, in proportion to the whole amount of the capital of a country. The actual proportion, perhaps, cannot be estimated with accuracy. In Great Britain, writers on this subject have greatly varied. Some have estimated it at the 50th, and others, at the 127th part of the whole capital. The latter is, probably, by far the nearer to the truth.

III. We see, then, that under given circumstances, in any country, a given amount of specie will be required to effect its exchanges; and that, that amount will depend upon the relative value of the precious metals with other things, and upon the number and the facilities of exchange. These latter circumstances remaining the same, the same *value* in specie will always be required, and no more. If specie, equal in value to ten millions bushels of wheat be required, no more *in value* can be used. If the *amount* be increased, its *value* will fall. If the *amount* be diminished, its *value* will rise. And this rise and fall will equally take place, whether the relative variation arise from a change in the cost of specie or of other products. Now, it is easy to see that these variations, if left alone, will regulate themselves.

We have seen, already, that the relative value of specie and of other products may vary. Let us suppose, in the first instance, that production, in any one year, is greatly increased, so that money in any country is dear, or, which is the same thing, that other products are cheap, Let us, for the sake of illustration, suppose, that in New York, flour is sold at four dollars per barrel. If, now, a merchant wished to import a cargo of wine from Bordeaux, since four dollars and a barrel of flour here, are at the same price, he can as cheaply send out the one as the other, with which to pay for his wine. But suppose that a barrel of flour will purchase more wine in Bordeaux, than four dollars or four ounces of silver. He will then send flour, instead of silver; and, as all other men in their senses will do the same, of course no specie will leave the country. On the contrary, a merchant in London, wishing to purchase cotton in New York, will ascertain the relative value of specie, and that of calico, or hardware, or iron; and will send specie in payment for his cotton, whenever he finds that, by a given value of this export, he can import a greater amount of cotton, than by the same value of any other. Other merchants in other places will do the same, until the requisite amount of specie has flowed in, and it has become as abundant here, as in other countries. Thus, when specie is high in any country, it goes out no where, and comes in from every where.

On the contrary; suppose an unproductive season to arise, and the relative quantity of specie in this country, to exceed the average in other countries. In this country, therefore, specie would be cheap; that is, every thing else would be dear. The merchant, who wished to import a cargo of iron, would compare the prices of flour and of money. If flour was at fifteen dollars the barrel, that is, if he could purchase, at the same price, a barrel of flour and fifteen dollars, he would easily ascertain by which, in Russia, he could procure the greatest amount of iron. If fifteen dollars would procure the most iron, he would send the dollars, instead of the flour. This would be an advantage to him and to the country, because, by this mode of exchange, he receives the largest amount in return ; and he procures it by means of that which is relatively the most abundant ; that is, which is manifestly the least needed. And a merchant in Liverpool, who knows the prices of our products, observing that he can exchange more profitably with us by receiving his payment in specie, at the relative prices which specie and products sustain to each other, will receive his payments in specie. Thus, by the sending abroad of our specie, which we do not so much need, we shall be supplied with other products which we more need ; and hence, the relative value of specie to other products, will be again brought to an equilibrium. In other words, when specie is cheap in any country, it comes in from no where, and goes out every where. Thus, among countries between which there is frequent intercourse, and a free circulation of mercantile information, the price of the precious metals can never, for long periods, vary much from the medium rate, or, the rate which is fixed by nature, in the costs of their production. Hence we see, that a provision is made, founded on the self-interest of man, by which any great fluctuation in the exchangeable value of the metals used as a circulating medium, is prevented.

IV. Hence, we also see what *is a real scarcity*, and *what an abundance of money ;* if, by the term *money*, we understand merely a metallic circulating medium.

Money, we have said, is the instrument by which we facilitate exchanges. Now, if we bear this in mind, it is easy to see what is a plenty, and what a scarcity of this instrument. A power-loom is an instrument for facilitating the operation of transforming yarn into cloth. Power-looms are too plentiful, when there are too many to perform the work that is required to be done ; in this case, we can buy them cheap ; that is, we have to give for them a less amount of cotton cloth, or of wool, or of silver. Power-looms are scarce, when there are not enough of them to perform the operations which are required; in this case, we find it difficult to purchase them; they are dear; that is, we are obliged to give for them more than the ordinary amount of cotton, or of wool, or of silver. The case is the same with vehicles for transportation, or with any other instruments.

Now, money is just such an instrument. It is required, to facilitate exchanges. To accomplish a given amount of exchange, a certain value in money is required, and, in ordinary times, this value always exists. And, the exchanges remaining the same, we cannot employ for this purpose more than this amount of value. If a quantity equal to one thousand ounces of silver, or of one thousand bushels of wheat, be required to perform the exchanges of a certain community, we cannot employ more than this amount of value. If we increase the quantity, we shall only decrease the value proportionally. If such a country be insulated from other countries, and we introduce into its circulation one thousand additional ounces of silver, equal to one thousand additional bushels of wheat, the value of the whole two thousand will be just equal to that of the one thousand ounces before; that is, the *value* will not alter. If, on the other hand, from such a country thus insulated, we remove half the circulating medium, the remaining half will accomplish the purpose of the whole; that is, it will double in value. This is evident, because there are neither more nor less exchanges to be made than before, and a variation in the instrument, does not vary the amount of the work which the necessities of the community require to be done. If there be a given amount of yarn to be woven by twenty looms, the quantity will not be increased, by employing forty looms. And, if we employ forty, we must work all of them but half the time; that is, each one will be of half its original value. If the work be doubled, we must work them day and night; that is, each one will be worth twice as much as before. But, manifestly, the quantity of work to be done being given, it can never be affected by varying the quantity of the instruments by which it is accomplished.

Now, suppose the exchanges, in a given community, be equal to fifty millions annually, and that there are required, to effect these exchanges, one million ounces of silver, and that this quantity of silver actually exists in its possession. Under these circumstances, there will be neither a plenty nor a scarcity of money, and it will be neither exported nor imported. But suppose, that, owing to a very productive harvest, or some rapid improvement in the productiveness of human labor, the amount of products to be exchanged arises to seventy-five millions. Here will arise a scarcity of money; there will be more exchanges than can be accomplished by the instrument employed for effecting them. The price of money will rise; in other words, the price of other commodities will fall, and every thing will be cheap; that is, though you cannot purchase more wool, or butcher's meat, or cotton, with a barrel of flour, than you could last year, you can purchase more wool, or meat, or cotton, with the money, which a barrel of flour cost last year. The same result will take place, if, while production continues as active, one half of the specie for any purpose, as the carrying on of a foreign war, were sent out of the country. In this case, as in the other, the price of money will rise; that is, money will be dear, and every thing else will be cheap.

But it is easy to see, on the principles already explained, in what manner this difficulty will be met. In the first place, inasmuch as money prices are lower than any others; that is, as specie retains its former value in all other places, but here, it is dearer: that is, will purchase more than any other commodity; other nations will send specie in exchange. This will be done, until the equilibrium is restored. And thus, this one nation shares the blessing of God's providence with its neighbors, since they receive its productions at a less price. In the second place, something else, as, for instance, notes of hand, will be, in part, substituted for specie; that is to say, as there is too much exchanging to be done in a given time by the instrument, at its utmost power of working, the work is spread over a longer time, and, instead of exchanging for specie now, the parties agree to exchange, but defer the payment for three or six months. Thus, when a weaver is unable to perform the work of his customers to-day, he promises to do it at a subsequent time; and, in the mean while, if his present instrument will not accomplish it, he procures others that will. So, the merchant spreads the exchange of to-day over a larger time, and, in this time, is able to secure the instrument to accomplish the object.

And thus we see, what is also an unusual plentifulness of money. If, while exchanges were at fifty millions, and one million ounces of silver were necessary to effect them, a mine were discovered, by which the quantity in circulation was doubled, the price of silver would fall, and we should give twice the usual price for commodities. Or, if, while the silver remained the same, production, and, of course, exchange, diminished one half, the result would be the same. In this case, as we have already seen, specie would be sent in exchange to other countries, because it was less needed, and its place would be supplied by other productions which were more needed.

Hence we see, that a plenty or a scarcity of money forms no occasion which calls for the interference of government, but that it is a matter, which, if left alone, will regulate itself. When money is really scarce, there is no need of prohibiting its exportation; for no one will be so unwise as to export it. When it is abundant, it is useless to prohibit its exportation, because it cannot be prevented; and because, if it could be prevented, by preventing it, we should deprive ourselves of the only method in our power of alleviating the evils which we suffer. The precious metals are relatively abundant in the states of South America; that is, they need other kinds of capital more than they need this. How absurd would be the policy in them, to forbid their exportation, and thus deprive themselves of all the conveniences of other countries, nay, of the very means on which progress in civilization and the arts, and in the real accumulation of wealth, depends.

Hence we see, that the notion, that the plenty or scarcity of money is an unfailing indication of the prosperity or of the adversity of a country, is, in the highest degree, fallacious. If the scarcity result from an increased productiveness of labor, it is an indication of prosperity; just as the business of weaving is most prosperous, when the weavers have more work than they can do. If it result from a casual withdrawment of specie, it is an ambiguous indication, and its effect upon the country will depend upon the use which is made of that which is sent abroad. If it be employed in wars, or in other unproductive consumption, it is just so much loss; and it matters not whether this amount of loss be in silver, or gold, or copper, or tea, or coffee, or cotton. If it be well invested, and return in the form of a profitable addition to the capital of the country, it is just as much a source of gain, as though the same profit were made upon any other article. It is profitable for an individual to give one thousand dollars for what is worth fifteen hundred dollars, although, for a month afterwards, he be obliged to live somewhat more economically. And what is profitable for the individual, is profitable for the country.

And so of the plentifulness of money. If a mine were discovered, by which the quantity of silver were doubled, and if this silver were produced at a fair profit to the miner, it would be an advantage, inasmuch as it would open a new and profitable method of employing both capital and labor. But, in this case, it could be of use only by its exportation, because, as the number of exchanges in the country has not been increased, only the former amount of value is needed for a circulating medium, and to increase the quantity, will be only to diminish the value. By being sent abroad, capital, in other forms, susceptible of change and increase of value, is imported; and thus, a country is made richer. If the plentifulness be the result of the diminution of exchanges, it is an indication of adversity, because it shows that productiveness has fallen off, that the means of living are less abundant, and that capital is in haste to flee to more congenial climes. When this is the case, it generally springs from oppressive legislation. In this case, it is better for a government to remove the cause, than to aggravate the evil by additional and aggravated wrong. To prohibit the exportation of specie, in such a case, is not only to oppress a human being, but to forbid him the use of any means by which he shall escape from your oppression.

Thus we see, that no indication of the prosperity of a country can be derived, either from the plenty, or from the scarcity of money. The only sure indication of its economical prosperity, is the increase of its productiveness; that is, an increase of the supply of objects of desire, at the same, or at a diminished amount of labor. The increase or diminution of the quantity of specie in circulation, is of importance, only in so far as it indicates this increase of productiveness, and no farther. We estimate a man's prosperity, not by the amount of money in his possession, but by his power to command a larger or a smaller amount of the objects of desire.

V. And hence, we may judge of the truth of that oft-repeated, but worse than puerile maxim, "It matters not what becomes of *property*, so long as the *money* is in the country." If a million of dollars be lost in an unprofitable canal, or ten millions are sunk by a profitless experiment in manufactures, we are told, and even by many persons are expected to believe, that it is all of no consequence; nobody is any poorer, because the money is in the country. That is, if a million dollars' worth of labor and capital have ceased to exist, we are no poorer than we were when this capital was existing, and yielding to its owners, and, of course, to the public, its annual production. If so, why not invest the whole capital in this manner, or why not pay men for throwing it all into the sea? The money was merely the instrument which we used to effect its destruction; and surely, we are but little better off, because the means of destruction remain. If a thief, in the night, had emptied your store-house with a wheelbarrow, you would not be very easily convinced you were no poorer, because he left the wheelbarrow behind him. In the late disastrous fire in New York, it is said that fifteen millions of capital were consumed. I did not hear that any specie was destroyed, and yet, I think it would be difficult to show to the sufferers, that no harm was done, because the money was all in the country. Now, it matters not in what *manner* property is rendered *valueless*, whether by fire, or by folly. It matters not, whether fire does the work for nothing, or whether you hire workmen to do it for heavy wages. It matters not, whether the fifteen millions be turned into ashes, and thus rendered valueless, or whether it be turned into a canal, which is equally valueless. If your store and goods are burned up, you would give away the ashes. If it be turned into a canal, which you would be equally willing to give away, in what respect are you better off in the one case, than in the other?

VI. We have already seen, that the natural price for the precious metals is the cost of their production, and that a given amount of them will be required for effecting the exchanges of the community. Suppose, now, these metals to be indestructible, and unchanged in quantity, and the quantity of other productions annually created, to be, for fifty years, the same; it is evident that specie and other products would, at the end of that time, bear the same ratio to each other, as at present; that is, the money prices of all commodities would remain unchanged. But neither of these is the case. In the first place, the productions of the earth annually increase; this is evident, from the increase of its number of inhabitants. And, on the other hand, the precious metals are annually produced, in large quantities, from the mines. But they are also destructible, and suffer from wear and tear, when used as coin; and they are also consumed in the purposes of the arts. Now, if these two causes exactly counterbalanced each other; that is, if the supply of the precious metals were precisely such as to correspond to the increase of productiveness, and the necessity of increased means of exchange, and to the amount consumed in the arts, prices would still remain as before. If the increase of the metals were not sufficient to supply the increased demand arising from increased productiveness, and other causes, the price of the metals would rise; that is, the price of other things would fall. And if, on the other hand, the increase of the metals were greater than the increase of productiveness, their price would fall;

that is, the price of other things would rise. Now it appears that, previously to the discovery of America, for several centuries, there was no great change in the relative value of specie and that of other commodities. That event, however, by throwing upon the world an immense amount of the precious metals, effected, at once, a great change in their value. As they are but slowly consumed, this diminution of their value continued for some time to increase. This depreciation was still more advanced, by the troubled condition of Europe, which prevented the development of her productive energies; and by the slow progress which she was making in the arts of civilization. But, of late, in consequence of the introduction of machinery and the division of labor, and of improvements in government and legislation, the increase of productiveness has more than kept pace with the increased supply of the precious metals. Hence, of late, prices have fallen; and this has been specially the case, in consequence of the peace of the world, for the last twenty years, since the fall of Napoleon.

These remarks are illustrated by the following facts:

The quantity of wheat, in France, which was exchanged in 1520, for 512 grains of silver, was exchanged in 1536, for 1063 grains; in 1602, for 2060 grains; and, in 1789, for 2012 grains; thus designating a variation in the prices of silver, according to the principles which we have suggested.

Now, as the progress of geology, mining and mineralogy, will probably greatly increase the production of the precious metals in future, it is probable that their price will continue to fall. Hence, when indefinite leases are given, it is wise never to fix a rent at a given amount of silver per annum, but at a given amount of some other less variable product, such as wheat. Or it would, perhaps, be better still, to average the rent at definite periods, on terms which should be equitable, and of which neither party could take any advantage. The oldest professorships in Oxford, were established upon a salary of £40 sterling a year. This was, probably, then sufficient to support a teacher handsomely; and was equal to the rent of an ordinary farm. If a farm had been leased then, at £40 per year, perpetually, the rent, at this time, would have been but a very small part of its value.*

SECTION IV.

OF THE AGENCY OF GOVERNMENT, IN RESPECT TO A CIRCULATING MEDIUM.

We have, thus far, said nothing concerning the agency of government, in respect to a circulating medium. The reason is, that, thus far, the necessity for the exertion of such agency has not been apparent. Two men use money, in exchange, for the same reason that a man uses a hammer for the purpose of driving a nail; because, he thus economises both time and labor. All men use money

* It is difficult to ascertain, with any degree of accuracy, the annual supply and the annual consumption of the precious metals. M'Culloch, a high authority, estimates the supply from the American, European, and Russo-Asiatic mines, at six millions pounds sterling per annum, and the consumption, for the purposes of the arts, at nearly four millions; leaving somewhat more than two millions pounds sterling of silver and gold, for the purposes of coining.

Dictionary of Commerce: Art., "Precious Metals."

in exchanges, for the same reason that all men use hammers for the purpose of driving nails; because they all find that they thus save time and labor.

Had governments no agency at all in the matter, the precious metals, as a circulating medium, might have been both introduced, and universally employed; and they *would* have been so introduced and employed, as they actually *were*, in the time of Abraham. We hence see, as we have before remarked, that a circulating medium derives its use, as money, from its inherent fitness, and the desire of men so to employ it, and not from any agency of government in establishing it. While, however, this is the case, and while this is always to be borne in mind, there is yet some agency, which society, or government, which is its agent, may exert, that shall increase the convenience of whatever may be used as a circulating medium.

This agency has reference to two circumstances.

1. Whenever any substance has been found universally adapted to the purposes of exchange, it is important that it should be used by all men, unless something to the contrary be specified by particular contract. If I owe a man for a hat, and when I come to pay him, he demand payment, not in silver, but in beaver skins, I may not be able to procure them, and he may hold me his debtor, and imprison me accordingly. If I, instead of paying him in silver, offer him leather, and declare that I will pay him in nothing else, he will be defrauded out of his due. Now, to prevent disputes without end, it is desirable that something be fixed upon, of which the tender shall discharge for ever the debtor's obligation. And, as this would most naturally and most justly be the substance, which all men have chosen for a circulating medium, this is, most properly, chosen. Hence, society, or govern-

ment, have a right to establish the precious metals as a *legal tender;* that is, to enact, that if a man declare that I owe him ten dollars, and I offer him ten silver dollars, if he choose not to receive them, I am under no obligation to give myself any more trouble about it. The tender, on my part, is a full release. I am under obligation to offer nothing else; and he has no right to demand any thing else. Nor is there, in this, any oppression. If a man wish to be paid in something besides money, he can always specify it in the contract; and thus his object can be accomplished. The whole effect of such a law is, to prevent disputes, and to enact what shall be a full and valid release from obligation, when nothing specific has been agreed upon.

But, secondly: If any substance be used as a circulating medium, it is evident that its utility will be greatly increased by several circumstances. Of these, the principal are:—

1. That it be of uniform *purity.* Were it otherwise, every piece must be tested by chemical analysis. This would be, of course, impossible; and hence, its utility would be greatly diminished.

2. That it be *divided* into portions of such a size, as shall be most convenient for the purposes of exchange. Were coins a foot in diameter, or as small as the head of a pin, they would, in either case, be almost useless. The former could be used only in large exchanges; the latter would be so small, as to be very frequently lost, and of so small value, as to consume a great deal of time in counting them.

3. That it should be so *prepared*, that each piece shall, on inspection, indicate its value, and also indicate, that no

change has been effected in that value, by design. To give to the precious metals these qualifications, is the intention of coining.

But, it is evident, from a moment's consideration, that the preparation of coin in this manner, for the public use, could never be safely entrusted to *individuals.* The temptations to dishonesty are too great for ordinary human virtue. It is evident, that such a work should be executed by those, whose interest would lead them to perform it with the greatest possible fidelity. Hence it is, that individuals have, in all civilized countries, surrendered the right of coining money to the whole society, that is, to government; and governments have executed it, by means of agents appointed for that purpose. These agents have been always placed under such circumstances, that their interest is strongly on the side of honesty; and the supervision over them is of such a nature, that any failure, either of skill or of integrity, could be easily detected.

Such are the limits, within which the powers of government, in respect to money, are restricted; and such is the reason, for which this power is conferred. Of the manner in which a government should execute this trust, it is only necessary to add a few remarks.

1. It is the business of the government to regulate the purity of money. Inasmuch, however, as this whole power is conferred for the public convenience, the exercise of this power, should never be on the ground of arbitrary enactment, but of public convenience. Thus, as money is liable to loss from wear, and as this loss is rendered less by the addition of a small portion of alloy, which renders it harder; and, also, as the purification of the precious metals from all alloy, would be a process of

great and useless expense, it is for the convenience of all parties, that some portion of alloy should be allowed to remain, when the metal is prepared for coining. The degree of this adulteration should, however, be fixed by law, and should thus be publicly known, and should be invariable.

2. The government should regulate the *form* and *size* of the coin.

1. The *size* of the pieces should be such, as shall best adapt them to the purposes of exchange.

2. Their relative proportions to each other, should be such as to adapt them, most conveniently, to the purposes of enumeration. On this account, the decimal system, adopted by the United States, is probably preferable to any other. The size having been once fixed upon, it should remain invariable.

In respect to the *form* of money, we may add:

1. It should be adapted to convenience for counting. On this account, flat coins are always preferred.

2. It should present the least possible surface to friction. On this account, the thicker the pieces are, the better, provided they be not inconvenient for piling.

3. The whole surface, or so much of it as is possible, should be so ornamented, that if any of the metal should be feloniously filed, or worn away, it may be easily discovered. For the same reason, the edges should always be milled.

4. To reduce the amount of friction, as much as possible, the rim of the edge should be so raised as to protect the face.

It would be of advantage, also, if the amount of pure metal in every piece were always stamped upon its face. This would be an additional check against any interference on the part of government with the purity or the weight of coin. It would also allow persons entering into contracts, to make them, either in weight or in denomination, as they chose; and thus, to give them additional means of protection against interference of this sort, even if it were attempted.

Inasmuch as a piece of metal coined, is worth more than a piece uncoined; that is, as it has an additional value, derived from the means of verification conferred upon it; as this additional value is the property of the owner, and as the conferring of it is a costly operation, it is right that the owner should pay for it. Were nothing charged for it, as it is worth more when coined than when uncoined, when it could not profitably be sent abroad in one form, it might be so sent in the other form; hence, when it could not be sent in bullion, it might be coined, and sent away in money. Hence, there would be, in such a case, a premium given to its exportation. But, on the other hand, the charge for this operation should be just sufficient to defray the expenses of the work. If more than this is charged, so that coining would be a profitable business, it would soon be done by private individuals, for gain; and the country would be flooded with coin made in other countries, and be thus liable to great imposition. The government would thus soon lose the business. If it be done at the lowest practicable price, as no one can make any thing by the operation, all temptation to private coining is taken away.

Inasmuch as money is liable to continual wear from friction, and as it is thus steadily, though slowly, diminished in value, it at last becomes so much worn, as to be unfit for circulation; because its impression is effaced, and also because it contains much less than the standard quantity of metal. When it becomes thus unfit for circulation; on whom is the loss to fall; on the last holder, or on the whole community? Doubtless, on the latter. The last holder has derived no more benefit from it than any one of the thousands of holders, each one of whom has contributed, by using it, to depreciate its value; and there is no reason why he, in preference to any other, should bear the whole loss. In other words, worn-out coin should always be received at the mint, at par, and exchanged for new. This remark, however, should apply only to *worn-out* coin; and not to coin which has been fraudulently diminished in value. Pierced or clipped coin, should not be exchanged. This will tend to prevent every one from receiving it; and will thus tend to keep it in the hands of those who have robbed it of a part of its value.

If such be the agency which a government is called upon to exert, in respect to a circulating medium, it will be seen that it has no right to interfere in any other respects. Hence, for instance:

1. It has no right to prevent the exportation or importation of specie. This, like any other commodity, if let alone, will regulate itself. Specie will never be sent abroad, unless it be for the advantage of the country that it should be so sent abroad. The actual monetary condition of a country cannot be affected by arbitrary acts. Besides, a man has the same right over whatever silver or gold he may possess, as he has over cotton, or wool, or any thing else; and he has just the same right to exchange it *with any one*, and *for any thing*, as he may think for his advantage.

2. A government has no right, *arbitrarily*, to alter the value of money; that is, to say that a dollar shall contain either more or less silver than it now contains. To do so, is, of necessity, to interfere with private contracts; and thus to expose one half of the community, a prey to the dishonesty of the other half. If A have promised to pay B, one thousand dollars; meaning by this, one thousand ounces of silver; and the government enact that the dollar shall hereafter contain only half an ounce of silver, and oblige B to receive half ounces, instead of ounces; they defraud him of precisely half his due. This will be the case, not only with B, but with all the creditors in the whole community. It is just the same interference, as though they should enact, that a debt of one thousand bushels of wheat should be paid with five hundred bushels; or, that a debt of a yard of broadcloth should be paid with half a yard.

If, however, the coin, by *common consent*, is found to need a change of any kind, and the public convenience actually require it, it is to be done by common consent, after sufficient notice of the change has been given, and be so done, that all contracts existing at the time, be left inviolate. If the amount of silver in a dollar, in this country, should ever be changed, it should be effected by exchanging, at the mint, the present dollar at *its* value in silver, for the new dollar, at *its* value in silver; so that all contracts now in existence, should be fulfilled according to the terms of the agreement. A still better method would probably be, to issue a new coin, with another name. This, I believe, has lately been done in Great Britain. Instead of the guinea, of twenty-one shillings, a gold coin, of twenty shillings, has been introduced, called a sovereign.

3. A government, I think, has no right to fix the rela-

tive value between the precious metals. This cannot be done, in fact, because their relative value is liable to continual fluctuation. If both are a legal tender, the debtor has the right of paying in that which he prefers; and, as he may be always expected to choose to pay in the cheaper, he may thus frequently defraud his creditor, to the amount of the fluctuation. It is better to have but one a legal tender, and leave the other, as any other matter of merchandise, to be exchanged by special contract between the parties. In this respect, I think the system of Great Britain preferable to our own. Gold, as has been remarked, is there the only legal tender, for all sums above twenty shillings; and silver, for all sums below that amount. Hence, whenever contracts are made, their amount determines the metal, in which the payment is to be made.

CHAPTER THIRD.

OF A CIRCULATION BY MEANS OF A PAPER CURRENCY.

SECTION I.

OF THE NATURE OF BANKS IN GENERAL.

PART I.

BANKS OF DEPOSIT AND EXCHANGE.

We have already treated somewhat at large upon the subject of division of labor; the circumstances in our constitution by which it is introduced; and the benefits which result to every class of the community from its introduction. We have also seen, that division of labor is always carried on most successfully, when it is united with the use of some natural agent. Thus, in the manufacture of cotton, by the union of steam or water power and machinery, with division of labor, production is greatly increased; and every class of society is enriched. And we have also seen, that the one could not be carried to great perfection, without the employment of the other; and also that, in the nature of things, the one actually suggests and renders necessary the employment of the other.

Now all these remarks apply, with the same force, to the labor of exchange, as to any other labor. From the necessities of society, it is evident that a very large portion of its labor must be the labor of exchange. The increase of this labor would naturally lead to the discovery of some natural agent, by which it might be executed at less expense of time and industry. At first, the rudest instruments, such as cattle, and the baser metals, were employed. These gradually gave place to the more perfect instruments, gold and silver. As the use of this more productive instrument increased very greatly the number of exchanges, and thus required more laborers, instead of fewer, in this department of industry, it was natural, in the next place, that division of labor should be introduced, in order to use the instrument, or natural agent, with the greatest degree of success; and also to accomplish, with a given amount of industry, the greatest amount of product; that is, of exchanges.

Division of labor, in this department of industry, as in every other, has proceeded from rude beginnings, to greater and greater perfection. At first, its benefits were but imperfectly appreciated. By experiment, they were more and more unfolded; and now, although its principles may not be generally understood, yet, it is coming into very general use throughout the civilized world. Instead of banks in none but the great marts of trade, as was the case a century or two ago, we find them, in free states, employed in towns and villages, over the whole community; and, when judiciously administered, their effects are the same upon the small, as upon the great sections of the community.

The word *bank*, is said to be of Italian origin. "In the infancy of European commerce, the Jews in Italy were wont to assemble in the market places of the principal towns, seated on benches, ready to lend money; and the term *bank*, is derived from the Italian word *banco*, a bench." When any of these money-lenders failed, his bench was broken. Hence, the origin of the word *bankrupt*.

1. We have shown how very great, in a civilized country, must be the amount of exchanges. We have also shown, that these exchanges are greatly facilitated, by means of the use of a metallic currency. But it is evident, that were the labor of exchanges to remain at the point to which we have carried it, every individual engaged in this business, would be obliged to keep constantly on hand, a great amount of silver and gold, in order to effect his exchanges. This would very greatly limit the number of exchanges which he could effect, with a given amount of capital. If a merchant were worth one hundred thousand dollars, and were obliged to keep constantly on hand, fifty thousand dollars' worth of gold and silver, he could effect exchanges only with fifty thousand, and must keep fifty thousand dollars constantly idle. If, by any means, he could diminish this amount, by so much as he diminished it, could he increase his amount of exchanges, and, of course, effect them cheaper.

2. Were men thus to keep on hand so large an amount of the precious metals, and actually to make their exchanges by means of metallic transfer, much time would be consumed in transportation. A large number of persons must be employed constantly, in no other business than in carrying silver and gold from one merchant to another, in the same place, and between the merchants in different places.

3. Were exchanges to be made directly, through the medium of money, it is evident that every payment must,

of necessity, be counted by both parties. This, in large payments, would consume much time, and cause great wear and tear of the coin. Were a large mercantile house, which transacts exchanges to the amount of from ten, to one hundred thousand dollars' worth in a day, obliged to count all the money paid and received, every one must see that more than thrice the present number of agents must be employed; and thus, the expenses of the establishment would be greatly increased. The effect of this additional expense for labor, would be very greatly to increase the cost of exchanges; that is, the price of products.

4. The precious metals are small in bulk, and, therefore, are very liable to be stolen. The pieces of the same denomination being of precisely the same form and impression; if stolen, they cannot be identified. Hence, more than usual care is necessary, in order to secure them against robbery. Were every individual, therefore, to keep on his premises, the whole amount of the precious metals necessary to effect his exchanges, every one would be obliged to guard his property with increased vigilance, both by day and by night. He would be his own banker, and must add to his present expenses, all those expenses necessary to the security of a bank.

But let us now see, by how simple an arrangement all these difficulties might be obviated. Suppose this labor were divided, and that all the merchants in a town, instead of being every one his own banker, agreed together to employ a single person to become the banker for all of them. Let us suppose this person to procure a safe repository for all the specie in the neighborhood, and to become responsible for its safe keeping. Suppose, also, that these merchants, instead of keeping their money themselves, all lodged it with him, and that he opened an account with each one, crediting him with whatever he deposited, and debiting him to all that he withdrew; and that every one was at liberty to withdraw, at any moment he chose.

It is manifest that, in such a case, if A owed B one thousand dollars, he would not send to the bank and withdraw the money for B to replace it again, but would give to B an order for one thousand dollars, which B would present to the banker, and the one thousand dollars would be withdrawn from A's account, and added to that of B. If B owed C, he would do the same. C would do the same to D, and perhaps D would owe A, and would pay him in the same manner. At the close of the day, their bank accounts would stand just as they were at the beginning; and yet, there have been four payments made and received, of one thousand dollars each. Yet, not one cent of the specie has been touched. Not a dollar of it has been counted. It has been all done by a few entries made on the books of the bank, and done in a very few minutes. Here, then, we see that the writing of a few lines saves all the labor of repeated transportation, of as frequent counting of coin, and also all the cost of wear which must arise from every such operation. Besides, inasmuch as no more vigilance is necessary to secure from depredation the whole sum of specie than any one part of it, it is evident that great additional labor is saved in this respect also.

But this is not all. We see, from the case above, that at the close of the day, although each one had made a large payment, yet every one stood with the bank, just as he did at the beginning. Though this will not be so in every case, yet it is evident that, supposing no great change in the value of products, such must be the general result. The reason is evident. Every man must sell as much as he buys, and he evidently must buy as much as he sells. When he buys, he pays money; when he sells, he receives money; that is, the money which every man receives, must be as much as he pays away, with the addition of the profit which he has made by the operation. So that, if all the exchanges of one hundred men were made among themselves, and all purchases paid for in cash, and their accounts were all kept at one banking-house, these accounts must all, at the close of every day, very nearly balance each other. Under these circumstances, it would very soon appear, that it was unnecessary to have so large a sum in deposit, in order to meet the emergencies of exchange. Instead of being obliged to have enough there to pay for every purchase, it would be sufficient, if every man had enough to meet any accidental variation between his purchases and sales. Thus, each one would be enabled to withdraw a large portion of his deposit, and employ it in active business. In this manner, the amount of *active* capital in a society would be greatly increased; inasmuch as, he who was formerly obliged to keep on hand, and out of employment, ten thousand dollars, might now accomplish the same purpose with one thousand dollars; and he might employ the remainder in active exchanges. Thus would all exchanges be cheaper, products would be at a lower price, and the whole community would be richer.

Suppose, now, the business of this society to become so extensive, that one banker is unable to transact the operation of all these transfers, and another is also employed, who opens another banking-house on the same principles. If we bear in mind the fact, that the purchases and sales must, in the end, be equal to each other; that is, that every man *receives* as much money as he *pays away*, the transactions of the day must, as before, equalise each other. If both parties transact their business at the *same* bank, this, as it has been just shown, will be the case. If they transact their business at different banks, it will but slightly differ. A pays B in a draft on the first bank, which B deposits in the second bank. B pays C in a draft on the second bank, which C deposits in the first bank. At the close of the day, these banks exchange drafts, and thus, without any labor or counting, or transportation, by merely writing a few words in a bank ledger, the whole transaction is completed. It is hardly possible to find a case, in which, by the division of labor, a greater increase of productiveness is given to human industry.

Now the case will be the same, if banks be established in different cities, or in different countries. It is to be borne in mind, that the sales and purchases of every society, as well as of every individual, must be, substantially, equal. The reason is obvious; for a man can buy only as much as he can pay for; and, as much as he can pay for, he will generally buy; and, if he buy skilfully, he will lose nothing by the exchange. In other words, all exchange is ultimately and substantially exchange in kind. And, as the things exchanged are, at the place of exchange, of equal value, the purchases and sales must be equal to each other. If Boston buy ten million dollars' worth, of New York, it must send ten million dollars' worth with which to pay for it. If both parties made these exchanges by means of money, not only the goods, but also the money, must be transported to and fro, at every exchange. If, however, banks be established in both places, and both parties transacted the payments by means of their agency, all this would be avoided. Thus, for instance, suppose A in Boston sells to B, in New York, ten thousand dollars' worth of domestic cottons; he is entitled to draw on B for that amount; that is, to order him to pay it, to whomsoever he will. Again: Suppose C, in New York, sells to D, in Boston, ten thousand dollars' worth of French silks; he, in like manner, is authorised to draw on D, for that sum. D, in Boston, may buy of A his draft on B, which he sends to his creditor, C. C presents it to B, who pays it at sight; that is, D pays A, and B pays C; and thus these debts mutually cancel each other, and all the labor consists in writing these drafts, sending them by post, and making the necessary entries upon the books of the bank.

We see, therefore, that if the exchanges between two places were equal, by means of banks, the whole business of payment might be made without the transfer of any specie whatever.

But, suppose the business between two places were not equal; that is, suppose that Boston purchased of New York more than it sold to that place; suppose, for instance, that Boston purchased of New York, ten million dollars' worth, and sold to that place only five million dollars' worth. In this case, one half the payments would be made in productions, in the manner we have already suggested. The remaining five millions must, however, be provided for, in some other way. One obvious way would be, to send this remainder in specie. But, it will be asked, how is this five millions of specie to be provided? We answer, by sending the five millions of products, which would otherwise have been sent to New York, to some other place, where specie can be had at the cheapest rate; and thus, paying for what we have purchased at New York, by two exchanges, instead of one. This is one method. Another method would be, for Boston to send five millions of her domestic products to some other market, say to the West Indies, and exchange it for some other product, say coffee, or sugar; and remit these to New York, to pay the balance of her debt. This would be sold, the proceeds deposited in the New York banks, and he who owed the New York merchant, would purchase a draft in Boston, of him who had imported the coffee or sugar; and thus the debt would be liquidated.

Now, it is manifest, that it is, to Boston, of no consequence, in which way she pays this debt; whether by sending directly to New York ten millions of her products; by sending five millions to New York and five millions to South America in exchange for specie; or by sending five millions to New York and five millions to Cuba, in exchange for coffee and sugar. In either case, she pays but ten millions; and the way in which it is paid is a matter of indifference. And, it is also obvious, in which manner Boston will choose to pay her debt. Every one, who has a debt to pay, will pay it in that which will liquidate it at the least expense to himself. If five millions of specie can be procured by four and a half millions of other products, it will be best to pay the debt in specie. If sugar and coffee, worth five millions in New York, can be purchased by four and a half millions' worth in Boston, she will choose to import coffee and sugar, in payment. And thus, the account will be adjusted, in every case, according to the interests and conveniences of the respective parties; that is, of the whole community.

This is the case, if we take into consideration two trading places in the same country. But, the case is the same with the trading cities over the whole world. And, by thus allowing every thing to regulate itself, the whole business of exchange is adjusted.

Suppose, for instance, that Great Britain has purchased of us, more than we receive in return. There will then be a portion of her debt unpaid; and there will then be a demand for something wherewith to pay it. In this case, drafts on America will rise; that is, those who have payments to make, will overbid each other, and drafts will rise in price. In this case, a French merchant, who has sent a cargo of silks to America, will find that he can get more for it, by selling, in London, drafts on his correspondent in New York, than by importing American produce. In this case, he will sell, to the London merchant, drafts to the whole amount of his cargo; that is, England pays France, for sending to America sufficient produce to pay the deficiency which she is unable, profitably, to supply from her own productions. In this manner, the deficiency of the exports of the first country to the second, is made up by the excesses of a third; and, as every one receives as much as he pays out, and imports, on the whole, as much as he exports, by free communication among themselves, the balance is speedily adjusted.

Hence, bills of exchange, or orders of payment for goods already delivered at any particular place, become an article of merchandise, as much as any thing else. If I send a cargo of cotton to Liverpool, and I can get more for the orders to pay the amount of it to some one, there, than for produce which I might bring back in return, I shall dispose of it in that manner; that is, receive from some one, perhaps a South American merchant, who is obliged to make payments in London, more than I should gain by the return cargo. In this case, I order my ship to return in ballast, or else to bring out a freight for some one who wishes to transport goods to this country, from Europe. This being the case, it is of importance that some persons should devote themselves to this branch of labor. By these means, both parties know how they can be best accommodated. The sellers know when to sell, and the buyers, when to purchase. This business is carried on, to a considerable degree, by banking institutions, and by men who devote themselves to the buying and selling of exchange. Those who transact this business, however, transact it, to a great degree, through the agency of banks, by means of the facilities derived from which, they are enabled to accomplish it, with vastly less expense of time and labor.

Such, I suppose to be some of the principal functions of banks, as offices of deposit. They, by means of division of labor, diminish the amount of the circulating medium necessary to carry on the exchanges of a country; they greatly diminish the labor of transportation and of counting money, in the same place, and almost remove the necessity of transporting it between different places.

The Bank of Amsterdam was purely a bank of deposit. It received the specie of the merchants of the city, and gave them acknowledgments, which were transferable, like specie; and by the transfer of these, on the books of the bank, all large payments were universally made. And, so great was the confidence in the management of the bank, that certificates of these deposits were current throughout Europe. Adam Smith attributes the origin of this bank, to the desire of the Dutch to prevent their coin from migrating into the surrounding states, and being replaced by the inferior and debased coin, with which they were liable to be inundated. That this might have been the idea, from which the first conception of such a bank originated, is very possible. But, whoever will observe the advantages of such an institution, as they have been stated above, must be aware, that when the transactions of a commercial city became numerous, and the exchanges became active, merchants could not long fail of falling upon some instrument which their necessities so imperatively required, and which all their habits of thought would be so likely to suggest.

From what has been said, it is obvious that when all

other methods fail of adjusting the differences of exchange between two places, specie must be procured, and remitted from the one to the other. This will *always* pay the debt, and equalise the exchange. Hence, the highest rate of exchange, which, under natural conditions, is possible, between two countries, is that which is sufficient to procure the specie, and to remit it to the place of payment.

PART II.

OF BANKS OF DISCOUNT, OR LOAN.

We have already seen, that all production is the result of the application of industry to capital. But, we also see, that the capital and the industry are frequently in the hands of different persons. One has capital, but does not wish to labor with it himself. Another has industry and skill, but has no capital, with which to create products. It will be at once seen, that it will be a great advantage to both parties, if the capitalist can loan his capital to the laborer, and receive from him a fair compensation; while the laborer, by uniting capital with his industry, will be able, after paying this compensation, to retain a handsome remuneration for himself.

For the accomplishment of this result, the introduction of a circulating medium presents great facilities. A flour merchant might have more flour than he wished, and would be willing to loan it to another person, who wished to establish himself in business; but, perhaps, the person who applies to him for the loan, understands nothing but the trade in iron. The capital of the one, therefore, in this case, could be of no service to the other. But, let the flour merchant convert his flour into money, and then he can loan it to any one who needs it, no matter what may be the occupation in which he hopes to be the most successful.

As men accumulate capital, they are enabled thus to loan. There are always multitudes of persons who wish to borrow. But, he who is willing to loan, is also frequently engaged in active business, and can rarely take pains to ascertain the character of the borrower; neither may he have any means of so observing his affairs, as to secure himself, in season, against the results of dishonesty. Hence, his risk of loss would be great; the rate of interest high; the time requisite to effect and to watch over loans, great; and, there would be, on the part of the capitalist, but little disposition to part with the immediate control of his means.

Thus, also, if a laborer wished to borrow of a private capitalist, he would not know, to whom to apply; much time would be lost in finding a capitalist; and, if the capitalist were timid and suspicious, it might be utterly impossible to satisfy him that the security was sufficient, unless it were in property with which he was acquainted; or, unless the money were to be employed in operations with which he happened to be conversant. Thus, a great inconvenience would be suffered, both by those who were willing to lend, and by those who wished to borrow money; that is, capital.

Now, it is obvious, that these inconveniences would be greatly relieved, if, by a division of labor, some persons were set apart for the express purpose of loaning money.

In this case, those who had more capital than they wished to employ, would exchange it for money, and place it in the hands of the money-lender; and those who wished to borrow, would go to him for such accommodations as they needed. He would attend to the whole business of loaning, and collecting both the principal and the interest, and would pay the interest over to the capitalist, receiving for himself a fair compensation for his expenses, labor and skill.

In this manner, banks perform the service of bringing together the lenders and borrowers, so that he who has any thing to lend, can lend it, if there be any one who wishes to borrow; and so that he, who wishes to borrow, can borrow, provided there be any one who wishes to lend. And thus, by bringing the wants of both parties to act upon each other, each has the advantage of loaning or of borrowing, on the most favorable terms.

Nor is this all. When this is once accomplished, the whole may be done, in the shortest possible time; because, the greatest part of the time, without such an arrangement, would be spent in bringing together two individuals who could agree upon the loan in question. Hence, a negotiation, which might otherwise have taken half a day from the labor of both parties, may now be perfected, in a very few minutes. This is a great saving of time and labor, and contributes greatly to the punctuality of the whole community, which is a still farther saving of time and capital.

Besides, we have already shown that when a man devotes himself to any occupation, and does nothing else, he will acquire a skill which can never be attained by him who only practises it occasionally. This principle applies, with full force, to the present case. He, whose only business it is to loan money, will keep himself, at all times, acquainted with the state of the money market; he will ascertain the character and responsibility of the individuals who are requesting loans; he will be the first to ascertain the indications of their failure, either in skill or in fidelity; and will, therefore, be the best prepared to decide, whether it be necessary to withdraw capital from a debtor. This will be especially the case, if there be interested in the management of the funds thus collected, several men engaged in the general monetary operations, and who, therefore, are likely to collect all the information on these subjects, that may, at any time, be afloat in the mercantile community.

Such is the nature of banks, as offices of discount. Some of the private banks of Great Britain, are of this character. They issue no notes of their own, but merely negotiate the bills of other banks, or of the Bank of England. Of the same nature, to some degree, are savings banks; of which the object is, to collect the capital from small owners, and loan it out, at interest, for their benefit.

OF BANKS OF CIRCULATION, OR ISSUE.

If banks were established on the principles which we have suggested, and if the depositors and contributors placed, in the hands of the banker, metallic currency, it is evident that the bankers or bank would soon collect the greater part of the metallic currency in the country. Now, were this the case, it is evident that they might do a very considerable service to the community, by furnishing the depositor, a certificate of deposit, which he might use, instead of the money which he had deposited. Thus, if I had deposited one thousand dollars in a bank in Providence, and wished to use it in New York; if their certificate that they owed me so much money, were as good in New York as the specie, the carrying of this piece of paper, or the sending it by mail, would save all the trouble and risk of carrying the specie. If he who wished to send the same sum of money to Providence, did the same, the exchange of these obligations by the respective banks, would perform the whole operation of the exchange. Or, the same might be accomplished, if the bank, upon sufficient security, loaned to me its obligation to pay on demand, and allowed me to use this obligation, in any place where it might be for my interest to do so. And, still more readily might this be done, if a number of individuals had deposited, in the bank, specie, for the purpose of having it loaned, at stated rates, to any persons who could offer a reasonable guaranty that whatever was borrowed, would be, at an appointed time, refunded. It is always to be understood, that the bank obliges itself, in all cases, to pay these obligations to the bearer, on demand, in the precious metals; and that hence, these notes represent the value in the precious metals, which their obligation designates. And thus, from the nature of the case, a large amount of the money in circulation, would soon become specie certificates, or notes of obligation of the bank. And they would get rapidly into circulation, because of their greater convenience for transportation; their diminished liability to robbery; and the greater ease, with which they could be identified, in case they were stolen.

But still further. It is manifest that many of these bills thus issued by banks, in this condition, would never require to be repaid in specie, but would be cancelled by an equal amount of similar bills from other banks. Again: Of those which required to be so paid, it is impossible that that they would all require to be paid, at the same instant. And, yet more: As some persons were receiving payments in specie, other persons would also be depositing specie, which would make good the deficiency which this withdrawal occasioned. Hence, from these causes combined, it is evident that a bank thus constituted, might, without violating its engagement to pay every certificate or bill in specie, issue a larger amount of such obligations, than it at any time contained of specie in its vaults. And, inasmuch as it redeemed every such note on demand, with the precious metals, these notes would have, in exchange, the same value as the precious metals, every where in the immediate vicinity of the bank; and they might have the same value in other places, if this bank were in correspondence with other banks of the same character, in the different places with which its customers transacted business.

Inasmuch as these notes possess some considerable advantages over specie; that is, as they are lighter, occupy less bulk, and are equal in exchangeable value to specie, they would be commonly preferred. That they are so preferred, every one proves, every day, by his own conduct. When we take a check to the bank, and can receive for it, either notes of the bank or specie, we never take the specie, except in such quantities as may be required for small exchanges. When we travel, we prefer the bills of the United States Bank, to specie, and would commonly give a small premium for them, in preference to specie, if they could not be obtained at any other rate. From these reasons, it is manifest, that under such circumstances, a large portion of the currency in a country, when banks were established which had the confidence of the community, would become paper, instead of metal.

Now, banks, in this country, and in Great Britain, generally perform all three of these functions. They receive and pay out money on deposit, and keep all the accounts necessary to these transactions; they loan money at interest, and collect monies so loaned; and they also issue their own promissory notes, payable in specie, on demand.

We shall close this section, by a brief notice of the manner in which banks are created in this country, and a statement of their sources of profit.

Banks, in this country, are chartered incorporations; that is, the privilege of banking is conferred on several associated individuals, by a special act of legislation. By these acts, banking companies are entitled to certain privileges, are subject to certain forms of legislative inspection, and are restricted, in their operations, within such limits as the wisdom of the legislature may see fit to impose. These privileges generally refer either to the mode of collecting their debts; or to the limit of the liability of the individuals, in case of failure; or to the power of issuing bills on demand. And the restrictions limit the amount of their circulation, in proportion to their actual captital, or their specie in actual possession.

When any number of persons desire to be incorporated as a banking company, they present a petition to the legislature of the state in which they reside, praying for such privilege. If the prayer be granted, they are thus incorporated, and the amount of their capital is fixed in the act. This sum is divided into shares, or equal portions, of such amount as may be supposed best suited to answer the wants of the community. At a given time and place, publickly notified, books are opened for subscription; that is, every one is allowed to subscribe for as many shares as he wishes. When the necessary amount is bespoken, the subscribers are called *stockholders*, as the shares are commonly, in mercantile language, called *stock.* The stockholders now meet, and choose, from their number, certain persons to conduct the operations of the bank, who are called *Directors*, and the whole of these together, are called the *Board of Directors*. These directors then choose, from their own number, a *President*, and some person not of their number, as *Cashier*. On these two last mentioned persons, the active duties of conducting the affairs of the bank depend; though the directors meet, at stated times, for the purposes of general consultation, and especially to decide upon the commercial character of those, to whom they are requested to loan their money.

The bank is thus organised. The subscribers are now required to pay to the cashier the sums which they have subscribed for; that is, that portion of the amount, which each has agreed to invest in the general business of the bank. Suppose the capital were one hundred thousand dollars, and each share were one hundred dollars, there would then be one thousand shares, and might be one thousand stockholders. As soon as each one had paid the portion for which he had subscribed, one hundred thousand dollars would be collected in the banking house, and this would be the capital, with which they would be prepared to commence their banking operations.

The manner in which these operations are conducted, is something like the following: The bank loans its own bills, payable in specie, to those who wish to borrow, and receives the notes of individuals, of equal amount, in return, and charges them interest, which is paid in advance. The payment of these notes is always guarantied by some other person or persons, called *endorsers*. The ordinary period of loan, is thirty or sixty days; at the close of which time, the notes are required to be paid, either in whole, or in part, at the discretion of the directors.

Hence, if it were necessary, the whole affairs of the bank might be closed; that is, all its bills might be called in, and all the notes it has received might be given up, and the bank remain as it was when it commenced, with the addition of whatever interest it might have acquired, in thirty or sixty days.

Suppose, now, the capital of the bank were all paid in, in specie, and that it issued notes only to the precise amount of its capital. In this case, there would be a double and full guaranty for the payment of all its bills. The first guaranty would be the specie in its vaults, equal to the amount of all its bills in circulation; that is, for every note it issued, there could be shown an amount of silver or gold, equal to what it had promised to pay. The second guaranty would be, the notes of the individuals, of substantial responsibility, for an amount greater than all the bills which the bank has issued, by the interest which was deducted from the note when it was received. Thus, suppose the capital of the bank to be one hundred thousand dollars, and that this has all been paid in specie. The bank loans one hundred thousand dollars of its notes, and receives one hundred thousand dollars' worth of the notes of individuals of sound pecuniary ability. The bank is then liable to pay one hundred thousand dollars, and it has, wherewith to pay it, two hundred thousand dollars; that is, one hundred thousand dollars in specie, and one hundred thousand dollars of the notes of individuals. I think that every one would be inclined to say, that such a bank was not only safe, but even superfluously safe. If *all the debtors failed*, and nothing was received for its issues, yet its notes would be safe; for it would still have, in its vaults, sufficient to meet every demand, as soon as presented, even if all its bills were presented for payment at *the same instant.*

Now, inasmuch as one perfect security is as safe as two, and, as this security is *more than* perfect, it might be diminished, and yet the bills of the bank be perfectly safe. Thus, it is morally certain, that all the bills of the bank can never be presented for payment at the *same instant.* If this can never be the case, as its debtors are continually paying back what they have borrowed, and, as it has, always, as much less to redeem, as it has already redeemed, it is manifest, that with something less than the amount of specie designated by its notes, it may always be prepared to meet every demand that may be made upon it. Again: If all its debtors failed, it would still have, in its specie, if equal to its bills in circulation, enough to redeem all its issues. But, with any tolerable management, its debtors would not *all* fail. It would be a very unusual occurrence, if one half of them failed. The bank would be then perfectly secure, if the proportion of its specie capital, in actual possession, were sufficient to pay all deficits which could arise, from the failure of its debtors. Hence, we see, that the security of a bank would always be perfect, if it always possessed enough, in specie capital, to redeem every bill as soon as it was presented, and also sufficient to guaranty the holder, against any injury which it might suffer, from the failure of its customers; that is, if there existed this ratio between the issues of the bank, and the capital in its vaults, such a bank would be of undoubted security.

If it went beyond this ratio, and just in proportion as it went beyond it, there would be danger that its notes would not be redeemed in specie; hence, that they would be of imperfect value, or even be valueless, and thus, that the holders of them would lose, to the full amount of their depreciation. Thus, we see, in general, if the capital in specie were equal to the circulation, though all the debtors of the bank failed, the holders of its bills would lose nothing, but the stockholders would lose all their contributed capital. If all the specie were stolen, and the bills were all paid, the holders would lose nothing, but the stockholders would lose all. But if there had been fraud, at the commencement, and no capital had been contributed, if the debtors of the bank all failed, the *holders* of the notes would lose *all*, and the stockholders would lose nothing. And, in general, if the debtors of the bank failed, the holders of the notes could lose nothing, unless the deficit thus created, were more than sufficient to consume all the actual capital of the bank. The capital of the bank, is the guaranty for the payment of all the notes which the bank has taken in exchange for its own bills; and, hence, the holders of these bills cannot suffer, until all this capital be first exhausted.

OF THE SOURCES OF THE PROFITS OF BANKS.

1. From deposits. As banks are extensively used for this purpose, they must have on hand, at all times, a considerable amount from this source, lying idle. This may be considered a part of their capital, which they may use in their business. If a bank have, on an average, fifty thousand dollars of deposits, it may issue bills to the amount of fifty thousand dollars beyond the amount which would otherwise be in its power, because, it has this additional amount of means wherewith to meet the demands made upon it. The first source of profit, is, therefore, interest gained on deposits.

2. From exchanges. As these are to be made between different places, and as they must be made in drafts or in specie; if two banks, in different places, undertake to transact this business in concert, they may greatly facilitate the means of payment between two places. For this

accommodation, they charge a per centage, varying with the rate of the market. This is another source of revenue.

3. From interest on notes discounted; that is, on its regular loans. This is its great source of revenue. The manner of this has been already explained.

4. As, from what has been said, it is evident that a bank may safely loan an amount of its notes, greater than that of its capital, the interest of this excess, is an additional source of revenue. Thus, if a bank have one hundred thousand dollars paid in, and issue notes to the amount of one hundred and twenty-five thousand dollars, it receives interest on twenty-five thousand dollars more than its stockholders have deposited. This is an addition to its revenue, by its amount, whatever it may be.

SECTION II.

OF THE UTILITY OF BANKS.

In stating the nature of banks, in the preceding section, we have, to a considerable extent, unfolded the principles on which their utility depends. The subject is, however, susceptible of a more ample development. We shall, therefore, pursue it through the present section.

We have shown that the functions of banks were of three kinds: *First*, As institutions of *deposit; Secondly,*

As institutions of *discount or loan;* and, *Third,* As institutions of *circulation.* We shall proceed to consider their *utility,* in each of these three respects.

I. *The utility of banks, as institutions of* DEPOSIT.

The utility of banks, in this respect, is derived from the saving of labor. They save the labor of transportation, of counting, and of vigilance. Of the manner in which this is done, I do not know that any thing further need be said. In so far as this is concerned, all that is necessary to be done, is, so to conduct their arrangements as to increase their utility in the greatest possible degree.

In so far as a bank is intended for a place of deposit for the circulating medium of any *particular community,* the arrangements which need be attended to, will at once suggest themselves. For instance, its location should be such, as to accommodate the greatest number of its customers. Its hours of business should be the same as those of the mercantile community. Its affairs should be conducted with the greatest possible regularity. Mistakes frequently produce the same effect as fraud, and they always present, either to the one party, or the other, a great temptation to it. The physical and moral security of the institution, should be as great as possible. Hence, a banking-house should possess every practicable security against fire and robbery; and, if necessary, should be always under the protection of a guard. Such is the case with the Bank of England. The officers of the bank, whether chief or subordinate, should be persons of tried integrity, and should also be so arranged in respect to each other, that collusion should, if possible, be impracticable; and their whole affairs should be so under the inspection of those, whose interest it is to detect any fraud, that dishonesty might be as difficult as possible. The chief officers should be men of property, so that their own interests would suffer more than they could gain, by any violation of faith.

The necessity of all these provisions will be at once apparent. It is for the interests of the community, as well as of the bank, that every one should transact his business by means of a bank; that is, that he should receive and pay money through means of its agency. But, no one will employ this agency, unless he is certain that his money will be appropriated as he directs, and that nothing shall be lost, either by carelessness or by dishonesty.

But, banks, as institutions of deposit, are designed also to facilitate the payments of money in *different places*, and, in the same manner, and on the same principles, to labor in transportation, counting and vigilance, and to diminish the amount of the circulating medium necessary, in order to carry on the exchanges of the community.

Thus, if a merchant in Boston pay one thousand dollars into a bank in that city, he sends the note of that bank to New York in payment of his goods. If the bank in Boston, be in correspondence with one in New York, the owner of the draft may apply to that bank in New York, and receive the money there, by paying the difference of exchange, if, at that time, there be any; that is, the bank at New York buys his bill, and, it then possesses one thousand dollars in the bank at Boston. If a merchant in New York have one thousand dollars to pay in Boston, he again purchases of the same bank, the draft on Boston, which it may have bought, perhaps, the day before. This is now sent to his creditor, who presents it at the Boston bank, and receives his payment accordingly. The same result would be accomplished at the bank at either place, bought drafts known to be good, but payable by other persons besides the banks. And still further, if two banks were well acquainted with the resources of each other, and were each confident that all the debts of the other would be paid, they might give orders on each other, for the facilitating of exchange. Thus, if A wished to pay money in New York, and a bank in Boston were authorised to draw on New York, it might furnish him with a draft which would be paid in New York, and receive the difference of exchange; and the same operation being performed by the bank in New York, each would receive, at every transaction, a moderate per centage, and yet add greatly to the convenience of the community.

On this account, I suppose it would be much better, to have several banks nearly connected, as the branches of a large bank; than to have them isolated, and independent of each other. When banks are, in some measure, responsible for each other, they must become acquainted with the standing of each other, and will, of course, be disposed to check each other's excessive transactions. Hence, they will also be more likely to give to each other every reasonable credit. When, on the contrary, each one is entirely isolated from all the rest, and no one bank either knows, or has a right to know the condition of the other; each is naturally fearful of the solvency of the rest; and thus, may not be willing to afford those facilities of exchange, which the transactions of commerce require. Hence, the price of exchange is liable to rise unnecessarily high; and, of course, an unnecessary expense is imposed upon the trading community. It is by means of its system of branches, and the supervision which it thus exerted over them, that the late United States Bank was enabled to carry on, so extensively, the business of exchange, with great profit to itself, and with great benefit to the community. Were banks, in general, constructed more upon this plan, I think it would greatly facilitate the business of exchange.

II. *The advantages of banks, as institutions of* DISCOUNT AND LOAN.

1. It may be proper to suggest, at the beginning of our remarks on this head, that banks add nothing to the capital of a country. Capital has been already defined. It is either the material on which industry operates, the instruments with which it operates, or the means of sustentation, by which it is supported during the operation. The capital of any country, at any one moment, consists of the amount of these which it then possesses. Now, it is evident, that the collecting this in one place, rather than in another; the loaning of it to one, rather than to another; or the loaning of it, instead of not loaning it at all; or the manufacture of printed or of written promises to pay money or any thing else; can never increase the capital, that is, the wealth, or the amount of objects of desire, possessed by any country. A man is surely no richer, because he *verbally* promises to pay me one hundred dollars; nor am I any the richer for his promise. And, if neither he nor I be the richer, I see not who else can be the richer for it. And, if he actually lend me one hundred dollars, and I return it, at the end of the week, if I have used it profitably, the capital of the country has taken a different direction from that which it would have taken; that is, it has been in my hands, instead of being in the hands of some one else, but this is all. The capital is the same, except that my industry may have added somewhat to it. Could a nation, or an individual, become rich by the issue of promissory notes, no one who could write a promissory note, ever need be poor. But it is manifest that this is not one of the methods by which the capital, that is, the objects of

desire, is, in our present state, to be increased. This subject is so obvious, that it seems really almost unworthy of serious consideration. The above remarks, however, have been made, because the contrary notion has been so frequently maintained, and even so frequently acted upon, to the great detriment of the commercial interests of the community. No one, who has the least practical acquaintance with the functions of capital and of money, can candidly reflect upon the subject for a moment, without coming to a correct conclusion.

2. But whilst it is allowed that banks add nothing to the existing capital of a country, it is also true that *they are capable of rendering the existing capital much more productive.* In this manner, the practical result may, to some extent, be the same as though they actually increased the capital of a country. If one million of capital be capable, under ordinary circumstances, of producing two hundred thousand dollars of annual revenue; and if, by means of any improvement in the manner of its distribution, it can be made to produce three hundred thousand dollars, the annual resnlt is the same as if, under the previous circumstances, the capital had been increased to a million and a half. And, it is because banks have frequently thus increased the productiveness of capital, that the notion has arisen, that they increase the capital of a country itself.

The manner in which banks may increase the productiveness of capital, will then be the subject for our present consideration.

Banks increase the productiveness oi capital, chiefly, by the facilities which they afford for *the extension of credit.* The *nature of credit* is, however, first to be considered.

"Credit is the term used to express the trust or confidence placed by one individual in another, when he assigns him money or other property in loan, or without stipulating for its immediate payment. The party who *lends*, is said to *give* credit, and the party who *borrows*, to *obtain* credit."*

That the extension of credit, in every manner which can be rendered consistent with the safety of the lender, must increase the productiveness of capital, may be seen from the following considerations:

1. It is manifest, that the labor of man, without tools, must be, in the smallest degree, productive. What man, by the mere labor of his *hands*, without tools, could ever maintain a family, or even maintain himself? Without an axe, he could neither cut nor cleave wood; without a hod, he could not even carry mortar. He could add but very little to productiveness, and hence, his revenue from that which was added, must be reduced to the lowest limit. But give him tools; that is, capital; and the productiveness of his labor, is at once greatly increased. As he receives an equitable share of this productiveness, his wealth is also increased. Thus, by the use of a small portion of capital, both he, and the community; that is, every individual; are rendered richer.

2. But this is not all. A man may have skill and instruments, but he may not have the material, on which to exert his industry. In this case, his industry and instruments will be useless. Thus, a cabinet-maker may possess both skill and tools, but if he have no mahogany upon which to labor, all his skill will be of no value. If he can procure materials, he can, by a week's labor, add

* M'Culloch.

very considerably to the total wealth, both of the community and of himself. A blacksmith may have skill and tools, but if he can procure neither iron nor coal, his skill and tools are valueless, Let him possess iron and coal, and his industry and skill will not only support him, but render the annual revenue of the society much greater. A merchant may have skill in the business of exchange, which might be a great saving to a whole neighborhood, but if he have no means of procuring a stock of goods with which to commence exchanges. his skill will add nothing to the wealth of the community. And thus, we see, that in order for the industry and skill of the community to operate most productively, it must be universally united with capital.

But, it may be said, let all these operatives labor in the employment of those who possess capital, until they have acquired sufficient to commence production on their own account. This, to a considerable extent, is always done; and, by this means, the productiveness of a country is annually increased. It may be proper, however, to show in what manner, by a different arrangement, and a wider dissemination of the benefits of capital, productiveness may be more rapidly increased.

I. *As to Capitalists.*

1. Were this plan universally adopted, it would oblige capitalists either to extend their business beyond their wishes, or else to leave many laborers unemployed. If a capitalist loaned nothing, he must invest all his annual revenue in the business of his own profession. Were he successful, in this manner, he would, in the course of years, be obliged so to enlarge all his means of production, that a large part of his affairs must be managed by subordinate agents.

2. The talent for conducting large transactions, is by no means universally possessed. Many men, who are capable of superintending an establishment of ten thousand dollars per year, would be utterly incapable of conducting one, of one hundred thousand dollars per year. And, in general, in proportion to the number of grades of agency necessary to the management of any concern, the ratio of profit diminishes.

3. Suppose capitalists always to employ their own capital, the burden of every man's business would increase with his years; and thus, the older he grew, and, of course, the more unfit for business, the more intolerable would the pressure of business become. This is unnatural. As a man advances in years, and is less adapted to labor, he is disposed to retire from it, and to seek for some method in which, without *active* employment, he may reap the advantage of his previous industry and frugality.

II. *As to Laborers.*

1. A laborer will work with skill and success, just in proportion to the personal advantage which he reaps from his own labor. Now, every one must perceive, that these inducements will operate with more success, when he is laboring with his own capital and reaping all the advantage of his skill, than when he is laboring upon the capital of another, and is paid only at a stipulated price. A hundred men, each possessing a capital of two hundred dollars, allowing each one to select his own place for labor, would add much more to the annual revenue of a country, than one hundred men, all laboring in the same place, under an employer, who himself owned the whole twenty thousand dollars.

2. Besides, were capital thus to accumulate, in a few

hands, it would confine the operations of industry to a few places, and thus materially add to the cost of productions, and diminish the conveniences of the community. Many of the trades require to be conducted very near to the residence of the consumer. The blacksmith, the carpenter, the cabinet-maker, the shoe-maker, the baker, and the retail merchant, must reside in the midst of the community for whom they labor. Were capital always to be employed by those who own it, it would, of necessity, be collected into large masses, and the consumer would lose a great deal of time in procuring the product which he needed. The farmer would be obliged to go to the city to have his horse shod or his plough mended, and thus, the labor of transportation, and the consumption of time would be greatly increased.

From these reasons, I think it evident that the productiveness of a country must be greatly increased, by any means which shall enable the skilful and industrious, in any profession, to obtain the use of capital, by means of which, they may labor on their own account, and, in any place which presents the strongest inducements of personal interest. They will thus produce more abundantly, and enrich more rapidly, the country, as well as themselves. And, if such arrangements can also be made, that those who loan them the capital shall be perfectly secure, it will be a mutual advantage to the capitalist and to the laborer. While the laborer is improving his condition, the capitalist is also enjoying, in security, the benefit of his former industry; and thus, without laboring himself, is enjoying all the advantages of labor. And, I believe, that arrangements of this kind are commonly found to be more advantageous to a capitalist, than to continue in active business. The general opinion of mercantile men, is, I think, that men in declining years, are more likely to lose, than to gain, by continuing in business beyond the period of active enterprise. The last ten years of a life, have frequently been destructive of the results of all the labors of the forty previous years.

The same principles apply to merchants, and to all other persons employed in active business. And hence we see, in general, that it is by means of credit, that those who possess more capital than they wish personally to employ, may, without labor, derive from it an equitable revenue; and that those who have less capital than they can profitably employ, may procure the use of such capital as they wish, and may thus be enabled to enjoy the full benefit of their skill and industry. It is thus that a poor man, with industry and skill, is enabled, at once, to reap all the advantages of riches; and a rich man, whose power of labor is past, to reap, to a considerable degree, the advantages of industry and skill. The benefit, to both parties, is great and mutual. And, it is manifest, that any institution, which contributes to accomplish such a result, must be of material service to the community.

Now, banks are such institutions. They stand in an intermediate place, between capitalists and laborers; and enable both to derive advantage from each other.

They do this, in the following ways:

I. They collect together, capital, which would, otherwise, be scattered and useless.

1. This has been, in part, illustrated before. The greater the difficulties of loaning, the less will always be the amount loaned. If he who has a few hundred dollars to loan, is obliged to wait until some one calls for it, it will lie, for the greater part of the time, idle. And, if he be obliged to observe the circumstances of a debtor, of

whom he may know very little, the time and labor thus spent will frequently be as valuable as the interest he is to receive. Hence, a large amount of capital will always remain unproductive; and, consequently, a large amount of industry, which might have been rendered productive by means of it, will languish.

2. But this is not all. A large amount of capital is always in the possession of widows, minors, and aged persons, who are unable to unite with it, that labor which is necessary for its productiveness. These persons can neither labor with it themselves; nor are they capable of superintending the loaning of it, either safely or profitably. Hence, the fear of losing all will deter them from loaning, and they will hoard it, and live upon the principal, until it is all spent, and they are reduced to poverty. Thus, the property which might have been useful to others, and might have supported themselves without any diminution of its amount, is, in a few years, dissipated; and the gains of a previous life, instead of being added to the capital of a succeeding generation, are abstracted from it for ever.

3. There is always, in every community, a large number of persons who are engaged in active industry, but whose gains cannot at present, and sometimes cannot at all, be invested in their employment. Such are laborers, whose gains cannot be of service to them, until they have accumulated a considerable sum. A laboring farmer, who saves from fifty to one hundred dollars a year, cannot, with this, buy a farm, until he have accumulated the earnings of several years. He cannot conduct a farm, profitably, upon borrowed capital, because the income of agriculture will rarely allow of it. If he can invest these gains as they accrue, and receive interest for them, they will annually add to his stock. If he cannot thus invest them, they must lie idle, doing good neither to himself, nor to

any one else. The same is the case with mechanics, and various other laborers.

Besides these, there is a very large class of the community whose employment cannot be increased by the addition of capital. The merchant can, by investing his annual gains in his stock in trade, increase his sales, and, of course, his profits. But, how can the physician, or the lawyer, or the clergyman, or any person who is paid by salary, do this? Hence, if there be not some means by which these annual gains can be conveniently collected and invested, they will be either foolishly squandered as fast as they arise, or they will be hoarded without any annual profit, either to their owner or to the community.

Now, for these evils, a bank provides the remedy. The stock of a bank is all divided into shares, of such amounts, that they are within the purchase of most persons who may wish to invest their capital. These shares are always for sale, at a price regulated by the interest which they annually pay. He who has one hundred dollars to invest, purchases one hundred dollars' worth of bank stock; that is, he invests one hundred dollars in the bank, in the place of the person who formerly owned this portion of the capital of the bank. He receives interest on this one hundred dollars, from the day he purchases it, until the day on which he sells it again. When he has accumulated any thing more, he purchases in like manner. And thus, he has a safe place of investment for all his gains, where they are both held securely, and without any trouble to him, and where they also pay him an annual revenue. When he wishes to withdraw these funds, and to appropriate them to some other use, he sells his stock; that is, some one becomes one of the stockholders, instead of himself; and he thus receives back the money which he formerly paid in. These shares are, every day, to be bought and sold in the market; and hence, he can, generally, invest or withdraw his money, any day in the year, at an hour's warning.

On this account, it will at once be evident, that the shares of banks should be of such amount as will best accommodate the communities for whose benefit they are specially designed. When they are intended for capitalists, they may as well be large as small. But when they are for the benefit of those who have but small amounts to invest at one time, they should be small. They will, in this manner, enable persons of small means, the more easily to invest; and, on account of this increased convenience, as their stock will be more eagerly sought for, it will bear a higher price in the market.

The utility of banks would be still further increased, if, besides this mode of investment, they were in the habit of receiving small deposits on interest, which might remain with them, to be drawn for, at the pleasure of the owner. Many persons, having small amounts of property to invest, are unacquainted with the process of buying and selling bank shares, and thus, either spend their money thoughtlessly, or allow it to lie idle. Were banks to receive all such sums on deposit, and allow for them a lower interest than they charge their customers, they might thus conduct a profitable business as the loaners of money for the public, and redeem a large amount of capital from unproductiveness. This is the practice of the banks in Scotland.

It is true, that this is accomplished, to a considerable degree, by the savings banks. But these might still be very useful, by receiving money in smaller sums than those received by the bank, and it might remain with them, until it became large enough to invest in a bank of discount. Thus, both institutions might assist each other; and the bank of discount would have this additional advantage, that it could allow of the withdrawal of money on demand, which a savings bank cannot always readily do.

In this manner, banks collect together the scattered and useless portions of capital, and place it in a form in which it may conveniently be used; and they also collect together that which would, perhaps, be used, but which, without their assistance, would be used in a much less convenient manner, both to the borrower and the lender.

II. Let us now see, in what manner, after this capital has been thus collected, banks enable the industrious classes to enjoy the benefit of it.

The most obvious method, in which, without banks, the capitalist would assist the laborer, would be to sell him goods on *trust*. Thus, suppose a mechanic wished to establish himself in a village where his services would command a high remuneration; he might purchase of the dealer in the material which he wanted, as much stock as he wished, at three or six months, or a year's credit; and, with this capital, he could commence his business. By converting this material into product, and selling it, he would be able to liquidate the debt; and all the surplus would be his own. Or, take the case of a wholesale merchant. Suppose such a merchant to import, into a large city, two hundred thousand dollars' worth of goods. If he shall wait for the individuals, who may need his wares, to come and purchase them, it may be a year or two before his sales are completed. There may, however, be fifty retail merchants, of small capital, in several of the surrounding towns, who are not able to pay in cash for his commodities, but who, if they can obtain them on credit, will be able, both to sell them to good advantage to themselves, and also to refund the money, in three, six, or twelve months. It will be of advantage to both parties, the one to sell, and the other to buy, on credit. And this is the manner in which very much of this business is commonly transacted.

But when the business of credit is managed in this manner, several things are to be considered.

1. The merchant, who sells in this manner, either charges interest from the date of the sale, or from a time agreed upon between the parties, or settled by common usage.

2. He knows, that when he sells, in this manner, he is liable to lose, either by the want of skill, or of fidelity in his debtor. Hence, to cover his risk, he always charges considerably higher for his goods, than he would charge, if he sold them for cash. Hence, merchants always have a cash, and a credit price, for their goods.

3. Besides all this, to this mode of sale there is a limit, in the ability of the wholesale merchant. If his capital be not large enough to allow him to sell his goods on credit, he must sell them altogether for cash; or, if he have capital, the extent to which it will allow him thus to trade, is limited. This limit will be extended very much, if either party can procure a loan of capital from some one who has it to spare, and who does not wish to invest it in any other business.

I. *Of the Retail Merchant.*

Suppose the retail merchant, in his own town, be known to be a man of skill, industry, and integrity. A local bank, knowing his circumstances and his character, will readily loan him a sum of money, at the ordinary rate of interest. With this loan, he will be able to make his purchases of the importer; and thus, he uses in his business the capital of the bank, instead of the capital of the seller. In doing this, there is a manifold advantage.

1. This capital in the bank, which would otherwise have been idle, is bringing in a revenue to its owners. This is an obvious saving to the community.

2. The buyer pays the bank a lower interest, than he would have paid the importer.

3. He procures his goods at cash, instead of credit prices; and hence, he is able to make a greater gain himself, and, at the same time, to sell them cheaper to his customers.

4. The importer, being able to pay cash for his goods, can himself import them cheaper; and hence, there is a still farther reduction of their price to the whole community.

The case of the retail merchant is the same as that of the mechanic, or of any other individual, who needs capital to unite with his industry. The use of the bank, in all these cases, is, to offer *its* capital to the industrious laborer, in the place of the capital of the *wholesale dealer;* and, as it can loan on better terms, and to the advantage of all the parties concerned, the whole community are benefitted by all the points of difference.

II. *Of the Wholesale Merchant.*

The case is the same with the importer. He can easily sell, with profit, an amount of goods larger than his actual capital. But if he import his own goods, on credit, from a foreign manufacturer, or merchant, to whom he is almost *unknown*, he must pay him interest, and receive his goods at credit prices. Using the capital of a bank where he is *known*, he can purchase them at cash prices, and thus import them more advantageously, both for himself and for the community. In this case, as before, he uses capital which would otherwise have been unproductive; and, while he pays for it a suitable remuneration, which would otherwise have been lost, he is enabled to reap an increased profit to himself, while he sells at a less price to the community.

It is in this manner, therefore, that banks quicken the industry of a people. They first collect together, and render available, all the capital of a country; and they so use it, that every one who needs it, and can give the requisite assurance that it will be well used, can obtain it. They thus, by giving facilities to the extension of credit, enable every individual to reap all the benefits which can arise from his *industry*, his *skill*, and his *moral character*. Without credit, if he possessed no capital, he would be left to the resources of his *simple industry*, or simple manual labor. In just so far, therefore, as they tend to the extension of credit, they confer a benefit upon the industrious. Thus, every one may have the opportunity, so far as the capital of the country will allow, to unite his industry with capital, and reap the resulting advantage; and, on the other hand, all the capital of the country is enabled to be united with industry, and thus it is all employed, in some way, in the business of production. The nearer any community approaches to such a state of things as this, the more intense will be its industry, and the greater its productiveness.

And still more. As banks are permanent corporations,

of which the laws and resources are known, they present an inducement for the investment of *foreign* capital. This is always an advantage to any country. Capital will never be invested, in any country, unless the rate of interest in the country where it is invested, is higher than in that from which it is sent. In this case, the former country derives the advantage from the difference. If money can be borrowed in London, at four per cent., and be loaned here, for six per cent., we have the benefit of the use of the money, and of two per cent. in addition. In this manner, money is constantly borrowed by a new country from an old, with great advantage to both, but specially to the new country.

If such be the utility of banks, in this point of view, it is of importance that their arrangements should be so made, as to loan, on the most convenient terms, to those who are able to give proper security. The mode, in this country, is by receiving a note of hand, with approved endorsers, and made payable at a specified time, say at sixty or ninety days. The bank, however, allows no interest on deposits made by the drawer of the note. This mode of transacting business, answers a very valuable purpose; but, it may be questioned, whether its convenience might not be very considerably increased.

Judging by these principles, it would seem that the Scottish banks were conducted more correctly, as well as more beneficially to the public, than any institutions of the kind at present known.

1. As offices of deposit, they receive all sums, not less than £10 sterling; and, for such deposits, allow interest. Less sums than this are placed in the savings banks, until they become sufficiently large to be deposited in a bank. These deposits are, generally, made by persons who labor

in agriculture or manufactures. The whole amount thus deposited, is equal to about twenty-four millions pounds sterling, or not far short of one hundred and twenty millions dollars. This large sum is thus redeemed from idleness, and added to the productive capital of the country.

2. They discount notes, as our banks do, but they have another mode of loaning, which is called *cash credits.*

When a man wishes a cash credit, he finds bondsmen, who promise to indemnify the bank for all that it may lose, by loaning to him within a certain sum; or else he places real estate in the power of the bank, to a sufficient amount to render it secure within the sum which he wishes to borrow. The bank then opens with him a cash account, or allows him to draw for any sum within the specified amount. He is charged interest only for the amount which he borrows. As fast as he is in funds, he deposits all he can spare, in the bank, and, for every thing thus deposited, he is allowed interest; so that his interest on deposits always diminishes the interest on his debt. Thus he borrows and pays, successively; and, at stated seasons, the accounts are adjusted.

The advantages of this system, are: 1st. That it enables an industrious man to procure credit to the amount of his real estate, and, hence, to do more business with the same capital, than any where else. 2d. That by rendering every deposit valuable, it stimulates him to frugality. 3d. It enables the bank to understand, more correctly, the state of his affairs, and, hence, to know how deserving he is of confidence. 4th. That this may be done with greater safety, than in any other mode, is evident from the fact, that while the Scottish banks have been liberal in their accommodations, and have, by the acknowledgment of all, been of the most important service to that country, but one of them has ever been known to fail. These are, surely, the best evidences of the wisdom of any practical system.

Such, I suppose, to be the advantages of banks, as institutions of discount or loan.

III. *On the utility of Banks, as institutions of* CIRCULATION.

I have already shown, in what manner it is possible for banks to issue notes for a larger amount than they at any moment actually possess, in specie, and that they may do so, to a certain extent, with entire safety to the community. Should banks be generally established, and all of them adopt this system, as they would naturally do, it is evident that there would be in circulation more paper than specie; that is, that the actual circulation would, to a great extent, become paper, instead of the precious metals.

But I have already shown, that a community, in any given condition of exchanges, requires no more than a given value of coin, for its exchanges. If the amount be increased, its value will diminish, and *vice versa.* If it need an amount equal to a million bushels of wheat, no more than this can be introduced, and if more be introduced, its value will fall, till it become equal to a million bushels of wheat.

Now, by issuing paper money, the whole amount of money is increased, and, hence, its price falls. But, as every paper dollar is redeemable in silver, its value is still equal to that of a silver dollar. Hence, the whole amount of currency, silver and paper together, falls in price, so that money becomes cheap, and you can buy more abroad with a silver dollar, than you can with a silver dollar, at home.

Now, in this state of things, if the paper and coin were equally valuable in foreign countries, either would be exported, at pleasure. But, inasmuch as only the metal is valuable abroad, this, exclusively, is sent out of the country, in the purchase of other articles. And, it will be sent out, until the price of the circulating medium at home, is reduced to its ordinary price in other countries.

Suppose that two-thirds could be thus sent away without impairing the soundness of the currency at home. Business would then go on as securely, and as well, as it did before. But, these two-thirds would procure in exchange an equal amount of other capital, by which the wealth of the country is by so much increased. In the mean time, all the exchanges of the country are carried on by means of the remaining one-third, *plus* the expense of the manufacture and management of the cheaper commodity, paper; that is, the given operation, exchange, is carried on by means of an instrument, which costs only about one-third of the expense, which the former instrument cost.

This, then, is the advantage of banks of circulation. They furnish to the community a cheaper article of exchange. And the extent of the benefit is easily estimated. If the *whole* of the metallic circulating medium were exchanged for paper, we should have the benefit of the interest of this *whole amount.* If twenty millions of specie were wanted to carry on the exchanges of this country, and the whole were exchanged for paper, we should be benefitted to the amonnt of the annual interest of twenty millions, or, at six per cent., of one million two hundred thousand dollars per annum. If three-fourths of it were sent away, our benefit would be equal to nine hundred thousand dollars per annum. This is the *whole* pecuniary advantage of a paper currency, over a metallic. It consists in substituting a *cheaper*, for a *dearer* circulating medium. And, our advantage, supposing the cheaper to be equally good, is precisely equal to the interest of the difference.

This deserves to be seriously considered. Banks do not *create* capital. The issuing of paper money, does not render money *abundant.* If it be issued to such an extent, that its soundness is doubted, it produces an effect precisely the reverse. If, while it is perfectly sound, it be issued to an amount beyond the wants of the community, specie will be exported, until the equilibrium is restored. If but twenty millions of value be needed in exchange, you can employ but the value of twenty millions. The only benefit of a paper currency, supposing it to be perfectly sound, over a metallic currency, is, *first,* its greater convenience in exchange; and, *secondly,* that it enables us to use a cheaper instrument instead of a dearer, and to employ the amount of the difference in the various operations of human industry.

SECTION III.

ADVANTAGES AND DISADVANTAGES OF A PAPER CIRCULATION.

Having thus endeavored to illustrate the *nature* of a paper circulation, it may be of some importance to explain, in as simple a form as possible, the *advantages* and *disadvantages* which appertain to it.

1. The advantages of a paper circulation. These are two, *economy* and *convenience.*

I. *Economy.*

1. The material in use, in a paper circulation, as we have shown, is of much less value than that in a specie circulation. A bill worth one thousand ounces of silver, may not cost more than two or three cents. Now, in just so far as a paper circulation accomplishes the same result as specie, and accomplishes it at a less price, the community is the gainer by the difference.

2. The wear and tear of paper money, as well as the original cost, is less expensive than that of silver and gold. Were silver and gold transported, as paper money now is, the friction would reduce the weight of coin so rapidly, that new emissions would be much more frequently necessary.

3. But, specially, as the introduction of paper money renders a considerable part of the specie formerly employed, useless, it may be exchanged for other capital. Specie is, in itself, incapable of production. If a part of it will answer the purposes of exchange, all the remainder may be changed for productive capital. Hence, the gain, as has been shown in the preceding section, is equal to the amount of this difference employed in productive, and the same amount employed in unproductive capital. If five millions can be, without injury, dispensed with, the benefit is equal to the difference between five millions in productive and five millions in unproductive capital.

II. *Convenience.*

1. Paper money is much more easily transported. To travellers, and men in the ordinary affairs of life, this is a matter of considerable consequence. Specie is heavy and burdensome. Any amount of paper money which a man

needs, may be comprised in as small a bulk as he chooses. When large transfers of money are to be made between distant places, the additional convenience and security are still more evident.

2. Paper money is less liable to robbery. As we can render its bulk whatever we please, it can be more readily concealed, if we doubt the honesty of our associates. Specie is heavy, bulky, and noisy, and, hence, its presence is unavoidably discovered.

3. Paper money, if stolen, is more easily identified, and, hence, more easily recovered. A man, by noting the number and marks of a bank bill, may safely swear to its identity; but, inasmuch as coin is intentionally all alike, this would be impossible in the case of specie.

These are the principal advantages, so far as I can see, of a paper currency. If there be any others, I have not been able to discover them.

On the other hand, its disadvantages are three, viz: Its liability to *forgery*, to *fraud*, and to *fluctuation*.

I. It is liable to *forgery*. The risk, in this respect, from the use of bank paper, is considerable. The security from signatures is small, since any good penman, by practice, can easily learn to imitate any signature. The principal security arises from engraving and paper. But, as this depends only upon its excellence, any one, who can engrave sufficiently well, can so engrave a false bill, that no ordinary examiner can distinguish it from a true one. Hence, every one is liable to be imposed upon, and to suffer a total loss, to the exact amount of the imposition. It is true, that coin is also liable to be falsified; but, the process is much more difficult and expensive than that of engraving. False coin, being liable to detection from its color, weight, and sonorousness, is more readily detected. Inasmuch, therefore, as the liability to counterfeiting, is greater in paper money than in specie, this difference is to be set down in the list of the disadvantages with which it is chargeable.

On this account, banks which issue paper money, are under obligations to take every precaution to render their bills as little liable to be counterfeited, as possible. The greatest security, as we have remarked, is in the excellence of the engraving, and in the peculiarity of the paper. Hence, they should employ, for the engraving of their bills, none but the best artists; and thus employ talent, which would be under no temptation to engage in counterfeiting. They should never use plates which have been so much worn, as to render the impression coarse, indistinct, and easily imitated. A bank which, to save expense, uses a worn-out plate, enriches itself, at the expense of the public. I see no reason why a bank, which issues bills of this description, and thus takes no pains to secure the public against fraud, should not be liable to pay the false, as well as the true bills. Were this done, more care would be used, and counterfeiting would become far less common.

II. *Fraud.* I have elsewhere shown, that if the capital of a bank be all paid in, and the notes which it holds against individuals, and which it has received in exchange for its bills, be all good, the holder of its bills has two perfectly good securities. Were all the capital stolen, he would be safe; and, were all the notes bad, the capital remaining, he would still be safe. We have also shown, that he would always be safe, so long as the capital actually paid in, was sufficient to cover any deficiency which might arise from a failure of the debtors of the bank.

And, it is manifest, that this is the utmost limit of the safety of the holder of the bill. And, with ordinary skill and fidelity, it is manifest, that the issues of a bank may always be kept within this limit, and thus the holder of its notes incur no risk.

But, neither the skill nor the fidelity of man, is always to be trusted. Hence, banks frequently fail, and inflict either a partial, or a total loss upon the community.

1. Banks may fraudulently commence issues, when only *a part*, or when not even *any part* of their capital has been paid in. Suppose that only a *part* of their capital be paid in; then, the public, instead of having a guaranty, over and above the notes of individuals held by the bank, equal to the whole amount of its capital, has a guaranty equal only to the amount of the part paid in. If the capital of a bank be one hundred thousand dollars, and only ten thousand dollars be paid in, and the bank issue one hundred and fifty thousand dollars in bills, it possesses only a guaranty of ten thousand dollars, to ensure the payment of one hundred and fifty thousand dollars by the debtors of the bank. In a time of commercial pressure, or in case of loss by accident, or robbery, such a bank must fail, and the holders of the bills must suffer a loss equal to the deficiency by the failure of the debtors of the bank, the costs of closing its concerns, and the loss of interest until its bills have been paid.

Again: Suppose that *none* of the capital stock were paid in, but that the stockholders simply gave their notes for their shares. The security would then be precisely equal to the average goodness of the notes of individuals, received by the bank, in exchange for its bills. It would have no capital on hand to redeem these bills, and, on the least pressure for specie payments, it must fail. The notes of individuals, in a time of scarcity of money, would be worth much less than par; and, as the stockholders would pay for their notes which they gave for shares, by surrendering up the shares for which they gave them, the whole loss would fall on the holders of the bills.

Again: Suppose that, as in the last case, no stock were paid in; that the stockholders were the directors themselves; and that they accommodated themselves with money, without ever requiring notes of each other. Here, there would be no security whatever, either in bank capital, or in the notes of individuals. In such case, the bank must speedily stop payment, and the whole loss of its issues would fall upon the holders of its bills. This, as well as the last case, is nothing more than a fraudulent arrangement for picking the pockets of the public, on an extensive scale. It is nothing more nor less, than downright swindling, and should expose a man to the same punishment as housebreaking.

Nor is this danger merely imaginary. The amount lost by the public, from the failure of banks, is actually enormous. Mr. Gallatin, a most able and competent authority on this subject, in his pamphlet on the currency, has made the following statement, which, from the character and accuracy of the author, is entitled to full credit:

"We have an account of one hundred and sixty-five banks which have failed, between the first of January, 1811, and the first of July, 1830. The capital of one hundred and twenty-nine of them, amounted to more than twenty-four millions of dollars, stated as having been paid in. The whole amount may be estimated at nearly thirty millions, and our list may not be complete. The capital of the state banks now existing, amounts to about one hundred and ten millions. On a total capital of one hundred and forty millions, the failures have amounted to thirty, or more than one-fifth of the whole. Of the actual loss incurred, we can give no account. There are instances in which the stockholders, by paying for their shares *in their own notes*, and afterwards *redeeming their notes with the stock in their name*, suffered no loss, and this loss fell, exclusively, on the holders of notes and the depositors. In many cases, when the whole stock has been lost, the holders of notes, nevertheless, suffered a partial loss. In the most favorable cases, the stockholders lost a considerable portion of the stock, and all the debts will be ultimately paid. But, even here, there has been a heavy loss to the community, the notes having been generally sold by the holders at depreciated rates, when the failure took place. We believe that the pecuniary loss sustained by government, on loans raised during the suspension of specie payments, and from bank failures, exceeded four millions of dollars."

Now, when a currency is liable to such results, from fraud or folly; that is, when skill and integrity must enter as an element into its goodness, the risk which a community sustains in the use of it, must certainly be placed in the list of its disadvantages.

Nor are these evils peculiar to this country. In England, in the year 1793, as we are informed by M'Culloch, *one third* of the country banks stopped payment. And we learn, by the daily newspapers, that the failures of private bankers, are matters of very frequent occurrence. Between the years 1809 and 1830, the number of commissions of bankruptcy issued against country bankers in England, was three hundred and eleven. "Exclusive of the above, many banks stopped payment, to the great injury of their creditors and the public, which afterwards resumed them; while the affairs of some bankrupt concerns were arranged without a commission." Yet, it would seem, there are means which may be devised to remedy this evil; for he informs us that, "during this whole period, *not a single Scottish bank gave way.*"

III. *Fluctuation.* In speaking of a metallic currency, we had occasion to remark, that it was essential to the character of whatever was used as money, that it be liable, as little as possible, to fluctuation. Hence, vegetable products, of which the amount created was liable to vary under the same amount of labor, with the different productiveness of seasons, could never be employed as money. The reason is obvious. He who contracted debts, when money bore one ratio to products, would pay them when it bore another ratio; and hence, though he might pay the same nominal amount, yet he would pay twice as much in value as he had promised. So, also, he who had loaned money while it bore one ratio, and received his payments while it was at another, though he might receive the same *nominal* amount, would not receive half the amount *in value* which he loaned. And hence, all civilized communities have denied to governments the right of altering, or in any manner interfering with, the value of coin; for the reason that this cannot be effected without causing a variation in the value of money, and thus interfering with private contracts. Were this allowable, it is evident that credit must be at an end; because, whatever a contract might mean *to-day*, no one could possibly predict what it would mean to-morrow. Hence, all fluctuation in the value of any substance, renders it, by the amount of this fluctuation, unfit for the purposes of a circulating medium. If gold and silver were as fluctuating in value as cotton or wheat, they would, their bulk only excepted, be as unfit for the purposes of money, as these substances themselves.

Now, these remarks apply, not only to gold and silver, but to *any thing* which may be used as money. They apply to silver, as much as to gold, and to gold, as much as to silver. If either of these substances were liable to great fluctuations in value, we should be obliged to abandon it, and to take the other. If both of them were so liable, we should relinquish them both, and find a better substance. And so, if paper be used as the circulating medium, the case is the same. By as much as it is liable to sudden or to great fluctuation, by so much is it unfit for the purposes of money. And, when once paper has supplied the place of gold and silver, it becomes the circulating medium as truly as gold and silver were, when they supplied the place of copper, or sheep, or cattle.

Now, the *disadvantage* to which, as we have said, paper money is exposed, is, that it is liable to sudden and great fluctuations in value.

The manner in which this occurs, is easily explained.

We have already shown that, in order to accomplish a given amount of exchanges in a community, a certain amount of value is necessary; and that no more than this amount of value can be employed for this purpose. If, to accomplish the exchanges of a community at a given time, one thousand ounces of silver, equal to one thousand bushels of wheat, are necessary, and twice this quantity be introduced, the value will remain the same, though the quantity varies; and the result will be, that the price of money, in relation to other products, will fall one half; that is, if we gave five dollars for a hat before, we shall give ten dollars now, and for other things in proportion. And, if half the quantity were removed, the reverse would be the case; that is, the price of money would be doubled; in other words, if we gave five dollars for a hat, formerly, we should give two dollars and fifty cents for it now; and so of other productions.

If we we bear this principle in mind, we shall easily see the nature of the fluctuations to which paper money is liable. Metallic money has a natural price, which is not liable to any fluctuation within short periods. This price depends upon the cost of mining, which is liable to very little variation. He who exchanges a thousand bushels of wheat for a thousand ounces of silver, knows that it will cost as much to bring an ounce of silver into the market, six months hence, as it does now, and hence, its cost being the same, it will bring for him as much of other products, six months hence, as it does now; that is, if this be the medium of exchange, and its value be not interfered with by the use of some other substance. Now, paper money has no such *natural* price; but the quantity of it in circulation depends, considerably, upon the hopes, wishes, and anticipations of men. Hence, the quantity may vary in almost any amount, and, as the *value* of the whole is not altered by the *quantity* in use, as the quantity increases, the value of each portion must decrease; and, hence, a paper dollar may be worth twenty-five per cent. more or less to-day, than it was a month ago, or than it will be a month to come. Hence, though there may be the same words written upon the paper, and it be called by the same name, yet it means, to him who pays it, and to him who receives it, a very different thing from what it did a month ago. And that it does mean differently, is very evident, from the facts of the case. A month ago, he could obtain one hundred dollars for six dollars a year; now, he would willingly give ten or twelve dollars for the same sum.

This fluctuation may arise, on the part of the bank,

innocently or viciously; from want of skill and forethought; or from want of integrity.

I. *Innocently.* Suppose that, at a given period, the circulating medium in a community is properly proportioned to the necessities of exchange, and that this medium, though paper, is perfectly sound; that is, that there exists, in all the banks, sufficient specie to pay all debts of the bank on demand, in the precious metals.

Let, now, from any cause whatever, the productiveness of labor be greatly increased, so that a much larger amount of annual products is brought into market; that is, offered in exchange. If the amount of money remain the *same*, while the amount of products is *increased*, the price of money will rise; that is, every thing will be cheap. As soon as products become cheap, every one is anxious to buy. Merchants will be desirous to borrow money, or, in other words, capital, with which to buy, because, when products are cheap, they may be reasonably expected to rise; and, if the rise in price be greater than the interest paid for money, the purchaser may reasonably hope to be able to repay what he borrowed, with interest, and yet realise a handsome profit. Besides, when an article is low in any country, then is the time to export it with advantage; and this prospect of increased advantage will induce men to borrow, in order to export, in the expectation that the unusual profit will enable them to realise far more than the interest they have paid for borrowed capital. Hence, in such a season, every one is desirous of borrowing, and banks can most profitably employ their capital. They are called upon to loan, to the utmost extent of their power, both by their own interest, and by the universal wish of the public.

Now, in such a state of things, it is not to be supposed

that the directors of banks are endowed with greater prudence than other men, or that they are not as likely to be influenced by the hope of large dividends. The example of one stimulates the others. The risk that one institution runs, another will be willing to run. No bank would be willing to make a dividend of six per cent., while its neighbor was making eight. And when disconnected banks, all over a nation, are animated by these principles, it is evident that a very large amount of loans must be effected; that is, a very large amount of paper money must be issued. But just so fast as, beyond the necessary amount, the quantity is increased, the value of each portion of it diminishes, and thus prices rise; that is, money becomes abundant, and the dollar will purchase no more than it would in a time of scarcity. Thus, the amount of the circulating medium becomes too great for the amount of exchanges, and money is cheaper than any other article in the market.

But, we have before seen, that the cheapest article in the market will always be exported. As this is now money, money will be exported. But, as the bills are redeemable in specie, specie is worth no more than bank bills; and, as the bills are worth nothing abroad, the whole exportation will be in coin. In a short time, a large portion of it has left the country. The banks then find themselves liable to pay in specie, a vastly greater amount than they were liable to pay, a month or two since, and they find that they have much less specie wherewith to pay it; and the demand for specie still continues. They are, of course, in danger of stopping payment, and their only means of safety is, in diminishing their loans; that is, loaning no more, and requiring payment of those who owe them. Hence, those who had borrowed, with the hope of paying by means of their sales, are called upon to pay, before these sales are effected, and, as the banks refuse to loan, very few are disposed to buy. Thus, the debtors of the bank are required to pay their debts sooner than they expected, and the means of making those payments are curtailed. The money goes back into the bank, and does not come out of it. Thus, with every day, the quantity of the circulating medium is diminished. The scarcity of money increases. The price of goods falls, as men will sell for lower and lower prices, rather than lose their credit. Every man, from necessity, presses his neighbor, and the bank, from the same necessity, presses them all. And thus, in a few months, the amount of circulating medium is greatly diminished; and money is worth twenty-five or fifty per cent. more than it was a short time ago. He who agreed to pay one thousand ounces of silver, when one ounce of silver was worth a bushel of wheat, pays it now, when it is worth a bushel and a half of wheat; that is, though he pay the same nominal amount, he pays fifty per cent. more in value.

The result of such a state of things depends, of course, upon the degree of the excess of these issues. If this excess have not been great, by means of mutual forbearance, the scarcity passes away; that is, holders of produce, being obliged to sell or to fail, sell at reduced prices. Thus, the price of money rises, and it becomes profitable to import it. It is then imported; the banks are thus enabled to discount; and things go on again, as usual; with, however, a severe loss to those who have purchased when goods were at high prices.

But, it is not always thus. Sometimes the pressure for money is so great, that those who have purchased products with borrowed capital, cannot sell them fast enough to make their payments. These are obliged to stop payment, or become bankrupts, and assign their effects to their creditors. But these were debtors to many others who were depending on the payment to be received from them, to pay their own debts. These, being disappointed in this expectation, also fail. Their failure leads again to the failure of others, and the panic becomes general. No one dares to trust his neighbor, and the banks dare not trust any one. An universal crash of mercantile credit succeeds, and none are able to withstand the shock, save those of the heaviest capital, and of the greatest financial ability.

This, however, at length works its own cure. When a debtor fails, he assigns his property to his creditors; that is, he pays them in *kind*, instead of in *money*. Hence, this being done, *his* need of money is over, and, by so much, diminishes the demand. His property is sold, at any price it will bring. This depresses, still more rapidly, the price of goods; that is, raises the comparative value of money; and hence, it will be the more readily imported. As soon as these causes have had time to operate; that is, diminished demand and increased supply; the equilibrium is restored, and credit is established on its ordinary basis.

In this manner, fluctuation may arise *innocently*. And every one knows that such fluctuations are constantly occurring in the mercantile world. But what occurs thus innocently, is liable to occur *viciously*.

II. *Viciously*. A bank, established in a town remote from the ordinary channels of business, or the banks in any one place, if combined together, as they furnish the paper money which is used for all the common purposes of exchange, have, to a considerable degree, the monopoly of the article in the market. Hence, by loaning very freely at one time, they may bring the whole district into their debt. When this is the case, if they see fit to curtail their discounts, they may reduce the amount of circulating medium, and raise the price of money as much as they will. They may thus, by enforcing payment, render half the population bankrupt, and possess themselves of their estates, at half price; or else oblige them to pay double or treble the usual per centage of interest. That such events have occurred, is, I fear, too much a matter of history. And it has given rise to a frequent and unwarrantable prejudice against banks in general.

While, however, all this is admitted, it deserves to be remarked:

1. That these disadvantages of fluctuation, both from unskilfulness and from fraud, do not belong exclusively to *banks*, but are liable to exist under any circumstances, in which money is loaned and borrowed. Were there no banks, and were money to be loaned by private capitalists, and even to be loaned in specie, the same inconveniences would be liable to result; for men are always tempted to borrow to-day, more than they will be able to pay to-morrow. And it is evident that collusion, for the sake of raising the rate of interest, is at least as liable to occur between individual money-lenders, as between banks. It is my impression that it more frequently occurs, inasmuch as it is more difficult of detection.

2. The blame, when such a state of things as has been described, exists, is always laid upon the banks. This is manifestly unjust. It belongs to the borrower, just as much as it does to the lender. Men are very willing to borrow, but they very commonly call upon the community for great commiseration, when they are obliged to pay. I by no means object to the extension of any commiseration which may be convenient, but it would be a very inconvenient extension of it, if it released a man

from the obligation to refund what he had borrowed, and, by the use of which, he has already, perhaps, realised a handsome revenue. The bank, by enforcing payments in a time of pressure, is really doing a great service to the community. This is evident. If the debts due to the banks were not paid, the banks would fail. In this case, not only the stockholders themselves, but every one else would be ruined. So that, if, by their exacting punctuality, some persons fail, it is better that a few should lose, than that the whole community should be ruined.

3. Again: In a time of scarcity, banks are sadly abused, because they will not loan more money. A bank, if it be honest, and mean to pay its debts, has its limit, beyond which it cannot safely pass, as truly as an individual. When it has arrived at this limit, its loans must cease. A merchant, who has involved himself in large transactions, expecting that he could borrow as much as he chose, is now disappointed, because his expectations are not realised. But what reason has he to complain? The bank never promised to lend him, when it had nothing to lend; nor to ruin itself, for the sake of saving him from the consequences of his own headlong improvidence; specially, when by doing this, it must involve, not only itself, but him also in ruin. The bank was no party to his engagements; it derives no benefit from them, and it is under no obligation to enable him to fulfil them. The only remedy for these evils manifestly is, for both parties to be willing to grow rich more slowly, and thus to assume less formidable risks. When a whole community has run into transactions beyond its means, and has become embarrassed, there is very little gained by the abuse of banks and of bank directors.

But, whatever may be the advantages or disadvantages

of a paper currency, one thing is certain, that it has, in all actively commercial countries, taken the place of a specie currency. This is a sufficient reason to believe that it is the more convenient circulating medium. It would not be so universally chosen, unless it were found to answer a better purpose than specie; and, if it be found to answer a better purpose, it ought to be chosen.

If these remarks be just, there will follow several very obvious conclusions.

1. That to lend money, is just as necessary to the good of the community, and is, therefore, as innocent and as honorable, as to borrow it.

2. That an institution, organised for the purpose of lending money, is, so far as its object is concerned, as beneficial to the community, as innocent, and as honorable as any other institution.

3. That a lender of money is liable to be dishonest and unskilful; but that a borrower of money is also liable to be dishonest and unskilful.

4. And hence, that the one, as much as the other, is entitled to all the benefits of equal laws, and the fair and unbiassed execution of them. If a bank conduct dishonestly, this is a reason why it should be dealt with according to just and equitable law; but it is not a reason why all the capital of the country should be oppressed, and every capitalist insulted. A carpenter may be dishonest, and this is a reason why he should be dealt with according to just and equitable law; but it is no reason why every carpenter should be oppressed, and his calling made a cause of opprobrium. The principle which applies to the one case, applies equally to the other.

SECTION IV.

OF THE AGENCY OF SOCIETY, THAT IS, OF GOVERNMENT, IN RESPECT TO A PAPER CIRCULATION.

I have already remarked, when treating of specie circulation, that coin was employed as a circulating medium, not in consequence of the act of a government, or of the stamp which it bore, but simply in consequence of its adaptedness to be employed for this purpose, and of the universal desire of the community so to employ it; and also, that the whole agency of the government is properly limited to the making of those arrangements, which would enable it to accomplish this purpose the most successfully; that what substance a community should employ, is none of the concern of the government; its only concern is, so to prepare the substance employed, that it may be used with the greatest common advantage.

Now, the same remarks manifestly apply to *whatever may be used as a circulating medium*, whether it be gold and silver, or paper. Hence,

1. A government has no right to interfere with this question, and enact any law, or take any measures in regard to it. If the people choose to use a paper currency, instead of a metallic currency, they have a right to use it, and no one, either individual or associated, has any right to control that use. If I present a check to a bank, and they offer me in payment either specie or bills, and I choose to take their bills, it is a matter wholly of my own concern. I ask permission to make this choice,

of no one on earth. If I have a thousand dollars to pay in New Orleans, and I choose to take the bill or the draft of a bank, and send this in payment instead of the thousand dollars in silver, and my creditor receive it in payment, if both he and I are satisfied, no one has a right to interfere. And, if any one, whether individual or society, whether government, judicial, legislative, or executive, see fit to interfere, my only and sufficient reply to each and to all of them is, that it is, distinctly and particularly, none of their business.

2. But, although a community may choose a paper, instead of a metallic currency, and although they have a right to choose it; neither any community, nor any individual of a community, chooses either a *worthless* or a *fluctuating* currency. While, therefore, a government has no right to enact that a currency shall be any thing *else* than the people wish it to be, they have a right to take all proper means to make it *such* as the people wish it to be. Hence,

1. They have a right to take such means as will be likely to give all reasonable *security* to a paper currency. These means have respect, in general, to the liability of directors and stockholders to redeem their bills. In what manner this security can be best effected, it must be left to practical men to decide. In some cases, all the property of all the stockholders is rendered liable for the debts of the bank. This would commonly be a perfect guaranty. In other cases, I believe, the property only of the directors is held liable. In what way soever security can be best and most equitably effected, I think a government has a right to effect it.

2. A government has a right to take all reasonable means to diminish the *fluctuation* of a paper currency.

We have seen that, inasmuch as a bank promises to redeem its bills in specie, and as hence, the amount of paper in circulation must always depend upon the amount of specie in a country, the fluctuation in the amount of paper must arise from fluctuation in the amount of specie. Hence, also, this fluctuation will always be less, when the proportion of specie to paper is great, and *vice versa*. The best method, therefore, of preventing this evil, is, so to construct the currency, that the proportion of specie to paper shall be too large to be affected by any thing but large and long continued exportations of the precious metals. This result may be easily effected by the prohibition of the issue of small bills. This will, by necessity, place in the hands of every individual, specie for every amount which he may hold of less value than the lowest note issued. Were no bank in this country to issue notes of a less denomination than five dollars, most of the sums held by individuals, in notes of one, two, and three dollars, would be in silver. If every individual of the twelve millions in the United States, possessed two dollars more in specie than at present, this would amount to twenty-four millions more of specie than we now possess. This would, of itself, be sufficient to prevent the evil arising from any ordinary fluctuation.

In addition to this, I suppose that an exact account should be kept, and at short periods made public, of the amount of specie imported and exported. This would give to the banks, timely notice of the danger, and, at the first intimation of excessive issues, they might curtail their discounts, in season to avert the evil before it became excessive and remediless.

So far as I can discover, the power of a government over a paper currency, is conferred solely for the accomplishment of these two objects; and, of course, it is restricted to the accomplishment of these two objects. A government has no right to interfere with it, for any other purpose. If it do interfere, such interference is manifest usurpation. It has, for instance, no right to interfere with the currency, because the people import too much, or because they import too little, because they buy too much land, or because they buy too little land, because they over-trade, or because they under-trade. Its power was conferred for no such purpose, and to use it for such purpose, is usurpation. To all such interference, the proper answer to be given by the individual to the government, is, that *all this is none of your business.*

Nor, is the principle, in this case, at all affected by the patriotism from which such interference proceeds, or the paternal solicitude by which it may have been dictated. The parental authority and the parental responsibility cease, when the child has become of age. And whoever may assume to be the Father of his country, it surely is not too much to claim for the people of these United States, that they have at least attained to the *period of majority.*

But, other grounds for legislative interference with banking institutions are assumed, which, if correctly assumed, are of a very extraordinary tendency. Some of these, it may be proper for us briefly to consider. For instance, it is said, that banks are the *creatures of the legislature;* and that bank directors are the *agents of the legislature;* and, therefore, that a legislature may rightfully exercise over them any authority which it chooses; and may impose upon them such laws as it sees fit. Such an assumption as this, deserves at least a passing notice.

1. It is asserted that *a bank is the creature of the legislature;* and, therefore, that a legislature may rightfully

impose upon *its creature* such laws, and subject it to such jurisdiction, as it pleases.

The assertion is somewhat figurative. What is meant, when it is said that a bank *is a creature of the legislature?* In what does a banking *company* differ from a banking *individual?* The only difference, that I can discover, is, that one *is incorporated* by a legislative act, the other *is not.*

What, then, is an *act of incorporation?* It is merely a power granted by a legislature, to several individuals, to do, as *a society*, some innocent act, which they may thus do more conveniently, but which any one of them *might*, if he saw fit, do without any act of the legislature. I say some *innocent* act, for what is not innocent, should be allowed neither to individuals nor to societies.

The necessity of such a provision is manifest. Many innocent purposes can be accomplished, only by many persons associated together. Such are purposes of charity, of science, of internal improvement, and many others. Without corporate powers, persons so associated could neither hold property, nor enforce any regulations upon each other; and, besides, without them, they could not be known in law, nor could a creditor have any claim upon the property which they might hold. Hence, when individuals wish to be associated for any innocent purpose, *they* may claim an act of incorporation as a right; and it is necessary, for the protection of the *community*, that it should be granted. And hence, from both of these considerations, it is incumbent upon a legislature to grant it. The simple principle involved is this: Is this an innocent means of promoting my own happiness? If it be, society is under obligation to afford it to me.

Sometimes, the corporate power is conferred by a separate act, in every individual case; at other times, a general law is passed, empowering any individuals to become a corporate body, by conforming to specified conditions. Under the latter case, come the laws of partnerships in general; or, more particularly, the law of limited partnerships, of the State of New York. By this last act, any number of individuals may unite in business, and be liable in no greater amount than they have contributed; that is, to all intents and purposes, become a corporation, by complying with certain conditions. Such is also the case with ecclesiastical corporations in that State.

Now, in what manner soever this is done, its effect is simply this: It gives to certain persons associated together, under certain circumstances, the power to act in the same manner as an individual might act, and places them under the same responsibilities as those under which an individual is placed. This is the meaning of an act of incorporation. And to make heavy charges, and exact bonuses for the passing of such an act, is unjust and oppressive. A man might as well be charged for the right of trial by jury.

This, then, is the meaning of an act of incorporation, and this is what is really meant by the figurative and mysterious terms, "*a creature of the legislature.*" If, then, a legislature possess unlimited power over a *bank*, because it has received an act of incorporation, it possesses the same unlimited power over all its *creatures;* that is, *over every thing that is incorporated.* If the power exist, and exist for this reason, it exists in every case to which this reason applies. Thus, he who owns a manufactory *alone*, may conduct it as he pleases, and buy and sell when he chooses; subject only to the ordinary laws of the land. But, if *ten men* become incorporated, as a manufacturing company, *they* are under the unlimited power of the legislature; and the legislature has an uncontrolled right to say when, and where, and of whom they must buy; and when, and where, and to whom they must sell; or whether they may buy or sell at all. Or, again: An *individual* has the right to worship God as he pleases. But, if *several* individuals wish to unite together in the worship of God, and, for their own convenience, desire to be incorporated for the promotion of this object, their rights of conscience cease; and, after they have erected their house of worship, a legislature may shut it up, command them to worship when and how it pleases, or may command them to worship Mahomet or Juggernaut; and all this is no oppression, but is a matter of simple, honest, common-sense justice; because these individuals have, for their own convenience, and for the security of others, become in law, a corporate body!

But even this is not all. Legislation never *confers* any right whatever; it only confirms those rights which previously existed. A legislative act can *confirm* me in the possession of a house which is my own property; but it can give me no right to *take possession* of a house which is the property of my neighbor. In the case of corporations, the same principle holds. A legislative act, only defines and establishes for several individuals, a right which they previously possessed. But the case is the same with almost all the rest of our possessions. We hold them under laws by which our right is defined and established. So that, upon this principle, every man is the *creature* of the legislature; that is, a legislature is the *fountain* of all power, the *creator* of all *right*, and deals out to its *creatures* and *vassals*, whatever of liberty or of possession it sees fit to confer. This is, surely, a novel doctrine to advance in the audience of a *free* people; and whenever it is advanced, the time has manifestly arrived, for a people which intends to *continue free,* to turn their attention to the consideration of first principles.

The simple truth in the case must be at once apparent. An act of incorporation, has no other effect, *per se*, than to place a society under the same protection as individuals, and subject it to the same responsibilities as individuals; that is, to place it under the common and universal laws of the land. If, together with this, a corporation enters into a contract with the legislature to do certain acts, this is another affair, and is subsequent to, and different from, the act of incorporation. By such contracts, both parties are equally holden. But this makes the corporation no more a creature of the legislature, than it makes the legislature a creature of the corporation. A legislature may agree with a contractor to build a wall; but this makes the builder in no respect a *creature* of the legislature; nor does it give them power over him in any other respect, than to oblige him to fulfil his contract, according to the laws of the land.

But it is also asserted, that bank directors are the *agents* of the government, or of the legislature, and hence, that they are under the unlimited control of the government, which is the *principal.* The reason for this assertion is, that the government has the right to control the circulating medium; that paper money is the circulating medium; that bank directors issue paper money; and that, therefore, they are under the control of the government.

To this, it may be replied:

1. The control of the government over the circulating medium, is limited in *degree;* and even *within this degree,* it is limited by *the object* for which it may be exerted. A government has a right to enact such laws

as may insure the payment of the debts of a bank, as well as of all other debts, and as may prevent excessive fluctuation in the circulating medium; that is, they have a right to take care that the circulating medium be *sound* and *convenient*, but, I see not that they have any other right over it. And this right is equally limited, whether the circulating medium be paper or money.

2. Suppose bank directors to issue this circulating medium, and that, on that ground, they are under the control of a legislature; they are then under its control only *within the limits*, and *for the purposes* above specified; that is, they are to be placed under *the general laws* for the regulation of the circulating medium. To exert any *other power*, or to exert a power for any *other purpose*, is tyranny.

3. But let us inquire in what sense bank directors are *agents* of government. The government, in their case, as in many others, requires, and has a right to require, that, in the conduct of their business, they shall conform to certain principles, made necessary for the good of the whole. But does *this* render them *agents* of the government? He who sells gunpowder, is obliged to sell it under special regulations; but is he, on this account, an *agent* of government? *Every man*, who buys or sells at all, buys or sells under some regulations of a legislature; but is *he*, on this account, their *agent*, over whom they have the right of unlimited control?

But, take a still more analogous case. Suppose an *individual*, or a mining *company*, to obtain from their mines, one hundred thousand dollars a year. This they appropriate to the business of loans. They have, however, no right to *coin* it themselves, but must have it coined at the mint;

that is, if they be a company, they must be incorporated, in order to carry their purposes into effect; and they must carry them into effect, subject to such rules as the good of the whole may demand. But does this render them, or their directors, the agents of government? or does this give to the government any other power, than that which it exercises over any other individual?

Suppose, now, several individuals have obtained one hundred thousand dollars in any other way than by mining, and that they wish to employ it in the business of loaning. They are under obligations to conform to the general laws made for the regulation of the circulating medium, but this is all. They do not, in this manner, become the agents of government, any more by loaning, than by doing any thing else. And suppose that their customers prefer to borrow paper, instead of metallic money. If they issue paper, they are under obligation to issue it in obedience to the laws enacted for the purpose of insuring its goodness and stability; but they are not, on this account, the agents of government, nor has the government any more power over them than it has over any other individuals. It seems to me, therefore, that the second assertion, namely, that bank directors are the agents of the government, is wholly gratuitous.

But, it is said that the banks have a monopoly of this article, money; and that, therefore, they are, of right, subject to *particular* legislation. To this, I reply; who creates this monopoly? Certainly not the banks, but the legislature themselves. If the legislature refuse banking privileges to those who deserve them, or grant them under such terms, that but few persons can accept of them, and thus diminish the amount of banking capital, and render it inadequate to the wants of the community, they are the authors of the monopoly; and they may not plead their *own wrong*, as an excuse for *injustice.** Were they to oblige a shoemaker to pay ten thousand dollars for the privilege of exercising his profession, and then, because there were but one or two shoemakers in a city, undertake to regulate his business, interfere with his concerns, and fleece him over again, on the ground that he possessed a monopoly; we should speak very mildly of such legislation, when we called it oppression and tyranny. He would very naturally say: "I do not ask you for your monopoly. It is all of your own imposing. It is *a creature of the legislature.* Let every one who chooses make shoes, subject to the common laws of the land; and both the monopoly, and your reasons for interfering with me in consequence of it, will cease together." And the case is the same with banks. Let all banking be

* The fact, no less notorious than disgraceful, I fear, is, that, in many of our States, bank charters are granted or denied for purely political reasons. They are reserved as the reward for services done to the dominant party. Hence, *one half* of the community at once, is, by this policy, excluded from the privilege of employing their capital in this manner. The charters thus granted, are frequently granted, not to those who are possessed of the necessary capital, but to those who have promoted an election. It is manifest, that neither activity nor skill, in political intrigue, will add any thing to the value of a bill, or afford any guaranty for the honest management of a bank. If, however, as is frequently the case, the applicants do not wish to hold the shares themselves, they sell them at an advance, before any of the capital has been paid, to persons of the other party. These last, therefore, are obliged to pay this advance, as a bonus to those who have obtained the charter; and thus, their property is taxed at the outset, to reward the industrious partisan. This advance, by its whole amount, reduces the value of banking capital, and prevents men from so investing their property. In this manner, the monopoly is created; and thus, very commonly, are spurious banks brought into existence. It will be found, I believe, in the greater number of instances in which fraud has been detected in the management of banks, that they have been banks, which have been decidedly partisan in their character. The evils resulting from this system, are, however, all charged upon banks and bank directors. No one thinks of arraigning the legislature, from which all these evils truly emanate.

governed by principles which shall insure the security of the community, and then let banks be multiplied at will. If they yield more than an average profit, they will thus be increased, until their profit is reduced to that of other business. If they yield less, they will be diminished, until they merely supply the wants of the community. Thus, the monopoly, and the reason for oppression founded on it, will terminate together.

I have pursued this subject, to a greater extent than I should otherwise have done, were it not that a very general disposition exists, and has always existed, to interfere with the rights of capital; and because no country can long be prosperous, where these rights are not respected. Men too frequently assume, that capital, devoted to the purposes of loaning, is owned by the rich; that, by overtaxing and oppressing it, the rich only suffer; and, as the rich are always the minority, they must bear it, without any redress. Now, setting aside the equity of such a notion, it is still proper to remark, that there is nothing which so readily eludes the grasp of oppression, as capital of this kind. It is, of all capital, the most easily transferred. If oppressed, it will be transferred to more congenial climates; the industry of the country from which it has been removed will languish; its population will diminish; and the majority will find, too late, that the blow which was aimed at the minority, has recoiled upon themselves. There is no better policy, either for nations or for individuals, than strict and even-handed justice.

BOOK THIRD.

BOOK THIRD.

DISTRIBUTION.

WE have seen that, in order to the creation of value, it is necessary that labor be united to capital. In some cases, both of these are the property of the same individual; that is, the same person both owns the capital and performs the labor. In by far the greater number of instances, however, they are the property of different individuals; that is, one person owns the capital, and another person performs the labor. As, when the same person owns both labor and capital, the whole increase of value becomes his exclusive property; so, when these belong to different individuals, the value belongs to them in common; that is, a share of it is the portion of each.

If, then, profit arise from any operation in industry, which has been the joint result of the labor of one man, and the capital of another man, it is a matter of some consequence to ascertain the principles, on which the division of this profit, or the *distribution*, shall be effected. And, besides, in every important operation, a great variety of laborers, is, of necessity, employed; and of these laborers, the skill and talents are very dissimilar. To these different persons, very different proportions of the profit, equitably belong. And, also, the value of the capital thus employed, may be different at different times, and in different occupations. Hence, there will arise a difference in the proportion of profit which shall, at different times, be assigned to a given amount of capital. And, if it be said, that the remuneration in these cases is always arranged among men by mutual consent; it may be still important to ascertain the principles, on which this mutual consent is founded.

This book would, therefore, naturally be divided into two parts: First, *Wages,* or the price of *labor;* and, secondly, *Interest,* or the price of *capital.* But, inasmuch as *Land* is a form of capital, in some measure peculiar, it may be more convenient to consider it separately. We shall, therefore, divide the present book into three chapters.

I. Wages, or the price of *Labor.*

II. Interest, or the price of *Money.*

III. Rent, or the price of *Land.*

CHAPTER FIRST.

OF WAGES, OR THE PRICE OF LABOR.

In this chapter, I shall consider, 1st. The general principles of *wages;* and, 2dly. The *special circumstances,* by which those principles are modified.

SECTION I.

THE GENERAL PRINCIPLES OF WAGES.

The price of any thing, is its exchangeable value, expressed in the form of money.

Exchangeable value, is cost, *plus* the effect of supply and demand.

In order, therefore, to understand the exchangeable value of labor, we must consider, 1st. Its *cost;* and, 2dly. The *effect* of supply and demand upon it.

I. *Of the Cost of Labor.*

Labor may be divided into two kinds: 1st. *Simple labor,* or that which is unconnected with previously acquired skill; and, 2dly. *Educated labor*, or that, in which industry is combined with the results of previous education.

FIRST. *Of Simple Labor.*

In order to produce this, all that is necessary is muscular strength, resulting from a properly formed body, and a sound mind, in ordinary health.

But, in order to the production of health and muscular strength, it is necessary that the human being be supplied with food, clothing, shelter, and, at times, with medicine and medical attendance. If a man have nothing to eat to-day, he cannot labor to-morrow. If, for a few days, he be deprived of food, he will inevitably die. If his food be insufficient in quantity, or of improper quality, his strength will diminish, and, of course, the muscular effort, of which he would be otherwise capable, will be decreased. If this be continued but for a very short time, he will become sick, and thus lose the power of laboring altogether. If he be not relieved, he will die. Hence we see, that there is a natural minimum of the cost of labor. The least cost, is that which is sufficient to give the laborer all the necessaries of life. If we give less, we not only diminish the power of labor, but, in a short time, take it away altogether. Hence, the minimum price of wages, does not depend upon the will of employers, but upon those physiological laws which regulate the existence of man.

2. But, this is not all. Man is short-lived. The species is kept in existence by succession. Unless children be reared, the race would soon become extinct. And children are, for several years, not only unable to earn any thing towards their own support, but they also require a

large portion of the time and labor of the parent. A mother, who has the care of several children, and who also provides for the domestic wants of her husband, is rarely capable of much additional labor. Hence, in order to keep the number of laborers the *same*, in any particular country, it is necessary that the parent or parents receive sufficient wages, not only to provide food, clothing, and shelter for themselves, but, also, for at least two children, until the children be able to support themselves.

But, this is not all. The life of man is often prolonged beyond the period of active labor. In old age, a man is either utterly disqualified for labor, or else his labor is insufficient to support him. Hence, he must either be supported by his children, or else he must, when in his full strength, have accumulated sufficient property to support him in his decrepitude. Hence, the wages of labor must be sufficient, not only to support the laborer, and at least two children, but also to provide for, or to sustain him, in old age, when the power of labor is exhausted.

If so much as this be earned by the laborer, the population of a country may remain stationary. If two children be reared by every human pair, these will supply, but will no more than supply, the ravages of death. This, therefore, is manifestly the lowest price of labor. If wages do not equal the amount necessary for this result, men will become sick, and will die; a less proportion of children than this will be reared; and population will diminish. The lowest price at which the labor of any animal can be procured, is the cost of rearing him, and of maintaining him in health and vigor.

But, it is the fact, that the natural rate of the productiveness of the human species is more rapid than that of two children to two parents. In favorable circumstances, two parents frequently rear six, eight, or ten children. The number of children who are born, does not depend upon the circumstances of the parents. More children are commonly born to the poor, than to the rich. The rich are often childless; the poor, very rarely. But, suppose that the laborer receive only sufficient wages to enable him to support himself and wife, and two children; and that his family amount to six or eight human beings, it is manifest that some of them must perish. The food of two, will not sustain six or eight. The others must starve, or, in some way or other, die of want. The manner in which this occurs, it is painful to contemplate; though, in most of the older countries, it is frequently seen. The pressure, in such a case, must fall upon either the parent or the child, and parental affection generally decides upon which it shall fall first. When parental affection is strong, the parent denies himself of the necessaries of life, in order to support his children, until his constitution, worn down by improper and insufficient food, sinks beneath the burden, and he dies in middle age, leaving his children helpless, unless they be relieved by public charity. When the parental feeling is less acute, the suffering falls directly upon the children. Their food being scanty and unhealthy, but few survive early infancy; and those who do survive it, grow up feeble and unhealthy. A human infant is a tender plant, easily cut down, and liable to frequent diseases. Measles, whooping-cough, croup, teething, chronic complaints of the lungs, head, and abdominal viscera, require assiduous attention, warm clothing, and suitable food for the patient, or else its chance of living is very small. When children, ill-fed, ill-clothed, and without medicine and medical attendance, are attacked by these diseases, they die by thousands. When a portion of a family is thus removed by death, a larger portion of the necessaries of life remains for those who survive; and, thus, their chance of life is increased. Thus, out of a very great number of births, frequently, but two or three children are reared. And this view of the subject is abundantly supported by facts. Adam Smith informs us, that it is no uncommon thing to see a woman, in the Highlands of Scotland, who has borne twenty children, of whom not more than two have arrived at adult years. The same author adds, that, although the children born in military barracks are numerous and apparently healthy, yet, officers have informed him, that rarely enough of them are reared, to supply the regiments with drummers and fifers.

Now, we can scarcely suppose that to be the condition of man which his Creator intended, when so large a number perish in infancy, from suffering, from hardship, and from want. Hence, I suppose the natural cost of labor, or, that cost which corresponds with the proper condition of man, would be that which allows of the rearing of such a number of children as naturally falls to the lot of the human race. This, however, presupposes the laborers to be industrious, virtuous, and frugal. If they be improvident, indolent, intemperate and profligate, and thus either do not earn a competency, or else, having earned it, squander it in vice, the fault lies, not in their wages, but in themselves. Of course, the correction must come, not from a change in wages, but from a change in habits.

It is, however, here to be remarked, that what is necessary to the sustentation and comfort of a human being, differs greatly in different climates. In northern latitudes, human beings seem to need a larger portion of animal food, in order to endure labor. The Esquimaux live upon animal food entirely, and Sir E. Parry informs us, that, while wintering at the North Pole, he observed that the appetite of both his officers and men was much stronger than usual, not only for animal food, but for animal food of the richest and most nutritious description. And as animal, is more expensive than vegetable food, the northern laborer, on this account, is more expensive than the southern. Again: In cold climates, clothing is much more expensive. A laborer must use both winter and summer clothing; it must protect him from the cold and wet, or he will become sick and die. In cold climates, much more expense is incurred, in the erection of houses. A comfortable house, in a northern country, costs the labor of several men for several weeks, and of some men of considerable skill. In India, a day or two are sufficient to erect a bamboo-house, which, in that climate, answers tolerably well for the purposes of a habitation. And, besides this, in a cold climate, fuel, which must be used from three to six months in the year, is a very great item in the bill of annual expense. In warm countries, fuel is used for no other purpose than that of cooking; and, for this purpose, there, a very small quantity suffices.

These circumstances are sufficient to account, in part, for the different prices of labor, in southern India, and in the northern parts of Europe, and of the United States. Laborers in Batavia are hired for four cents a day; and, in India, I believe, they are hired for the same sum. This would scarcely pay for the fuel, with which the meals of a northern laborer are cooked.

It would seem, at first view, from these facts, that the laborers in southern latitudes would have a great advantage over the laborers at the north, and must, of necessity, undersell them in every thing. But such seems not to be the case. The enervating nature of the climate, unfits them for labor; and indisposes them to the putting forth of intellectual skill. Hence it is, that this labor is mere muscular force, accompanied by scarcely any of the advantages derived from natural agents. The rigors of a northern latitude compel men to invention, and invigorate them for continued effort. Hence, although a northern laborer receives one dollar, or one dollar and fifty cents per day, and the Hindoo receives only four cents, yet the former is, in fact, the cheaper laborer; that is, it is the most economical to employ him. And the evidence of this is seen in the fact, that raw cotton is, at present, carried from India, manufactured in Great Britain, and then, carried back to India, and sold cheaper than it can be made in India by the native workmen.

SECONDLY. I have, thus far, treated only of *simple* labor; that is, labor with which no such skill is united, as requires a previous education.

But, this is only a part of the labor which is employed by man. A large portion of it, requires special and peculiar training. This, of course, adds to its cost. Suppose, as I have already stated, that the natural price of simple labor were merely sufficient to sustain a family, consisting of the ordinary number of persons. A man would, therefore, by labor, without any education, under such circumstances, earn this amount. But, if another labored for the same number of hours, but labored at an operation which he could not learn to perform, without spending six or seven years in acquiring an education, it is manifest that the second would be entitled to additional wages. Thus, suppose the laborer must spend seven years in acquiring a knowledge of his trade. During this time he is earning nothing. Now his wages, at compound interest, if he had been at profitable labor, would amount to a considerable sum, specially if they had been invested in capital, which might have been united with his own labor. He is entitled, therefore, to such an addition to his wages, as would pay the interest upon this amount. Besides, in many cases, the learner not only earns nothing, but is obliged to board and clothe himself. This amount is to be added to the capital which he has expended, and for which his wages should pay the interest. Nor is this all. The learner is frequently obliged to pay a large sum for instruction. This, also, is to be added to his investment, for which he is to be paid when we employ him. Thus, in the learned professions, a student is obliged, commonly, to spend two or three years in preparing for college, to spend four years in college, and three years in professional studies, before he is permitted to practise. During the whole of these nine or ten years, in which he earns nothing, he must be fed, clothed, and furnished with books, and must pay a very considerable sum to his instructors for tuition. He must, in most cases, also possess the means to meet all these expenses, before he commences. Now, had he used such a sum skilfully, from the time at which he commenced, to that at which he concluded his studies, it would have amounted to a small competency. He is, therefore, fairly entitled, in addition to the price of simple labor, to such wages as would pay the interest of whatever such a sum would have amounted to, had it been used with ordinary skill.

Wages, which, in addition to the price of simple labor, would pay the interest of whatever is expended in procuring the necessary education, would hence be the lowest cost of such labor. And, it is manifest, also, that these should vary with the cost of the investment necessary for acquiring the skill. Thus, the wages of him who was obliged to *sustain himself* while a learner, should be higher than those of him, who, though he earned nothing, was boarded and clothed by his teacher. The wages of him who was obliged to pay for his tuition, should be higher than those of him, who, though he boarded and lodged himself, received his tuition for his services. And, if such wages be not generally paid, such labor will not ordinarily be produced. Parents who have capital to bestow upon their children, are generally desirous of investing it to the best advantage. If the capital necessary to furnish a professional education, will not improve the condition of a child, the parent will not invest the money in a professional education, but will employ it, for the advantage of his child, in some other way. In this manner, the supply of such labor will be diminished, until necessity obliges men to offer greater inducements to produce it.

II. *Of the supply and demand for Labor.*

FIRST. *Of the supply of Simple Labor.* I have before stated that the number of children *born*, does not depend either upon the riches or the poverty of the parents; but that the number born, is generally greater among the poor, than among the rich. I have also stated, however, that the number *reared* does depend, very greatly, upon the circumstances of the parents. When the wages of parents are barely sufficient to rear two children, but two will be reared; the rest will die in infancy. When wages will allow of rearing four, four will, *on an average*, be reared; and so on, until we arrive at the natural limit of fecundity of the human race, supposing the habits of the parents to be virtuous, industrious, and frugal. Now, as simple labor requires nothing but healthy human beings, it is manifest that the supply of this labor will be in proportion to the demand; that is, if wages be such as to indicate an actual demand for a large increase of labor, a large increase of labor will be the result. If wages be such as to demand only a diminished amount of labor, a diminished number of laborers will be reared. And this result will take place, until, on the one hand, it reaches the limit of the natural increase of the human race; or until, on the other hand, the number of human beings be so reduced by death or by emigration, that it can be sustained by the wages which industry can command.

If this first limit be reached; that is, if wages be so high as to support all the children that are born, and yet there be a want of laborers, wages will rise very high; and the deficiency will generally be supplied by imigration. Laborers from less favored countries will then flow in, to supply the demand. The overburdened population of an older country will be drained off, and the surplus capital of a new country will be profitably employed.

2. Such is the case with simple labor, or that which is produced by the mere multiplication of human beings. The same principles apply, in substance, to that sort of labor which consists of industry, directed by previously acquired skill, but which requires no special natural endowment. In this case, as has been remarked, if the investment made in education will afford sufficient emolument, in addition to that obtained by simple labor, it will be produced. If this additional emolument be insufficient, it will not be produced; that is, men will not be educated for this particular occupation; or, if they have been educated for it, they will leave it, and devote themselves to some other pursuit.

3. But, it frequently happens, that not only an education, but also peculiar native talent is necessary, in order to arrive at eminence, in a particular pursuit. When this is the case, the supply is limited by the gift of the Creator, and cannot be increased by the agency of man. No pecuniary emolument could create the talent of a Milton or a Shakspeare, a Cicero or a Demosthenes, a Watt or a Fulton. Hence, the demand for such talent being great, and the supply limited, and by human effort incapable of in-

crease, the exchangeable value of its productions is frequently great. The emoluments of Sir Walter Scott were princely. It not unfrequently happens, however, that this sort of talent is in advance of its age, and its value is not appreciated until after the death of its possessor. Although, however, demand cannot create unusual genius, yet it is the fact, that, whenever the demand is greatest for any particular talent, then, that talent is most likely to arise. The reason I suppose to be, that, in proportion to the encouragement which it receives, the less is the liability that any portion of that which the Creator has bestowed will be lost. Military talent, which is commonly held in high estimation, seems to be of very frequent occurrence. A nation has rarely any real need for it, without producing, in a short time, as great an amount of it as can be desired. The same remarks apply, in a considerable degree, to the talent for invention; for scientific investigation; for eloquence; and many others.

SECONDLY. *Of demand for Labor.* We have already divided labor into two kinds, viz: First, *Simple labor*, comprehending, under this term, that which requires only that skill which every person may easily acquire; and, secondly, that which requires some *peculiar talent*, and is perfected only by long and expensive training. We shall here, as above, consider these separately.

I. *Of Simple Labor, and that which requires only such skill as may be easily acquired by all.*

This is the sort of labor required to produce the necessities of life; that is, labor in the several departments of operative industry. For this labor, the desire is incessant and universal. Every one in the community needs, at every hour of his life, the results of that labor which produces food, clothing, fuel and shelter. Unless these can be procured, the human being will die; and, as these articles perish with the using, the demand is not only imperative, but unremitting.

Now, such being the fact, he who possesses capital, knows that, if he can transform it into such products, he can always reasonably anticipate a profit. But he cannot transform it into such products, without labor. Hence, as incessant and imperative as is the demand for the necessities of life, so incessant and imperative must be the demand of the capitalist for that labor, by means of which alone they are produced. If a community need clothing, and a capitalist have all the means for making clothing; and want nothing but workmen to create the product; just in proportion to the demand for clothing, will be his demand for the workmen, by whose agency alone this demand can be supplied, and his capital rendered profitable.

Such being the fact, there must always be a demand for such labor; hence, when there is any capital, such labor will always bring something. The rate at which it will be paid at different times, and in different countries, is next to be considered.

We have already stated, that wages are the result of a partnership, formed between the laborer and the capitalist, in which the one receives a portion of the value created, in return for his labor; and the other, the remainder, in return for the use of his capital. Both of these parties are equally necessary to each other. If the laborer could not procure work, or could not exchange his labor for some value which he created, he must starve. If the capitalist could not create value from the employment of his capital, he must starve also. He could neither eat, nor drink, nor wear his looms, spinning-jennies, ships, iron, or cotton.

Both, therefore, come into the market on equal terms; each needs the product of the other; and, under these circumstances, they will each receive either less or more, in consequence of the conditions under which the exchange is made.

Every capitalist wishes to have all his capital united with labor; for, that which is not thus united, will be useless to him; nay, it will generally diminish in actual value. On the other hand, in a given state of the arts, the labor of a single man can be applied to but a given amount of capital. Hence, the number of laborers whom any single capitalist will require, will be in proportion to the amount of his capital. If a capitalist of ten thousand dollars require ten laborers, one of one hundred thousand dollars will require one hundred laborers. And so, in general, the greater the amount of capital employed in a country, the greater, of course, will be the number of laborers required.

As now, every capitalist will wish to employ all his capital, if the number of laborers be insufficient to supply the demand, there will be a competition among capitalists for laborers, and they will offer higher wages; that is, rather than have any portion of their capital useless, they will offer a larger share of the profits to the laborer. The first class of workmen will be all employed at a high price, and a portion of the second class will be raised one grade, in order to supply the demand. The second class will, therefore, be still more insufficient to supply the demand for their description of labor, and their wages will rise, and the increased deficiency be supplied from the third class. And, at last, those who were before employed only at simple labor, will be taken up and taught; and thus, the whole class of workmen will be raised one grade in labor and in wages.

And the reverse will take place in the opposite case. Suppose the number of laborers be too great to be employed by the existing amount of capital. A capitalist whose capital will occupy but one hundred, cannot employ one hundred and fifty laborers. Hence, there will be a competition among laborers for work. After as many of the first class have been employed as are needed, there will remain a portion of them out of work. These must fall into the second class, and receive the second rate of wages. This will cause an excess still greater in the second class; their wages will fall, and a still greater number will fall into the third class. The lowest class will thus be supplied from the classes above it, and it must betake itself to simple labor, or labor of the cheapest kind, while many of those whose only support is derived from simple labor, must be out of employment, either wholly or in part; that is, the whole class of laborers will fall one grade, and their wages will depreciate in proportion. Hence we see, that, at any given time and place, the demand for labor, and the wages of labor will be in the proportion to the ratio that the active capital of a country bears, to the number of laborers in that country.

But provision has been made, in our physical constitution, for the rapid increase of the human race. It is capable of doubling, once in twenty-five years, as is seen to be the case in the United States. And, provision is also made, for the rapid accumulation of capital. The earth, every year, if it be properly tilled, and if capital be properly employed, produces more than its inhabitants consume. This surplus may be turned into fixed capital, and may thus give employment to a larger number of laborers. Hence we see, that the average rate of wages, in any country, for a number of years taken together, must depend upon the ratio which the annual accumulation of capital in any country, bears to the annual increase of human beings. If wages be high, and capital increase as fast as the human species increases, wages will, for any period that may be contemplated, continue as they are at present. If wages be low, and capital does not increase faster than the human race, they will continue low. If the increase of capital be more rapid than the natural increase of the human race, wages, however high, will rise, until they be so high that production can yield no profit. The deficiency would then be supplied by foreigners, who would emigrate to the more favored country. If the increase of capital be less rapid than that of the human race, the price of wages will fall, distress in the working classes will ensue, and they must either emigrate or starve.

Hence we see, that the prosperity of a nation does not depend simply upon the *absolute* amount of its capital, but upon the ratio which its capital bears to its population, and the ratio which is maintained between the increase of both. If the increase of capital be so rapid as to allow the simple laborer sufficient wages to support and rear as many children as, under ordinary circumstances, form a human family, there will be no distress in any class; all will be well supported; there will be no beggars from necessity; and every one will have the additional advantage arising from his skill and his education. If the increase of capital be more rapid than this, every one will have, besides support and maintenance, many of the conveniences of life; and a large proportion will be continually rising from a lower, to a higher grade of employment. When the increase of capital is less rapid than the ordinary increase of the human race, there will be, in the lowest class, continual distress; children will die in great numbers; the average duration of human life will be shortened; and many persons will be sinking from the higher, into the lower grades of employment and comfort.

The former seems to be the condition of this country. Hence, distressing poverty, or poverty which shortens life, except it arise from intemperance, or from some form of vice or indolence, is very rare. The common laborer, if industrious, virtuous and frugal, may not only support himself, but, in a few years, accumulate a valuable little capital. And, notwithstanding the great immigration of foreigners, the wages of labor are annually rising. Hence, it is evident, that the increase of capital more than keeps pace with the natural and imported increase of the human race.

In Ireland, the case is reversed. There, the lowest classes are, and have been for a long period, in the most abject poverty. Multitudes of them are said to die, annually, of famine. He is considered in tolerable circumstances, who is able to furnish his family with a hovel, with one full meal of potatoes a day, and with a sufficient supply of straw to be spread upon the earthy floor for bedding. The reason I suppose to be, that, in addition to the deplorable ignorance of the people, the land is owned in England; and the rents, collected by rapacious underlings, is annually carried away and spent in England, instead of being turned into fixed capital in Ireland. Hence, the annual increase adds but little to the capital of the country; and the people must starve or emigrate.

This subject illustrates the connexion between capital and population. Population always follows capital. It increases, as capital increases; is stationary, when capital is stationary; and decreases, when capital decreases. And hence, there seems no need of any other means to prevent the too rapid increase of population, than to secure a correspondent increase of capital, by which that population may be supported.

Several conclusions naturally belong to this part of this subject, to which it may be proper in this place to allude.

1. If the above reasonings be correct, we see the great importance, both of individual and national frugality. It is by many persons supposed, that luxury and expensiveness in individuals are specially useful to the poor; and that economy and frugality are injurious to them. We see, however, that nothing could be more evidently erroneous. He who consumes upon horses, and dogs, and equipage, ten thousand dollars' worth of value, is annually putting out of existence a value, which, if united with industry, might support several families in comfort; and he is thus rendering it impossible, that so many can be supported. He who saves this sum by frugality, and invests it in some profitable enterprise, employs the persons whom it will support the first year; and, by so doing, is enabled to support a larger number the next year, and thus on, indefinitely. The one is destroying, for ever, a fund for the support of industry; the other is annually rendering that fund larger and more productive.

2. The same is true of nations. The annual revenue of a nation, must, of course be derived from the annual revenues of the people. If a man, this year, pay one hundred dollars in taxes, he has precisely ninety dollars less to unite with the industry of the next year, than he would have, if he paid only ten dollars. And thus, if the annual expenditures of a nation be fifty millions, these fifty millions are just so much abstracted from the fund which has been collected during that year, for the purpose of supporting the addition which this year has made to the number of the human race. If the whole revenue of the nation were barely sufficient to employ and support the annual increase of its inhabitants, those who would have been supported by these additional fifty millions,

must perish. Such is the natural and necessary result of national prodigality.

I do not, however, by any means, intend to assert, that taxes are not always necessary. A government necessarily involves expense. And, if the government be well administered, no mode of expenditure yields a richer or more valuable product than taxes. What I have to say, is merely this: that while all the expense necessary to good government should be met, and met cheerfully and liberally, yet expense, *beyond this*, is a benefit to no one ; it diminishes the comforts of all, and destroys the lives of multitudes. Hence, we see the evil of any form of government, which, by necessity, involves great expenditure. Hence we see, also, the evil of laws of entail, and of all other arrangements, by which immense amounts of capital are accumulated in the hands of single individuals, or of families, in perpetuity. In this manner, the annual productiveness of a country is greatly decreased, and, in consequence, the annual revenue of the whole, is by the difference lessened.

3. Of all the modes of national expenditure, the most enormous is that of war. In the first place, the expense of the munitions of war is overwhelming. In the next place, the most athletic and vigorous laborers must be selected for slaughter. Of these, the time and labor are wholly unproductive. The operations of industry, in both belligerent nations, are thus greatly paralyzed. The destruction of property, in the district through which an army passes, is generally very great. All this must be taken from the earnings of a people; and, is so much capital absolutely destroyed, from which multitudes might have been reared, and have lived in prosperity.*

* To illustrate the vast expenditure of war, I here insert an estimate of the expenses of some of the latest wars. I do not vouch for its entire

If the considerations which have been adduced above be correct, there is no need of seeking any further for the cause of that distress among the lower classes, of which we hear so frequently in Europe. If the capital which a bountiful Creator has provided for the sustenance of man, be dissipated in wars, his creatures must perish for the want of it. Nor do we need any abstruse theories of population, to enable us to ascertain in what manner this excess of population may be prevented. Let nations cul-

accuracy, but, I presume it will be found, in general, correct. It is from one of the publications of the Peace Society, and seems to be made up from authentic documents :

GREAT BRITAIN.

War expenses, for the year 1815, - - - - - - - -	£54,317,767
Interest on debt, for that year, - - - - - - - - -	6,200,000
	£60,517,767
Military and naval expense, for 1818, - - - - - -	15,155,000
Difference of the two years, - - - - - - - - - -	45,362,767
Equal to - - - - - - - - -	$201,362,898

FRANCE.

Military expenses for 1809, - - - - - - - francs.	656,500,000
Contributions on foreign nations, - - - -	330,000,000
Total, - - - - - - - - - -	986,500,000
In 1817, the military expense was, - - - - - - -	228,000,000
Expense of one year's war, - - - - - - - - - - -	758,500,000
Equal to - - - - - - - -	$142,218,750

The estimated cost to Great Britain, of 22 years' war,	£720,000,000
Equal to - - - - - - - -	$3,200,000,000
War expense of France, for same period, - - -	3,130,000,000
Austria, about - - - - - - - - -	2,000,000,000
Three years' war of the United States, - - -	120,000,000
	8,450,000,000
Expense of other European Powers, - - - - - -	4,550,000,000
	13,000,000,000

This is nothing but the national expense, without estimating the prodigious and incalculable losses to individuals.

tivate the arts of peace. Let them reduce the unnecessary expenses of governments. Let them abolish those restrictions which fetter and dispirit industry, by diminishing the inducements to labor. Let them foster the means by which the productiveness of labor may be increased, and the annual gifts of the Creator will so accumulate, that the means will be provided for the support of all the human beings which are annually brought into the world. As soon as this accumulation bears a suitable ratio to the number of inhabitants, we shall hear no more of the evils of excess of population. It is vain to throw away the food of a million of people in a single day, and then be astonished that a million of people are starving for the want of it.

Hence, we see the economical evils of every form of vice, as, for instance, of intemperance. The money spent in intemperance, is so much absolute waste of capital. This is, of itself, in most civilized countries, enormous. But besides this, it unfits the individual for labor; it is the author of numerous diseases, both in parents and in children. It is the cause of almost all the crime and pauperism in the community. All these together, if they could be correctly estimated, would form a total amount, which would seem almost incredible; and they are altogether exclusive of that loss of social, intellectual, and moral happiness, which results from this vice.

To sum up what has been said. We see that the demand for the labor employed in the production of the neccessaries of life; and, of course, the wages of labor, must be in proportion to the ratio which the amount of capital in any given community, holds to the number of laborers; and to the ratio which the accumulation of capital bears to the increase of the human race. And these being at any time fixed, wages will rise or fall, as this ratio varies. If capital be increasing more rapidly than human beings, wages will rise. If it be not increasing so fast, wages will fall. And if, from any sudden change in the affairs of a country, this ratio be suddenly affected, wages will be affected accordingly.

II. I come now to consider that sort of labor, which requires special and expensive education, and some peculiar natural endowment; such, for instance, is the labor which is bestowed upon the fine arts, and which is employed in some of the professions.

1. The desire for this labor, varies with the state of society. In the beginnings of a nation, when every one is interested in providing the means of subsistence, there is little time or capital to spare for the cultivation of a taste for the fine arts. And, at a yet more advanced period, when the wages of labor are universally high, and every one may reasonably cherish the hope of attaining to independence, the love of gain is too absorbing a passion to allow of the development of any habit that does not conduce to pecuniary acquisition. It is only in the later and more advanced stages of society, where hereditary fortunes have been built up, and where accumulated property gives opportunity for leisure and refinement, that much desire is manifested for those productions of the fine arts, which are considered the offspring of the rarest and most highly gifted talent.

2. The ability to gratify this desire, depends also upon the social condition of a people. The productions of the fine arts are generally very costly. Hence, where property is nearly equally divided, where no one is poor, though no one may be exorbitantly rich, such productions could have but few purchasers. Whether wages were high or low, whether there were no beggars, or whether there were ten

thousand beggars, would have no effect upon the probability of the sale of a statue which cost one hundred thousand dollars. The demand, of necessity, is limited to the wealthy; and that form of social organization which is most favorable to the accumulation of large estates, and to the retaining of them in the hands of single individuals, will always be most favorable to the cultivation of the fine arts. In this country, where we have few beggars, and where, but for intemperance and vice, we should have none, a first-rate sculptor or painter would starve. In many of the countries of Europe, where the poor are frequently famishing, and where a large proportion of the population are beggars, you may frequently find, in the gallery of a single gentleman, a finer collection of paintings, than could be made from all the pictures in the whole United States. Hence, I think that the prospect for the arts, in this country, is by no means encouraging.

SECTION II.

OF THE SPECIAL CIRCUMSTANCES BY WHICH, IRRESPECTIVELY OF THE INFLUENCE OF CAPITAL, THE WAGES OF LABOR ARE AFFECTED.

In the preceding section, I have endeavored to show in what manner wages, or the price of labor, are affected by capital. The general principle there illustrated, is, that wages will be high, when the proportion of capital to labor is great; and low, when the proportion of capital to labor is small. And that wages will be rising or falling, as this proportion of capital to labor is increasing or diminishing. On this principle, I suppose that the difference of wages, in different countries, under the same physical conditions, may be explained.

And the same principle may be carried a step farther. Whenever, in any country, capital is removed from one kind of employment to another, the wages, in that form of labor to which capital is transferred, will be raised. Thus, if a people find it for their interest to employ their capital in manufactures, instead of navigation; the wages of manufacturers will rise, and those of sailors will fall. This will continue, until the demand for manufacturing labor is supplied. But, when once the current is set in any direction, it frequently continues to move, after the force which was originally applied has ceased. Hence, it will frequently happen, that a change of this sort will abstract from navigation too large a number of laborers, so that there will not be a sufficient supply to meet even the diminished demand. In this case, the wages of seamen will rise again, somewhat above the proper average.

But, supposing all these circumstances to be adjusted; there will yet remain others of a different kind, to affect the wages of labor. We do not find that the wages of all laborers are the same, whether labor be high or low, and whether the productiveness of labor be great or small. A captain receives higher wages than a sailor; a master manufacturer, higher wages than his journeyman; and a merchant, higher wages than his clerk. The circumstances which cause these differences, remain now briefly to be noticed.

1. The price of labor is affected by the ease or difficulty, the pleasure or pain, of the employment.

When the employment requires great muscular effort, the number of persons who can accomplish it, is comparatively small. This diminishes the supply, and, of course, increases the price. When this is the case, as men are not usually attracted by the prospect of hard labor, a smaller number apply for this kind of employment. This still further diminishes the supply. Hence, the price will rise, as the wages must be increased sufficiently to overcome this repugnance. On the contrary, when the labor is easy, the number of persons, both able and willing to perform it, is increased; thus, the supply is large, and wages fall in proportion.

The same effect is produced by the general estimation of the pleasantness or unpleasantness of the employment. Any kind of industry, which, from necessity, is uncleanly, commands higher wages than one which can be performed without interfering with personal neatness. One which is considered disgraceful, can be supplied with laborers, only by paying an unusual price. The business of a public executioner, though not difficult, is disagreeable, and generally considered disgraceful; and hence, in countries where it is made a distinct profession, it commands high wages. The labor in the learned professions, is considered honorable; and, therefore, it is less highly recompensed than the same degree of labor and skill in other employments.

2. Wages are affected by the *skill* required in performing the operation. This arises from two circumstances: *First,* skill can be acquired only by practice and education. This, as has been explained, is in itself costly, and is an investment, for which the possessor of right receives an emolument. And, *secondly,* unusual skill generally supposes some unusual endowment. But, in proportion to the rarity of the endowment, must be the smallness of the supply, and, of course, the rise of price which must be paid for the product.

3. *The confidence reposed.* Wherever a great amount of capital is employed, it must, to a very considerable degree, be placed in the power of some one or more agents. Hence, if this power be abused, or used unwisely, the whole is liable to be lost. If the manager be careless, he may destroy it by negligence; and, if he be dishonest, he may convert it to his own emolument. Now, this union of judgment with incorruptible integrity, is absolutely necessary in many of the operations of production. But, such a union is rarely to be found. Hence, while the demand is imperative, the supply is small. On this account, the wages of such persons are high; and it is generally found more economical to secure such persons at any price, than to entrust important affairs to the incompetent and the vicious. This is one of the rewards, which, in the course of human events, God bestows upon wisdom and virtue.

4. *Certainty or uncertainty, constancy or inconstancy,* of employment. Division of labor requires that a man devote himself exclusively to a single employment, and, therefore, that his whole emolument be derived from that employment. Hence, when the opportunities of employment are rare, the wages for each particular operation must be greater; since we must pay, not only for the time actually employed, but also for that time which is lost to the laborer, while waiting for employment. We pay more for riding a mile in a hackney-coach, than for riding the same distance in a stage-coach; because the hackney-coachman may stand half a day in waiting, before he finds another customer. For the same reason, although horse keeping is higher in the city than in a country town, you pay less for coach hire in the former case, than in the latter, because of the greater steadiness of the employment. Thus, also, when a trade can be exercised for only a part of the year, as in the case of a

brick-layer, you pay to the laborer higher wages; because he must receive enough to compensate for the time in which he is obliged to lie idle.

5. Another circumstance which affects the price of wages, is the *certainty or uncertainty* of success. In most of the ordinary avocations of life, if a man acquire the requisite skill, he will invariably find employment. In the professions, it is not so. Those who have prepared themselves at great expense to exercise them, unable to find employment, sometimes relinquish them for other pursuits. When there is such a risk, the wages of labor should be greater; for the laborer is entitled to a remuneration for the risk of this loss of time and of capital.

These, I believe, are the principal circumstances on which, irrespectively of the influence of capital, the price of labor depends. It will be at once seen, that they are susceptible of very great variety of modification, and combination; and that, frequently, several of them require to be taken into the account, in order to explain the reason of the high or low price of any particular form of labor. I think, however, that by such combination, the various phenomena of wages may be generally explained.

The preceding remarks are intended to apply to those cases, in which the individual is supported *wholly* by his own labor. When an individual, or a class of individuals, have any other means of support, the price of labor, of course, falls, and can be subjected to no general rule. Thus, a large portion of the laboring class of females are supported, in part, by their relatives; some of them receiving house-rent, others, both house-rent and board, for nothing. Hence, they are enabled to labor for a price far less than the actual cost. This is one reason why the price of female labor, especially of that labor which requires but little skill, and which can be done at home, is so low. Another reason is, that the customs of society restrict the modes of production in which female labor may be employed. Hence, in these modes of production, the supply of labor is greater than the demand. Hence, also, the establishment of a manufactory, or the introduction of any kind of labor, which furnishes a new mode of female employment, advances the price of female labor. This, also, is the reason why the labor performed in nunneries, monasteries, and state prisons, is sold below the market price. The fact is, that the laborers are supported, either in whole or in part, by a separate fund; and hence, there is no *natural* price for their products, since it is not regulated by the *cost.*

CHAPTER SECOND.

THE PRICE OF MONEY, OR INTEREST.

SECTION 1.

OF THE BENEFIT OF CAPITAL TO THE LABORER.

Having, in the preceding chapter, endeavored to illustrate the principles which regulate the rate of wages, we now proceed to illustrate those which regulate the rate of interest, or the price of capital.

We have already stated, that when two persons were engaged in creating a product, a part of the profit belonged to the labor, and a part to the capital. Let us first consider the benefit of capital to the laborer.

Suppose a laborer to be endowed with health, and also with skill sufficient to perform an operation in any mode of production. His power is made up of two things, first, mere *muscular force;* and, secondly, *skill.* By the one, he is enabled to exert mere brute force, as in lifting, carrying, or drawing. By the second, he is enabled to avail himself of the use of natural agents; for, skill in production, is little else than this ability. But it is evident that his labor of the first kind, is vastly less productive than that of the second kind, as the simple labor of a man's hands, is less productive than that labor which is employed in directing the agents of nature.

Suppose, now, a man entirely deprived of the use of capital; his labor must be wholly of the first kind; of course, it must be of the least productive quality, and it must earn the lowest rate of wages. Suppose a blacksmith, of ever so great skill, destitute of forge, hammer, anvil, and of all his tools, and also of iron upon which to employ them; he can, in no manner, avail himself of his skill, or of the use of the natural agents with which he is acquainted, and he must either perish, or else earn his livelihood by simple labor; that is, by the putting forth of mere brute force, without any benefit from his skill, though it be ever so great. But, let some one loan him a shop and tools, with iron and coal sufficient to carry on his business, and he can, at once, avail himself of his skill; that is, of the use of those natural agents, with which he is acquainted. His labor will now become vastly more productive; that is, he can, in a given time, create a vastly greater amount of value than before, and will, of course, receive a much larger recompense. If his simple labor were worth one dollar per day, his labor and skill will now probably be worth at least two dollars; that is, the capital which he uses, has at least doubled his wages. This, at the rate of three hundred working days in a year, would be equal to three hundred dollars, which he receives for the use of the capital which was loaned to him. Suppose that this capital were worth, originally, five hundred dollars; and that he paid for the use and wear and tear of it, ten per cent. per year, he might then pay fifty dollars for the use of it, and have two hundred and fifty dollars nett profit, over and above the wages which his simple labor could earn. In two years, he might, besides paying the interest, pay for the whole capital, and thus own it himself. He would then be entitled to all the profit derived from the three several sources: first, his *labor;* secondly, his *skill;* and, thirdly, the use of the *capital*, upon which his labor was employed.

I have, in the above case, supposed the laborer to *borrow* the shop, tools and materials. This is not the ordinary way in which capital is borrowed. It is much more common, and much more convenient for him, who wishes to borrow the capital with which to employ his skill, to borrow it in the form of *money*, which he immediately transforms into that kind of capital, which his occupation requires. Hence, contracts of this kind are always estimated in money. And hence, *interest* is commonly called the *price of money.* It is evident, however, that it is not the *money*, but the *capital*, which is wanted; because, as soon as the man obtains the *money*, he at once exchanges it for *capital.* This, therefore, should always be borne in mind, that when we speak of the price of *money*, we always mean the price of *capital*, for which the money is always exchanged.

Hence we see, that the laborer may derive very great benefit from the loan of money; that is, of capital. He is thus enabled to employ, advantageously, all his *skill;* and thus, a loan for a few years is very frequently the commencement of a fortune. And hence we see, as we have said before, how very absurd is the prejudice so commonly excited against money-lenders, and money-lending institutions. Were there no money-lenders, there could be no money-borrowers; and were there no money-borrowers, the industrious artisan would surely be the greatest sufferer. It is not denied that the money-lender, loans for his own advantage. But, I do not see why it is any more odious for one man to *lend* for his own advantage, than for another man to *borrow* for his own advantage. It is not pleaded, that the one, any more than the other, is *benevolent.* This is another question. All that is pleaded is, that both, in so far as the things themselves are concerned, are equally honest and honorable. In both cases, the man benefits himself while he benefits others; and this is all that can be said in favor of any other exchange. It is not, of course, denied, that the lender may be oppressive, tyrannical, and avaricious; nor that the borrower may be fraudulent, indolent, and profligate. But this affects not the nature of the transaction *per se.* We here speak of the thing itself, and not of the manner in which either party may act, in consequence of, or in connexion with, it.

I have stated but one form in which the laborer is benefitted by the use of capital. Another form of equal advantage is equally common.

Suppose that a village were destitute of capital, and that its inhabitants were therefore obliged to be employed in simple labor, or in that which required the least skill, and, therefore, produced the lowest wages. They would, consequently, be poor, and would be able to accumulate very little; since, their whole earnings would be scarcely more than sufficient to provide them with the necessaries of life. Let, now, an opulent man come among them, and establish a manufactory which should employ every inhabitant capable of labor. Every one knows, that, by this means, the wages of labor would be doubled, and all the comforts of living would be incomparably increased. The reason is the same, in principle, as in the other case. The capitalist furnishes the materials and the tools, by which the laborer is now enabled to use his skill, in addition to the simple labor, which he used formerly; that is, by which he is enabled to labor, not with his hands, but also with the agents of nature. The result is, a great increase of the productiveness of industry; and, of course, a much larger amount than before, becomes the portion of the laborer. In the division of the profits, the owner receives payment for the use, wear and tear, and risk of his instruments, for the use and risk of his material, and for his own labor and skill in supervision, if he superintend; or for the labor and skill of another, if he does it by a deputy. The workman receives payment for his labor and for his skill, according to the principles illustrated in the preceding chapter. We see, that, in this case, the laborer is as truly benefitted by the use of capital, as in the preceding case. The only difference is, that *here*, he receives payment only for labor and skill; and *there* he received payment for the use of capital, deducting the rate of interest and the risk of loss. It will be easy to apply the principle here illustrated to other cases. When a merchant borrows capital, he is thus enabled to use his skill in exchange. Hence, the use of capital, makes the difference between his wages as a merchant, and what his wages would be, were he a common laborer. And so of any other case.

Hence, we see how incorrect is the notion frequently advanced, that when property is destroyed by fire or flood, or in any other manner, it is of no consequence to the community; since it was nothing but the possessions of the rich. The rich may, or may not, suffer in their comforts and conveniences, by such a loss; but the poor always must suffer. The very means by which their wages are raised from those of simple to those of skilful labor, from the wages of labor with their hands alone, to the wages of labor with the agents of nature, is thus taken away. Remove capital, and they have nothing to offer in exchange, but mere physical force. Hence, it is always to be remembered, that, in the destruction of property, the poor are always the greatest sufferers.

It is evident, then, that capital loaned, should be paid for. Interest is no extortion, and no unreasonable demand. It is for the advantage of the skilful laborer to borrow it, at a reasonable interest, as much as it is for the advantage of the capitalist to loan it; and it is as much for the advantage of the laborer as of the capitalist, to enter into that partnership, by which they share the profits of the operation between them. It is by reason of this partnership, as I have said, that the laborer receives the wages of *skill*, instead of the wages of mere *physicial force;* and the capitalist is able to employ *all* his capital in production, instead of employing only *that portion* of it, which he could employ with simply his own personal industry and skill.

We next proceed to consider the circumstances which vary the rate of interest at which capital may be borrowed. These, I suppose to be three, viz: 1st. *Risk;* 2d. *Convenience of Investment;* and, 3d. *Productiveness of Capital.*

SECTION II.

OF RISK, AND CONVENIENCE OF INVESTMENT.

I. *Of Risk.* When a man loans his property to another, there is always a risk of his never being repaid. Now, the greater this risk, the greater will be the interest which a capitalist may justly demand. He who would loan to one man, for six per cent., when he was sure of being repaid, would not, surely, loan to another man, for the same sum, when there were fifty chances in one hundred, that he would lose both principal and interest. At any rate, he who did so, would very soon cease loaning altogether.

This risk depends upon several circumstances. Of these, the principal are: the nature of the employment; the character of the borrower; and the character of the government.

1. There is a difference in risk, arising from the different modes of employing capital. For instance, property at sea, is more liable to destruction than property on land. Hence, the ancient Athenians made a difference between land and marine interest. The former was at twelve, and the latter as high as sixty per cent. per annum. Property in merchandise is more liable to be destroyed, than property in houses; property in houses, than property in farms. A house in the country, is safer than a house in town; and a stone house is safer than a wooden house. Property employed in the manufacture of cotton, is less liable to be destroyed than property employed in the manufacture of gunpowder. Now, when a capitalist loans property to be invested in some one of the above forms of capital, and his only security for payment consists in his hold upon the property in which it is invested, it is evident that his risk, other things being equal, will depend upon the safety of that property. Hence, it is reasonable that his remuneration for risk, should correspond with the greatness of that risk.

It may also be remarked, that the principle is the same, whether capital be used by the owner, or by some other person. If a merchant borrow capital, under the circumstances above mentioned, he pays according to the nature of the risk. If he use his own property, he is entitled to remuneration for that risk. He may, if he please, have it insured, and then he pays for the insurance, and charges this in the cost of the articles which he sells. Or he may leave it uninsured; that is, insure it himself, and then he is entitled to an advance on his profit, equal to that which he would have paid to an insurance company for insuring it. Thus, if a merchant import one hundred thousand dollars' worth of teas from Canton, he may have it insured; and then he will charge this insurance upon the cost of the tea, when he makes up his prices for sale. But, if he do not have it insured, he is entitled to the same amount himself; because he takes the risk himself, and is entitled to the premium.

2. The second circumstance which enters into risk, is the personal character of the borrower. This is made up of industry, skill, knowledge of business, pecuniary ability, and moral character. When these have not been tested, or where, having been tested, they have been found insufficient to the safe conduct of business, there will be a correspondent indisposition in his neighbors to loan; because, every one feels that there is, in such a case, more than a usual risk. Hence, such an individual cannot borrow, unless at an advanced premium, or at a higher rate of interest. On the contrary, if a man have conducted an extensive business, for a long period, with undeviating success, he attains to a high mercantile credit, and is enabled to borrow money at the lowest rates. But, if a merchant be known to be frequently embarrassed; if he have ever, or specially have more than once, failed; mercantile confidence in him is destroyed. No one will lend him, except on the most unfavorable terms; hence, he can do business with nothing but his own capital, and, of this, he is generally destitute. Hence, a failure, and specially a second failure, is commonly fatal to mercantile success. Firm credit is rarely afterwards established.

I am aware that these two causes of variation of risk are apparently modified, by the practice of endorsing private notes. If I want money for the most hazardous investment, or am of the most doubtful credit, if I can offer my note, endorsed by persons of established mercantile character, it is raised, at once, to par; that is, the extra risk is immediately removed. But this modification is only apparent. The endorser will rarely do this for nothing. He either himself receives a premium for it, directly; that is, he is paid for taking the risk of default of payment; or else, two persons mutually endorse for each other, and thus, the risk which A assumes for B, is paid for, by B's assuming a similar risk for A. It is singular that any one should ever ask another to endorse his note merely as a matter of comity. It should always be a matter of business, and liable to be paid for, like any other business transaction. A merchant should no more ask another to endorse his note gratuitously, than he should ask him to insure his house gratuitously. The nature of the transaction is precisely the same. The risk in the one case, is frequently as great as in the other; and it should always, as much in the one case as in the other, be a matter of compensation. Such, at least, seems to me the nature of the case.

3. The risk incurred in lending capital, is affected by the character of the government. This affects both private and public contracts.

If justice be well administered, and every man have all reasonable security that he will have the whole power of the society at his disposal, in order to enforce a just contract; of course, the risk is less, and the rate of interest lower, than when experience has shown, that no such security exists. Hence, we see the economy of good legislation, and of a wise, just, and incorruptible Judiciary.

The additional interest on capital, incurred in consequence of the bad administration of justice in a country, would annually pay the expenses of all the courts of law, ten times over.

The same results flow from confidence, or the want of confidence, in the stability of a government. A revolution not unfrequently dissolves contracts, dissipates security, and renders obligations valueless, both by destroying the evidence of their existence, and annihilating the means of enforcing them. Hence, when such an event is feared, men will not loan, except at an exorbitant premium; and they generally prefer removing their property to some other country, to subjecting it, for any premium whatever, to the risks of a revolution.

The same may be said of public contracts. Governments, in whose stability undoubted confidence is reposed, borrow the most enormous sums, at the lowest rates of interest. Those, which are in daily danger of being overthrown, can scarcely borrow at all, or, if they do borrow, it is at the most ruinous premium. The South American governments can scarcely borrow at any interest. Great Britain, notwithstanding her present enormous debt, borrows at three or four per cent., to any amount she pleases. Nay, so great is the public confidence in her permanency and integrity, that, probably, there is scarcely a civilized nation on earth, which does not at present own some share of her national debt. The greater the civil commotions of other countries, the more easily can she borrow; because, capitalists naturally invest their property where they are confident of its security; and confident that its interest will, under all circumstances, be regularly paid.

II. The rate of interest is varied by the *convenience* of the investment. The convenience of an investment depends upon several circumstances.

1. *Facility of transfer.* When a man loans capital, he is, of course, ignorant of the future, and does not know how much he may need it, at some subsequent time. If he loan at six per cent., for two years, he may, in six months, find some investment in which it would yield him eight per cent.; but, having loaned it for two years, he cannot now withdraw it. Hence, it is a great advantage, if it can be so invested, that he may, without loss, recall it at any moment; while it is yet accumulating interest for just so long as it remains invested.

2. *Permanency of investment.* If a man does not wish to withdraw a loan, it is an advantage to him to have it continue for a long period; because, he is thus saved the loss of interest which would occur during the time of transfer, and the trouble and inconvenience of finding another borrower. This is of special benefit to widows, orphans, persons retired from business, and all those persons who wish not to labor with their own capital themselves, but only to live upon the interest of it.

3. *Punctuality* in the payment of interest. It is a great convenience to those who invest capital, to be able to calculate with certainty on the payment of interest. They can thus, with ease, adjust their expenses, both to the amount of their income, and to the time of their receipt of it. If they wish to re-invest the interest, they can make their arrangements with certainty; and thus invest it with the greatest advantage. They are also saved the trouble of looking after their debtor, and they avoid the inconvenience of that personal altercation, which is liable to arise respecting pecuniary transactions.

When any form of investment possesses these advantages, men are found to prefer it to one which is destitute of them; and hence, they will loan their money on these terms, at a lower rate of interest than on any other. When a debt is in this form, it is said to be *funded;* and the creditors are said to hold *stock.* Hence, public debts are generally thus arranged. The various companies, formed for banking purposes, and purposes of internal improvement, are constructed on the same principles. Every one who contributes a share towards the capital of such a company, receives a certificate that he owns such a share of that capital. He is entitled to his share of the profits at stated times. He may retain this certificate himself, as long as he pleases; or he may sell it, at any moment, to any purchaser who may want it. Hence, money may always be borrowed, under these circumstances, at the lowest rates.

SECTION III.

OF THE RATE OF INTEREST, AS AFFECTED BY THE USE OF CAPITAL.

When, however, the risk is the same, we find interest higher in some countries than in others; and higher in the same country at one time, than at another. Thus, when the security is equally good, interest is higher in this country than in Great Britain; and, in this country, it is higher in the new, than in the older states. And, we also find, that it is lower now, in Great Britain, than formerly; and that it generally becomes less, as a community grows older.

This shows that there must be causes of variation in interest, aside from that of risk. A few of these remain to be considered.

I. *The average profit of Capital.* The profit of capital, is that annual value which it yields to the possessor, after he has deducted the principal, and paid the expenses incident to his actual operation. Thus, if, by the use of one thousand dollars for a year, I am, after replacing the principal and all the cost of my operation, one hundred dollars richer, this one hundred dollars is the profit of my capital. Now, the greater this is at any time, the greater will be the sum which I shall be willing to pay for the use of one thousand dollars. If, by the use of capital, I can, after paying all expenses, realise twenty per cent., I can afford to pay more for the use of it, than if, after paying all expenses, I could realise only five per cent.

To specify the various causes on which the difference of profit of capital depends, perhaps would be impossible. Those which seem to me of the most general importance, are:

1. *Fertility of land.* He who wished to borrow money to invest in agriculture, could afford to pay higher interest, when the land produced fifty bushels to the acre, than when it produced only twenty-five bushels to the acre, provided he could procure the land for the same purchase money.

2. *Productiveness of industry.* The use of natural agents, adds greatly to the value annually produced from a given amount of capital. This will tend to raise the price of capital; since a man will give more for money to invest in a machine which will produce one thousand dollars a year, than in one which will produce only five hundred dollars. It is true that the influx of capital will tend

to bring any one branch of industry, in process of time, to the general level. But that progressive increase of productiveness, which belongs to the progress of civilization, tends to keep up the price of capital, which would, otherwise, fall unreasonably low.

3. *The demand for exchange.* The greater the demand for exchange, the more profitable must be that capital which is invested in exchange. In a town where mercantile business is brisk, and a man can sell all his stock at a good profit, two or three times in the course of a year, money will bear a higher interest than in a town where exchanges are slow, and he must keep his goods on hand, for a year or two.

II. *The ratio between supply and demand.* This produces the same effect upon the rate of interest, as upon every thing else. Whatever be the profit of capital, if the supply be very small, the price will rise in proportion; since he, who by employing it at a high price, can make a small profit, will rather so employ it, than, by doing without it, make no profit at all. Thus, if by the use of one thousand dollars for a year, I could realise five hundred dollars, I might be willing to pay two hundred dollars for the use of it, rather than not have it; for, in the one case, I should gain three hundred dollars, and, in the other, I should gain nothing. If, then, there were but little capital in the market, and many persons were as willing to give this rate of interest as myself, I should be obliged to give it. But if, on the contrary, there were many persons desirous of lending, and much capital in the market, and I were the only person who would be willing to give this interest, they would underbid each other, and I should be able to procure it of him who would loan it to me at the lowest rate. I might then be able to borrow it for one hundred and fifty, one hundred, or sixty dollars per annum.

Hence, the rate of money will vary in any country, according to the effect of these two circumstances. In a new and prosperous country, interest is always high. This results from several reasons.

1. Land is very *cheap*, and, at first, is all of very nearly the same market price. In many cases, it can be had for almost nothing.

2. Land is very *fertile*. The produce of a soil when *new* is generally greater than ever afterwards.

3. The soil, never needing manure, requires but small investments of capital, and these are very richly repaid.

4. The inhabitants of a new country can carry with them but few of the conveniences of life. These must be purchased after they arrive there, and they must either be made on the spot, or be imported. To do either, requires capital. And, as the demand for these conveniences is imperative, and, as the income of land is abundant, the settlers are willing to pay a high price for them. Hence, the profit, both of mechanical labor and of exchanges, is very great; and the price which is paid for capital is very high.

5. The inhabitants of a new country have generally very considerable exchanges with the aborigines. Such exchanges are exceedingly profitable. But these cannot be carried on without capital; and, of course, capital, on this account, always bears a very high price.

On the contrary, the supply of capital, in a new country, is generally small.

1. Emigrants are, by no means, the most wealthy classes of a community. Those who are living in peace and prosperity at home, are not generally those who are most willing to brave the perils and hardships of the wilderness.

2. Those who are not disposed to expose their *persons* to the hardships of a new country, are not disposed to send their capital where they are not present to watch over it themselves. Hence, it is difficult, for a while, for a new people to borrow; and they can overcome this difficulty, only by the payment of high interest.

These are, as I suppose, the causes of the high rate of interest in new countries, on the borders of civilization, and generally, wherever savage and civilized nations intermingle.

As a country becomes settled, however, these causes begin to operate less powerfully; and thus, the rate of interest gradually diminishes.

1. The annual produce of the earth is, year after year, changed into fixed capital; and thus, the demand is supplied from themselves.

2. The fertility of the soil diminishes, so that it will afford to pay less interest.

3. Land is sold at different prices, according to its fertility; and, as it rises in price, the degree of profit to the purchaser is diminished.

4. The wants of the natives are supplied; and, hence, one source of gain is dried up.

5. A more perfect knowledge of the country, and more

perfect confidence in its prosperity, diminish the unwillingness of persons in older countries to loan; and hence, capital from abroad, may be procured with greater facility.

Hence, the gradual operation of these causes, must tend to reduce the rate of interest in different countries to the same average.

Hence, we see that the constant tendency of civilization is to the reduction of the rate of interest. As capital becomes more abundant, in proportion to the uses that are to be made of it, it commands a less price; that is, a man can gain less than formerly with a capital of one thousand dollars; and hence, he is willing to pay a less interest for it. But, it is also to be remembered, that a much larger proportion of men is worth one thousand dollars than formerly, and that, for one that was worth one thousand dollars fifty, years ago, there are fifteen or twenty who are worth ten thousand dollars now; that is, men, with the same labor, are able to secure as many, or more comforts, than formerly; but they are obliged to do it by the use of a larger amount of capital. They are obliged to labor with a larger capital, but that large amount is more easily procured, than a less amount was formerly. Hence, we see that the complaint so frequently heard of the increasing difficulty of accumulating property, is really unfounded; and that, taking the difficulty or ease of procuring capital into the account, the more advanced periods of society are the most favorable to the industrious classes.

III. *The rate of interest is affected by the freedom of capital.* By *freedom of capital,* I mean the unfettered liberty of the individual to employ his capital in any innocent way that he pleases. When this liberty is enjoyed, every one chooses that way in which he supposes that he shall be most successful; that is, in which he will reap the largest profit. The larger the profit he realizes, the larger will be the interest which he will be willing to pay. When he is obliged to withhold it from a mode of investment which he prefers, and to employ it in one which he does not prefer; he must, therefore, divert it from a more, to a less profitable mode of investment. Hence, as he is obliged to employ it in a less profitable, instead of a more profitable investment, he can afford to pay less interest; and the price of interest, by the effect of this interference, must fall. Such must be the effect of all monopolies, and of all means by which the active power of capital is diminished.

IV. *The rate of interest is affected by taxation.* A tax abstracts its whole amount realized, besides the cost of collecting it, from the annual profits of capital. If a mechanic realize, from a capital of one thousand dollars, a nett saving of one hundred and fifty dollars, and is obliged to pay fifty dollars of this sum in taxes, he is in the condition of one who, without being obliged to pay taxes, realized a saving of only one hundred dollars. Hence, he would be able, if he conducted his business upon a hired capital, to pay only a diminished rate of interest. And, if it be said that he may raise the price of his labor, and thus repay himself, it may be answered: 1st. By raising the price of his labor, he diminishes the demand, and his profits are thereby reduced, so that he will be no better able to pay the former interest. And, 2dly, as other men, being taxed, will raise their prices, he is obliged to pay more for every thing that he consumes; and thus, again, his ability is lessened. Every one must see, that the immense sum which Great Britain annually pays, as the interest of her national debt, is so much abstracted from the profits of her capital; and that the amount of profit to the individuals must be greater, just in proportion as that is diminished; and that the profits of the capitalist and the producer would rise accordingly.

From what has been said above, we come to the following general conclusions:

1. That, other things being equal, interest will be high, when the risk is great; and low, when the risk is small.

2. That interest will be high, when the profit of capital is great; and low, when the profit of capital is small.

3. That both of these affect each other, within certain limits; that is, when profit is great, if the risk be also great, interest will be very high; because, the increase of risk diminishes the supply.

4. But, when profit is low, and risk is great, there will be no loaning whatever; because, what is paid for risk, will be more than can be gained by use, and, hence, men could not profit by borrowing.

5. And, hence, we see that the rate of interest will be always affected by every circumstance, which affects either *risk* or *profit* of capital. War, or the rumor of war, by increasing the risk, raises the rate of interest in property affected by it. In property not affected by it, the same cause depresses the rate of interest; because it diminishes the means and opportunity for production, and, of course, diminishes the profit of capital. On the other hand, the discovery of any new mode of profitably employing capital, raises the rate of interest, by creating an increased demand for capital.

6. And hence, again, we see that the rate of interest, at any particular time or place, is not of itself any indica-

tion of the prosperity, or of the decline, of a country. The indication is to be sought for, not in the *rate* of interest, but in the *cause* by which that rate is affected.

1. Whenever the rate of interest is raised by increase of risk, this is an indication of adversity. Rise of interest, from such a source, benefits no one. It is of no service to the *lender*, because he receives no profit from the premium which insures him against loss. It is as profitable for him to loan for five per cent. without risk, as to loan for ten per cent., when five per cent. is for risk, and five per cent. for use. It is an injury to the *borrower*, because, one hundred dollars are worth no more to him when he pays five per cent. for risk, than when he pays nothing for it. Whatever, therefore, is paid for risk, is always a loss to both parties; and the more that is thus paid, the worse it is for both. Hence, the rise of interest caused by bad government, civil commotion, revolutions, wars, and general immorality, is always an indication of national decline; and the fall of interest, produced by the contrary causes, is an indication of national prosperity.

2. On the other hand, the temporary rise of interest caused by increased productiveness, and the development of new national resources, is an indication of national prosperity. It shows that some more than ordinarily valuable modes of employing capital have been discovered, and, that men can afford to pay a larger price for the use of capital. I have, however, called this a *temporary* rise; because, a rise from such a cause, will soon equalise itself. Increased productiveness will soon supply capital, or it will be imported from less favored countries. Thus, in new countries, the rate of interest is high; but this is by no means an indication of adversity, for such countries, while paying so high a rate for capital, yet grow rich faster than those from which they borrow.

3. Again: The gradual fall of the rate of interest caused by the diminution of risk, and the greater abundance of capital, is an evidence of prosperity. It shows that a larger proportion of the means of subsistence is falling to the share of every individual; that every man can more easily procure capital; and that every man, in order to support himself, produces a larger amount than formerly, of whatever will contribute to the comfort and convenience of his neighbor.

4. On the other hand, the fall of the rate of interest, caused by a suspension of the means of production, is an evidence of national adversity. Suppose a war to occur between this country and France. The capital now employed in transportation, must be almost wholly unproductive. The capital employed in producing our exports to that country, must also be useless. Hence, the rate of interest would fall; for, many men would have no business in which to employ their capital. The case would be the same, were a fall in the price of capital to proceed from civil commotion, or any similar cause. And, the adversity would remain, until the cause were removed. For, if capital were removed out of the country, until, from reduction in the supply, the rate of interest rose, the industry of the country would still be depressed, until, by peace, order, and good government, it regained its natural advantages.

Hence, we see that, in order to form any correct opinion respecting the condition of a country, from the present rate of interest, we must always seek for the causes of that rate, instead of deciding from the mere rate itself.

It is almost unnecessary, after what has been already advanced, to state that, in the view of the political economist, laws regulating the rate of interest are injurious to the prosperity of a country. Some of the reasons for this opinion, are the following:

1. Such laws violate the right of property. A man has the same right to the market price of his capital, in money as he has to the market price of his house, his horse, his ship, or any other of his possessions.

2. The *real* price of capital cannot be fixed by law, any more than the real price of flour, or iron, or any other commodity. There is, therefore, no more reason for assigning to it a fixed value, than there is of assigning a fixed value to any other commodity.

3. The price of capital, or money, is really *more variable* than that of any other commodity. Most other commodities have but one source of variation, namely, *use* or *profit.* But capital, in the form of money, is liable to two sources of variation, *risk*, and *use.* These vary, at different times, in different investments, and with different individuals. There is, therefore, *less* reason why the price of money should be fixed by law, than why the price of any thing else should be so fixed.

4. These laws, instead of preventing, give rise to great and disastrous fluctuations in the price of money.

Suppose that, to-day, money is worth, in the ordinary operations of business, ten per cent., and it is worth six per cent. in loan. A man will as soon loan, as employ it in business, if he have more than he wishes to use. There will then be a fair supply of money in the market. But, let the profits of capital rise, so that, in the ordinary operations of business, capital is worth twenty per cent. If, now, the rate of interest rose with this increased rate of profit, the same individuals would be as willing to loan, as before; and thus, the supply following the demand, there would arise no peculiar scarcity. The high rate of interest, would also attract capital from abroad; and thus, in a very short time, it would, in this particular place, be brought to the general level.

But, suppose that six per cent. were the highest legal rate of interest, and that he who loaned at a higher rate, was liable to lose both his principal and interest, and also his mercantile character. In this case, as soon as the profit of capital in business rose to fifteen or twenty per cent., no one, who could thus employ it, would loan it at six per cent. Hence, as soon as it thus rose, the supply would be immediately diminished; and this would, of course, cause a greater rise of interest. Those who, from honor or conscience, obeyed the laws, would withdraw from the market, and employ their capital in some other way; and no one would loan, but those who were willing to risk the consequences of detection. These, having the money market in their own hands, will, of course, charge for the use, and for the risk of detection; and, hence, the price, in a few days, may become doubled or trebled. And, at the same time, although the real value of money may be fifteen or twenty per cent.; yet, because the *legal* price is six per cent., there is no inducement for capital to come in from abroad, to supply the demand. Hence, the change in the money market has, by reason of this law, no tendency whatever to regulate itself.

Hence, I believe all enactments establishing a legal rate of interest, are injurious, and unwise. The only enactment of any value would be, one which should define the usual rate, when nothing was said on the subject in the contract. The use of this would be, to prevent disputes. This is always an advantage to both parties.

I shall conclude this chapter, with a few remarks on the nature and price of *stocks*.

I have already remarked, that, when a company is formed for any purpose requiring capital, and yielding interest, the capital is divided into portions called *shares*, and, that any one has a right to subscribe for as many of these as he pleases. If the shares, for instance, are one hundred dollars each, he who takes one share, pays one hundred dollars, and so of any other number. For every share, he receives a certificate of ownership, and, so long as he owns this certificate, he is a member of the company; his proportion of the capital is governed by the laws of the company; he is entitled to the same rights as the rest; and receives his proportion of all the profit. These certificates are called *stocks*. They are transferable, like any other property, and the owner, as in any other case, sells them, if he wishes to do so, for whatever they will bring. The owner for the time being, is the stockholder; is amenable, in his proportion, to all the rules of the company; and is entitled to his proportion of all the benefits accruing from the use of the capital. Such is the nature of bank, insurance, railroad, canal, and other stocks.

The same principle is frequently applied to loans. Suppose a government wishes to borrow five millions of dollars at five per cent., for twenty years, the interest to be paid quarterly. The conditions of the loan are specified, and subscription books are opened, in different places throughout the nation. The whole sum is divided into shares, of which every one may subscribe for as many as he will. Every subscriber thus, in fact, loans the government, on the terms proposed, as much as he subscribes for. When his subscription is paid, he receives a certificate, which contains an obligation of the government to pay the money at the appointed time, and which entitles him to receive the interest for the sum which he has loaned, at the rate and times specified. These certificates are also called *stocks*, and are transferable, like any other property. Hence, they are an article of merchandise, like any thing else; and, as persons are wishing both to buy and sell, every day, they are every day bought and sold, in great numbers, in all commercial capitals.

Now, suppose money to be loaned in this way; it is so much capital at interest, and it is affected by the same circumstances as other capital at loan. As the convenience of investment is, however, in all cases the same, the rate, at which such stocks sell, will be affected wholly by profit and risk.

1. Supposing the risk to be the same; these stocks are affected by the profit annually paid on the investment. Thus, suppose the risk to be nothing, and the common rate of interest in a community to be six per cent. If I own a share equal to one hundred dollars, and it pay six per cent. interest, this share will always sell for one hundred dollars. Suppose that the ordinary rate of interest being the same, this share pays twelve per cent. interest. I can then sell it for two hundred dollars; because, he who pays two hundred dollars for it, will receive interest at the rate of six per cent., which is as much as he would receive from any other investment. On the contrary, if this share paid but three per cent. interest, I could get but fifty dollars for it; since three dollars is the interest of no more than fifty dollars. Thus, other things being equal, the price of stocks will always depend upon the interest which they pay; and they will always sell for that sum, of which the interest or dividend which they pay is the regular interest.

This, however, is sometimes affected by the anticipations of men. A stock which pays very little *now*, may *be expected* to pay largely, at some future time. Its price will, therefore, be kept up by this circumstance. On the other hand, a stock may pay largely now, but there may be a fear that it will soon be *worthless ;* this will, of course, depreciate it in value.

So, also, of risk. The profit of stocks being the same, their price is inversely as the risk. If a stock pay the usual interest, but is in danger of sinking the principal, it will be depreciated accordingly. If a government pay good interest for a loan, but there be danger that it will be overturned by a revolution, the stock will, of course, fall. Thus, insurance stock never rises to the value of bank stock, when it pays the same interest, on account of the greater risk. Thus, also, steam-boat stock may pay twenty or thirty per cent., and yet sell at no advance ; that is, it will be at par, because of the danger from fire and other accidents, and from the rapid wear of the principal.

It is by circumstances like these, that the prices of stocks are determined. When a stock sells for what it cost ; that is, when a hundred dollars worth of the original shares, sells for one hundred dollars, that stock is said to be *at par.* When it sells for more than this, it is said to be *above par ;* and when it sells for less, it is said to be *below par.* Thus, if stock be sold for thirty-seven per cent. above par, a share that cost one hundred dollars, sells for one hundred and thirty-seven dollars ; that is, one hundred dollars receives an interest, which, at the ordinary rate of money, is as much as one hundred and thirty-seven dollars would receive. And so of any other case.

Now, it must at once be perceived, that the opinion of the value of stocks is made up very much from expectations of profit or loss, or anticipations of increase or diminution of risk. Hence, a rumor of a war; of the failure of a company, or of a bank; of the probable insolvency of a government; or the news of the gain or loss of a battle, may make a very considerable difference in the price of those stocks which would be affected by such information. Hence, the great liability to fraud, in all the operations of the stock market. If a capitalist can get up a rumor which will depress any stock two per cent., and buy one hundred thousand dollars' worth, during this depression, he may sell it again the next day for its original value, and thus, in the course of twenty-four hours, realize two thousand dollars, without either risk or trouble; while the unfortunate seller is cheated out of this amount, without reason and without remedy. I do not say that all rumors affecting the price of stocks are thus fabricated. I only say, that such is the *liability;* and it is not very unlikely, that what can so readily be done, has actually happened. And, when such rumors actually arise without collusion, it requires great sagacity to judge of the probability of their truth, and thus to buy or sell, according to the true judgment to be formed from the facts actually in possession of the community.

And besides this, another method may frequently be resorted to, for the sake of transferring money from the pockets of one class of citizens, into those of another class. Suppose a particular stock to be worth no more than fifty per cent.; that is, to be capable of yielding no more than three per cent. on the original interest. Suppose there be only two or three hundred thousand dollars' worth of this stock in the market. If, now, a few individuals of large wealth combine together, they may easily, by means of agents, buy up the whole of it, at this reduced price. The scarcity will at once excite inquiry, and will tend to create some demand for it. If, now, by means of other agents, they put small quantities of it into the market, and buy it in, themselves, at gradually increasing prices, every one will become desirous of buying this stock, which, for a succession of days, has been rapidly rising in value. By careful management, it may thus be raised, in a few days, to seventy-five or one hundred dollars per share. If, then, these present owners carefully keep up the price, by buying and selling until they have disposed of the whole of their purchase, they will, in a few weeks, find themselves to have doubled their money. In the mean time, the cause of this rise having been removed, the effect ceases, and the present holders, who have purchased at seventy-five or one hundred dollars a share, find that their stock is worth no more than fifty per cent. Thus, fifty dollars per share, is, with great adroitness, transferred from the pockets of the many, into those of the few, and many are ruined, while a few are rendered enormously rich. I again say, that the rise and fall of stocks, are not always to be attributed to such causes. But, every one sees that such events are *liable* to happen. It is, moreover, said by some persons, that they actually have happened. Of the honor or the honesty of such a transaction, it is not necessary here to speak. We will only take occasion to remark, that it behoves the uninitiated, who wish to escape these dangers, to be somewhat careful how they speculate in stocks.

CHAPTER THIRD.

OF THE PRICE OF LAND, OR RENT.

As the *principal* demand for land, is for the purposes of agriculture, we shall first consider *Rent*, specially with reference to this form of utility.

Land is the instrument, by which the farmer produces the various vegetable and animal substances, which he offers in exchange.

Like any other valuable instrument, it of course commands a price according to its productiveness. He who hired a loom, would pay more for a loom with which he could weave twenty yards a day, than for one, with which he could weave but ten yards a day. The case is the same with land.

Now, the productiveness of land is made up of two things: 1st. *Fertility;* and, 2dly. *Situation.*

1. *Fertility.* We all know, that the productiveness of different soils is very diverse. Some soils will produce thirty, or forty, or fifty bushels of wheat to the acre, while others will produce, at the cost of more labor, not more than ten or fifteen bushels to the acre. Some soils will produce the most valuable vegetables; and others, only the most common, and comparatively valueless.

Some soils will produce no wheat whatever; and others will, without manuring, produce a luxuriant crop, every year. Some, wholly unfit for tillage, can be used only for grazing; and, even when thus employed, yield to their stinted flocks, but a meagre subsistence. Hence, we see a reason for a great diversity in the price of land. And we see, at once, that a farmer might more profitably pay a rent, for one farm, than occupy another farm for nothing.

2. *Situation.* The products of the farmer are all bulky, and, of course, acquire a very considerable addition to their cost, by transportation. Hence, if A raise wheat, within a mile of a market town, and sell it for one dollar a bushel, and B live one hundred miles off, and bring his wheat to the same market, he must sell it at the same price. The merchant who buys wheat, can give no more than the market price for wheat, whether it have been raised near or far off. It is no more valuable to him, for having been brought one hundred miles. If, now, the price of bringing a bushel of wheat one hundred miles be fifty cents, B actually receives but fifty cents a bushel for his wheat, while A receives one dollar for his. If the farms of both were of equal fertility, that is, if both produced twenty bushels to the acre, the farm of B would be only half as productive as that of A; that is, he would receive only ten dollars per acre, while A received twenty dollars. This amount of difference in situation, would be the same as a difference of one half in fertility, or actual productiveness.

Hence, we see, that, fertility being the same, productiveness would be as situation; and, situation being the same, productiveness would be as fertility. And we see, that these circumstances would always, when opposed, counterbalance each other; that is, land at such a distance from the market that it cost one half the price of products to transport them, would be of the same value, or actual productiveness, as land of half its fertility, contiguous to a market. And, hence, in estimating the productiveness of land, these circumstances are always to be considered together. And, we see, that land of the greatest fertility may be so far from a market, that the cost of transportation will leave a profit insufficient to repay the cost of cultivation. In such a case, such land will be worth nothing.

With these principles in mind, we can easily see in what manner rent will be paid, for the different lands in a country.

1. In the first settlement of a country, land is of no exchangeable value; for every one may have as much as he pleases. Every one, therefore, being at liberty to choose for himself, will select such a portion as he supposes most productive. Under these circumstances, land would bring no rent; since no one would pay another for the use of that, which he could have for nothing. This would continue to be the case, until all the land of the first quality was occupied. Let us suppose, for the sake of illustration, that this first quality of land were capable of producing one hundred bushels to the acre, and were all contiguous to the place of settlement, and that the second quality of land were capable of producing but eighty bushels to the acre.

2. Suppose, now, this settlement to increase so rapidly that the inhabitants could no longer be supplied with products from the land of the first class; or, that these products were in such demand, for the purpose of exchange with other countries, that these lands could no longer yield the requisite supply. The price of grain would rise, so that

a farmer could support himself by lands of the second quality; and, as those of the first quality were all taken up, and he could obtain those of the second quality for nothing, he will proceed to occupy these. Although this quality of land would bear no rent; for it will barely support him; yet, it is better than starvation, and he will proceed to till it. But, as soon as this is the case, the lands of the first quality will begin to command a rent; because, it is as well for a farmer to pay twenty bushels a year, for land yielding one hundred bushels an acre, as to have land producing only eighty bushels, for nothing. And, yet more: As soon as land will pay a rent, it will at once command a price; because, if a man wish to invest capital, he will be as willing to pay for land as for stocks, or any thing else, that sum, of which, at the ordinary rate of profits, the rent would be the interest. Thus, if land pay six dollars a year rent, per acre, if money be at six per cent. interest, it is worth one hundred dollars an acre; since six dollars is the interest of one hundred dollars. And so, if the occupier have the capital, it is as cheap for him to buy the land, and receive the interest himself, as to hold the money himself, and pay the interest to another.

3. Suppose, now, the price of grain, either for home, or for foreign consumption, to have risen so much, that the lands of the third quality, or producing sixty bushels per acre, could now be tilled, and support the agriculturist. As soon as this became the case, lands of the second quality would yield a rent and would bear a price; because, it would be as profitable for a farmer to pay twenty bushels a year for land of eighty bushels, as to cultivate land of sixty bushels for nothing. And, as soon as land of the second quality brought a rent, the rent of land of the first quality would also sustain a corresponding rise. It would be as cheap for a farmer to pay forty bushels a

year for land of one hundred bushels, as twenty for land of eighty bushels, or as to have land of sixty bushels for nothing.

4. It is evident, that as the settlement of the country advanced, rent and the price of land would go on augmenting, according to these principles. Land, which will *merely support* the cultivator, will bear no rent. But, all land of a greater productiveness than this, will yield *some* rent; and, this rent will be precisely as its productiveness exceeds that of the poorest soil which is worthy of cultivation. And, so soon as any soil is tilled of a *poorer* quality than any which was tilled previously, all the soils of a *better* quality will rise in rent, and in price accordingly.

5. Suppose the land of any nation to be limited by situation, or by territorial lines; it is evident that the demand for food, increasing with the increase of the number of inhabitants, the land would, of course, become all occupied. As soon as the poorest land was capable of yielding something, besides supporting its inhabitants, it would also pay rent. And thus, as before, the price and the rent of land would go on increasing, until it was arrested by some counteracting cause. Such causes are the following: If the grain were exported, its rise of price would gradually limit the foreign consumption; since other nations would begin either to raise it themselves, or else to procure it elsewhere. Or, if trade were free, as soon as its price rose so high that the nation itself could procure its supplies cheaper abroad than at home, it would import it instead of raising it. As soon as this became the case, the price of grain would rise no higher; and, at whatever rate of rent land may have been when this change took place, from this time it would, at that rate, remain stationary.

6. It is, however, to be observed, that this effect upon the occupation of land, would be rather a change in the manner of use, than in the utility of the land itself. It is evident that it could affect the demand for land, only for the production of those commodities that are capable of distant transportation, such as bread stuffs in general. But a very large part of the productions of the earth are not capable of such transportation; such are butcher's meat, which forms so large a portion of the food of man; green vegetables; milk and butter; and the food of animals, both for slaughter and labor. Now, just in proportion as a population increases, the demand for all these will increase likewise. Hence, it is reasonable to suppose, that as the importation of foreign grain checked the growth of domestic grain, the increased demand for these other domestic products, would keep the prices of land in a state of progressive increase.

Nay, more. It is evident that the demand for these recent and untransportable productions of the earth, must be in proportion to the number and the wealth of the population. We have already shown, that the number of the population must be as the means of subsistence. Hence, the cheaper grain and bread stuffs are, the more rapid will be the increase of population, and the greater will be the demand for those products, of which the agriculturist at *home* must, from his locality, enjoy the monopoly. Hence, it may reasonably be doubted, whether the corn laws of Great Britain, of which the object is, to keep up the price of land, and to sustain the agricultural interest, have really had this effect; and, whether they have not, in reality, had the contrary effect. Had the price of corn been as low as it might have been, for the last fifty years, but for the duties on imported grain, the population of Great Britain would have been probably doubled, both from the greater cheapness of living, and also from the stimulus given to her manufactures, by the diminished price of all her products. In this case, the increased demand for all the recent productions of the earth, would have been more than equal to all the good which even the agriculturist is supposed to have reaped, from the exclusion of foreign bread stuffs. If this be so, it is another illustration of the universal law, that a selfish policy always in the end defeats itself; and reaps its full share of the gratuitous misery which it inflicts upon others.

7. From the view which has been taken, it would at first seem, that the point of earliest settlement of a country, or at least its maritime frontier, would be its centre, where land would be of the highest price; while all the lands of the interior, in proportion as they receded from it, would gradually decrease in value, until the cost of transportation of products, at last reduced their value to nothing. Such would be the case, were it not for various circumstances, which greatly modify this result. Some of these modifying circumstances, it may be proper here to notice.

1. As a people thus spread over a large territory, and are devoted to agriculture, it becomes necessary that other persons should devote themselves to manufactures, and to exchanges. Those who are thus employed, by necessity collect together, into towns and villages. Thus a large portion of the population arises, which raises nothing from the earth; and hence, their wants must be supplied by the agriculturists in their neighborhood. Hence, immediate markets for produce, are created in every district; that is, although the farmer cannot remove his farm nearer to the market, the market has removed nearer to him; and the diminution of distance has increased the productiveness of his farm, as much as though its fertility had been increased, or it had been removed to the sea-board. It is not fifty years, since land in the vicinity of Utica, New

York, was valuable only for raising produce, which was sent to the city of New York, by the way of Albany; and the rent, and consequent price of land, depended on what could be made by a harvest, after deducting from the market price of wheat, in New York, the cost of transportation between the two places. But, while the *land* has remained *unmoved*, population has *moved* toward *it;* and Utica itself is a populous city, demanding for its supplies, the productions of all the surrounding country; so that land, in its vicinity, bears, I presume, a very considerable proportion to the price of land in the vicinity of the city of New York itself.

2. I have mentioned above, that productiveness of land, depended not only on *fertility*, but also on *situation*, or facility of communication with a market. Fertility being given, productiveness will be as situation; that is, the greater the ease of transportation, the greater the actual productiveness; and of course the higher the value of land. Thus, if land produce one hundred bushels per acre, and it costs half its market price to convey it to the place of sale, it is only as valuable as land of half its fertility, contiguous to the market. If then, the cost of transportation can be, by any means, reduced, the productiveness of lands affected by this reduction will rise in proportion. If, when the price of wheat is a dollar, it costs fifty cents to transport it, and the cost of transportation can be reduced to twenty-five cents, it is as good to me, as if the *price* had been raised twenty-five per cent., or my land had increased twenty-five per cent. in fertility. Now, in the progress of a country, a great improvement is generally affected in roads, and ordinary modes of transportation, by which the value of the lands at a distance is generally enhanced. This result is however signally effected by canals and railroads. The effect of these means of transportation is, to raise the prices of

products in the interior, and of course the price of land in general, in the manner above stated. A very intelligent gentlemen of Geneva, New York, informed me, that, in the year 1821, the price of wheat in that town was thirty one cents per bushel. In 1822, the price was thirty seven and a half cents. The canal was opened during the next year, and it rose to sixty-two and a half cents. It has never since fallen below this latter price, and at the time of the conversation 1835, it was selling at one dollar and thirty-one cents per bushel. The price of land, of course, has risen in proportion. And this change has been for the benefit of all parties. The farmer is greatly enriched; the laborer is better paid, a great number of persons are very profitably employed and supported by labor on the canal, and wheat has been sold at a *lower price to the consumer*, than ever before.

So far as we have treated of this subject, we have considered the fertility of land, as, on an average, equal; and the facility of communication gradually diminishing, with the increase of the distance. Under these circumstances, it is manifest, that the price of land, in the interior, could not rise, unless the price of land on the seaboard had first risen. And, as land came into market, farther and farther from the older settlements, it would always indicate a rise of price in the land which had first been cultivated; or in the most favored localities.

But it is manifest that the case may be far otherwise.

1. The land in the interior may be much the most fertile, and may enjoy the most favorable climate. The increased *fertility*, will, of course, counterbalance within a certain limit, the *inconvenience of situation;* and mildness of climate, will render a less exertion necessary to procure the necessary provisions for the sustentation of animal

life. Hence, the profit of labor will be greater, and the difference, in these respects, may be such, as to counterbalance entirely, within a given distance, the disadvantages of position. In this case, the interior will be settled without advancing the price of land on the sea board. The advantages of both, though dissimilar, are, so far as productiveness is considered, equal ; and, of course, there is no reason why any one should pay any thing for a choice.

And, secondly, as I have shown before, the difficulty of transportation may be so reduced, that it forms but a small part of the cost of whatever is raised in the interior. When it costs but a few cents more a bushel, to transport wheat three hundred miles than fifty miles, and the fertility of land three hundred miles from the market is twice as great as that in the vicinity, it is evident, that the productiveness of land three hundred miles off will be greater than of that only fifty miles from the market. Hence, the price of the one might rise, without producing a rise in the price of the other. Nay, it is evident, that it might produce a contrary effect. If a farmer in the interior could raise wheat at a fair profit, and bring it to market for one dollar a bushel, and the farmer in the neighborhood of the market could not, at a fair profit sell it for less than one dollar and twenty-five cents, as the latter must sell his wheat at the current price, of course, he could not raise it at all. Hence, as a source of profit is cut off, the annual produce is less, and the price of land will fall.

Such has been, to some extent, the course of events in this country. The lands on the seaboard were first settled, and cultivation gradually extended to the south and west. At first, the average fertility of the lands newly occupied was no greater than that of those first cultivated ;

and the price of the old lands rose, as the new lands were occupied. By degrees, cultivation passed over the Alleghany mountains, and entered the Valley of the Mississippi. Here the soil is exuberantly fertile, and the climate mild; but, the difficulty of communication with the interior, operated as a severe check upon the growth of the new States, and the price of lands in the old States was not materially affected. As soon, however, as the use of steam opened the navigation of the Mississippi, the whole scene was changed. The inland States, became, in position, almost sea board States. Their fertility was relieved from the inconveniences of position, under which it had formerly labored; and the productions of a new and rich soil could be brought to market, with as little cost for transportation, as that, of lands within one or two hundred miles from the sea board. The result has been, that the western farmers have undersold the farmers of the north and east; and now, but little wheat is raised in any part of New England. This result has been increased, by the vast emigration to the west, which has diminished the number of laborers; and at the east, by demand for laborers for manufactures and internal improvements, which has withdrawn men from agriculture, and raised the wages of agricultural labor in the New England States. Hence, by the increased wages of labor, and the reduced price of grain, the profit of agriculture has been reduced, and the price of land has fallen. I suppose that land, at present, in New England is not generally as dear as it was twenty or thirty years since.

Yet, it by no means follows, that this depreciation will increase. The settlement of the western States creates a vast market for manufactures, and a vast demand for mercantile exchanges. These require capital, which is more abundant in the older States. The older States, also, have by nature, the greater facilities for such employments. Hence, the western States will become their customers, and the older States will become thickly peopled with a manufacturing and mercantile population. Land will be in demand, for supplying the immediate wants of such a population, and, it will probably again soon rise. Each manufacturing establishment will become a centre, which will confer a high value on land in its immediate vicinity. By the multiplication of such centres, the price of the whole will be augmented.

I have thus far considered the price of land, only in so far as its mere productiveness is concerned. This will, of course, be the most ordinary and general cause of the variation in its price, and in its rent. There are, however, other circumstances, which have a material effect upon its value, even in the same country, and under substantially the same laws.

1. *Beauty of situation.* Of two farms, equally productive, many men would give a decided preference to that which commanded a view of the richest and most beautiful prospect, or of which the trees and shrubbery were so arranged, as to give the greastest *pleasure* to the beholder. For this preference, most men would be willing to pay a considerable additional price. This additional price, will increase with the wealth and the improving tastes of a community. This is a circumstance which should always be borne in mind by the occupiers and owners of land. It costs but little more labor, to lay out an orchard regularly and beautifully, than to lay it out irregularly and clumsily. It costs nothing, to let a tree stand, where it adds beauty to a prospect, and it costs very little to plant one, where it will have the same effect. A neat and convenient house, consumes neither more lumber nor nails, nor labor, than a slovenly and inconvenient one. And yet, on these differences, very much of the exchangeable value of a farm depends.

2. The price of land depends much, on the intellectual and moral character of a neighborhood.

Of two farms of equal productiveness, but in very dissimilar moral and intellectual communities, almost every one would prefer that, which, in these respects, possessed the greater advantages. A man who has in any degree cultivated his own intellect, prefers the society of those whose intellects are also cultivated. A parent would always prefer a neighborhood, in which his children could receive the advantages of education. A man, who had been accustomed to religious observances, would choose to remove, where he could enjoy the benefits of religious instruction. And, every man, let his dispositions be what they may, will chose to reside in a neighborhood, in which the moral character of the people is a protection from dishonesty and robbery; and where his children will be, as little as possible, liable to the contamination of vice. It is manifest, that each of these considerations, would form a ground of preference for one situation over another, and, for this preference, every reasonable man would be willing to pay. Were these two farms thus differently situated, there would be many more buyers for the one than for the other, and the advantage would all be on the side of the most intelligent and moral community.

Hence we see, that, besides the advantages which intelligence and virtue confer upon the character of a people themselves, there is also an additional advantage, in the rise of property which they produce. It may be fairly questioned, whether this, of itself, be not sufficient to repay the whole expense of literary and religious institutions. There are towns in New England, in which, within a few years, the price of real estate has doubled, for no other assignable reason, than that of the literary and moral advantages which they hold out to residents. This, is a mode of increasing the value of property, which seems to me deserving of more attention than it has generally received.

Land is used for other purposes besides residence, and agriculture. The principles upon which its value is determined in such cases, are substantially, the same as those mentioned above.

1. Thus, in cities, land, for the erection of buildings, has a two fold value; 1st. For dwelling houses. And, 2dly, for ware houses, and places for the transaction of business. Its value, in both of these respects, depends not on *fertility*, as it is not wanted for cultivation, but wholly on *situation*. A man needs a house which will furnish the necessary conveniences for his family. He also wishes one, within a convenient distance from his place of employment. The farther his dwelling is, from his shop or his counting room, the longer time is occupied in passing from the one to the other, and the less are the conveniences of his residence. Hence, he will be willing to pay for the choice, and thus, the price of land gradually diminishes, from the centre to the circumference of a thickly settled town.

But, in a place of mercantile business, edifices have another value, besides that of dwelling houses. They are needed, for the transaction of business. Where many exchanges are to be made, in the course of a few hours, every day, it is of importance that the exchangers should be as near together as possible. And, where a large number of strangers, are daily collected for the sake of making purchases, it is important to the seller, to be so situated as to be in their immediate vicinity. A merchant whose store is in the centre of business, can easily sell ten times as much in a day, as one, who is half a mile off from the centre. Hence, he is able, from the mere fact of difference in situation, to realize a much greater annual profit, in the one place than in the other. For this difference of productiveness, he will be willing to pay a price; and, hence, in large cities, the most central situations, or as they are called the best stands for business, command a very high rent; and a correspondent price. A few square feet of land in the centre of the city of New York, will sell for more than several hundred acres of the most productive soil in any part of the Union. And, as the price of land, in such cases, is owing entirely to the demand for the purposes of facilitating trade, it can only rise with the increasing prosperity of the place. Hence, the rise or fall of real estate, in any town, is one of the surest indications of its mercantile prosperity or of the reverse. And, moreover, the rise of rents, in any given place, proceeds upon the same principles as those which we have already illustrated. Suppose the places of business, in a town, to be all occupied, within a given circle, and that they are sufficient for the accommodation of all the merchants who need them. If the town be prosperous, in five years, these accommodations will be insufficient, and buildings without this circle will come into demand, for this purpose. Their rent, in consequence of this additional value, will rise. But this rise will be accompanied by a rise in the rent of the more favored situations. Those persons, whose employment requires a central situation, will occupy the centre, at a price which will exclude those, to whom such a situation is less essential, and this process will go on, until those who are the least able to come into competition, pass out of the original circle, and thus create a new demand and raise the price of rent as it has been suggested.

2. Land frequently possesses an additional value, in consequence of its proximity to water falls. A water

fall provides for the manufacturer, a constant supply of momentum, which he can use by means of very simple machinery. Suppose the interest of capital employed in the construction of furnaces, and steam machinery, and the annual expense for fuel and attendance in a given situation, were one thousand dollars, and the same power could be procured at the same place, by appropriating a water fall, by means of machinery of which the interest was no more than one hundred dollars; the labor of the water fall would be worth nine hundred dollars per year. Hence, supposing it to be in a situation, in which there was a demand for this power, the land which gave the legal right to the use of it, would possess a value proportioned to the value of the power. Of course the price which it would command, would depend upon the annual value of the privilege. This would be determined, by the amount of applicable power, and by the situation. A power sufficient to move a dozen mills, would be twelve times as valuable, as that which could move only one. A water power near the sea board, would be much more valuable than one in the interior. If it were at tide water, its annual value would be equal to the difference between its annual expense and that of steam. If it were at a distance from tide water, or the market, it would be equal to this difference, *minus* the expense to be incurred, in the transportation of the material and of the manufactured fabric. As soon as the cost of transportation, was equal to the difference of expense, between the two modes of producing power, it would become valueless; because it would be as cheap to erect a manufactory at tide water, and pay the expense of building and fuel, as to have the power for nothing, and pay the same expense for transportation. Hence, in the erection of mills and the establishment of manufactures, both of these circumstances are to be maturely considered, before a situation is decided upon. For want of such consideration, much property has been totally lost.

3. *Mines.* These depend upon the same principles as those which have been already illustrated. A water privilege is a mine of power, a bed of ore is a mine of metal. The former is frequently the most valuable possession.

Suppose a farm to be worth the ordinary price of land; and the owner discovers on it, a bed of iron ore, which, after deducting the necessary expenses of working it, and paying the labor and skill necessary to the operation, will yield one thousand dollars a year. The farm, or the land necessary for the mining operations, will rent for one thousand dollars a year, or will sell for such a sum as will yield, at the ordinary rate, one thousand dollars as interest. In this case, it is manifest, that the original owner of the property will be a gainer by the discovery, to the full amount of the increase in the price of his land. But, here, the *peculiar* gain ceases. To other holders who may come after him, it is merely an investment, of the same nature as any other investment; and will yield no more than the ordinary rate of profit.

The case is the same with a copper, a silver, or a gold mine. The owner of the land at the time of the discovery, becomes greatly enriched, in consequence of this new product, which may be derived from his property. But, after this rise, when a new purchaser comes into possession, the *peculiarity* of the gain ceases. A rich gold mine, will rent, or will sell for more than a poor one, and its price, or its rent, will be in exact proportion to its productiveness, just as a farm, a mill-privilege, or any other property. It is a somewhat remarkable fact, that mines of the precious metals, are in general, singularly unprofitable, after they have passed out of the hands of the original owners. It has grown into a proverb in South America, that, if a man own a copper mine he will grow rich, if he own a silver mine he will gain nothing, but if he own a gold mine, he will certainly be ruined. The fact however may be easily accounted for. The imaginations of men are always strongly excited by the contemplation of the precious metals; and it is rare that any thing but experience can teach them, that they may buy gold too dear. Hence, they do not compute the chances of profit in the production of gold, as coolly as they do in any other case. But the production of gold, is governed by as fixed laws, as the production of wheat. Gold can no more than wheat, be produced by an effort of the imagination. It is the result of labor, and skill, and expense. And, if these be greater than the revenue, a man will as assuredly be ruined by producing gold, as by conducting any other unprofitable business; his imagination to the contrary notwithstanding.

Such are, I believe, the principle circumstances which effect the distribution of the profits of capital, and the wages of labor. It may be useful to illustrate the mode in which they operate, in an individual case. Let us take, for instance, a yard of calico.

1. The price of a bale of cotton, is made up of the rent of the land on which it grew, the wages and expense of the laborers, who were employed in its cultivation, the labor and skill of the agriculturist, who superintends the labor, the cost of seed, manure, utensils, &c. He who buys the cotton, pays a price sufficient to remunerate these laborers, pay the interest on the investment, and replace the expenditure for materials. He who raises the cotton, distributes the money which he has received, according to the principles which have been above suggested.

2. The cotton is sent by the merchant in Mobile to New York, and sold at an advanced price to the merchant, in this latter place. This advance, is sufficient to remunerate the merchant in Mobile, and to pay the cost of transportation. The merchant at Mobile is thus paid for his labor and skill in selecting and stowing the cotton; and for the use of his capital whilst it was invested in cotton. The cost of transportation, is made up of cost of investment in the vessel, in the wear and tear which it undergoes, in subsistence of mariners, and cost of insurance. This remuneration, is distributed as we have stated, according to the skill and labor of the several persons, by whom it has been performed. This is paid by the merchant in New York, and adds so much to the price of the cotton. When paid, it is divided between the owners of the vessel and the mariners, according to the laws which govern the wages of labor and of capital.

The cotton is bought by the manufacturer, who pays the merchant in New York, what he paid to the merchant in Mobile, with an addition for transportation, agency, and the use of capital whilst it has been in his hands. He removes it to his manufactory, cards, spins, and weaves it and prepares it for the calico printer, to whom it is next sold. The calico printer, pays the manufacturer, what he paid the merchant, and an additional sum for the value which he has confered upon it. This additional sum, is the compensation to the manufacturer. With it, he remunerates himself for his use of capital, labor and skill, and pays his workmen, for their labor, according to their skill and industry.

It now goes through the process of printing, and is then sold to the merchant at an additional advance. This advance, is sufficient to replace the price paid by the calico printer to the manufacturers, and also to pay the calico printer for the use of his capital, and the labor of his workmen. It is by the merchant sold to the consumer. The consumer pays the merchant the price paid by him to the manufacturer, and an additional sum, sufficient to remunerate him, for the use of his capital, skill, and labor. So that, when the article comes to the consumer, it is charged with all these previous prices, which have, in these various processes, accumulated upon it. The consumer pays what has been paid to the agriculturist, the mariner, the cotton merchant in Mobile, and the cotton merchant in New York, the manufacturer, the calico printer, and the calico merchant. Each several amount has been charged upon it in its progress, and the consumer at last, pays enough to replace the whole. The case is the same with a watch, a knife, a plough, or any other article of merchandize.

I shall conclude this chapter with two general remarks.

I. The interest of land, or real estate in general, is commonly less than that of other property, that is, if any particular stock costs one hundred dollars, and yields as interest, but three per cent., it would not sell for one hundred dollars but for fifty or sixty dollars. But land which costs one hundred dollars, although it yield but three per cent., will sell for ninety or one hundred dollars. That is, men are willing to receive less interest for money invested in land, than in other property. It may be worth while to suggest the reason of this difference.

1. Property in land, is considered more secure than any other property. The principal may be considered indestructible. Hence it is the safest of all investments, and *nothing* is paid for the *risk*.

2. The title to land can be more definitely secured, than that of any other property. The legal instruments, by

which it is secured to the individuals, are a matter of public record. The boundaries of land, can be, and commonly are, ascertained with entire precision. The land itself cannot be removed. Hence, the ownership of it, can be always ascertained and conveyed to posterity.

3. Men generally derive some influence and consideration from the ownership of land, which they do not derive from any other possessions. In many places, the right of suffrage is restricted to landholders. Where this rule exists, it, of course, shows the degree of consequence which is attached to this sort of possession. And the fact, that it has so frequently existed, while the contrary rule has never existed, shows the general tendency upon the subject.

4. There is, I think, in the human race, a strong disposition to become the owners of land; and a natural love to the pursuit of agriculture. Men of all professions, look forward to some period of life, in which, relieved from the toils of business, they may retire to the quiet country. To whatever extent this disposition exists, it of course tends to raise the price of land, above that of other property, paying the same rate of profit. If a man receive a part of his remuneration in pleasure, he will be content to receive less in the form of money.

5. And lastly the natural progress of society tends to increase the value of landed property. This has been already illustrated in general, in the remarks which have been made upon rent. And it must be evident, that land, remaining the same, and the population continually increasing, the demand for land must continually increase. And, besides this, the progress of society creates not only a more extensive demand for land, but a much greater variety of demands. As such is the tendency, men are

willing to hold land at a less interest than other property, in the hope that the rise of price at some future time, will compensate for their present loss. Thus, men frequently invest money in wild lands, expecting to reap no profit from them for many years, but calculating upon a rise of price at some time or other, which shall abundantly repay both principal and interest.

II. The second remark relates to a different subject.

From what has been said upon the nature of credit, it is evident that a merchant may easily carry on a business, greatly beyond his actual capital, and even with no capital at all. For instance, he may sell wholly the goods of another, by purchasing entirely on credit. Or he may borrow capital of an individual, or of a bank, and pay cash for his stock, and interest on his purchase money. In this case, he uses the property of the lender, instead of the property of the merchant, of whom he purchases. Or, he may have capital, say ten thousand dollars, of his own, and may effect credits to twice or thrice this amount. Or lastly, he may employ in trade no more capital than that which he actually possesses.

Now, it is manifest, *that the profit* must be, in these cases, very dissimilar. When a merchant owns all the capital he employs, he receives as profit, interest on his capital, and remuneration for his labor and skill. When he owns but a part, he receives interest for that part, and remuneration for his labor and skill in managing the whole. When he owns nothing, he receives nothing for interest on the capital, but only remuneration for his labor and skill in the management of the capital.

The risk of failure, and the liability of injuring others, are also dissimilar. He who owns all the capital he uses, can injure no one; because, he cannot lose more than all, and as he owns all, he is the sole sufferer. His payments may possibly be delayed, but he will, in the end, be able to pay every one his due.

When a merchant owns a *part* of the capital which he employs, he is not liable to injure his creditors, unless his loss be sufficient to absorb more than the portion which he himself possesses. But when a merchant trades wholly upon the capital of others, if his losses are more than sufficient to cover the advance due to his labor and skill, he must fail, and his creditors must suffer.

Hence the moral and economical principles which should govern men in the transaction of business, under these circumstances, are somewhat dissimilar.

1. If a man choose to squander or to risk *his own* property, though there may be a moral question in respect to his duty to God, there is none in respect to his duty to man. If he pay all his debts, no one has any claim upon him. Yet, so far as his own interest is concerned, he may do well to remember, that men will very naturally suppose, after having wasted all that was his own, that it will not be safe to trust him with what belongs to others.

2. If a man trade with the property of another, he is bound so to conduct his affairs, as to expose their property to no risk that can be foreseen. Hence, if their guaranty against loss, consist in that part of his stock which he owns, he is bound to guard against every risk, which could not be made good, by the sacrifice of his own property. This principle affects both the kind, and the amount, of business which he undertakes. It should be of such a *kind* as is exposed to no greater risk than may be covered by his own property. It should be only to such an extent,

that no ordinary fluctuation of business, will endanger those who have confided in his skill and integrity. If he, knowingly, act otherwise, he is dishonest. Nor is this all. If he really expose others to no risk, yet if he so enlarge his business, that he is continually obliged to call upon his neighbors for assistance, and to throw himself on their mercy, to save him from loss of mercantile character, he trifles with his credit, and makes an unfair use of their kindness. A man who is always exposing himself to extreme risks, will generally expose himself once too often.

3. He who trades upon the capital of another, should consider himself essentially in the character of an agent, and at liberty to expose the property of his principal, to no risk which the principal would not permit were he present; or which an unprejudiced person would not consider reasonable. He is to remember that if he succeed, the owner of the property derives no benefit beyond the fair and ordinary profit, but if he fail, the owner suffers all the loss, and therefore, he has no right to seek to benefit himself, at the risk of impoverishing another.

4. The same rule should govern the expenses of him who is engaged in business with the capital of another. He derives from his trade nothing more than the wages of his skill and labor. Within the amount of these wages, his expenses should be restricted. If he expend more, he is living dishonestly on the property of another. If he expend the whole of these wages, he is accumulating no capital, but at the end of the year will be as poor as he was at the beginning. He can only become rich by reducing his expenses as far as possible below his income, and thus having, every year, something to invest as capital, which shall give stability to his credit, and increase to his annual revenue.

Of Insurance. When property of any kind is consumable, it is liable to be consumed by accident. Thus houses, being combustible, are liable to be destroyed by fire. Ships are liable to be destroyed by storm and tempest. This liability is called *risk.* It is evident that it may, under given circumstances, be estimated. Thus, if we know the value of all the houses in a given city, and the amount of value in houses, which, on an average, for several years, has been destroyed by fire, we may estimate how great the risk of fire in that city is. The case is the same with ships, or with any other property.

Now this risk being thus known, one person may bear it as well as another. If I have a ship at sea, I may either bear the risk of losing it myself, or I may pay another person for bearing the risk for me. This transfer of risk is found convenient, and either companies or individuals are easily found, who, for a small addition to the actual value of the risk, are willing to insure any property that may be offered.

From this view of the case it is manifest, that insurance has no effect upon the fact of the loss. If a ship and cargo worth one hundred thousand dollars be sunk, precisely one hundred thousand dollars' worth of value is destroyed. The only effect of insurance is, to make the loss fall upon one person instead of upon another. The benefit of this transfer consists in this, that the loss is thus equalized. It is better for a community to divide a given loss among a great number of persons, than to suffer it to fall exclusively upon one.

And hence, inasmuch as every one has the power of avoiding risk, by paying a small premium; every one whose property is small, and liable to be lost by a single accident, is culpably negligent if he suffer it to remain a moment uninsured. Specially is this the case, when he holds the property of others; or when their only security for payment, depends upon the stock in trade which he possesses.

And again. As insurance has no effect upon the *fact* of loss, the higher the premium of insurance the greater is the annual loss to a country; because it shows us, how great an amount of property is annually destroyed. Hence a sound policy would always dictate the importance of taking every means to reduce the rate of insurance as low as possible. This can be done only by reducing the risk of the accidental destruction of property. On this account, the abundant supply of water, is a matter of inestimable economical importance to a city. The difference in the amount annually paid for insurance by the two cities of New York and Philadelphia is enormous. Nor is this all. New York in one single night, has lost by fire, property sufficient to pay the expense of abundantly supply herself with water, three times over. The same principles would teach us the importance of accurate surveys of the coast, the erection of light houses, and of wise and judicious laws for the government of pilots.

If the principles illustrated in the above chapter be correct, they will lead us to a few important practical conclusions. They teach us:—

1. That the capitalist and the laborer are equally necessary to each other. And hence that all attempts to excite the prejudices of the poor against the rich, or of the rich against the poor, are no less injurious to the interests of both classes than they are wicked and detestable. They most commonly emanate from unprincipled men, who can rise to notoriety in no other manner than by agitation; and who are willing to gratify their own lust of power at the sacrifice of the best interests of the community.

2. That the *accumulation* of capital, is as much for the interest of the laborer as of the capitalist himself. The manufacturer who is worth five hundred thousand dollars actually possesses but few of the real comforts of life more than may be possessed by one of his industrious and frugal workmen. Let it all be destroyed, and by his skill and industry, he could still gain a comfortable subsistence. But let it be destroyed, and one or two hundred families would be thrown out of employment; and be thus reduced to poverty. Let the property of all the capitalists of a country be destroyed, and thousands of laborers would, in a few weeks, die of starvation.

BOOK FOURTH.

BOOK FOURTH.

OF CONSUMPTION.

CHAPTER I.

OF THE NATURE AND DESIGN OF CONSUMPTION.

Of the nature of Consumption. Consumption is the destruction of value. By this is not meant the annihilation of the *material*, but only of a *particular form of utility*. Thus, if gunpowder be burned, if bread be eaten, if a tree be felled, the *particular utility* which each originally possessed, is destroyed forever. And this destruction of value takes place, altogether independently of the result, which may, in different cases, ensue; because that destruction is as truly effected in one case as in another. A load of wood, when it has been burned, as truly loses its utility, that is, its power of creating heat, when it is destroyed in a conflagration, as when it is consumed under a steam boiler, or in a fire place, though the result, in the two cases, may be very dissimilar. If bread be thrown into the sea, its utility is destroyed, just as much as if it were eaten; though, in the one case, there is no result from the consumption, and, in the other, it is the means of creating the vigor necessary to labor.

Hence consumption, viewed simply by itself, may be considered in the nature of a misfortune. It is the destruction of so much wealth as is consumed. A man, if he had his choice, would rather create one product without destroying another; or enjoy a gratification, if it were possible, without rendering the thing enjoyed useless. But, inasmuch as it is the law of our Creator that we shall obtain our possessions, and gratify our desires, on no other conditions than that of the destruction of value, we have no choice. We cannot cut up a hide of leather for the purpose of making shoes, without destroying forever its utility as a hide of leather. We cannot cut down a tree, and saw it into boards, without destroying forever its utility as a tree. We cannot enjoy the pleasure of eating an orange, without destroying forever the power in that orange of affording to any one else the same pleasure. And thus, in general, consumption is one part of an exchange, in which we surrender one value with the hope of obtaining another; and whether the hope be realized or not, the thing consumed is surrendered, and surrendered forever.

When, however, it is said that the *utility* consumed is destroyed forever, we mean only to speak of *this particular* utility. There may yet remain some valuable quality which has not yet been affected. Thus, if a linen garment be worn out, its utility as a *linen garment* is destroyed forever. It may however still possess an important utility, as a material for the manufacture of lint or of paper. Wood may be consumed for fuel; and its utility *as fuel* may be destroyed forever. A quantity of ashes however remains, which possesses an utility for the manufacture of soap. A pair of india rubber shoes, may be worn out, and yet possess a valuable utility to the manufacturer of india rubber cloth. Hence we see the importance, in all cases, of entirely exhausting all the values contained in any product before we surrender it up as worthless. For the want of this care, millions of property are annually wasted. The difference between the cost of two establishments, in the one of which *every* utility of every substance is consumed, and in the other of which, only the first utility is consumed, is frequently as great as the nett profits realized in the ordinary employments of industry.

1. Consumption may be either *of labor or of capital.* A mechanic who bestows a days labor upon a table, consumes that amount of labor upon it. He also consumes the material upon which he has labored. He has received in return the table, and, if his labor and capital have been well employed, the result will recompense his consumption, both of labor and capital. So he who employs laborers to work for him, consumes all the labor which he purchases. And, as every man who has skill and health, is capable of labor, the consumption of *time* uselessly, is the same as the consumption of labor; since this time, if not wasted, either would have been, or ought to have been, occupied in labor. Hence we see that every day spent, is, in fact, so much value *consumed.* If it bring no profitable result, it is so much value wasted.

2. Consumption may be either *voluntary* or *involuntary.* It is *voluntary* when it is effected by *design.* It is *involuntary* when it is the result of *accident.* In either case, if there be consumption, there is value destroyed. The difference is, that, in the one case, there is a profitable result expected; in the other case there is none. If a loaf of bread become mouldy by neglect, its value is destroyed, just as much as though it were eaten. The difference is, that, in the one case, the loss is total; in the other case, the consumption of value creates a power to labor, which is of more value than the loaf itself. If, for the want of a fender, the fire fall out of the fire place, and

burn the carpet, the carpet is as effectually consumed, as by the wear of several years. The difference is, that, in the one case, it affords a substantial convenience, and in the other it affords none. If, by forgetfulness or neglect, a gate is left unlatched, and it is beaten in pieces by the wind, it is as effectually consumed, as by the wear of several years. The difference is, that, in the one case, it answers for several years the purpose of inclosure, in the other case it answers no purpose at all. Hence, the necessity of care and vigilance in all the business of life. Almost every thing is constantly tending to consumption. Vegetable matter decays. Animal matter putrefies. Most of the metals are corroded. Almost all our possessions are liable to accidental destruction, from fire, or flood; from the cold of winter or the heat of summer. Hence, without our continual care, a continual process of consumption will be going on, by which our capital will be diminished.

3. Consumption, is either *rapid* or *gradual.* The consumption of wood for fuel is rapid. The consumption of wood, in consequence of the wear of a dwelling house, is gradual. But gradual consumption is as sure and as certain as though it were rapid. Hence, in estimating cost and expenses, unless an allowance be made for wear and tear, our calculations will not agree with the fact. If a man's furniture be wearing out every year, this average of loss, is as much to be taken into account, in estimating his expenses, as the cost of the fuel which he consumes.

The annual consumption of an individual, is the sum total of all the values which he destroys. Hence the materials upon which he operates, the tools which he wears out, the expenses of his household, both for materials and for labor, are all to be reckoned as parts of his annual consumption. So, also, the values destroyed by a nation, are the national consumption. The exports of an individual or of a nation, are a part of individual or of national consumption, since value to the full amount of the exports, is abstracted from the capital of the country. On the contrary, the imports are the product, or what the country receives back again in return for its exports, or consumption.

Every man in the country is a consumer. Without consuming he could not sustain life a day. He must consume the food which he eats, the clothes which he wears, and the dwelling that shelters him. Hence, if he do not produce any thing, he is an absolute and useless burden upon the community. If he do not produce as much as he consumes, he is by the whole amount of that deficiency an unprofitable member of the body politic.

A man cannot, honestly, consume more than he produces. And the more he produces, the more will he consume. Hence, the more industrious and the richer the community, the greater will be the consumption, and of course the demand. Hence, as we have said before, the richer the community, the better will it be for every class of producers.

II. *Of the design of Consumption.* Consumption, as we have said, is the destruction of value. But no man in his senses, will consume value without *some* expectation of advantage. Hence, the design of consumption is always some advantage which cannot be obtained in any other way.

This advantage is of two kinds. 1. *The increase of value;* or, 2. *The gratification of desire.*

1. *The increase of value.* This is the design of consumption in all the departments of industry. Thus, the farmer consumes seed, utensils, rent, manure, labor and sustenance of laborers. These all are abstracted from his

capital, and their value is destroyed, either wholly or in part, forever. But he consumes them cheerfully, in the expectation that the crop which he reaps, will replace them and repay both the interest of his capital, and his various outlays for materials and labor, and leave him also a suitable recompense for his industry and skill.

The manufacturer, consumes raw cotton, instruments, machinery, and labor. The value of these various products, is destroyed forever. But, by means of this destruction, he produces a fabric which repays all his consumption, and yields him a reasonable profit.

The merchant collects the productions of this country, and sends them abroad in his ship. He thus consumes these products, and also the wear and tear of his ship, and the labor, skill and subsistence of his officers and crew. His return cargo, if the voyage have been successful, replaces his cargo exported, pays the expense of transportation, and affords him a compensation for his labor and skill.

And thus, in all the operations of industry, the process of consumption, or the destruction of particular values for the sake of producing other and greater values, is continually going on. And men consume values in this manner cheerfully, because they are aware that *increase of value* is to be effected in no other way.

2. *The gratification of desire.* In this case, the value of a product is commonly destroyed, without the anticipation of the creation of any other product by which it is to be replaced. The purposes for which values are consumed in this manner are various.

1. For the gratification of those desires which are necessary to the preservation of life and health. In this

manner, we consume food, clothing, and shelter. In this case, there is combined with the gratification of desire, a substantial benefit, in the health and vigor which we derive from sustenance.

2. The mere gratifications of the *senses*. These are of two kinds, the *lower* and the *higher*. We consume values in the lower gratifications of sense, when we expend money for shows, for mere delicacies of the table, and for any thing of which the only result is, the gratification of a physical appetite. In this case, our only recompense consists in the pleasure experienced in the organ of sense. The *higher* gratifications of sense, are those which are called the pleasures of taste, and which are gratified by painting, statuary, architecture, and music. In this case, besides the gratification of the taste, there is also an additional result, in the mental cultivation and refinement, which such pleasures promote.

3. *Intellectual gratifications*. We consume money, for this purpose, in the purchase of books and philosophical instruments, and we consume time in the study and use of them. We here enjoy the pleasure of intellectual exercise, and also obtain that knowledge, by which we are enabled to perform the duties of life with greater success.

4. *Social pleasures*. We gratify our social instincts, by hospitality to our friends; and thus strengthen the ties which bind us to the human race.

5. *Moral pleasures*. In benevolence we expend money for the good of others. In this case, we receive gratification in the act itself, and also cultivate in ourselves those dispositions, which make us more worthy of the regard of our fellows, and more well-pleasing to our Father who is in heaven.

We have said that, by consumption, value is destroyed; but it is destroyed with the expectation of realizing a more valuable result. Hence, we see that the character of this consumption, is to be decided by ascertaining how far this expectation has been realized. If a product of more value than the time and labor consumed, be created by the consumption, such consumption is called *productive.* Such is the case when a farmer consumes labor and capital, worth one hundred dollars, and realizes a harvest worth two hundred dollars. If the product be not equal to the consumption, such consumption is called *unproductive.* If no product at all be realized, the consumption is then a total loss.

And, the same principles apply when consumption is effected for the purpose of gratifying a desire. If no such result be realized, it is a total loss. If the gratification be of less value than the value consumed; or if we have obtained a less amount, or less excellent gratification than we could have procured by some other mode of expenditure, there is always a loss, although it may not be total, and the consumption is unwise.

From what has been said, we may easily see the rules by which expenditure of all kinds should be governed.

1. Inasmuch as consumption is a destruction of value, and annihilates forever the particular value which we consume, our consumption for the purpose of producing a *given result*, should be as *small* as possible. Whatever is consumed beyond what is necessary to accomplish our purpose, is so much absolute loss.

2. The consumption being given, it should be our object, to derive from it *as large a product*, or as *valuable a gratification* as possible. Whatever is consumed, that

does not conduce to this result, in every way of which it is capable, is so much utility thrown away.

When these rules are perfectly obeyed, we enjoy as much as our circumstances allow; and we also enjoy it, with as little expense to the means of happiness of others as the nature of the present constitution permits.

Consumption is of two kinds, *Individual* and *Public*. *Individual* consumption, is what the individual consumes for his own personal profit or gratification. *Public* consumption, is what is consumed by the society, for the benefit of the whole.

CHAPTER SECOND.

OF INDIVIDUAL CONSUMPTION.

The consumption of the individual, is the amount of value which each individual destroys either for his own personal *profit* or for the *gratification of his desires.*

Individual consumption is then of two kinds; first what he consumes for the sake of reproduction, and secondly what he consumes for the gratification of desire; or in other words, what he consumes in personal and domestic expenditures. We shall consider these subjects separately.

SECTION I.

OF INDIVIDUAL CONSUMPTION FOR THE SAKE OF REPRODUCTION.

This is the consumption, which every individual effects, who carries on the operations of production. The farmer, the mechanic, the manufacturer, the merchant are all consumers, and are such in a greater or less degree, according to the extent of their production.

Productive consumption requires both skill and labor, while consumption for the sake of gratification requires neither. It requires labor and skill, so to consume seed and manure, &c., as to produce a loaf of bread, but it requires neither skill nor labor, to eat it after it has been produced. It requires labor and skill so to consume wool and dye-stuffs as to produce cloth; and so to consume that cloth as to produce a suit of clothes, but it requires no skill or labor to wear them out after they have been produced.

On the other hand, consumption of which the design is production, is commonly attended with no immediate gratification. The farmer may prefer agriculture to manufactures, but he would not commonly labor for the mere pleasure of the operation. Could he secure his crop with half the present labor, or with no labor at all, he would doubtless do so. The case is the same with the manufacturer, or any other producer.

Now, these two things are manifestly set over against each other, by the law of our Creator. We cannot use the same value for these two distinct and opposite purposes. If a man consume one hundred dollars in amusement, or in ostentation, he cannot have it also as capital, to be employed in his trade. And, not only can he not have it *now*, but he can never have it *again*. If it be invested in reproduction this year, it may, by the next year, amount to one hundred and fifty dollars, and the year after to two hundred dollars, and in twenty years it may become five thousand dollars. If it be spent on an entertainment or a journey of pleasure, it is lost, and all that it might have subsequently become, is lost forever. This should be borne in mind by every man who wishes to rise to independence. Every dollar which is spent in self gratification, is so much capital placed forever out of his power. And, on the contrary, every dollar which he invests in reproductive employment, may at any future time minister to gratification, or it may provide the means of much more valuable gratification in subsequent life.

Consumption is either of capital, or of labor.

I. Consumption of *capital.*

The principles which we have already endeavored to illustrate would suggest the following rules, respecting this part of consumption.

1. Our *consumption of capital,* in order to produce a given result, should be *as small as possible.* The ordinary maxim is as true as it is common, *a penny saved is a penny earned.* In estimating the profits of any operation, it is manifest that he who has produced a value worth one hundred dollars, at an expense of sixty dollars, reaps a profit of twenty dollars more than he who has produced the same value, at an expense of eighty dollars. Thus, the farmer should economize to the utmost all his materials. He who saves half a bushel of seed, in sowing an acre, enriches himself as much, as though he had reaped half a bushel more per acre. It is said that, in China, sowing is always done by drilling. One of Lord Macartney's suite estimated that the *saving*, throughout the whole empire, from this improvement, is sufficient to *feed* the whole population of Great Britain. The same principle applies to mechanics, manufacturers, and all consumers whatever. It is, unfortunately, the case that from want of care and ingenuity a much larger portion of value is commonly consumed, than is necessary for the production, required. This is specially the case with fuel. Probably not more than one tenth of the heat given off by wood, is rendered serviceable by the common fire place.

2. We *should employ capital, of no greater value than is necessary* to effect the production intended. Hence, every producer should make it an object of inquiry to ascertain, so far as the present state of knowledge may enable him, in what manner he may effect his purposes, by the least costly materials. The merchant, on this principle, should, before making an exchange, ascertain what is the cheapest product at home, with which he will be able to procure a given amount of a product from abroad. Very much of the success of a producer must of course depend upon his skill in this respect. The discovery of a cheaper dye stuff, of equal goodness, or the exchange of one export for another, may frequently, of itself, be sufficient to render a man independent. I do not, of course, suppose that any man will be so simple as knowingly to expend more in production than he supposes necessary. To guard him against this folly is not my object. It is rather to incite every man to a more thorough and intimate knowledge of the principles, on which the operation which he conducts, depends. It is only by such knowledge, that improvements in the various departments of industry are to be effected. And hence we see the importance of knowledge, to every man in the community.

3. It is important that *every utility possessed by any substance, be entirely consumed.*

In order to secure this result, attention must be paid to two circumstances. *First.* All the *fragments and remnants* should be, so far as possible, employed to some valuable purpose. This principle is well illustrated in the various uses to which the horns of cattle are applied. The horn consists of two parts, an outward horny case, and an inward conical shaped substance. The first process consists in separating these two parts by means of a blow against a block of wood. The horny exterior is then cut into three portions, by means of a frame saw.

1. The *lowest of them*, next the root of the horn, after undergoing several processes by which it is rendered flat, is made into combs.

2. The *middle of the horn*, after being flattened by heat, and its transparency improved by oil, is split into thin layers, and forms a substitute for glass, in lanterns.

3. The *tip of the horn*, is used by the makers of knife handles, and of the tops of whips.

4. The *interior* or *core* of the horn, is boiled down in water. A large quantity of fat rises to the surface. This is sold to the makers of yellow soap.

5. The *liquid itself*, is used as a kind of glue, and is purchased by the cloth dressers for *stiffening*.

6. The bony substance which remains behind, is sent to the mill, and, being ground down, is sold to the farmers for manure.

7. The clippings and shavings, are also sold to the farmers, for manure, or are used in small quantities, for the manufacture of toys." *

Now, it is evident, that if any part of this material were wasted, the cost of the manufactured articles would be higher, and the gain of the producer less. And, we also see that he who first discovered the mode of rendering any one of these portions of a horn useful, must, by this single discovery, have made himself rich.

* Babbage, on Manufactures.

And *Secondly. All the values must be consumed in the most profitable manner.* It frequently happens that a producer wants but one value from a substance for *his particular purpose*, while another and an important value remains unappropriated. It is always a matter of importance, to employ in the best manner every value which a substance is known to possess. Thus, after we have derived from wood, all the heat which it can evolve, it leaves ashes which possess an important value. After the oil manufacturer has expressed all the oil from flaxseed, the residuum is a valuable food for cattle. The employment of this utility, of course lessens the price of oil, and increases the demand for it. Hence, we see the superior economy of large establishments to small ones. A large manufacturing establishment, can carry on several distinct operations, for the sake of using these secondary utilities. In a small one, this would be impossible, and much must in consequence be wasted. Thus, in connexion with a large slaughter house, I have seen a soap and candle manufactory, a manufactory of glue, and one of neats foot oil; while a large number of hogs was fattened with the refuse of these several establishments. In this manner, every part of the slaughtered animal was profitably consumed. In small establishments, a large portion of the fragments is, by necessity, wasted.

II. *Consumption of labor.*

The principles above illustrated would teach us :—

1. To employ *precisely as much* labor as is necessary to accomplish the intended result.

We should never employ *more* than is wanted. This generates idleness and negligence. One supernumerary laborer, is not only an useless expense himself, but he generally requires the time of two or three others, to bear him company in idleness.

We should never employ *less* labor than is wanted. This produces confusion, and destroys the advantages of correct division of labor. It is no saving to employ one person less than is necessary in an establishment, and to suspend the labor of others several times in a day, in order to do the work which that one should have accomplished.

In general, provided of course the work be well done, the less the consumption of labor the better for the producer. Hence the economy of labor saving machinery. He who, by an ingenious contrivance, is able to save the hire of one laborer, will find himself, at the end of the year, richer by precisely this amount saved.

2. We should employ labor at *no higher price*, than is necessary to accomplish our object.

Every important operation consists of several subordinate operations, requiring very different degrees of skill in their execution. According to these degrees of skill, the wages of labor are adjusted. Now, economy requires, that labor of no higher price should be employed on each several operation, than the importance of the operation requires. He who is able so to arrange his laborers, as to entrust, safely, to labor worth fifty cents, what was formerly executed by labor worth one dollar, makes a gain of fifty cents a day. Thus, in the power press, the labor of press work, which formerly employed two able bodied men, is executed, in part by animal force, or by steam power; and the remainder by women. The reduction in price, thus effected, is very considerable.

But while this is the fact, it is also the fact, that we never gain by employing laborers incapable of accomplishing the result. If a particular part of an operation require skill and labor worth five dollars per day, it is better to give this price, than to confide it to an incompetent person, who is willing to work for two dollars per day. Thus, a good painter of calico patterns, a good calico engraver, or dyer, is cheaper at five dollars per day, than an inferior artist, even if the latter would offer to perform the labor for nothing.

We hence see, again, the importance of an accurate knowledge of principles, to every one engaged in extensive production. It is by deep and thorough reflection upon every part of the process which he conducts, that a manufacturer is able to keep up with, and specially to add to, the improvements of the age, and to prevent himself from being undersold by his more enterprising and intelligent neighbors.

3. The labor *paid for, should all be performed.*

Time, as it is frequently said, is money. It is surely money to him who pays money for it. And of course every hour for which he pays, that is spent in idleness or uselessness, is so much useless consumption; or so much absolute loss.

The causes of the waste of labor are various. Some of the more common are :—

1. *Want of superintendence.* It cannot be supposed that laborers, if left alone, and if paid by the day, will labor as faithfully as if laboring for themselves. Hence the necessity and the economy of efficient superintendence. He who employs twenty men by the day, to perform a

particular piece of work, will find that an efficient superintendent will, by preventing idleness, sauntering, and story-telling, save much more than his wages. And, hence, I suppose that commonly, where the labor is of such a nature as to allow of it, it is cheaper to pay by the piece, than by the day. In the one case, if a laborer be idle, he wastes his *own* time ; in the other case, the time of his employer. It is easy to perceive which case is the most favorable to industry.

2. *Irregularity.* This is a great source of waste of labor. Where tools are allowed to get out of place, materials to be deficient or unsuitable ; or where several laborers are obliged to stand idle, to wait for the completion of an operation which is done out of season, much time must, of necessity, be lost. In a shop containing a dozen workmen, if each one spend, on an average, half an hour a day in looking for misplaced tools, or in waiting for materials not at hand, this is a loss of more than half the wages of one laborer a day. This, in a year, would be sufficient to purchase the clothes of a small family.

3. *Defective tools.* In order that the economy of labor may be as great as possible, the tools by which labor is saved, should be as perfect as possible ; otherwise, we derive only a partial benefit from the invention. He who employs a man to chop wood, would certainly see the importance of furnishing him with a sharp axe. He who erects a fence, to save the labor of guarding his cattle, will certainly do wisely to keep his fence in good order. It is surely less labor to *mend a gap in a fence*, than to be obliged to plant a field a second time, because the grain has been destroyed, by cattle which that gap permitted to enter. It takes less labor to mend a leakage in a mill dam, than to rebuild the dam after it has been, by means of that leakage, carried away. Hence, we see the import-

ance, of keeping every part of an establishment in perfect order, and of allowing nothing to be out of repair, if it be possible to repair it.

"I remember," says Say, "being once a witness of the numberless misfortunes which a neglectful housekeeping entails. For the want of a small latch, the gate of the poultry yard was forever open, there being no means of closing it externally, and many of the poultry were lost in consequence. One day, a fine young porker, made his escape into the woods, and the whole family, gardener, cook, milkmaid, &c., presently turned out in quest of the fugitive. The *gardener*, in leaping a ditch, got a sprain that *confined him to his bed for a fortnight*. The cook, found the *linen burnt that she had left at the fire to dry*. The milkmaid forgot, in her haste, to tie up the cattle in the cow house, and one of the loose cows *broke the leg of a colt* that was kept in the same shed. The linen burnt, and the gardner's work lost, were worth twenty crowns, and the colt as much more, so that forty crowns were, in a few minutes lost, for want of a latch that would not have cost more than a few sous." [Pol. Economy, Book 3d, chapter 5.]

Illustrations of the importance of having every instrument in order, and in place, are occurring in most establishments every day. They teach us, that economy of capital, as well as of labor, requires that every thing should be done in time, and in season; that if a thing need to be done, to day, we have no means which shall enable us to estimate the loss that may ensue, by putting it off until tomorrow; and, that negligence is as much at variance with the laws of our Creator, as absolute wastefulness, inasmuch as it exposes us to equally severe punishments. Is would be well, if men would remember this, not only in the affairs of this life, but still more, in the affairs of another.

Supposing now that both labor and capital, have been invested upon the most economical principles. The object for which they have been thus invested, is the creation of products. Hence, the greater this product is, the more successful the investment, the better is it for the individual, and the better is it for the community. The object of the farmer is, with a given soil, a given expenditure of labor, of seed and of manure, to raise the greatest amount of *value* in a harvest. This will *generally*, though not *always*, be as the *quantity*. Fifty bushels of common apples, will not sell for so much as forty bushels of good ones. One hundred pounds of coarse wool, will sell for much less than one hundred pounds of fine wool. Hence, his object should be, from a given expenditure, to derive the greatest amount of profit. It is, by thus adjusting his expenditure, and thus calculating the results, that an intelligent and thoughtful farmer will grow rich; while all around him are remaining stationary or are growing poor.

So, it is the business of the manufacturer to create, with a given expenditure, the greatest amount of value. If he can succeed in giving to his cloth a better dye, or can produce a more durable or a more tasteful fabric, or can adapt it better to the satisfying of any human want, its value is, by so much, increased, and he and the community are the better for the increased value of his production.

In like manner, the merchant having arranged his exports with the greatest economy, should labor to import, with this expenditure, the greatest amount of value. He should send to the country, and at the time, in which his own product will exchange for the greatest amount of whatever he wishes to procure.

It is evident, that, in order to do this, a systematic knowledge of the principles of any employment is necessary to the individual by whom it is carried on. A man, in order to be a skilful producer, must be acquainted with the laws of production, that is, those laws of nature and of society, which govern the transaction in which he is engaged. Hence, we see the importance of accurate knowledge, and sound mental discipline to all the classes of society.

We see, in the above remarks, another illustration of the truth, that the benefit of one is the benefit of all, and the injury of one is the injury of all. If a man economize labor and capital, he increases his own wealth, and he also rescues as much as he saves, from actual destruction. The whole of this amount may go to the farther increase of production, or to the satisfying of human wants. The more he produces, the greater is his wealth ; and the greater is the value which is created for the good of the whole community. Hence, we see, that he who is honestly promoting his own welfare, is also promoting the welfare of the whole society of which he is a member.

And as it is manifestly for the interest of the individual, so is it for the interest of the society, that every producer should consume as little value, and produce as great value, as possible. Hence, we see the impolicy of those restrictions, which will not allow the individual to purchase and to sell where he pleases. If he must give a higher price than is necessary for his material, this is, by the difference, unprofitable consumption. If he cannot dispose of it where he pleases, this is, by so much, unprofitable production, because he is unable to realize from his production as much he would be able to realize, were he left to himself.

SECTION II.

OF CONSUMPTION FOR THE GRATIFICATION OF DESIRE.

By means of the productive consumption, above treated of, a man procures the means for this second kind of consumption. This means however, it is always to be remembered does not consist of his whole production, but only of the excess of production over consumption. If he live on capital loaned at interest, the case is the same. The money loaned is, for the time, consumed. The interest paid, is the excess of the production over the consumption, and this, of course, is all that he has to appropriate to the gratification of his desires.

Consumption for the gratification of our desires, may be considered from two points of view. *First.* Without reference to the circumstances of the individual, or to the relative value of the various modes of gratification ; and, *secondly* with reference to these circumstances.

I. *Of consumption for the purpose of self gratification simply.*

These purposes have been already alluded to. They are generally comprehended under the following particulars :

Expenditures for the necessaries and conveniences of living, as food, clothing and shelter ; for the gratification of the senses and the tastes ; for the pleasures of intellect ; for the pleasures of society ; and for moral pleasures. Under one or other of these simply, or under several of them combined, I believe almost all of our expenditures may be classed.

Now if these be considered, irrespective of our circumstances, or of the intrinsic value of the gratifications themselves, the principles of expenditure will be, essentially, the same as those which have been already illustrated. That is to say, if a particular mode of living, or the enjoyment of a particular gratification *be determined upon*, whether that determination be wise or unwise, economy teaches us to obtain it most perfectly, and at the least possible expense. The question of its wisdom or folly, belongs to another part of the subject. A particular mode of living having been resolved upon, economy will teach us to sustain it, at the least possible expense. Hence, in regard to capital, the rules will be:

1. That the consumption of values be as small as is consistent with the accomplishment of our purpose. This is opposed to several errors.

To purchasing *more* of any value than is wanted. The articles ordinarily consumed in a family, are rapidly destructible. If more be purchased than is wanted, it is liable to become useless, and, in this case, the loss of this excess is total. By having a superabundance of any thing consumable, it becomes, in the eyes of those who use it, less valuable, and is used less carefully. And, if neither of these results be experienced, if an article be purchased a year before it is wanted, the purchaser loses the interest, for a year, of the money expended. Hence, it is generally as economical to purchase at retail, as at wholesale.

Hence it is commonly wasteful to purchase any thing because it *is cheap*. If a man *need* any thing, its cheapness is a reason why he should buy it. But, if he do not want it, its cheapness is no reason at all. A man may buy stones very cheap, but it is doubtful whether he would be either enriched or made happier by the purchase. Many a garret is filled with great bargains; which were purchased because they were cheap, and then laid away to rot.

2. The consumption should *be as perfect as possible.* When we have possessed ourselves of a substance, it should not be thrown away, until every utility which it possesses has been exhausted.

Thus, an article of clothing which will not answer any longer for one purpose, may answer very well for another. An article of food, which may not be used in one form, may be used in some other form. And hence, in general, nothing should come into a house, unless it be wanted, nor in a larger amount than it is wanted; and nothing should leave it, until all its utility is exhausted.

3. All the means should be provided for the most perfect production and consumption of values. Hence, every useful utensil should be furnished, and should be the most perfect of its kind. It is cheaper to buy a coal hod, than to carry coal in a basket, and by saving a dollar in a utensil, ruin a carpet worth fifty dollars. It is cheaper to have every description of culinary vessel that may be needed, than to have food spoiled by being cooked in an unsuitable instrument. It is cheaper to have a bad fire place altered, at an expense of fifteen dollars, than to consume annually ten dollars more worth of wood than is necessary.

Hence, it is also important, that every article purchased, be of such a nature as will admit of the most profitable consumption. If a man buy fuel which gives off very little heat, because it is at a low price, it is by no means certain that he has made a successful purchase. It should always be remembered, that we want a given amount of utility, and not the mere form in which it seems to reside. It is cheaper to purchase a dollar's worth of utility for a dollar, than half a dollar's worth for seventy-five cents. Hence, the lowest priced products, are by no means always the cheapest.

The same principles apply to labor.

Economy directs, that in a household, we should purchase as much labor as we need, and of the kind that we need, but no more than we need. When we pay for useless labor, we throw money away ourselves. When we employ incompetent labor, we pay others to throw it away for us.

These, I suppose to be the principal circumstances, which should govern our expenditures. And, it will be seen, that they apply to all the conditions of men. Whether our expenditure be large or small, it should be conducted with economy. The object to be attained is, to secure as large an amount of gratification, at as small an expenditure as possible. To the man who has but two hundred dollars per year to spend, it is certainly important to spend it economically. To the man who has ten thousand dollars per year, it will generally be found convenient.

Hence it will be seen, that, in order to enjoy the comforts or the luxuries of life, at the least expense, care and superintendance, and knowledge of the various operations performed in a household, are absolutely necessary. And, as this department of consumption, in general, devolves upon the mistress of a family, we see how important to the execution of it, with success, must be vigilance, care, intelligence and industry. The husband, by the employment of capital, labor and skill, in productive consumption, secures an annual revenue, for the purpose of consumption in the various means of gratification, whether necessary or superfluous. The expenditure of this annual revenue, or the making of those arrangements which govern the expenditure, generally devolves upon the wife. If that expenditure be made without economy, either the gratifications which it might procure are never enjoyed, and by all the consumption, neither comfort nor pleasure is obtained; or else, if the gratification sought for be obtained, it is obtained at an expense absolutely ruinous. Hence, it will be seen, that the physical comfort, as well as the means of happiness of both parties, depends more on the domestic education of the female sex than is ordinarily supposed. Affection will rarely exist in the atmosphere of self inflicted poverty. No man can respect a woman, by whose caprice and ignorance of her appropriate duties, he is plunged into disgraceful bankruptcy, and wedded to hopeless penury. Nor, let it be supposed, that no talent is requisite skilfully to superintend a household. It requires at least as much ability to direct, with skill and on principle, the affairs of a domestic establishment, as to select a ribbon or dance a minuet; to finger a piano or to embroider a fire screen.

II. *Consumption considered in respect to the relative value of the desire.*

The various objects of desire, by the possession of which our happiness may be promoted, may, with sufficient accuracy for our present purpose, be divided into moral, intellectual, social, and sensual.

The attainment of happiness from either of these, commonly involves some expenditure of time, or of property, or of both. Thus, we cannot by reflection improve our own hearts, without the consumption of time, nor cultivate our benevolent sentiments, without the consumption of property. The improvement of our minds by reading and study, demands both time and books. We cannot enjoy the society of our friends, without the consumption of both time and of property. And every one knows, that the gratification of our senses, whether intellectual or corporeal, consumes a large portion of the income of every individual.

It belongs to the teacher of ethics, to show in which mode of expenditure a man may best secure his *future* happiness, and act most worthily of the *moral* nature with which he is endowed. The political economist, looks upon the various modes of expenditure, simply as they affect the *wealth* of the individual, and of the public. Yet, even in this view, it may not be inappropriate to offer a single suggestion. Inasmuch as we have been created with aptitudes for all these different modes of happiness, it is manifestly the intention of the Creator, that we should enjoy, not merely *one*, but *all* of them. As we are not merely sensual, but also moral and intellectual beings, it is *as* reasonable that we should expend a part of our time and property, in the pursuit of moral and intellectual, as that we should spend a part of it, in the pursuit of sensual gratifications. He who argued from the superior dignity of our nature over that of brutes, might perhaps urge that the former was the *more reasonable* mode of expenditure. But the dignity of the race not belonging to the province of the political economist, we shall not consider the subject in this point of view.

The principles upon which political economy would teach us to *select* our modes of gratification are, I suppose the following. *First.* Where the amount of gratification in two cases is equal, it is wise to choose that which is the least expensive. The reason for this is too obvious to need much illustration. If a particular gratification can be procured for one hundred dollars, and another, which will afford an equal amount of happiness, can be procured for ten dollars, the cheaper is to be preferred; because, while, in this case, we obtain an equal gratification, we have ninety dollars remaining with which to purchase other objects of desire. *Secondly.* When two modes of gratification are, in themselves, equally productive of happiness, but, of which, one *tends* to the wealth, and the other to the poverty, both of the individual and of society, the former is to be preferred. Thus, if it cost the same sum, to spend an evening in intellectual improvement, that it would cost to spend it in a drunken frolic, and the pleasure in the two cases were the same; inasmuch as intellectual cultivation tends to knowledge, which is a valuable consideration to every producer, and a drunken frolic has no such tendency, economy would teach us to spend the evening in intellectual cultivation.

If, now, we compare the various modes of expenditure most common among men, I think that we shall find, that the economy of the moral and intellectual pleasures, is somewhat overlooked.

The expenditures for all the real wants and conveniences of a human being, may, by industry and frugality, without great difficulty, be supplied. It does not cost much, to provide all that we need for wholesome and palatable food, for comfortable clothing and shelter, and for all the furniture demanded for convenient domestic arrangements. Our greatest expenses are for those objects, which yield no other utility than the mere gratification of the senses, or, which are rendered necessary, by command of fashion, or the love of ostentation. Thus, in the purchase of a garment, or of an article of furniture, a part of the price is paid for the real utility which it possesses, and the remainder, for that particular form, or color, or workmanship, which is designated by fashion. Now, it frequently happens, that this latter portion of the price, is far greater than the former. The same may be said of many of our expenses of the table and of various others.

Now, that men should not, if they have the ability, in any manner gratify their senses, and yield obedience to fashion, it is not necessary here to affirm; nor is it necessary that political economy should prescribe the limit, within which these gratifications shall be confined. A few considerations for the sake of illustrating the comparative economical advantages of other modes of gratification is all that will be here attempted.

1. Moral and intellectual pleasures are by no means expensive. To spend time in moral cultivation, is no more expensive than to spend it thoughtlessly and frivolously. The time consumed in thoughtless dissipation, if employed in moral culture, would be sufficient to effect great changes in our habits and tastes.

The pleasures of benevolence, so far as pecuniary consumption is concerned, are less expensive than those of the senses. Were the sums lavished in thoughtless caprice, in obedience to fashion, or in the gratification of appetite, to be reserved for charity, how great an amount of happiness might be created both in the benefactor and the recipient.

The same may be said of intellectual pleasures. Books and all the means for intellectual gratification, may be had at an expense within the reach of a very large class of the community. The useless ornaments of a drawing room, would frequently purchase a considerable library. The sums of money annually paid, by most families, to satisfy the demands of fashion, would provide them with as much reading as they would desire. Now, when these two kinds of pleasure are equally set before us, and when the one may be procured at so much less expenditure than the other, it surely is worth the attention of every man, deliberately to inquire by which mode of investment he will best secure his own happiness. There seems something ill-adjusted, when the habitation of a moral and intellectual being, reminds us of every thing else, than that he is either moral or intellectual.

2. Moral and intellectual pleasures tend to the wealth both of the individual and of society.

The exercise of benevolence has several important economical tendencies. For instance, it tends directly to cultivate the habits of self-denial and self-government, which are so essential both to industry and to frugality. Sensual self-indulgence, tends directly to produce both indolence, and capricious and reckless expense.

Again. The habit of benevolence tends to moderate and correct that intense love of gain, which is so frequently the cause of ruin to enterprising men. In the management of any hazardous business, he will be the most likely to succeed, who looks with entire coolness on the chances of loss and gain. The too eager, governed by their imagination, rush into needless danger. The too cautious allow a fair prospect of advantage to pass by unimproved. The one is as liable to fail as the other. He who, by the practice of benevolence, has learned a more accurate estimate of the blessings of wealth, will more probably than either, judge correctly. The miser and the sensualist will fall into opposite extremes, one upon each side of him.

Besides, the social benefits of benevolence are incalculable. It unites together the various classes of men, by the strong ties of affection and gratitude. By bringing all classes of men more directly under the view of the whole mass of society, social responsibility is increased, and the encouragements to virtue and the restraints upon vice are strengthened. When the rich are hard-hearted and luxurious, the poor are disaffected, anti-social and destructive. In so far as benevolence, therefore, tends to the improvement of the social dispositions of men, it may lay claim to great economical advantages.

And the same is true of intellectual pleasures. A man cannot enjoy these without improving his mind, and rendering it a more valuable instrument both for the production of his future happiness, and the accumulation of wealth. Knowledge is power, in what sphere of life soever it be exerted. The gratification of the senses enervates the body, enfeebles the mind, and tends to render intellectual exercise unpleasant, and to unfit us for any important or highly responsible exertion.

CHAPTER THIRD.

OF PUBLIC CONSUMPTION.

SECTION I.

OF TAXES, OR, THE MANNER IN WHICH PUBLIC EXPENDITURE IS PROVIDED FOR.

We have thus far treated of individual consumption, or of that destruction of values affected by the individual, in the accomplishment of his own purposes; and for the gratification of his own desires. But, all the capital produced by a society, is not expended in this manner. A part of the annual revenue of every individual, is contributed in some manner to the public, and is expended by the agents of the public, that is, by the government. This part remains to be treated of, under the head of public consumption.

This expenditure is provided for, by means of *taxation.* When a given sum is to be raised for the accomplishment of any object, it is, by some mode of assessment, distributed among the various individuals of the community, and every one is obliged to pay the proportion with which he is charged. The sum thus collected, is then for the accomplishment of particular purposes consumed by the agents into whose hands it is delivered. The consumption itself is of precisely the same nature as that effected by individuals, that is, the value is destroyed; and the utility consumed, is annihilated. If an individual burn gunpowder, the value in time and material by which it was produced is destroyed; if a hundred, or a thousand men do it, the result is the same. If a man in the digging of a ditch consume the labor of a thousand workmen, and use the provision for their sustenance, the whole value, thus expended, is annihilated. And, if a thousand men unite in the undertaking, the annihilation is the same. This is really so evident, that to illustrate it at length, seems almost childish. Does any one doubt when a house is burnt down, whether the value of a house is or is not consumed, because the owner did not set fire to it *himself*. Does any merchant doubt, whether his property is diminished or not, when it has been wasted by a profligate clerk. In a word, government is nothing but a system of agencies; and property consumed by the government, is as really consumed, and its value as really destroyed, as though the individual citizens consumed it themselves.

Now, this being the fact, the rule by which consumption is to be judged of, is precisely the same, whether it be public or private. If the product created by the consumption, whether that product be material or immaterial, be of greater value than the product consumed, it is profitable consumption; that is, the public receive in return a greater value than they parted with. If a less valuable product be created, than is consumed, it is unprofitable consumption, and the value might better have remained in the hands of the individuals. If no product whatever be realized, it is a total loss; and the value taken from the individual might as well have been thrown into the sea. Nay, had they themselves thrown the value consumed into the sea, there would have been a gain, in the amount of the expense of collecting and consuming it. And still more, if the value consumed produce no valuable result, but, on the contrary, be employed to promote the purposes of oppression and misrule, the evil is enormous. The possessions of the individual are taken away, not only without rendering him any equivalent, but for the sake of employing other men to torment him, and deprive him of his dearest rights.

It is very frequently asserted, and therefore some of those to whom it is told, I suppose, must believe it, that public expenditure enriches a country, or that, at least, it is wholly innocent, since it quickens the circulation of money, and does no harm, inasmuch as all the money always remains in the country. To obviate sueh an objection, let us trace, from first to last, the passage of a product towards ultimate consumption, on the public account. The government exacts from the tax payer, the payment of a given sum in the shape of money. To meet this demand, the tax payer exchanges part of the products at his disposal, for coin, which he pays to the tax gatherer. A second set of government agents is busied, in buying, with that coin, clothing and other necessaries for soldiery. Up to this point, there is no value either lost or consumed; there has only been a gratuitous transfer of value and a subsequent act of barter, but, the value contributed by the citizen, still exists in the shape of stores and supplies in the military depot. In the end, however, this value is consumed, and then the portion of wealth which passes from the hands of the tax payer, into those of the tax gatherer, is destroyed and annihilated.

"Yet, it is not the *sum of money*, that is destroyed; *that* has only passed from one hand to another, either with or without any return, as, when it passed from the tax payer to the tax gatherer; or in exchange for an equivalent, as when it passed from the government agent to the contractor, for clothing and supplies. The *value of the money* survives the whole operation, and goes through three or four, or a dozen hands, without any sensible alteration. *It is the value of the clothing and necessaries that disappears*, with precisely the same effect, as if the tax payer had, with the same money, purchased clothing and necessaries for his own private consumption." *

The consumption, then, is of the same nature, whether it be public or private. It is a destruction of value, and the rule by which we are to determine, whether it be profitable or unprofitable is the same, in both cases. It is, by inquiring, whether the benefit created by the consumption, is greater than, equal to, or less than, the value of the product consumed.

While, however, this rule is always to be adopted, it is, as in the case of individual consumption, to be interpreted with a liberal and intelligent forecast. It must not, of course, always be expected, that the product created by consumption, will be a visible, tangible, material substance. Thus, we see no physical, tangible product, as the result of taxes for the support of civil government. But, we receive the benefit in security of person, property and reputation; or in that condition of society, which, though it be incapable of being weighed and measured, is absolutely essential both to individual happiness, and individual accumulation. The same may be said, in substance, concerning the taxes paid for general education. Here, whether the tax payer receive his remuneration in instruction given to his own children, or not, he yet receives it, in the improvement of the intellectual and social character of his neighbors, by which his property is rendered more secure, the labor for which he pays is better performed, and the demand for whatever he produces,

* Say.

is more universal and more constant. The same may be said of that public expenditure, by which the moral and social character of a community is elevated, the taste of a nation refined, and an impulse given to efforts for the benefit of man. With this view, no one could oppose the expense incurred in bestowing upon public edifices elegance, or even, in some cases, magnificence of structure; in the public celebration of remarkable eras; and in the rewards bestowed upon those who have by their discoveries enlarged the boundaries of human knowledge, or by their inventions, signally improved the useful arts. Political Economy is opposed to none of these forms of expenditure; all that she requires is, that a valuable consideration be received in return for the consumption; and that the consumption be not disproportionate to that consideration,

Of the different modes by which the public expenditure is provided for.

Taxes are of two kinds, *direct* and *indirect.*

A direct tax, is a certain amount assessed upon every individual, in proportion to the property which he is known to *possess.* In many of the towns of New England, an annual tax list is made out, in which the portion which every taxable inhabitant must pay towards supporting the expenses of the district, is specified. The apportionment is made out by persons appointed for the purpose, called assessors. If any individual consider himself as taxed too highly, he is at liberty to appear, and declare upon oath, the amount of property of which he is possessed. His assessment is then graduated, according to the amount to which he has sworn.

An *indirect* tax, is levied upon articles of production, at some period during their passage from one possessor to another. Thus, a tax or as it is called a duty, is laid by this country on various goods imported from abroad, immediately on their arrival. This duty, is paid by the merchant who receives them; and he adds this duty to the cost of the goods, when he sells them to the next purchaser. Thus, the price of the product is raised, by this amount, when it comes into the hands of the consumer. If broadcloth pay a duty of two dollars a yard, he who buys a yard of broadcloth pays two dollars a yard more for it than he would pay if there were no duty to be paid. If coal be taxed two dollars a ton, as it is at present, every consumer of foreign coal pays two dollars a ton more than he would pay if no such tax were exacted. The effect of this tax is also to keep the price of all other coal two dollars a ton higher than it would otherwise be.

Now, supposing the same sum were to be demanded for the service of the public, it may be asked, which mode of raising it is to be preferred.

1. In favor of an indirect tax it may be urged, that it is raised with more *convenience*, and less liability to personal collision, between the tax payer and the tax gatherer.

The imports of a country are all received at a comparatively small number of places, denominated ports of entry. Goods arriving at these places are all charged with the duty on their arrival; and thus, the collection may all be accomplished in a short time, and with very little trouble. Besides, as the importer, who pays the duty, receives it back again from the purchaser of the goods, it seems to him a matter of small importance, whether it be high or low, and he is disposed to make but little trouble about it. The case is the same with every succeeding purchaser, until it comes at last to the consumer. The consumer may feel, that the product is dear, but if it be no dearer than he has always paid, he thinks but little about it; and, if it be somewhat dearer than formerly, the rise and fall in the price of goods is so common a thing, that he imputes the difference to any other cause, as soon as to the additional duty paid to the government. Hence, it is frequently said, that people do *not feel an indirect tax*, which means, I suppose, that they do not know, either how much they pay, or when they pay, or whether they pay or not.

On the contrary, it is, doubtless, the fact, that men *feel* direct taxes more sensibly, that is, they know when they pay them, and how much they pay. Here, then, is liability to ill feeling, and sometimes to resistance; and, moreover, there is a possibility that an excessive parsimony may restrict the public means in such manner, as to prevent the execution of works of real utility, if not of imperative necessity.

2. There is, however, a somewhat greater liability of injustice, in indirect than in direct taxation. As, when duties are laid upon goods, the tax payer knows very little of the amount paid, and is hence less careful to inquire on what principles the revenue is raised, there is a greater opportunity afforded, in this manner, of imposing the public burdens unequally, and of imposing them for purposes at variance with the principles of the social compact. Hence, a majority may impose taxes for the benefit of a part, and not for the benefit of the whole; and the matter can easily be so mystified, that the sufferer can excite but little sympathy. I do not deny that direct taxation is liable, in some cases, to the same abuse; as, for instance, when the city and country interests strive to shift the burden of taxation upon each other. I only say, that the evil is not

so liable to happen in the one case as in the other, and when it does happen, it is more readily exposed.

3. Aside from irregularity in the assessment of indirect taxes, it may be observed, that, in their very nature, they are liable to objection, because they do not impose the public burden, in any manner in proportion to the share which the individual receives of public protection. The *indirect tax*, is paid by the *consumer*. Hence, he pays, not according to the benefit which he *receives* from the existence of civil government, but according to the amount of production which he *consumes*. Hence, he who possesses a million dollars worth of property, if he consume no more than he who lives by his daily labor, will pay no larger share of the public burden. Hence, a manifest inequality is involved in the original conception of an indirect tax. To this, I know, it may be answered, that the merchant also pays part of the tax, inasmuch as the rise of price, in consequence of the duty, diminishes his sales, and he is thereby so much the poorer. But to this it may be replied: 1. Every man is not a merchant, and, hence, the answer is not of universal application, and does not remove the difficulty ; and, 2dly, while, in this manner, the merchant is made poorer, no one is made richer. It is true he loses, but from his loss no one gains. The public burden is by no means the less, because he sells less than he would otherwise sell. Hence the answer merely asserts, that both parties suffer equally, though only one suffers with any benefit to the public, while the suffering of the other is wholly gratuitous.

The same remark may however be applied in part to direct taxation. It may be said, that the tax payer here raises his price, in such a manner that he only pays a part of the tax assessed upon him, and that the remainder is paid by the consumer. This is, in part, true, but I think not by any means to the extent that it is true of indirect taxation. He whose actual property is taxed, cannot raise the price of his commodities, with such accuracy as the merchant, but must bear his proportion without the ability of so readily shifting it upon another. Hence, direct taxes, if equally imposed, are commonly more just; that is, they derive the support of government from the individuals, more in proportion to the degree of benefit which each desires from the government.

In favor of direct taxation, it may also be added, that it is decidedly more in harmony with the genius of a republican or representative government. Such a government, proceeds upon the principle, that the people are the fountain of power, and are competent to govern themselves. Now, such a government ought not, surely, to act upon the directly opposite principle, that the people ought *not to know what they pay, or when or how they pay. They* are the *party*, from which, specially, nothing of this sort should be concealed. They should know *what*, and *how much*, they contribute; and, also, in what manner, whatever they contribute is expended. It is in this knowledge, and in the judicious use of it, that their safety consists. To me therefore, the consideration, so frequently urged in favor of indirect taxation, that the people do not feel it, is one of the strongest arguments against it. The more a people feel taxation, and the more jealously they watch over the public expenditure, the better it is for them and for their rulers.

Of the principle by which taxation should be regulated.

I have already stated that the several members of a society should be taxed in proportion to the benefit which they receive from a government. Thus, if a government protects for one man, one hundred thousand dollars worth of property, and for another only one thousand dollars worth, the former should pay one hundred times as much towards the public expenses, as the latter. So far as this is evidently just. But it may be questioned whether justice might not go somewhat farther, inasmuch as, a percentage of his income, which would not abridge even the luxuries of the rich, might materially curtail even the necessities of the poor. But whether the rich ought to be taxed *more* than a pro rata proportion or not, I think it evident, that taxes should be so arranged, that individuals should, in so far as possible, pay in proportion to their property; that is, in proportion to the amount of protection which they receive of the government. Now, inasmuch as indirect taxation, if laid *indiscriminately*, would apportion the public burden on no such *principle*, it is evident, that such taxation, should be made *discriminately;* that is, that articles of necessity should be either exempt from taxation, or taxed very lightly; and articles of luxury, or those used chiefly by the rich, should bear the greater part of the burden.

This would lead us to the following conclusions.

1. Property below a certain amount, might very properly be exempt from taxation.

The *poor man's* clothes and bedding, his cow and his pig, should never be enumerated among taxable property.

2. The necessaries of life, if taxed at all, should be taxed at the lowest rates. Of these, the rich and poor must consume nearly equal quantities. But they require only a fraction of the rich man's income, while they demand almost the whole of the poor man's earnings. A tax on bread stuffs, fuel, coarse clothing, or iron, dimin-

ishes, essentially, the comforts, and even the necessaries of life, of a very large proportion of every community.*

3. Taxation should be the heaviest upon articles of *luxury and ostentation;* not for the sake of interfering with these modes of pursuing happiness, but because those who are able to expend in this manner, are able to bear, with the least inconvenience, the expenses of government. The *conveniences* of living, and the means of accumulation, should bear the next portion of the burden. He who is able to furnish himself with the *conveniences* of living, is always able to pay a portion of the expenses of government; and he who possesses means of accumulation, can always devote some part of that which is annually accumulated, to pay for the protection which he receives. Thus, carpeting, is a more fit subject for taxation than bread stuffs or fuel. Thus, also, a farmer's wagon, or a merchant's ship, may justly be taxed, but they ought not to be taxed in the same proportion as a

* It is somewhat singular, that, with a surplus revenue on hand of forty millions of dollars, we are, at the present moment, in this country, paying a duty of six cents a bushel on imported coal, from five to eight cents per pound on candles, four and five cents per pound, on cordage, three and a half cents per square yard, on cotton bagging, from ten to thirty dollars per ton, on iron, ten cents per bushel on salt, one dollar and fifty cents per one hundred and twelve pounds,on steel,andfour cents per pound together with forty per cent. ad valorem, on wool. And what is still more surprising, while the best land in the world, in the vicinity of navigable waters, may here be had for one dollars and twenty-five cents per acre, we are importing bread stuffs from every port in Europe, flour is at ten or eleven dollars a barrel, and we are paying a duty of nearly twenty five cents a bushel on wheat, and fifty cents a hundred pounds on flour. These are all, absolutely, necessaries of life, and by far the greater portion of the consumption of them, must be among the poor. On the contrary, *coffee, tea, dried fruits, and spices* are admitted duty free, and wine and silks at the very lowest duties. And this is, at a time, when all the articles of prime necessity are excessively dear. To render evident either the wisdom or the justice of such a policy would require a great many *words*. I fear it could not be done by *arguments*.

gentleman's coach. I have spoken of the expenses of civil society, as a public burden. It ought however to be remarked, that this is one of the burdens, which a good citizen should be the most willing to sustain ; as it is a mode of expense, for which he receives a most abundant equivalent. If any one doubt this, let him ask himself, what expense would be necessary to secure for him, and his property, that protection which he now receives in return for the trifling sum which he pays in taxes. The sum paid for the necessary expenses of civil government, is very trifling, when compared with that which is annually expended in journeys of pleasure, in luxuries of the table, in ornaments of dress, nay, in profligate amusements and vicious indulgences. Every good citizen, while he is under obligation vigilantly to watch over the *manner* in which public money is appropriated, is bound to contribute, cheerfully and liberally, for every purpose required by the public good.

It will scarcely be necessary to add, after what has been said, that a surplus revenue is a public nuisance. It gives to the government a control over the monetary affairs of the country, at the best dangerous ; and a control which is very liable to be exerted for the promotion of party purposes. It hence gives an additional, an unnecessary, and a dangerous power to a majority, and gives them the means of perpetuating that power, indefinitely. It is taking productive capital from the hands of the owners, and vesting it in hands where there is every temptation to spend it uselessly, if not viciously. The world has never yet seen a government so pure, that it would not become corrupt, if a surplus revenue were permanently placed at its disposal.

SECTION II.

OF THE PURPOSES FOR WHICH THE PUBLIC REVENUE IS COMMONLY EXPENDED.

Of these, the most important are; the support of civil government, education, national improvements, the support of the institutions of religion, war, and pauperism. Of these, we shall now procecd to treat in their order. The principles which we have already illustrated, will, however, render it unnecessary to consider them at great length. A few remarks upon each, will be all that we shall here attempt.

I. *Of expenses for the support of civil government.*

This is by far the most necessary of any of the objects of public expense. Without government, there could be no society; and without society, there could be neither redress of wrong, nor security of property. But, government cannot be administered without officers, and no one will devote himself to the discharge of the duties of civil office, unless he be paid for it.

The principles which should govern this branch of expenditure, are therefore few and simple.

1. Economy requires, that precisely such talent should be employed, in the various offices of civil government, as may be necessary to insure the discharge of the duties of each office, in the best possible manner. Many of these offices, can only be discharged, successfully, by the first order of human talent, cultivated by learning and discipline, and directed by incorruptible integrity. Now

it is certainly bad economy, to employ inferior talent to do badly, that which can only be of any service when it is done well.

2. Hence, the salaries of judicial, legislative, and executive officers should be such as will command the services of such talent as the duties of each office require. It is most unwise parsimony, to give to a judge such a salary, as will command the services of nothing more than a third rate lawyer; and, it is mean, to ask an individual to do a service for the *community*, at a lower rate than that at which he would do it for an individual.

In answer to this, it may be said, that by bestowing large salaries upon the offices of government, we present temptations to avarice. But, I reply, the reduction of salaries, by no means diminishes the evil. Were emolument to be reduced, there would always be a contest for office. The only question then is, whether we shall have the contest between men of *high*, or between men of *low* character, between those who are capable of *serving us to our advantage*, or those who are only capable of serving us to our disadvantage. Were the most important trusts in the government to command no higher salaries than the wages of day laborers, there would be as great competition for them as at present, only, then, the contest would be between day laborers, instead of being between men of professional ability.

Here, however, I am willing to allow, that the principles of wages formerly illustrated, should have their full effect. For instance, where an office confers rank, or dignity, or indicates professional eminence, the emolument should be less, than would otherwise be paid for the same amount of service. Again, when an office is permanent, the emolument should be less, than when it is temporary.

But, on the other hand, if it be insisted upon, that neither rank nor consideration shall be allowed to the public officer, but that all men are, and must show themselves to be, on a level; the remuneration of office should be higher. And also, when an office is temporary, and the having held it, disenables the incumbent from subsequent professional employment, the remuneration should rise accordingly. In such cases, a pension should be attached to the office, if its duties, for a given time, have been faithfully discharged.

II. *Of expenses for the purpose of education.*

1. Education is of two kinds, common and scientific. Common education, is limited to the teaching of those branches, of which a knowledge is necessary in the pursuit of the ordinary occupations of life. This is a proper object for national expenditure, because it is for the interest of every man, that every other man should be acquainted with the elements of learning. Specially is this the case in a representative government.

A question however occurs, both as to the manner in which such a revenue should be raised, and the manner in which it should be distributed. It may, for instance, be raised like any other tax, and paid into the public chest, and the teachers be paid as officers of the government. Or, it may be raised in the different districts, in which the schools are to be supported, and paid into the hands of district officers, who both oversee the schools and employ the teachers. The latter seems to be by far the preferable method. In this manner, there will be by far the most lively interest maintained in behalf of schools, the appropriation of money will be more vigilantly guarded, and the teachers will more probably be appointed on account of their skill and ability. The appointment of so many teachers, could rarely be effected by a central government, with either skill or fidelity. And, the community, having no interest, either in the selection or the remuneration of the teacher, would rarely take that interest in the subject of education, which the good of the pupils requires.

On this subject, the principles to be kept in view seem to be simple. It seems necessary, that every district sufficiently large to maintain a school, should be obliged to maintain one, and that, for this purpose, the necessary funds be raised by the authority of the public. When, however, these funds have been raised, they may safely be left in the power of each district itself, in the belief that those who have, themselves, earned and contributed the money, will be more likely than any other persons, to disburse it skilfully and economically. Besides this, as upon such a system, teachers will be wanted in large numbers, it may be desirable that seminaries be established for the special purpose of educating them. This will give uniformity to the system of instruction, and enable the science of education, throughout a whole community, the more easily to keep pace with the progress of science, in other departments of knowledge.

2. Of scientific education.

That the cultivation and the diffusion of science is greatly advantageous to a whole community, does not, I trust, require proof. Nations are, at present, principally enriched by the result of discovery and invention; and in consequence of the general diffusion of knowledge and intelligence. That a portion of the national revenue should be directed to the promotion of these objects, seems both equitable and wise.

As both the *cultivation* and the *diffusion* of science may be performed by the same individuals, and, as the same instruments are needful for both purposes, these two objects have been commonly united. The design of an establishment for scientific education is two fold. 1st. To *diffuse abroad* the knowledge already existing, and 2dly, to *add to the amount* of knowledge that now actually exists. Seminaries of learning have rarely been successful in accomplishing either one of these objects, when they were not also successful in accomplishing the other.

The only question to be considered here is this. In what manner, and how, at the least expense, may a government promote the cultivation and diffusion of science, by means of seminaries of higher education.

1. I have remarked when treating of production, that the instruments, the books, and the buildings necessary for the accomplishment of these objects, are very expensive, and can rarely be possessed by individuals. Or, if they were possessed by individuals, the cost of the investment would render education so expensive, as to restrict it entirely to the rich. Hence, we see that public provision for scientific education, instead of benefitting the wealthy, is, specially, a benefit to the poor. The furnishing of these means, is the most important duty of a government, in so far as scientific education is concerned.

2. Whether teachers should pay for the use of such means, may be easily decided. If they pay for such use, they must charge a proportionally higher price for tuition. If they have the use for nothing, their charges for tuition will fall in proportion.

3. The emolument of the teacher should be made to depend upon his professional skill and ability. In no other

manner, will the necessary stimulants be presented to professional industry; and, in no other way, will it be rendered impossible for a man to support himself in this profession, without performing its duties with skill and and fidelity. I have no doubt that the mode, in this country, of remunerating all college officers by a fixed salary, is exceedingly unfavorable to the progress of education. If, for the sake of promoting the study of a particular science, funds be provided for the partial support of an instructor, they should always be so managed, as not in any manner to conflict with the principle here advanced.

4. If, in addition to this, funds be provided for the education of a certain number of those who are indigent, I think that this should be done upon the following principles:—

1. The provision should be so made, as *to benefit merely the indigent,* and not to reduce the price of tuition, *to the whole.* If tuition be so expensive that A cannot procure it, and it be desirable to educate *him,* it may be well to make provision for him. But, this is no reason why the price of tuition should be reduced, in an equal degree, for B, C, D, and the rest of the community, who are able to pay for it at its natural cost.

2. The provision should be so made as not to interfere with the principle above advanced, that teachers be rewarded according to their skill and fidelity. If it be so made that a college, on account of its cheapness, will always be full, and its officers be paid, whether they perform their duties or not, it will retard, instead of promoting, the cause of education.

3. It might be of advantage, supposing a series of schools were established, if gratuitous admission to the higher seminaries were the reward of talent, diligence and good conduct in the lower. This would be a strong stimulant to effort in the lower schools, and would be more likely than any other mode, to limit the bounty of the public, to those who are the most deserving of it.

It may not be amiss here to add, that the success of public efforts for the purpose of promoting scientific education, will depend very greatly upon the mode in which those efforts are exerted. If they be directed to the single object of *reducing the cost of education*, nothing but this object will be effected. Pupils will pay the smallest possible sum for tuition, and the instructors will receive the smallest possible remuneration for their services, and their services will be of the smallest possible value. A man would be considered very simple, who flattered himself that he could purchase twenty-five dollars worth of broadcloth, or flour, or coffee, for five dollars. Let him please himself with his own fancies as he may, it will be found, in the end, that for five dollars he has received no more than five dollars worth. The case is the same with education. Men may have teachers worth five hundred or one thousand, or two thousand, or three thousand dollars per annum. But they will greatly mistake, if they suppose, that, by any process yet discovered, services worth three thousand dollars can be procured for five hundred dollars.

By merely reducing the cost, education will decrease in quality as it increases in quantity. As the article is found to be less valuable, it will, in the end, be less in demand; and thus, at last, not merely will the *quality* have deteriorated, but the *quantity* produced will also have diminished.

On the other hand, if the efforts of the public be directed to *improvement of education*, the increased value of an education will induce a greater number to avail themselves of its advantages. The literary taste of the community will be elevated; the demand for education will increase, and thus, not only will the quality of the product be improved, but the amount disposed of will be greatly augmented. If these views be correct, it will follow, that the efforts in behalf of collegiate education in this country, have not always been wisely directed, and, that, if much that has been done to render education cheap, had been done to render education good, it would have been far better for the cause of science, and of professional learning among us.

III. *Of expenses for maintaining religious worship.*

These expenses need to be borne by men in some manner associated together. It, however, by no means follows, that they are to be borne by men as members of civil society. It cannot be proved that the Christian religion needs the support of civil government, since it has existed and flourished when entirely deprived of this support. And, if it be said, that every man derives benefit from religious services, inasmuch as these services improve the moral and intellectual character of his neighbors; and hence that every man ought to pay for their maintenance; the argument may be easily met as follows. It is granted, that every man is benefitted by the regular administration of the ordinances of religion, but this is not the *reason* for which these ordinances are established. Men unite with their neighbors to procure religious instruction, for *their own* benefit, and not for the benefit of others. If it happen, accidentally, that others are benefitted, it does not follow that they are obliged to pay for this benefit. If my neighbor erect a building for his own profit, on his own land, and thus improve my property, I am not obliged to unite in defraying the expenses of his building. I am entitled gratuitously to this accidental advantage. I think the same principle applies to the case in question.

The only ground on which the support of religion by public taxation can be defended, is, that its existence is necessary to the support of civil government, and that it can be sustained in no other manner than by compulsion. The first assertion we grant to be true. The second, we utterly deny. Hence we do not believe that any taxation for this purpose is necessary. All that religious societies have a right to ask of the civil government, is, the same privileges for transacting their own affairs, which societies of every other sort possess. This, they have a right to demand, not because they are religious societies, but, because the exercise of religion is an innocent mode of pursuing happiness. If these be not granted, religious men are oppressed, and the country where such oppression prevails, let it call itself what it may, is not free.

IV. *Of national improvement.*

Another purpose, for which the public funds are frequently expended, is national improvement. The principles which seem to apply to this case, have been already stated. They are briefly these. Improvements of coasts, and habors, and all that is necessary for the security of external commerce, must be done by the public. Internal improvements, such as roads, canals, railroads, &c., may, in general, be safely left to individual enterprise. If they would be a profitable investment of money, individuals will be willing to undertake them. If they would be an unprofitable investment, both parties had better let them alone. The only case in which a government should assume such works, is that in which their magnitude is too great for individual enterprise, or that in which the power which they confer, is too great to be entrusted to private corporations. Whenever they are undertaken, the principles on which the expenditure should be made, are the same as those which govern the expenditure of individuals.

V. *Of the expenses of pauperism.*

To relieve the sick, the destitute and the helpless, is a religious duty, and therefore should, like every other religious duty, be a voluntary service. Hence, charity in a moral and religious community should generally be dispensed by individuals from their own resources, or from the resources of voluntary associations.

Nevertheless, as cases frequently occur which could not, with sufficient promptness, be relieved by the aid of individuals, or in which the burden would press too heavily on the most charitable, it may be proper that some public provision should be made for the relief of those whom old age, or infancy, or sickness, has deprived of the power of providing the means necessary for sustenance.

By far the greater number of persons requiring such aid, are however capable of some labor, and are also possessed of some skill. They are also far happier, when engaged in suitable labor than when idle. It is therefore the dictate of benevolence, as well as of economy, to provide them with means of profitable occupation. This labor and skill, if judiciously employed upon capital, will commonly defray the expenses of the support of paupers. Hence, the best method of relieving the poor, is to provide some establishment furnished with sufficient capital, in which, all the poor who need assistance, may be employed and supported. In many cases in New England and New York, farms have been purchased by towns or by counties, for this purpose. It has generally been found, that the only expense necessary to be incurred is the purchase of the farm, or the first investment of the capital. The establishment, after this, under judicious management, has generally paid its own expenses, and, in some cases, as I have been informed, has even yielded a revenue to the public. The expenses of pauperism, if they be defrayed in this manner, must of necessity be very moderate; while a competent and convenient provision may be made, for every individual who actually deserves assistance.

VI. *Of War.*

The cheapest defence of nations, I suppose to be the exercise of justice and benevolence. If however a nation resolve to rely upon its military prowess, and to encounter the dangers to its liberty, which necessarily arise from the existence and employment of military force, economy would direct that both its plans and means of defence should be extensive, scientific and complete. Its territory and its coasts should be accurately surveyed with reference to this object. Its assailable positions should all be strongly fortified. Munitions of war should be provided in abundance. Schools for instruction in the art of war, should be supported at the public expense, and the persons so educated should be maintained, either in whole or in part, at the public expense, so that their services may be commanded, whenever they may be required. In this, as in every other case, economy teaches us, that if a given object is to be effected, no expense is unreasonable, which is necessary to effect it in the most perfect manner. The manner of expenditure is to be learned from the teachers of military science. Economy therefore directs that the most valuable talent should be employed, at whatever expense, for providing the plans of defence, that these plans should be fully and perfectly carried into effect, and that all should be done at no greater cost than is necessary to the accomplishment of the object.

NOTE.

[The subject of the Currency occupies, at present, so prominent a place in the public attention, that I have added, in the form of a note, the article on the Precious Metals entire, from Mr. McCulloch's Dictionary of Commerce.]

To enter fully into this interesting and difficult subject would require a long essay, or rather a large volume. Mr. Jacob has recently published an "Historical Inquiry into the Introduction and Consumption of the Precious Metals," in which he takes up the subject at the earliest period, and continues it to the present day. This work, though neither so complete nor satisfactory as might have been expected, contains a good deal of valuable information, and deserves the attention of all who take an interest in such inquiries. We confess, however, that several of the learned author's statements and conclusions seem to us to be not a little wide of the mark. We shall notice one or two of them in the course of this article.

1. *Supply of Precious Metals.*—Since the discovery of America, the far greater part of the supplies of gold and silver have been derived from that continent. Previously to the publication of Humboldt's great work, *Essai Politique sur la Nouvelle Espagne*, several estimates, some of them framed by individuals of great intelligence, were in circulation, of the quantities of gold and silver imported from America. They, however, differed widely from each other, and were all framed from comparatively limited sources of imformation. But these have been wholly superseded by the more extensive and laborious investigations of M. Humboldt. This illustrious traveller, besides being acquainted with all that had been written on the subject, and having ready access to official sources of information unknown to the writers already alluded to, was well versed in the theory and practice of mining, and critically examined several of the most celebrated mines. He was, therefore, incomparably better qualified for forming correct conclusions as to the past and the present productiveness of the mines, than any of those who had hitherto speculated on the subject. His statements have, indeed, been accused of exaggeration; and we incline to think that there are grounds for believing that this charge is, in some measure, well founded, particularly as respects the accounts of the profits made by mining, and of the extent to which the

supplies of the precious metals may be increased. But this criticism applies, if at all, in a very inferior degree, to the accounts M. Humboldt has given of the total produce of the mines, and the exports to Europe. And, making every allowance for the imperfection inseparable from such investigations, it is still true that the statements in question, and the inquiries on which they are founded, are among the most valuable contributions that have ever been made to statistical science.

According to M. Humboldt, the supplies of the precious metals derived from America have been as follows:—

	Dollars a Year at an Average.		Dollars a Year at an Average
From 1492 to 1500 - -	250,000	From 1600 to 1700 -	16,000,000
— 1500 — 1545 -	3,000,000	— 1700 — 1750 -	22,500,000
— 1545 — 1600 -	11,000,000	— 1750 — 1803 -	35,300,000

(*Essai sur la Nouvelle Espange*, tome iii. p. 428. 2d ed.)

The following is M. Humboldt's estimate of the annual produce of the mines of the New World, at the beginning of the present century:

Political Divisions.	
Vice-royalty of New Spain,	$23,000,000
Vice-royalty of Peru,	6,240,000
Captain-generalship of Chili,	2,060,000
Vice-royalty of Buenos Ayres,	4,850,000
Vice-royalty of New Granada,	2,990,000
Brazil,	4,360,000
Total,	$43,500,000

Taking the dollar at 4*s*. 3*d*., this would give 9,243,750*l*. as the total annual produce of the American mines. M. Humboldt further estimated the annual produce of the European mines of Hungary, Saxony, &c., and those of Northern Asia, at the same period, at about 1,000,000*l*. more.

The *quantity* of gold produced in America at the beginning of the century, was to the quantity of silver as 1 to 46; in Europe, the proportions were as 1 to 40. The *value* of equal quantities of gold and silver were then in proportion of 15 or 15½ to 1. Latterly, the quantity of gold produced has increased, as compared with the quantity of silver.

From 1800 to 1810, the produce of the American mines was considerably increased; but in the last-mentioned year the contest began, which terminated in the dissolution of the connection between Spain and the South American colonies. The convulsions and insecurity arising out of this struggle; the proscription of the old Spanish families, to whom the mines principally belonged, who repaired, with the wrecks of their fortunes, some to Cuba, some to Spain, and some to Bordeaux and the south of France; have caused the abandonment of several of the mines, and an extraordinary falling off in the amount of their produce. There are no means of accurately estimating the precise extent of this decline; but according to Mr. Jacob, who collected and compared all the existing information on the subject, the total average produce of the American mines, inclusive of Brazil, during 20 years ending with 1829, may be estimated at 4,036,838*l*. a year; being less considerably than ½ of their produce at the beginning of the century!—(*Jacob*, vol. ii. p. 267.)

Since the publication of Mr. Jacob's work, some further light has been thrown on this subject, by the publication of returns obtained by the British consuls in South America, of the produce of the mines at different periods. They differ considerably from those given by Mr. Jacob. The following is an abstract of their results, comparing the 20 years ending with 1809 with the 20 years ending with 1829 :—

Mines.	1790 to 1809	1810 to 1829
Mexico,	£98,952,681	£47,301,804
Panama,	223,518	23,603
Chili,	1,808,710	2,782,702
Buenos Ayres,	21,149,786	10,057,782
Total of America,	£122,134,695	£60,165,891
Russia,		5,206,724
		65,372,615

There are so many sources of error attached to all investigations of this sort, that these results, though deduced from what may be reckoned good authority, cannot be altogether depended on. The consular returns contain no account of the produce of the Peruvian mines, except in so far as they come under the head of Buenos Ayres; and in this respect they differ very widely from the statements given by Mr. Jacob, who estimates the produce of the mines of Peru and Buenos Ayres, during the 20 years ending 1829, at about 18,500,000*l.*! We also incline to think that the mines and washings in Colombia are not quite so neglected as they are said to be by the consul. It will be observed, too, that the account does not include the produce of the Brazilian mines. They are supposed to have yielded, since 1810, about 1,500,000 dollars a year; but is this not more than adequate for the wants of the country. The produce of the Russian mines was comparatively trifling till 1810; but it has since increased, and is continuing to increase with considerable rapidity.

Adding to the produce of the American, that of the Russian mines, and separating the gold from the silver, their total produce, according to the consular returns, during each of the 4 decennial periods, ending with 1829, has been about—

	Gold.	*Silver.*	*Both.*
Ten years ending 1799	£3,295,000	£59,290,000	£62,585,000
—— 1809	4,180,000	55,367,000	59,547,000
—— 1819	3,955,000	29,953,000	33,908,000
—— 1829	5,752,000	25,712,000	31,464,000

This gives 3,146,000*l.* for the average annual supply of the American and Russian mines during the 10 years ending with 1829. But the returns show that the produce of the Mexican mines had begun materially to increase in the latter years of this period; and we have to add to the above the produce of the Hungarian and Saxon mines. Hence, allowing for the increase that has taken place since 1829 in productiveness of the Mexican and South American mines, exclusive of Brazil, and adding to their produce that of the Russian and other European mines, we may safely estimate (assuming the consuls not to have under-rated the American returns) the present annual supply of gold and silver from these sources at considerably more than 4,000,000*l.*

Exclusive of the sources now mentioned, the United States have recently begun to afford considerable quantities of gold. It was first discovered in North Carolina, in 1804; and from that period till 1829, about 109,000 dollars had been found. It has since been discovered in other States. The following Table exhibits the value of the gold annually produced in the United States since 1829.—(*American Almanac* for 1834.)

States.	1829.	1830.	1831.	1832.
Virginia,	$2,500	$24,000	$26,000	$34,000
North Carolina,	134,000	204,000	294,000	458,000
South Carolina,	3,500	26,000	22,000	45,000
Georgia,	- -	212,000	176,000	140,000
Alabama,	- -	- -	1,000	- -
Tennessee,	- -	- -	1,000	1,000
Total,	140,000	466,000	520,000	678,000

This Table shows a considerable increase; the produce in 1832 being above 135,000*l.* It is principally obtained by washing the soil in the valleys. Taking this new supply into account, and including, as was done by M. Humboldt, the produce of the Brazilian mines; and further adding 500,000*l.* to the sums given in the consular returns, to cover the deficiencies which they certainly involve;* we may safely estimate the entire annual produce of the American, European, and Russo-Asiatic mines, as amounting, at this moment, to about 6,000,000*l.* a year; being 6-10ths of their annual produce when greatest.

2. *Consumption of Precious Metals.*—Gold and silver are supplied either to serve as coin, or made use of in the arts. There are no means whatever by which to discover the proportion in which they are applied, at any given period, to these purposes; and the proportion is perpetually varying with the varying circumstances of each country; as, for example, with the greater or less abundance of paper money, and the degree in which the use of coins is saved by the various devices resorted to by means of banking and otherwise for economising currency, the greater or less wealth of the inhabitants, the fashion as to plate, the feeling of security at the moment, and a thousand other circumstances,—all of which are liable to great and sometimes sudden changes.

According to Mr. Jacob, the value of the precious metals annually applied to ornamental and luxurious purposes in Europe, may be estimated as follows: viz. Great Britain, 2,457,221*l.*; France, 1,200,000*l.*; Switzerland, 350,000*l.*; remainder of Europe, 1,605,499*l.*; making in all, 5,612,711*l.* And adding to this the sums directly applied to the same purposes in America, the whole will be about 5,900,000*l.*

The data upon which this estimate has been founded, are in the last degree vague and unsatisfactory. It can hardly, indeed, be looked upon as any thing better than a mere guess; and as such, we do not think

* Even with this addition, their produce is materially under the sum mentioned by Mr. Jacob.

that it is a very happy one. M. Chabrol (whose researches are far more worthy of confidence than those of M. Chaptal, to which Mr. Jacob refers) estimates the consumption of gold and silver in the arts at Paris at 14,552,000 francs a year—(*Recherches Statistiques sur la Ville de Paris*, 1823, Tab. No. 85.); which corresponds with the elaborate estimate of M. Benoiston de Chateauneuf—*Recherches sur les Consommations de Paris en* 1817, 2de partie, p. 78.). Both these authorities agree that the consumption of the precious metals in the arts at Paris is double that of the rest of France; so that we have 21,828,000 francs, or 866,190*l.* for the consumption of the whole kingdom, which is 333,810*l.* a year under Mr. Jacob's estimate.

We have been assured, by those who have good means of forming a correct opinion upon such a point, that the quantity assigned by Mr. Jacob for the consumption of Great Britain is over-rated in about the same proportion as the consumption of France, or about ¼ part. There has, no doubt, been a considerable increase of late years in the consumption of plate and gilt articles; but it would require far better evidence than any hitherto laid before the public, to warrant the conclusion that so large a sum as 2,457,000*l.* is appropriated to such purposes.

The consumption of Switzerland, as set down by Mr. Jacob, is probably not far from accurate. But the sum assigned for the aggregate consumption of the rest of Europe seems to be quite as much exaggerated as that allowed for France and England.

According to this view of the matter, the consumption will be,—Great Britain, 1,842,916*l.*; France, 866,190*l.*; Switzerland, 350,000*l.*; rest of Europe, 1,204,118*l.* in all, 4,263,224*l.* To this must be added 300,000*l.* for the consumption of America making the entire consumption 4,563,224*l.*

Probably this valuation is still too high. According to M. Humboldt (*Nouvelle Espagne*, 2d edit. tome iii. p. 464), the total consumption of the precious metals in Europe, for other purposes than those of coin, amounts to only 87,182,800 francs equal, at the exchange of 25·20, to 3,459,714*l.*: and adding to this 300,000*l.* for the consumption of America, the grand total will be, in round numbers, 3,760,000*l.*; being 803,000*l.* under our estimate, and no less than 2,140,000*l.* under that of Mr. Jacob!

But a portion of the gold and silver annually made use of in the arts is derived from the fusion of old plate, the burning of lace, picture frames, &c. Here, however, we have to lament the impossibility of ascertaining the proportion the supply from this source bears to the total quantity wrought up. Mr. Jacob estimates it at only 1-40th part, or 2½ per cent.; but so small a sum seems to be quite out of the question. Most part of the precious metals employed in plating, gilding, &c., is certainly destroyed; but the quantity of metal so made use of is admitted by every one to be decidedly less than the quantity used in the manufacture of plate, watch-cases, and other articles of that description. And these, when they either become unfashionable, or are broken or injured, are, for the most part, sent to the melting pot. According to the statement of Necker, quoted and sanctioned by Humboldt, a *half* of the gold and silver used in France by goldsmiths and others in the arts, is supposed to be obtained from the fusion of old plate, &c.—(*Nouvelle Espange*, tome iii. p. 467.)

But, notwithstanding the high authority by which this estimate is supported, we believe that it is nearly as much above the mark as Mr. Jacob's is certainly below it. Assuming, therefore, that, at a medium, 20 per cent. or 1-5th part of the precious metals annually made use of the arts is obtained from the fusion of old plate, we shall have, by deducting this proportion from the 4,563,000*l*. applied to the arts in Europe and America, 3,650,000*l*. as the total annual appropriation of the new gold and silver dug from the mines to such purposes, leaving about 2,000,000*l*. a year to be manufactured into coin.

It is not much more easy to determine the consumption of the precious metals when manufactured into coin, than when in plate. Mr. Jacob has entered into some curious details (vol. ii. c. 28.) to determine the abrasion or loss of coins from wear, which he estimates at 1-600th part a year for gold, and, and 1-200th part for silver coins. This, however, does not give the total wear and tear of the coins. To determine the latter, the quantities lost by fire, shipwrecks, and other accidents, must be taken into account. The loss from these sources can only be guessed at; but adding it to the loss by abrasion, perhaps we shall not be far wrong in estimating the whole at 1 per cent.

It is singular that, in estimating the consumption of gold and silver, Mr. Jacob should not have made the slightest allusion to the practice which has uniformily prevailed in all countries harassed by intestine commotions, or exposed to foreign invasion, of burying treasure in the earth. Of the hoards so deposited, a very considerable proportion has been altogether lost; and there can be no doubt that this has been one of the principal means by which the stock of the precious metals has been kept down to its present level. Every one is aware that, during the middle ages, *treasure trove*, or money dug from the ground by chance finders, belonged to the Crown, and formed no inconsiderable part of the royal revenue of this and other countries. The practice has always prevailed to a very great extent in the East.—*Bernier, Voyage de Mogol*, Amst. 1710, tome i. p. 209.; *Scrafton on the Government of Hindostan*, p. 16. &c.) But it is not confined to that quarter. Wherever property is insecure, it is invariably resorted to. Mr. Wakefield tells us that is common in Ireland.—(*Account of Ireland*, vol. i. p. 593.) It has always prevailed to a considerable extent in Russia and France; and in the latter during the revolutionary anarchy, immense sums were buried, of which it is abundantly certain a large proportion will never be resuscitated. The wars and convulsions by which Europe was desolated for more than 20 years extended the practice to all parts of the Continent; withdrawing in this way from circulation a very considerable part of the increased produce of the mines.—(*Storch, Economie, Politique*, tome i. p. 221. Paris, 1823.)

3. *Exportations of the Precious Metals to the East.*—It must be well known to all our readers, that from the remotest era down to a comparatively late period, bullion has always formed one of the principal and most advantageous articles of export to the East. Humboldt estimated that, of the entire produce of the American mines at the beginning of this century, amounting, as already seen, to 43,500,000 dollars, no less than 25,500,000 were sent to Asia,—17,500,000 by the Cape of Good Hope, 4,000,000 by the Levant, and 4,000,000 through the Russian frontier.—(*Nouvelle Espange*, tome iii. p. 443.) Latterly however, this immense drain has not only entirely ceased ; but *the current has, in fact, began to set strongly in the opposite direction.* Thus it appears that the total imports of gold and silver from Europe and North and South America into Bengal, Madras, and Bombay, during the 3 years with 1830-31, amounted to 479,388*l.*; whereas the total exports of the precious metals from these 3 presidencies to Europe and America during the same 3 years were 1,119,973*l.*, being an excess of 640,585*l.*; so that India, instead of importing, as formerly, very large quantities of bullion from the Western World, supplied, during the period in question, about 213,000*l.* a year to its markets !—(*Parl. Paper*, No. 390. Sess. 1833.) The same is the case with China. During the year ended the 31st of March, 1832, silver was exported from Canton to England to the amount of 1,976,930 dollars, or 390,000*l.*, besides about as much more exported to India !—(See *ante*, p. 237.) A considerable part of this large export consists of native silver, of which there are mines in several provinces. China has also mines of gold ; and in some late years her exports of that metal have been considerable : she is, however, an importer as well as an exporter of gold, having for a lengthened period drawn considerable supplies of that metal from Borneo, Celebes, and the Malay peninsula. It appears, too, that the efflux of bullion from Russia to China has ceased ; and that there, also, the current is setting the opposite way.—(*Jacob*, vol. ii. 320.) And if there be any sums still exported by way of the Levant, which is doubtful, they are certainly quite inconsiderable.

4. *Influence of the diminished Productiveness of the Mines on Prices.*—It has been customary in this country to ascribe almost the whole fall that has taken place in the price of most commodities since the peace, to the diminished supply of bullion from the mines. But we doubt whether this circumstances has not been fully counterbalanced by others, and whether it has had influence in the way now mentioned. The cessation of the drain to the East, even admitting that M. Humboldt has somewhat over-rated its amount, would of itself have gone far to counteract the decreased productiveness of the mines ; but we have just seen that it has not merely ceased, but that we are, in fact, deriving considerable supplies from that very quarter. In addition to this, the greater security and tranquillity enjoyed on the Continent since the peace, has not only checked that burying of money, formerly so prevalent, but has caused the bringing to light of a good many of the subterranean hoards. The institution of savings' banks, now so common every where, has also,

no doubt, tended to prevent hoarding, and to bring a good deal of coin into circulation, that would otherwise have been locked up. These circumstances, coupled with others that might be mentioned, such as the cessation of the demand for military chests, the greater employment of bills in mercantile transactions, &c., afford the best grounds for doubting whether the quantity of the precious metals annually applicable to the purposes of circulation be not as great at present, as in 1809 or 1810. It is further to be observed, that the falling off in the produce of the mines has been in silver only; and that the supply of gold, instead of being diminished during the last 10 years, has been *very materially increased*: and as gold is the standard of our currency, it is obviously false to affirm that its value has been increased from its being less abundant than formerly. It is contended, indeed, that in estimating the value of the precious metals, we cannot separate gold and silver; and that the fall that has taken place in the prices of *all* commodities since 1815, proves that the value of money has sustained a corresponding advance. But the value of gold is in no way dependent upon, or connected with, the value of silver. The exchangeable worth of each metal is wholly determined by the peculiar conditions under which it is supplied; and the circumstance of gold falling in value when silver is rising, is no more to be wondered at, than that lead should fall when iron rises, or conversely. Neither is it true that the fall in the value of commodities since 1815 has been universal. We admit it has been very general; but we venture to affirm that there is not, without any exception whatever, a single commodity that has fallen in price since 1814, the fall of which may not be satisfactorily accounted for without reference to the supply of gold and silver.—(See *ante*, p. 75.) Multiplied proofs of what is now stated, will be found in various articles throughout this work. And we have little doubt that those who investigate the matter with any degree of care, will agree with us in thinking, that, even without distinguishing between gold and silver, were the influence of the decreased productiveness of the mines on prices estimated at from 3 to 5 per cent., it would be very decidedly beyond the mark. We believeits influence has been hardly perceptible.

5. *Probable future Supply of Gold and Silver.*—Nothing but conjectural statements can be made as to the probable future supply of the precious metals. On the whole, however, we should think that a very considerable increase may be fairly anticipated. The anarchy in which the new South America States have hitherto been involved, will come to a close; and, with the increase of population and capital, renewed attention will, doubtless, be paid to the mines. It is reasonable also, we think, to anticipate that the supplies from the Russian mines will continue to increase.